Studies on the Civilization of Islam

By
Hamilton A. R. Gibb

Edited by
Stanford J. Shaw and William R. Polk

Princeton University Press
Princeton, New Jersey

Published by Princeton University Press, 41 William Street,
Princeton, New Jersey 08540
In the United Kingdom: Princeton University Press, Guildford, Surrey
Copyright © 1962 by Hamilton A. R. Gibb

First Princeton Paperback printing, 1982

LCC 81-47987
ISBN 0-691-05354-5
ISBN 0-691-00786-1 pbk.

Published by arrangement with Beacon Press
Printed in the United States of America by
Princeton University Press, Princeton, New Jersey

Editors' Note

The following articles have been drawn from a wide variety of publications over a span of nearly four decades. As a result, the reader will note differences of style, treatment and utilization of sources. In an endeavor to achieve consistency, the editors have unified systems of transliteration somewhat; to achieve readability for the non-Arabist, they have simplified the transliteration; to retain the special character of the volume, they have left all the notes contemporaneous with the articles to which they refer.

The transliteration system involved here does not indicate some differences between Arabic letters, as for example between the hard and soft *d*. Those wishing to check the Arabic original are referred to the following original journal article sources:

1. "An Interpretation of Islamic History." *Journal of World History*, I, no. 1 (Paris, 1953), 39-62.

2. "The Evolution of Government in Early Islam." *Studia Islamica*, IV (Paris, 1955), 1-17.

3. "Arab-Byzantine Relations under the Umayyad Caliphate." *Dumbarton Oaks Papers*, no. 12 (Cambridge, Mass., 1958), 219-233.

4. "The Social Significance of the Shuubiya." *Studia Orientalia Ioanni Pedersen dicata* (Copenhagen, 1953), 105-114.

5. "The Armies of Saladin." *Cahiers d'Histoire égyptéenne*, série 3, fasc. 4 (Cairo, 1951), 304-320.

6. "The Achievement of Saladin." *Bulletin of the John Rylands Library*, 35, no. 1 (Manchester, 1952), 44-60.

7. "Tarikh." (Arabic and Persian Historiography.) *Encyclopaedia of Islam, Supplement* (Leiden, 1938), 233-245.

We should like to express our grateful thanks to the editors
and publishers of these journals and books for their kind permis-
sion to reprint these articles.

We also wish to thank Dr. Shaikh Inayatullah, Professor

Emeritus at the University of the Panjab, Lahore, Pakistan, for his contribution to the bibliography of Professor Gibb's publications, and Miss Brenda Sens for her assistance with the index.

S. J. S.
Cambridge, Massachusetts   W. R. P.
November 1961

ABBREVIATIONS used in footnotes and bibliographies

BEO	*Bulletin d'études orientales*
BGA	*Bibl. Geographorum Arabicorum*
BSOS	*Bulletin of the School of Oriental Studies*
BSOAS	*Bulletin of the School of Oriental and African Studies*
GJ	*Geographical Journal*
IA	*International Affairs*
IC	*Islamic Culture*
JAOS	*Journal of the American Oriental Society*
JCAS	*Journal of the Central Asian Society*
JNES	*Journal of Near Eastern Studies*
JRAS	*Journal of the Royal Asiatic Society*
JRCAS	*Journal of the Royal Central Asian Society*
JTS	*Journal of Theological Studies*
MEJ	*Middle East Journal*
MSOS	*Mitteilungen des Seminars für orientalische Sprachen*
MW	*Muslim World*
RAAD	*Revue de l'Academie Arabe de Damas*
REI	*Revue des études islamiques*
RMM	*Revue du monde musulman*
RSO	*Rivista degli studi orientali*
SI	*Studia Islamica*
WI	*Welt des Islams*
WZKM	*Wiener Zeitschrift für die Kunde des Morgenlandes*
ZDMG	*Zeitschrift der Deutschen morgenländischen Gesellschaft*

Preface

One of my prized possessions is a copy of a reissued volume of essays by Dr. Taha Husain, inscribed by the author "To H. A. R. Gibb, who restored life to this book." This collection of articles should similarly be inscribed "To William R. Polk and Stanford J. Shaw." Its contents are largely their selection; it is they who persuaded me into a kind of honorary patronage of the reprint and who have undertaken all the material tasks involved in its preparation. Apart from some assistance in minor details, my responsibility scarcely goes beyond the writing of this Preface.

Even this, it may be said, was imposed not by the editors but by the publishers, who felt that the American public (by which, I suspect, is meant the hypothetical American reviewer) would want to know in what way the diverse articles could be so related as to form a coherent body of writing. The answer is not difficult. In so far as they possess any unity at all, it has been imposed on them by a slowly maturing conviction that literature and history, both being expressions of a living society, cannot be studied in isolation from one another without distortion of the underlying reality.

The majority of the articles selected for reprinting in this volume are surveys on broader or narrower lines. They are open, consequently, to the criticism that generalizations on such a scale may distort or even falsify to some extent the complexity of the actual data. There has been a tendency (entirely justified in itself) in pursuing sociological analysis into the medieval Islamic world to stress the degree of variety concealed beneath the outward uniformities. It is true that a civilization spread in medieval conditions of communication over so vast an area necessarily included many "little societies" with their own traditions, social customs and intellectual attitudes. Yet the most convinced defenders of the "little societies" must admit, however reluctantly, that the steady pressure of the ideas, practices and values of the

"Great Society" gradually ate into them so that they survived, if at all, only as communities with locally recognized "usages" within the multicolored and tolerant complex of Islamic society. On any general view there is no alternative to taking the development and advance of Islam in its community aspect as the warp of Middle Eastern history and literature. Perhaps it may be necessary to assure the reader that behind each generalization there lies a considerable body of detailed study of the original sources, of which the article on "The Armies of Saladin" in this volume may serve as a specimen.

The four essays grouped under the title of "The Structure of Religious Thought in Islam" therefore, as a broad sociological analysis of Islam, may serve in some measure as a basis for the other essays on history and literature. The history of the political institutions of the Middle East, however, is characterized by an increasingly wide divergence from Islamic norms and an increasing difficulty of accommodation between them. The stages in this development are studied in a series of essays, beginning with "The Evolution of Government in Early Islam," continuing with "The Social Significance of the Shuubiya," and the essays on al-Mawardi and "Constitutional Organization." Nevertheless, if the political institutions trace a discordant pattern upon the warp of Islamic society, emphasizing the failure of the Islamic civilization to achieve the unity and coherence that it sought as its ideal, the continuing vitality of that ideal is illustrated in the essays on Saladin and "Some Considerations on the Sunni Theory of the Caliphate."

In contrast to the articles on medieval history and literature, the four studies in contemporary Arabic literature illustrate one strand in the complex bundle of new ideas and forms introduced into the Arab world at the turn of the nineteenth and twentieth centuries. Written around 1930, they reflect something of the optimism and assurance of that period. The broader survey contained in "The Reaction against Western Culture in the Near East," written some twenty years later, may serve in some measure as an index of the rapidity of changing moods and phases in modern Arab society.

All the essays have been reprinted as they originally appeared, except for the correction of printing errors. A careful reader may detect contradictions or inconsistencies here and there; it would indeed be strange if in an output spread over more than thirty years no shift had occurred in points of view or bases of judgment. But even where the author would express himself somewhat differently if he were writing today, it has seemed superfluous to burden the text with meticulous footnotes advertising the fact.

Finally, it is a gratifying privilege to express my sincere thanks to my colleagues and to the publishers for their sacrificial endeavors to "restore life" to these essays.

H. A. R. GIBB

Contents

Part Three Contemporary Intellectual Currents

Part One   Medieval Islamic History

1. An Interpretation of Islamic History

I

Islam is a concept which, phenomenalized in a number of linked but diverse political, social and religious organisms, covers an immense area in space and time. In different regions and epochs it has presented differing features under the impact of and in response to local geographical, social and political forces. Western Islam for example, in northwest Africa and medieval Spain, though it was closely related to the Muslim heartlands in Western Asia and its culture was an offshoot from their culture, yet evolved several distinguishing characteristics, some of which in turn influenced Islam in Western Asia. In other large and self-contained geographical areas, such as the Indian subcontinent and Indonesia, or in the steppe lands extending from southern Russia to the borders of China, parallel factors produced similarly distinguishing forms. Yet each and all of these retain a certain easily recognizable common Islamic stamp. It is impossible within the limits of a single essay to deal with all these diverse regions. The present article is therefore confined to Islam in Western Asia with the double object: (1) of tracing the development of Islamic culture and the gradual evolution which by the end of the fourteenth century had transformed its inner structure, and (2) of examining the processes by which its institutions were molded into a coherent unity and given their specifically Islamic stamp, however widely Islam might spread and however various their external forms. It should thus supply a provisional framework within which (corrected or adjusted where necessary) other studies devoted to particular aspects and relations of Islamic culture may be coordinated.

The rhythms of Islamic history are curiously inverse to those of European history. Both arose from the breakdown of the Mediterranean empire of Rome. While Europe slowly and imperceptibly, and only after several centuries, grew out of the anarchy of the barbarian invasions, Islam suddenly emerged from Arabia and with incredible speed fashioned in less than a century a new imperial structure in Western Asia and the southern and western shores of the Mediterranean. But the contrast goes much deeper. The challenges to the ancient Mediterranean empire and institutions were of two kinds. On the northern borders, the barbarian invaders challenged the Roman political power, but entered into its new cultural system, the Catholic Christian Church, and accepted its basic social and religious institutions, upon which ultimately the new European political structures were erected. On the southern and eastern borders, the challenge was not to Roman political power but to the cultural centralization of the church, and manifested in popular rejection of Catholic orthodoxy in favour of dissident creeds, Donatist, Monophysite and Nestorian. Islam, after establishing a political system which embraced all these areas of dissidence (together with Persia, which had for centuries maintained against Rome a political struggle backed by a religious rival creed), was confronted with the task of bringing them into a common cultural and religious system, based upon its own universalist concept. To achieve this, it had to counteract and, as far as possible, extinguish the influence of the earlier universalist concept (Christianity) in Western Asia and the southern half of the Mediterranean, to destroy Zoroastrianism and the other dualist religions of Persia and Mesopotamia, and oppose a barrier to the extension of Buddhism in Central Asia.

The whole of medieval Islamic history is dominated by the effort on the part of the Sunni or "orthodox" religious institution, first, to maintain its universalism against internal and external challenges, and second to realize the widest possible measure of religious, social and cultural unity throughout the Islamic world. The second of these objects was not achieved until the political unity of Islam had been disrupted, partially recreated, and disrupted again; but in the effort to achieve it a vast area of interaction was created between peoples of diverse stocks and traditions, and in this process—almost, indeed, as a by-product of it—the medieval Islamic culture was brought into existence.

II

The social teaching of Muhammad was basically a reaffirmation of the ethical ideas common to the monotheistic religions: the brotherhood of all members of the new Islamic community, their equality in intrinsic personal worth in spite of differences of temporal status, function and wealth, and all the mutual relationships and duties following from these principles, deepened by being stated in terms of inward loyalty and outward obligation to the one God. Furthermore (and this was to prove of fundamental importance for the future development of Islamic culture), it included certain social and ethical obligations—but not the full freedom of brotherhood—towards members of other religious communities, provided that these accepted the political control of the Islamic community.

As in all religious movements, the concrete social results of this teaching were determined by its impact on the actual historical environment. In Muhammad's own lifetime, it was received at three different levels. The first was at the level of total conversion, producing religious personalities, whose activities and decisions were motivated by a complete inward acceptance of its spirit and principles. This group, the nucleus of the future religious institution, was in the nature of the case relatively small to begin with but steadily increased with the expansion of the community. The second was that of formal adhesion, of willing acceptance of the outward prescriptions and duties, without assimilation of their spirit, but because of the advantages to be gained by incorporation in the new community. Its leading representatives were the later Meccan adherents, to whose mercantile temper the external demands of Islam were eminently suited, requiring only the dedication to religious duties of a proportion of time and wealth, and leaving the rest free for personal activities and interest. A further commendation of Islam in Meccan eyes was the firm control which it established over the Bedouins, whose acceptance was on the third level, that of enforced adherence maintained by threat (and after Muhammad's death by the application) of military sanctions.

Since, however, inescapable economic forces made any permanent stabilization of inner-Arabian conditions virtually impossible, the mere suppression of Bedouin opposition—with the implication that the forces of Islam would be used up in an interminable and sterile struggle with the tribesmen—was an inadequate solution for the problem set by them. It was necessary to find the terms on which the tribesmen as a whole could be swung, if not up to the first level of assimilation, at least on to the level of identifying Islam with their own interests. Hence the trial expeditions deliberately organized by Abu Bakr after Muhammad's death, when groups of tribesmen were despatched under Meccan commanders towards the frontiers of Syria. The first successes led to a coordinated and organized military campaign which quickly achieved the conquest of the whole country; and the comparative lack of success of the simultaneous campaigns in Iraq under tribal leadership reconciled the tribesmen to a similarly organized campaign under Meccan leadership against the Persian empire, with equally decisive results. The policy of Abu Bakr and his successor Omar thus not only achieved their first purpose, of bringing the tribesmen to an enthusiastic acceptance of Islam as the palladium of victory and to unite their forces under commanders appointed by the caliph, but also a second and not less important result, that the conquests were made with the minimum of disturbance to the economy of the conquered countries and were followed by the rapid establishment of organized central control.

Nevertheless, the material interests of the two main parties to the victory, the tribesmen and the Meccans, were still in opposition to one another. The natural instinct of the tribesmen was to appropriate the conquered lands for their pastures, while the Meccans wished to exploit their resources for their own commercial profit. Although the structure of an agricultural economy was unfamiliar to the Arab leaders, they quickly understood its significance as a source of revenue. If it was not to be exposed to injury, the obvious solution was to leave its administration in the hands of the former officials who were familiar with it. While the tribesmen were still engaged in the campaigns and still amenable to the moral authority and control of the caliphate, they were persuaded to relinquish their claims to the occupation of lands, and to receive in compensation a fixed share of the revenues in monetary stipends and produce. This also enabled the central government to keep the tribesmen concentrated in garrison settlements, instead of spreading in nomadic fashion over the country, and by this means to maintain more effective supervision and control over them.

It was not long before the consciousness of the loss of their independence, combined with the unnatural conditions of life in the garrison cities, generated an increasingly violent feeling of resentment amongst the tribesmen, exacerbated by the Meccan exploitation of "their" conquests. The Meccan merchants had not been slow to seize the dazzling prospects opened up by the commerce of Iraq, Syria and Egypt. They were already active in supplying the needs of the new garrison settlements for consumption goods, in forming partnerships with local producers and merchants, and especially in the huge operations of exchange and banking required in the distribution of stipends and transfer to Medina of the fifth of all revenues, and were forming vast commercial establishments manned by slaves and clients.[1] In Medina also, after the first satisfaction with the great increase in wealth and prosperity, there was growing resentment at the rapid affirmation of Meccan political control under the third caliph, Othman, and the economic exploitation of the empire.

Open discontent was first expressed by several religious personalities, whose conscience was shocked by the worldliness and grasping materialism displayed in the name of Islam. But these only provided a rallying-cry and a cloak for the material grievances of the tribesmen and Medinians, who swung into line behind them. The assassination of Othman by the tribesmen provoked a civil war, in which the religious party at first joined the tribesmen of Iraq, in whom they saw the supporters of the cause of unity on Islamic religious and ethical terms. Opposed to them stood the Meccan governor of Syria, Muawiya, supported by his tribesmen, more disciplined and sedentarized, and less exposed to exploitation than those of Iraq. It soon became clear to the religious leaders that the tribal interpretation of Islam carried with it a threat to the whole principle of religious authority and to the system of mutual rights and obligations upon which rested the unity and stability of the community. The conflict turned out to be one, not between the religious basis and the secular basis of unity, but between unity on modified Meccan terms which at least respected the religious foundations of the community, and the disruptive forces of tribalism. When the issue was underlined by the emergence in Iraq of the violently sectarian and anti-Meccan group called the Kharijites (*Khawarij*) the choice could not long remain in doubt, and the religious party gradually drifted to the side of Muawiya.

III

The establishment of the Umayyad Caliphate of Damascus (661) was thus the outcome of a coalition or compromise between those who represented the Islamic ideal of a religious community, united by common allegiance to the heritage of the Prophet, and the Meccan secular interpretation of unity, against the threat of anarchy implicit in tribalism. But this was only a modus vivendi reinstating a central authority over the loosely bound provinces of the Arab empire. Three major questions remained to be solved; the relations of the government with the tribes, its relations with the religious party, and the relations between Arabs and non-Arabs in the conquered lands.

In their relations with the tribes, the Umayyad Caliphs at first returned to the old Meccan policy of conciliation by coordinating the interest of the tribesmen with their own, combined with a renewal of the Medinian policy of wars of expansion and distribution of booty. The survival of irreconcilable Kharijite and anti-Umayyad tribal opposition in Iraq stood in the way of their success from the first, and the rapid development of tribal factions forced on them a complete change of policy. The administration was increasingly centralized, and its control tightened over the inner provinces (Iraq, Syria and Egypt); tribal risings were repressed and Syrian garrisons established to maintain order in Iraq and Persia; most important of all, the tribesmen of Iraq were gradually demilitarized, and were beginning to be absorbed into the new mixed urban societies which were developing in the former garrison cities.

Religious factors entered into this process of centralization on both sides, partly in opposition, but partly also favoring the growth of an organized central authority. Their awareness of the secular tendencies in the Umayyad house, together with the influence of their religious idealism, inclined the religious leaders in a general way against the Umayyad regime, but their difficulty was to find an alternative that would not disrupt the community. The excesses of the Kharijites and of the activist Shiites discredited them with all but a minority, and an anti-caliphate set up during a second civil war (684-691) proved incapable of maintaining order.[2] At the same time, the Umayyad Caliphate itself was moving towards the universalist Islamic view, as the religious and ethical principles of Islam percolated in the course of the century more deeply into Arab society and affected its outlook and principles of conduct. The outcome of this symbiosis was the emergence of a semi-official interpretation of Islam, supported by a considerable body of religious opinion,[3] and it is noteworthy that the first condemnations for heresy took place under the later Umayyad Caliphs.[4]

By the end of the first century, however, non-Arabs were beginning to enter the ranks of religious teachers in growing numbers. These naturally accepted Islam in its most universalist interpretation, without any qualifying admixture of Arab ideas; as they were emotionally opposed to the Umayyads because of the grievances and social inferiority of the non-Arabs, they rejected the conformist attitude of the Umayyad supporters, as well as the other Arab sectarian interpretations, and remained on the whole on the neutral ground of doctrinal rigorism.

The most difficult problem for the Umayyads was to integrate the social structure of the Arab state as organized after the conquests with the agricultural economy of the conquered provinces, and to do so in a manner consistent with the ethical principles of Islam. What gave the problem a peculiar intensity was the movement of conversion to Islam among both landowners and cultivators, who continued nevertheless to suffer from their former social and economic disabilities. It was eventually solved towards the end of the Umayyad period (but only after bitter struggles) by assimilating new Arab landowners to non-Arab landowners, and by exempting converted cultivators from the poll tax payable by all non-Muslim subjects. Both measures led towards an assimila-

tion of Arabs and Muslim non-Arabs, and at the same time towards
uniformity of administrative practice in the Arab empire; but they
came too late to check the accumulated sense of grievance against
Umayyad rule, which in the eyes of the developing "religious
institution" stood for the political domination and social privilege
of the Arabs. Both the activist and neutralist religious oppositions
joined with a revolt of the Yemen faction of tribesmen to bring
down the Umayyad Caliphate (750); and thus, after having (in
alliance with the Umayyads) dissociated the religious polity of
Islam from the extreme sectarian and fanatical interpretations of
the Kharijites and the ultra-Shiites, now also publicly dissociated
it from the concept of Arab predominance.

IV

The new Abbasid line of caliphs, although themselves, as
relatives of the Prophet, also of Meccan Arab origin, clearly recognized the importance which the religious leaders had assumed
in the framework of the empire, and made it one of the corner-
stones of their policy to associate them with the new regime. The
evolution which had begun under the Umayyads towards centralized monarchical institutions and the merging of the hitherto
privileged Arabs into the general Muslim population would have
continued in any case, but it was accelerated and given a more
definite direction by the fact that the dynasty was brought to
power and maintained in it by an alliance of the Arab colonists
and Islamized Persian aristocracy of Khurasan. The increasing employment of non-Arabs in the administration favored the revival
of the old Sasanian court ceremonial and administrative traditions,
while the constitution of a Khurasanian standing army freed the
monarchy from the pressures of the Arab tribal structure. The
Arab landowners were integrated in the Persian feudal system, and
the expansion of industry, commerce, and material and intellectual culture in Iraq and Persia brought Arabs and non-Arabs
together in social, economic and intellectual activities.

The religious policy of the Abbasids also was affected by the
same influences. They not only placed a new emphasis on the

religious status and functions of the caliphate, and by their patronage of the religious leaders gave an impulse to the propagation
of an "official orthodoxy," but also, on lines reminiscent of the
Sasanid Zoroastrian organization, began to centralize the religious
institutions under state control.

In all these developments, however, there were implicit
certain dangers for the principle of Islamic universalism, the maintenance of the unity of the Muslim community in its religious and
ethical attitudes by acknowledgement of one common authority,
although at first sight it might seem to be favored by the establishment of the universal empire of the Abbasids. The rapid social and
economic development in Iraq and Persia was not paralleled in
Syria and the African provinces, where the Arab tribal structure
persisted with little change, and the solutions to the problems of
faith and order worked out in the former might be inapplicable to
or even rejected by the latter. Still more, too close an association of
orthodoxy with the Abbasid Caliphate might well lead, and did in
fact lead, to the rejection of orthodoxy by sections politically opposed to Abbasid rule, as in the adhesion of the Berber opposition
in Northwest Africa to Kharijism and the increasing attraction of
the Arab tribesmen in Arabia and the Syrian desert to Shiism. The
dangers could not be averted by the maintenance of Abbasid political authority by force, but only if religious authority were
clearly distinguished from political authority and if necessary in
opposition to it.

The problem was probably not at first explicit to the religious leaders in these terms, but it is a proof of the vitality of the
Islamic religious impulse that their activities tended, even if un-
consciously, in this direction. Although they accepted on the whole
the Abbasid "official interpretation" for some seventy or eighty
years, and supported the measures employed by the state for religious unification and against heresy, yet there was from the first a
current of opposition to some of its manifestations and to state control of religious functions, and an insistence on the free personal
responsibility of the religious teacher. The conflict was brought into
the open by the attempt of Caliph al-Mamun and his successors to
impose the Hellenizing doctrines of the group of religious teachers
known as the Mutazila as the "official interpretation," and their

persecution of the leaders of the opposing orthodox school. The struggle ended with the victory of the orthodox, and proved once and for all that the religious institution of Islam was independent of the caliphate or any other political institution, that its sources of authority could not be controlled by political governors but were possessed by the community in its own right, and that the caliphate itself was only an emanation of that authority and its political symbol.

This episode was fundamental for the whole future of Islam in freeing it from identification with any political regime, and allowing the religious institution, and the community with it, freedom to develop along the lines of its own inner logic and temperament. But simultaneously—in a more complex and less explicit manner—the conflict between the religious and political institutions was being fought out on another field, and this time with a less favorable outcome for the religious institution.

The introduction of the Persian monarchical tradition and political philosophy into the Muslim state resulted in a conflict of social and ethical ideals, which was fought out largely in a "battle of the books." The Persianizing movement, known as the *Shuubiya* movement, is usually regarded[5] as a current of reaction among the Persians against Arab dominance. But this is too narrow an interpretation. Its representatives were the class of secretaries in government service, whose influence had greatly increased under the Abbasid Caliphs owing to the rapid expansion of the bureaucracy and the growing power of viziers and heads of administrative departments (*diwans*). From late Umayyad times the secretaries had found their models in the court literature of Sasanian Persia, and the significance of the Shuubiya movement is that it represents the efforts of the secretarial class (while avoiding an open conflict with the religious institution) not only to establish the dominance of the Persian tradition at the court, but to revive the old Persian social structure with its rigid class divisions, and to substitute the spirit of Persian culture for the surviving influences of the Arab tradition in the new and rapidly developing urban society in Iraq, by the spread of translations and popular works of Persian origin.

Its first effects were to encourage the revival of the latent Manichaeism in Iraq, and the spread, in much wider circles, of religious indifference or concealed disrespect for Islam. While the official institution tried to stamp out heresy by persecution, the more advanced and rigorous group of the religious leaders, known as the Mutazila, sought and found in Greek philosophical litera- ture and Christian-Hellenistic apologetic works the dialectic equip- ment to meet and overcome the dualist arguments and to reinforce an ethic based on the Koran. At the same time, as the Shuubiya movement passed into a phase of open attack on the Arabs and sarcastic criticism of Arab traditions and pretensions, it brought the whole body of the religious institution up in defence of Arabic studies on religious grounds, since it was these studies which sup- plied the basis of the developing "religious sciences." Out of the effort to counteract the literary activities of the Shuubis, a new Arabic humane literature was born, steeped in the traditions and institutions of Arabia, both before and after the rise of Islam; and the force and weight of the double counteattack quickly checked the dangers implicit in the Shuubiya movement.

By this victory the Islamic religious institution, which had already rejected any domination of its ideals of faith and order by Arab social traditions, now equally rejected the Persian interpreta- tion of Islam as a state religion and the dominance of Persian social traditions. But the victory was bought at a price. On the one hand the link between the religious sciences and Arabic philology had now been expanded into something not far from identification of the religious culture of Islam with the Arabic humanities. It is a strange phenomenon that while Islam began as a protest against Arab culture and tradition as a whole, by the end of this period the literary heritage of ancient Arabia was indissolubly linked up with Islam, to be carried with it to the ends of the old world. On the other hand, the influence of the secretarial class had been strong enough to force a measure of compromise. Several of the principal elements of the Sasanian tradition were incorporated in the litera- ture of the Arabic humanities, and acquired an established and permanent place in Islamic culture in relation to the principles of government, in spite of their conflict with its inner spirit.

This concession was highly characteristic of the orthodox religious institution, which, while standing fast on the principle of its spiritual independence and its right and duty to assert Islamic ethical standards, yet recognized the facts of the actual situation and the dangers of an excessive rigidity to the maintenance of unity. At the same time, by admitting this discordant element into the general fabric of Islamic culture, it brought a kernel of derangement into Muslim society. Its immediate effect was to bring to the surface the hitherto latent or concealed division between the religious institution and the ruling institution, and to set the latter free to pursue its own course of development with relatively little control from the side of the religious institution; ultimately, as it diverged more and more widely from the ethical standards of Islam, the orthodox *ulama* themselves were to find their spiritual independence endangered by the still further concessions and compromises wrung from them for the sake of the principle of unity.

V

The process analyzed in the preceding sections, by which the orthodox religious leaders disentangled Islam from political and racial interests and traditions, involved a parallel and simultaneous process of definition of its content. Islam was at first an orientation of life in all its aspects in a particular ethical direction, dictated by the acceptance of certain general beliefs on the authority of Koranic revelation. In the early struggles, the religious leaders aimed to maintain that orientation against a variety of challenges, external in the sense that their motivating forces were derived from other systems of values, though issuing from within the community and expressed in terms of a particular interpretation of Islam. In meeting each challenge, therefore, they were compelled to oppose its particular interpretation, but their tendency was at first to reject what was opposed rather than assert positively what was to be accepted, and thus maintain the widest possible measure of moral unity. This policy, consciously and consistently pursued, became a marked characteristic of orthodoxy; unlike the fissiparous and exclusive groups which upheld the rejected doctrines, its leaders were unwilling to draw hard and fast lines (beyond the simplest test of adherence to the community) and tolerated a considerable degree of freedom of interpretation and even of divergence in external institutions.

With the development of the religious organization and the advance from defence against deviation to positive definition of doctrine, involving the creation of a theological science, a step of decisive importance was taken for the whole history of Islam.[6] For this was its first intellectual adventure, it absorbed the energies of most of its intellectual leaders in the second, third and fourth centuries, and consequently gave a permanent bias to Islamic intellectual culture.

The origins of its methodology are to be found in the practical problems with which the community was confronted rather than in any philosophical tendencies. Although the authority of the Koran was absolute and unchallenged, the development of doctrine and law from its religious and ethical contents involved a process of elucidation and interpretation. The first problem appears to have arisen in regard to the application of law. By the end of the first century, separate and diverging rules of law were being applied in different cities and provinces, based on the independent interpretations of local teachers, and complicated by survivals of customary law and administrative regulations. The religious leaders saw in this a danger, especially when local rules appeared to diverge from the ethical principles of the Koran. The method by which they proceeded was to produce "Traditions" from contemporaries of the Prophet which related the decisions of Muhammad on specific points, and to claim for these binding authority scarcely inferior to that of the Koran. Although at first the authenticity of many Traditions was disputed by the jurists, and much confusion was caused by the production of contradictory Traditions, the strength of religious feeling behind the movement ultimately forced a general acceptance of the principle.[7] This in turn involved the elaboration of a new science, whose objects were the collection, criticism, classification and co-ordination of Traditions, and the attainment as far as possible of an agreed and generally accepted corpus. This task absorbed much of the energies of religious and legal scholars in the third century, and was achieved with such success that henceforward the Tradition of the Prophet ranked as a second authoritative source of law and doctrine.

The same method was then applied to dogmatic theology, in the conflict with the speculative reasoning applied by the Mutazilite school to the interpretation of Koranic doctrine. The orthodox leaders proceeded not so much by argument as by production of Prophetic Traditions in support of their positions, and in the same way swung the main body of Muslims into line behind them. There can be little doubt, however, that the classical collections of Prophetic Traditions made in the third century do substantially represent the views of the general body of orthodox religious teachers of the first three or four generations, and it is almost as certain that the views expressed in them faithfully reflect the teachings and ethical attitudes of the Koran.

The Muslim doctors who elaborated this defence of unity against disruptive deviations were still aware of its artificial foundations, and the techniques of study included in the "sciences of Tradition" were designed to authenticate the whole structure by a system of formal criteria. But this was not enough. In conformity with the general trend of Sunni thought, the foundations were underpinned by the principle that once agreement on any main issue of doctrine or law had been reached by responsible scholars, it was final and conclusive, and to reopen controversy on it was heresy. On lesser matters, diversity of opinion and practice was permissible. By this principle the orthodox institution was enabled, in spite of the absence of any formal organization, to hold together in all later centuries, and to remain essentially one in the face of political pressures, calamities, and the influx of new ideas and peoples.

On the other hand it was this combination of (1) a God-given and unchallengeable sacred book, interpreted and supplemented by (2) an artificial creation of Prophetic Tradition, itself canonized by (3) the doctrine of consensus (*ijma*), and thereby excluded from any but formal study by predetermined methods and rules, which established the basic character and attitudes of Muslim theological studies, however widely the range of theological discussion might extend in the future. By confining scholarship within the limits of a body of accepted teaching, it gradually diminished and finally inhibited the independent examination of authorities, sources and methods, and condemned it more and more to mere transmission of the known and given, and the elaboration of subsidiary detail in commentary and supercommentary. The habit of transmission of what had been accepted on authority, inculcated first in the sciences of law and theology, ultimately extended its influence over all Muslim studies in every field of learning, to the exclusion of personal investigation.

But these results were not immediate. The first systems to become crystallized were in the field of orthodox law (*Sharia*), and the importance of this early and relatively rapid stabilization of legal norms, with their effects upon the social ethics of the community, will be seen later. In dogmatics, however, while universal agreement had been reached by the end of the third century on fundamentals, principles and authorities, there was still room for variety in interpretation. This was of great significance in the history of Islamic culture; for although there were currents of rigorism in some of these interpretations, the majority of orthodox leaders continued to admit a certain range of individual freedom. Thus they not only gave room for the development of cultural and intellectual activities which found expression in the "Islamic Renaissance" of the fourth, fifth and sixth centuries, but themselves participated in them in a certain measure.

VI

The credit for the "renaissance" itself, however, is not to be given solely to the toleration of the orthodox institution. Even in its intellectual and religious aspects, much of it was due in a positive sense to unorthodox and sectarian influences, and to the widespread growth of material culture resulting from economic development and prosperity. These also, during the preceding centuries, had been developing independently of the orthodox religious culture; and at the time when they came to fruition, in the fourth century, the orthodox were the less able to control their intellectual or material activities because, from the fourth to the middle of the fifth century, almost the whole of the central Islamic lands were governed by Shiite princes.

There may be a certain causal relation between these facts and a very remarkable feature of the Islamic Renaissance: the personal and individual character of most of its cultural achievements. Orthodoxy from the first stressed the "collectivity" as against the individual; even the individual personalities who played a leading part in the evolution of the religious institution were more often representatives of collective tendencies than creative thinkers. The great biographical dictionaries of orthodox scholars are concerned very little with their individuality as persons, but only with their contributions to the transmission of the collective heritage. It is a tempting conclusion that it was the other currents of intellectual activity, outside the orthodox institution, which were mainly responsible for the appearance and activity of those individuals whose personal contributions swelled the total of achievements of medieval Islamic culture, even when they were themselves orthodox.

It may be surprising, at first sight, that many of the most active movements and personalities in the third and fourth centuries have Shiite attachments, since Shiism in its organized dogmatic institution is even more authoritarian than orthodoxy. But Shiism at this time was more of a widely diffused emotional or intellectual tendency, sometimes combined with Sunni orthodoxy, and it is erroneous to visualize hard and fast lines of sectarian division as already solidified in the fourth century. It was natural that individuals who were emotionally or intellectually opposed to the developing tendencies within orthodoxy should find more freedom in the looser and vaguer current of Shiism. Moreover although the orthodox institution had asserted its spiritual independence of the political institution, it still continued to be associated with the civil authorities, partly as a result of the historical factors outlined above, partly because of its horror of disunity, and partly owing to the government's control of religious patronage. For similar reasons, the bureaucracy and the feudal landowners were as a whole strongly orthodox, and thus the leaders of orthodoxy not only were classed, but classed themselves, among the elite (al-khassa), in contradistinction to the merchants, troops, artisans, peasants and nomads (al-awamm). Many religious leaders and teachers, as will be seen later, were embarrassed or dissatisfied with this situation, and while their strong feeling for the cohesion of the community kept most of them loyal to orthodoxy, the more extreme or more independent were liable to be attracted into one or other of the opposition movements.

The phenomenal expansion of industry and commerce had in the meantime created a network of cities in the eastern provinces, with a highly developed urban life and prosperous merchant communities, possessing knowledge of the world, intelligence, boldness and independence. Their interests (as usual in flourishing commercial civilizations) were mainly secular, even while they remained attached to orthodoxy; but they no longer found adequate intellectual nourishment in Persian romances or the classical Arabic humanities. With the political unification of Western Asia and the multiple interactions between its cities, there came a rapid and widespread revival of the traditions of Hellenistic culture, followed by a general expansion of intellectual curiosity, the transplantation into Arabic literature of the physical and natural sciences, astrology, Hellenistic themes in tales and romances, and a new interest in geographical works and travels in foreign countries.

At the other end of the scale was an urban proletariat of poor artisans, freedmen and slaves; in between, there grew up a floating population of commission men, agents, traveling teachers, poets and vagrants of all kinds. The social and economic grievances of these classes were exploited by the Shiite opponents of the orthodox institution, but their successes among the Bedouins of the Syrian desert, the cultivators in Lower Iraq, and the proletariat of the cities created only nuclei of social disorder, without constructive objects or cultural ideals. Far more important for the development of Islamic culture was the "reformed" Fatimid Ismaili movement towards the end of the third century, which deliberately aimed at building up a new religious institution on the basis of the integration of Islam with Hellenistic culture, and at enlisting the new educated classes in its support. The leaders of the movement set up regular centers for systematic instruction and organized an extensive missionary propaganda; the popular masses were not neglected, and in the city lodges or guilds were constituted for craftsmen.[8] By the date of the transfer of the Fatimid Caliphate from Tunisia to Cairo (973) the whole Muslim world was honeycombed with Fatimid agencies.

The significance of the Fatimid movement in the Islamic Renaissance is not to be measured only by the contributions of its professed adherents or sympathizers (such as Abul-Hatim al-Razi and al-Farabi in philosophy; Ali b. Yunus in astronomy; Ibn al-Haitham in physics and optics; Masawaih and Ali b. Ridwan in medicine; the treatises of the Ikhwan al-Safa in the natural sciences), but by the encouragement which it gave to intellectual activities of all kinds, even among its political or religious opponents, and its influence long survived the fall of the Fatimid Caliphate in 1171. It spread a spirit of free enquiry, individual endeavour, and interaction of ideas, which expressed itself in the works of almost all the outstanding writers of Persia and Iraq in the fourth century, and most notably in Ibn Sina (Avicenna), and found echoes even in Muslim Spain, in spite of the restrictive tendencies of the orthodox Maliki school and the Almoravid rulers.

For a short time, this advance and diffusion of learning took on something of the character of an organic movement, spreading to every part of the Islamic world, irrespective of political and sectarian boundaries. A new power of intellectual organization was manifested, new methods or combinations were tried out, new types of production evolved in which to present the results of scientific study and literary culture in intelligible form to men of general education,[9] great libraries were built up, hospitals and observatories founded. The old social divisions between Arab and non-Arab were obliterated in the new civilization and even those which separated Muslims from non-Muslims were softened. Jewish and Christian scholars participated in all intellectual activities on an equality with Muslim scholars; this reflected also upon their social status, and admitted them to an honorable place in the bureaucracy and the public services, though they continued to be exposed from time to time to popular excesses. The leaders of orthodoxy themselves were drawn into the general current to the extent of underpinning its dogmatic foundations by a natural theology derived from prevalent scientific theories; but they were fully conscious of the heretical tendencies present in many branches of study and maintained a jealous independence of the inverse efforts of men like Ibn Sina to relate the prevailing philosophical theories to the principles of Islam.

In general, therefore, the consequence of this intellectual expansion was to broaden out the whole range of the Arabic humanities by the incorporation of the legacy of Hellenistic culture, which survived as a permanent element in the Arabic-Islamic cultural tradition, uneasily yoked with the religious and old Arabic disciplines. In the arts and architecture also there was a parallel expansion, as the old pre-Muslim arts, Hellenistic, Syrian and Persian were revived, developed and diffused, with the requisite adaptations, to create a new Muslim art, whose cultural foundations and significance, however, have not yet been adequately studied.[10]

The Islamic Renaissance suffered, on the other hand, from serious weaknesses. It was a culture and civilization of the city, which confirmed the already marked urban character of the orthodox culture, arising out of the association of the orthodox institution with government. The immense economic development of the cities completed this process by the concentration of wealth and intellectual activities in them, to the exclusion of the countryside, which had little or no share in the developing civilization, and remained divided from the cities by a widening social gulf. Furthermore, even within the cities, the instability and inorganic character of the political institutions, and the social tensions which prevented the development of municipal institutions, offered a constant threat to cultural activities outside the range of orthodoxy, which itself maintained an ambiguous attitude towards them. Hence, with all the remarkable intellectual achievement of the Islamic Renaissance, its foundations remained shallow, rooted neither in the deep soil of the Islamic movement nor in strong social organisms. It was confined to a narrow (if for the time being widespread and prosperous) layer of urban society, and dependent on temporary factors. So long as a flourishing urban civilization existed, local retractions in one region might be counterbalanced by expansion in another, but its survival was bound up with the survival of the temporary factors to which it owed its existence.

VII

The orthodox revival in the fifth century of the Hijra (the eleventh of the Christian era) marks the turning-point in the history of Islamic culture. It began as a systematic effort to remove or to counteract all the factors of instability and disunity, political, social, religious and moral, within the Muslim Community, but led ultimately as will be seen, to a thoroughgoing revolution.

The peculiarly inorganic character of the political institutions during the two preceding centuries was due partly to the conflict with the orthodox institution in the third century and partly to the composition of the military forces. The result of the former had been to delimit sharply the functions of the political institution, confining the activities of the governors to maintenance of order and public security, military policy and financial administration. All other functions—the administration of law,[11] education, social institutions—remained the jealously guarded preserve of the religious authorities. The religious institution thus interposed between government and subjects, and claimed their exclusive loyalty as the true representatives of Islamic authority. So long, however, as the army was recruited from among the subjects directly or through the association of the feudal nobles with the government, there still remained a positive link between rulers and people. When this was removed by the formation of professional armies of slaves and mercenaries no organic relation was left; the only remaining connection was the tax-gathering function. It has been well said that in medieval Islam there were never real "states" but only "empires" more or less extensive, and that the only political unity was the ideological but powerful concept of the *dar al-Islam*, the common homeland of all Muslims.[12]

The indifference, passing into hostility, of the general population to the political organizations made the existence and survival of rulers, dynasties and regimes dependent, with rare exceptions, on the quality of their military forces. Since the religious institution was, for the reasons already given, precluded from acting effectively as a mediating force, the political history of the later third and fourth centuries was mainly occupied by the struggle between the caliphs, princes and armed forces for power,

eventually won, in every case, by the army commanders. Thus the
fourth century saw the complete breakdown of the political organization built up by the caliphate on the Roman and Persian
foundations.[13] The final blow was given during the century of
Shiite governments in Western Asia, an era of widespread misrule
and anarchy, which bore most heavily on the countryside, although
the disorders and ideological divisions affected the cities also in
varying degrees.

The urban communities in all parts of the medieval Muslim
world have one remarkable feature in common: the development
of more or less organized popular parties, and the frequency of
violent outbreaks either between them or against the government.
This may be explained partly by the nomadic heritage of many
citizens, partly by the existence of a large proletariat, whose grievances were championed or exploited by local reformers or agitators, often in combination with anti-Sunni movements. Examples
may be found in the standing feud in Baghdad between the Sunnis
and the Shiites, and the anti-Ismaili riots of the Karramites in the
Persian cities.[14] But as often the rival parties were of the same sect,
or of different orthodox schools, as in the feuds between Hanafites
and Shafiites in Khurasan. Lawlessness on the part of the troops
led repeatedly to the formation of citizen organizations for defence
and reprisals, which sometimes became no more than robber gangs.
This lack of internal unity in the cities, sharpened by the mutual
suspicions of proletariat, merchants and governors, even found
physical expression in their organization in separate and independent quarters, with their own defences. In such features, as well
as in the absence of leadership by the merchant classes (who were
inclined to keep out of public life), are probably to be found the
reasons for the failure of the medieval Islamic cities to develop
organized municipal institutions.

The orthodox revival began at the end of the fourth century
in Khurasan, the one important region in Western Asia which had
not fallen under Shiite government, apparently in response to the
challenge of the organized missionary activities of the Fatimids on
the one hand, and the consolidation of "Twelver" Shiism into a
rival religious institution during the century of Shiite rule in
western Persia and Iraq. Early in the fifth century, the Shafiites

were organizing orthodox colleges (known as *madrasas*) in imitation of the Fatimid missionary institutions.[15] But the revival had also a political aim: the liberation of the caliphate from Shiite control. In pursuance of their object, the Sunni leaders formed what amounted to an alliance with the Seljuk leaders of the immigrating Turkish tribes from the East, an alliance formally ratified by the caliph himself after the Seljuk conquest of western Persia and Iraq (1055).

The renewed association under the Seljuks of the ruling and orthodox institutions was drawn still closer by the initiative of the vizier Nizam al-Mulk in founding *Nizamiya* madrasas. These were not only religious seminaries for directing and systematizing higher education, but training colleges in the Arabic humanities for a new class of administrators, the "orthodox bureaucracy" which replaced the former secretarial class, and in the Seljuk empire and its successors held a place as directors of civil administration alongside the military governors of provinces and cities. Yet at the same time the functional division between the ruling and religious institutions was more sharply defined than ever by the formal constitution of the sultanate, as the organ of political and military administration, alongside (though ideally subordinate to) the caliphate, as the head of the religious institution. It was the same Nizam al-Mulk who reaffirmed this duality by restating in his *Siyasat-nama*[16] the old Persian tradition of monarchy, with its independent ethical standards based on force and opportunism, thus perpetuating the inner disharmony which has always proved to be the principal weakness of Islam as a politico-social organism.

Nevertheless, by the device of forming an administrative class belonging to the religious institution and setting it alongside the secular governors, it is probable that something more was aimed at than a merely formal link between them. It is reasonably certain that one object was to preserve the spiritual independence of the orthodox institution against the increasing power and absolutism of the temporal princes, and at the same time to maintain (or to recreate) the unity of the community. Each party was expected to find its own interest in supporting the other; "kingship and religion are twins." A further measure of Nizam al-Mulk indicates his strong sense of social order. Both the military organization and the bureaucratic institution were assimilated to the old (and by now almost extinct) Persian landowning class by a reconstructed feudal system. Thus by the dual means of association with the religious institution and tying the army to the soil, the ruling institution would regain in some measure the organic character which it had lost. By the same association the religious institution would gain the support of the ruling institution in its efforts to recreate unity; for it must not be forgotten that the orthodox revival was a deliberate reaction against the experience of division during the period of Shiite governments.

The same pursuit of unity is manifest in the gradual concentration of all higher education, both for religious and public service, in the new madrasas. It is improbable that this was deliberately designed to narrow down education and circumscribe intellectual activities, by control and patronage, to the religious and philological sciences. The fact of narrowing down was rather the natural consequence of this concentration combined with other factors. First, it was inevitable that the attempt should be made to bring all other studies into an organic relation with the religious and literary interests of the madrasa; this involved some degree of standardization, and the teaching of these standardized materials in the authoritarian manner already described. Second, once the Hellenistic elements were assimilated into the Arabic humanities, there were no new elements from outside which could be brought into Islamic culture to challenge the established disciplines or give a fresh impulse to intellectual development.[17] Third, the inner decline of urban culture (to be described later) brought with it a narrowing down of intellectual interests.

For some centuries, however, the influences of the Islamic Renaissance remained active within the orthodox institution, and were not entirely crushed out by the process of standardization. Intellectual energies found new outlets in place of philosophical, scientific and secular studies. It is instructive to observe the consequences of the Sunni revival movement in Syria and Egypt under Nuraddin and Saladin and their successors (under whom a powerful orthodox bureaucracy maintained an exceptionally close association with the rulers). After the general decay of cultural life

in the later Fatimid period, the introduction of the organized
Nizamiya type of education brought an outburst of intellectual
life, literature and cultural activities of many kinds, including a
revival of art and architecture. For two centuries they remained at
a high level before beginning to be affected by the germs of decay
from standardization and the increasing subordination of the
orthodox institution to the Mamluk military aristocracy.

At the same time, the Sunni revival aimed at eradicating
Shiism not only as a political force, but as an element of moral
disunity. This proved to be, on the whole, surprisingly easy. In the
intellectual field Shiite dogmatics were smothered by the formulation of orthodox dogmatics in final and authoritative treatises.
Among the general public the earlier sympathetic attitude towards
Shiism was largely dissipated by the century of Shiite misgovern-
ment and the weakness of the later Fatimids. But the orthodox
leaders wisely gave satisfaction to the emotional attachment felt
for the house of Ali by incorporating the Shiite shrines as objects of
veneration within the orthodox community. Shiism survived only
in fragmentary groups, particularly among the tribesmen of lower
Iraq; and the activist movement of neo-Ismailis or "Assassins,"
organized in the mountainous fringes of northern Persia and
northern Syria, gained no following in spite of its terrorist campaign against the orthodox rulers and bureaucracy, but rather
strengthened the movement of Sunni reunion by the hostility
which it aroused.

The Sunni revival, linked with Seljuk expansion, achieved
by these means a striking success in reuniting and integrating at a
common level the whole urban culture of Western Asia and Egypt.
The rapidity of the process, however, and the solidity of the results
indicate that it did not so much create this unity as bring to
fruition already existing trends. The foundations had in fact been
laid during the preceding centuries by the slow but persistent pressure of the standardized Sharia law in remoulding the social ethics
and institutions of all Muslims, and substituting its common
processes and attitudes for their divergent older traditions. There
still remained, however, the problem of the social divisions and
antagonisms within the cities, and, related to it, the problem of

extending the influence of the orthodox religious movement to the populations outside the urban radius.

VIII

Among the established agricultural populations within the Islamic lands, it is generally possible to trace the gradual advance of the influence of the Sharia.[18] But from the fifth century conditions were radically changed in all parts of the Muslim world by the resurgence of the nomads: the irruption of Turkish tribes in east and north Persia, Mesopotamia and north Syria, Arab tribal movements in Syria, Egypt and North Africa, Berber movements in North Africa. In large areas the substitution of pastoral for agricultural economy led to economic retrogression; and although the nomads were kept in relative check at first by Seljuk imperial power, from the middle of the sixth century they were throwing off all control, and reducing the cities in Persia and the northern provinces to islands of "oasis culture," dependent for their survival on armed garrisons of imperial troops or the forces of local princes. Thus at the very moment when the orthodox institution had succeeded in integrating the urban culture of Islam under its aegis, that culture itself was increasingly hemmed in by the nomadic expansion and endangered by the immigration of new Turkish tribes who were not even nominally Muslim.

In these circumstances, the leaders of the orthodox institution began to realize the value of the revivalist missions led by sufi preachers among the urban proletariat and in the countryside, which they had hitherto regarded with some suspicion and hostility. The pietist missionaries who labored to produce conversions among the artisans and proletariat were inclined to share the proletariat's suspicions of the orthodox institution, as too closely identified with the political powers, even if they were still more strongly opposed to sectarian divisions and activist movements of all kinds. They disliked, moreover, the intellectualizing tendencies in orthodox theology, which seemed to emphasize external profession to the detriment of personal devotion. The orthodox leaders, for their part, distrusted the mystical and gnostic currents which were flowing into Sufism from the older Asian religions, the theosophical claims to union with the Divine, and the organized religious exercises for its adherents which threatened to displace the mosque rituals.

But the spiritual vitality of the sufi movement could not be denied, and indeed some accommodation with it was forced upon the orthodox leaders by imperative circumstances. Long before the Seljuk invasion, sufi missionaries had extended their activities into and beyond the frontier areas, and had been instrumental in the conversion of the Turkish tribes, among whom consequently their influence was greater than that of the orthodox doctors. The association of the Sunni reaction with the Seljuks thus reopened the question of the relations between the sufis and the orthodox institution. It was not an easy problem for the theologians, however, in their quest for unity, to integrate the sufi movement in the orthodox religious institution, until the great theologian al-Ghazzali (d. 505:1111), in his most important work,[19] demonstrated the truly Islamic foundation of Sufism, and reconciled both by the argument that orthodoxy without the revivalist leaven of Sufism was an empty profession, and Sufism without orthodoxy dangerous subjectivism.

Henceforward, in the movement of reunion the religious institution is represented both by the orthodox institution (including the religious bureaucracy) and by the sufi shaikhs, with the special function of missionary work in the cities and countryside. Everywhere sufi convents were founded simultaneously with madrasas, and on the whole the leaders of both wings co-operated with relatively little friction or jealousy. Gradually, however, the sufi movement, organizing itself as a rival institution, drained the orthodox institution of most of its vigor and vitality, and finally, when the dwindling of the religious bureaucracy in face of the encroachments of the ruling military classes in Egypt and India reduced the orthodox institution to a dangerous dependence on the ruling institution, found itself the champion of spiritual independence against both the rulers and the official ulama.

From the ninth to the thirteenth century, moreover, Sufism increasingly attracted the creative social and intellectual energies within the community, to become the bearer or instrument of a social and cultural revolution—a process hastened on by the destruction of the still vigorous centers of Islamic culture in north Persia during the Mongol invasion of 1220, and the Mongol occupation of all Western Asia (except Syria) after the capture of Baghdad in 1258. The orthodox institution was eclipsed under the rule of heathen princes, and though it gradually revived in the following century its social and political foundations were too weak to allow it to recover its former influence. Its function of maintaining the unity of the community thus passed to the sufi movement, in new and difficult circumstances. This fact itself determined that the sufi methods of operation would differ from those of the orthodox institution, but was also in keeping with their own historical origins. In contrast to the orthodox institution, the sufi movement was based on its popular appeal, and its new structure of religious unity was built on popular foundations. It would be difficult to prove (or even to imagine) that the sufi leaders consciously formulated a plan of action, and the result was achieved in a manner which gives the impression of spontaneous action, initiated independently and almost simultaneously in both the eastern and western lands of Islam.

This development arose out of two cardinal elements in Sufism: the close personal relation between the sufi shaikh and his disciples, and its missionary spirit. Whereas in the early centuries, however, the sufi circles were individual and dispersed units, the loose proliferation of individual activities was now replaced by more organized structures. Regular colleges were founded, with the aid of benefactions and alms, by particular shaikhs, who commissioned their leading disciples, after training in the special rites and rules of the "order," to organize daughter colleges in other centers and regions, and these maintained a close association with the original college and the successors of its founder.

Such networks of affiliated colleges and convents constituted a "path" (*tariqa*). Their function was not only to train initiates but to serve as centers of religious instruction and spiritual influence among the general population, who were associated with the order as "lay members." At some stage, not yet definitely established, lay membership was integrated with the guild organizations of artisans and other professions, each guild or corporation being affiliated to a particular *tariqa,* and extended also to village and tribal areas. While many *tariqas* had only local importance, the greater orders (such as the Qadiri, Shadhili and Suhrawardi) spread over the whole or a large part of Islamic territory. Thus they contributed, even more effectively than the orthodox institution (but at the same time building upon the foundations laid in earlier centuries by the common authority of the *Sharia*), to maintain the ideal unity of all Muslims, in spite of the existence of a very few Shiite *tariqas* and of deviation from strict orthodoxy among the initiates of some more extreme orders.

It was not only the physical expansion of the great *tariqas,* however, that served the cause of unity. Teachers and disciples journeyed from end to end of the Muslim world, bearing the seeds of interchange and cross-fertilization within the sufi framework. While this had been a characteristic of Islamic culture from the early centuries, its importance was now immensely increased. One consequence of the Turkish immigrations and Mongol invasions was to harden the division of the Muslim lands into separate Arabic, Persian and Turkish linguistic regions, between which literary intercommunication was confined to restricted circles of the educated. Although the effects of this division can be seen also in the distribution of the *tariqas,* the activities of the sufi teachers did much to counteract them by furnishing a means for the transference of ideas across linguistic frontiers and guiding their further development on parallel lines.

How effective the communication of ideas was between the initiates in every region is strikingly shown by a development which was to prove of decisive significance for the future cultural action and influence of Sufism—the evolution of its own intellectual system and literature. In its pure essence, Sufism, being a personal religious attitude emphasizing intuitive experience as against rational knowledge, could, in so far as it added to or diverged from the *Sharia* basis of Islam, present no common body of doctrine. But it was inevitable that as institutional forms developed with organized teaching, certain doctrinal tendencies should crystallize within them. The general trend was towards pantheism; but in the major orders these tendencies were stabilized in either one of two related philosophies. One was illuminationist, deriving ultimately from Asiatic gnosticism and systematized by Yahya al-Suhrawardi;[20] the other was monist, deriving from popular Hellenistic philosophy (probably through the Fatimid literature), and expounded by the Spanish Arab Muhyid-din Ibn al-Arabi.[21] The former was widely disseminated in the eastern provinces; the latter at first in the Arabic and Turkish orders, but later also in the east.

The intellectual consequences of this were extremely grave. Instead of revitalizing the inert matter of scholastic instruction in the madrasas, it drew intellectual energies off into subjective and antirational speculation, leaving the former more inert than ever and supplying no rigorous intellectual discipline in its place. On the other hand—emphasizing the social function of Sufism as an expression of cultural unity—these mystical institutions and adumbrations were enshrined in a new poetical literature, which utilized popular literary forms (wine songs, love songs, romances, apologues) and transposed or transformed their imagery into religious symbolism. These productions spread all over the Muslim world, in Arabic, Persian or Turkish, were appreciated by all classes, and for several centuries all but monopolized literary and aesthetic creation. The greater part of prose literature followed in their wake, furnishing in its higher ranges commentaries (in the true scholastic tradition) on the works of the masters and their successors or on the great Persian poems, and in its lower ranges lives and legends of the saints and other devotional works.

Finally the sufi movement, in spite of its original quietism and pacifism, took too firm root in the social organization of the Muslim peoples not to have also political effects. Especially in regions, such as Persia and Anatolia after the collapse of Mongol rule, where centralized political institutions had broken down by dynastic disruption or nomadization, the sufi brotherhood was often the only form of social organization left. It naturally served, in consequence, as the basis of association for self-defense against the violence of local tyrants or tribesmen, and in favorable conditions developed into a fighting force, emulating the achievements of the primitive Muslim armies "on the path of God." The inner history of northern Persia in the fourteenth and fifteenth centuries is obscure, but it seems probable that most political movements had sufi affiliations of some kind. In contemporary Anatolia, the town artisans were organized in *akhi* guilds, the tribal revolts were led by sufi shaikhs, and most of the small principalities were *"ghazi* states," devoted to war against the infidel and organized in corporations led by amirs but frequently, if not in all cases, associated with a sufi *tariqa.* Of the two great empires which were to divide Western Asia between them until the twentieth century, it has been shown fairly conclusively that the Ottoman Empire began as such a *"ghazi* state,"[22] and there is no question that its rival, the Safavid kingdom of Persia, was created by the shaikhs of the Safavi sub-order of the Suhrawardi *tariqa.*[23]

Thus through the influence and activity of Sufism the Islamic world was entirely transformed from the thirteenth century onward—spiritually, morally, intellectually, imaginatively and even politically—and only the orthodox madrasas preserved a tenuous link with the cultural tradition of medieval Islam.

NOTES

[1] The invested capital of Talha (d. 656) amounted to 30 million dirhams, and the daily yield of his enterprises in Iraq was a thousand dirhams or more (Ibn Sad, *Tabaqat,* III, 157-158); that of his fellow Meccan and collaborator, Zubair, was 35 millions, from investments in Iraq and Egypt *(ibid.,* III, 77) .

[2] See J. Wellhausen, *Die religiöspolitischen Oppositionsparteien* (Göttingen, 1901) .

[3] See *Encyclopaedia of Islam,* s. v. Murdjia.

[4] *Ibid.,* s. v. Djahm ibn Safwan.

[5] Especially since the studies of I. Goldziher in *Muhammedanische Studien,* vol. I, (Halle, 1888) .

[6] For an analysis of this process see A. J. Wensinck, *The Muslim Creed* (Cambridge, 1932) .

[7] This development is studied more particularly in J. Schacht, *The Origins of Muhammadan Jurisprudence* (Oxford, 1950) .

[8] The evidence for this is inferential, but fairly convincing; see B. Lewis, "The Islamic Guilds" in *Economic History Review,* vol. VIII, no. 1, Nov. 1937.

[9] See F. Rosenthal, *A History of Muslim Historiography* (Leyden, 1952), p. 171.

[10] See, e. g., Sir T. W. Arnold, *Painting in Islam, A Study of the Place of Pictorial Art in Muslim Culture* (Oxford 1928) ; Ernst Kühnel, *Die Arabeske* (Wiesbaden, 1949) ; Arthur Lane, *Early Islamic Pottery* (London, 1947).

[11] Except for special administrative courts for the army and bureaucracy.

[12] J. H. Kramers, in *Proceedings of the XXII International Congress of Orientalists* (Istanbul, 1953), p. 94. See also the article "Dar al-Islam" in *Encyclopaedia of Islam*.

[13] It survived under the Fatimid Caliphs in Egypt until the middle of the fifth century, but then broke down there also.

[14] See R. Levy, *A Baghdad Chronicle* (Cambridge, 1929), esp. pp. 160, 171, 179; and *Encyclopaedia of Islam*, s. v. Karramiya.

[15] The lead in this development had apparently been taken by the now obscure Karramite sect.

[16] Edited and translated by Ch. Schefer (Paris, 1891-1893).

[17] The only exception to this was the Chinese influence mediated at a later date through the Mongols, but this was fleeting and peripheral, and left an effective mark only in the domain of art in the further eastern provinces.

[18] For example, in the disappearance of Qarmatism in Iraq and of dualistic heresies in Persia, and the slow conversion of the Copts in Egypt.

[19] Entitled *Ihya ulum ad-din*, "The Revivification of the Religious Sciences." In his earlier works al-Ghazzali had summed up and consolidated the intellectual foundations of the orthodox revival in relation to dogmatics, the Hellenistic sciences, and the argument against the Shiites. See A. J. Wensinck, *La Pensée de Ghazzali* (Paris, 1940).

[20] Executed for heresy at Aleppo in 1191. See *Shihabaddin Yahya as-Suhrawardi: Opera Metaphysica et Mystica*, ed. H. Corbin, vol. I (Istanbul, 1945), Introduction.

[21] Died at Damascus 1240. See A. E. Affifi, *The Mystical Philosophy of Muhyid din-Ibnul Arabi* (Cambridge, 1939).

[22] See on this, and on conditions in Anatolia generally, P. Wittek, *The Rise of the Ottoman Empire* (London, 1938), especially pp. 33-40.

[23] See W. Hinz, *Irans Aufstieg zum Nationalstaat im fünfzehnten Jahrhundert* (Berlin-Leipzig, 1936).

BIBLIOGRAPHY

(in addition to works cited in the footnotes)

J. Sauvaget, *Introduction à l'histoire de l'Orient musulman*, 2nd. ed., Paris, 1961. Indispensable bibliographical work, with critical notes.

R. Levy, *The Social Structure of Islam*, 2 vol., London, 1933.

A. Mez, *Die Renaissance des Islams*, Heidelberg, 1922.

G. von Grunebaum, *Mediaeval Islam*, Chicago, 1946. Sometimes out of focus, but valuable for Byzantine and Hellenistic relations.

B. Spuler, *Iran in Früh-Islamischer Zeit*, Wiesbaden, 1952. Very detailed bibliography.

A. J. Arberry, *Sufism*, London, 1950.

F. Rosenthal, *The Technique and Approach of Muslim Scholarship* (Analecta Orientalia 24), Rome, 1947.

2. The Evolution of Government in Early Islam

The reign of Hisham (105-25:724-43) has long been recognized as the crisis of the Umayyad Caliphate, that is to say, the moment at which the political organization of Islam was confronted with the problem which every expanding organism must meet when it reaches the limits of its expansion. There are in history uncountable instances of imperial expansion, but very few in which the empire so created was able to attain to relative permanence and stability. To achieve this calls for a transformation of hitherto normal processes and habits of action, and the direction of energies into new channels designed to promote internal development, assimilation and cohesion. To use a biological simile, the organism which has furnished itself with the means and instruments for capturing its prey has to bring into play a new set of organs for assimilating it.

The problem which confronted Hisham was therefore not of his own making, but the outcome of a century of history, going back beyond the Umayyads to the Patriarchal Caliphs of Medina. The political organization which the first caliphs had created was essentially a military organization for the purposes of expansion and enjoyment of the fruits of conquest, and was furnished with no administrative organs for other purposes. The Umayyads inherited this organization and improved its efficiency. It suffered however from two factors of instability: (1) the instrument of conquest was an association of Arab tribesmen, atavistically resistant to control and easily stirred to rebellion; and (2) rival Meccan families (and even other Arab nobles), jealous of the power and material gains of the Umayyads, used every opportunity to exploit the resentments of the tribesmen. By a necessary and inevitable reaction to these challenges, there had resulted an increasing concentration of power in the person of the caliph and the emergence of new administrative organs designed to strengthen his control over the tribes.

The Umayyad Caliphate was therefore, in a manner, forced into becoming the symbol of a certain type of political organization, sometimes called *étatisme* or pursuit of the interests of the state, and became in consequence suspect on two counts. To the Arabs in general, with their inveterate interpretation of political concepts (like other general concepts) in personal terms, the "interests of the state" meant the interests of the Umayyad family,[1] and to the developing religious thought they implied thrusting the interests of Islam down to a secondary plane of consideration. Umar II tried to reverse the emphasis ("Muhammad came to summon men to the Faith, not to collect taxes"), and failed. The natural trend of development could not be arrested, and under Hisham the assertion of *raison d'état* reached a new climax. But simultaneously the basis upon which the power of the Umayyads rested had been steadily narrowing down, until in Hisham's time it came to depend only on the support of the Syrian forces and the new professional army organized by his cousin Marwan b. Muhammad. Since a large part of the old *muqatila* organization in Asia had fallen into disuse, it was no longer capable of continuing its former function of expansion and conquest; what remained of it could do no more than hold what had been gained.

There are ample evidences that Hisham was conscious of the changed situation of the Arab empire, both internally and externally, and set himself to meet it. By a general fiscal reorganization he removed the immediate grievances of the *mawali*[2] who had been supported in large measure by religious sentiment, and apart from this he cultivated the religous leaders to a greater extent than his predecessors had done, both positively, by personal association with them, and negatively, by active measures against heresy. On the other hand, he showed an open interest in the principles of the former Sasanid organization and the development of the administrative services in the direction of the Sasanid system.[3] But since the Sasanid traditions, with their centralized monarchy, powerful aristocracy, and organized religious hierarchy, were deeply uncongenial to Islamic thought, they could only emphasize still more strongly that monarchical evolution which scandalized religious opinion. Though the extent of the opposition to the Umayyad house, even by the time of Hisham, must not be exaggerated, it is clear that it was widely diffused, and by the fact of its wide diffusion made it difficult for the Umayyads (and for Hisham's successors, impossible) to carry out the structural readjustments which were demanded of the Arab empire by the new internal forces of social development, even more than by the limitations of its military power.

Yet the Abbasid caliphs, though in practice they were still more autocratic than the Umayyads, and their administration was still more closely adjusted to the Sasanid model, were able to satisfy Muslim feeling to a degree never attained by the Umayyads. It seems a paradox that the universal charge traditionally laid at the door of the Umayyads is that they transformed the caliphate into a kingship, whereas no Umayyad exercised such personal power or maintained such royal state as did the early Abbasids. The paradox itself suggests that if we are to understand the real nature of the crisis, we have to penetrate more deeply below the surface of events, and more especially free ourselves from the habit of the Arabic chroniclers to view the historical process in terms of personal action, without consideration of the relevant circumstances within which individuals acted and by which their action was circumscribed. The argument here to be presented is that the Umayyads were, so to speak, the victims of a dialectical process within Islamic society, a process of self-criticism by which its political ideals were gradually adumbrated; but since the society itself lacked the means or the will to define them and to articulate them in a political system, it tried to evade its own responsibilities by fastening the blame for its failure on the Umayyads, as convenient scapegoats.

I begin by drawing what seems to me an important distinction between different types of political tradition. The units which constitute the bodies politic of modern Western history are in origin either political or racial. In Eastern history, on the contrary, as also in the doctrine of the Christian church, the basis of the body politic is, as a general rule, ideological. As the result of the spread and acceptance of certain doctrines—which may or may not be religious in the strict sense (as, for example, the traditionalist ethic of Confucius)—there is evolved a new type of social order. This new social order is, at bottom, an adaptation of the pre-existing social organisms in the spirit of the new doctrines or ideology, and finds expression in a series of appropriate institutions which are created by the labours of successive generations of its adherents. At a relatively early date, for example, an institution for self-propagation is developed, i.e., an educational system; at a later stage, the older class structure or class groupings of its members are dissolved, in whole or in part, and new and more congenial groupings are substituted for them. Simultaneously, for the regulation of social relations, a new code or system of laws is evolved and brought into operation, and so forth. All of these institutions are interrelated, as being outgrowths or expressions of the ideological principle; but all are autonomous, subject only to the overriding authority of the ideological principle itself. "Tyranny" arises when any one of these institutions usurps control in a field outside its own, whether by upsetting the internal balance or by confusing or undermining their basic principles.

Among the institutions so created is the institution of government, which is primarily the organism serving the function of internal and external defence of the new society and its principles. Although the head of this institution is vested with a certain general power of supervision and control, the governing institution by itself (in the theoretical view of the matter) is in no way superior to the other institutions deriving from the ideology or its doctrinal principles, but is co-ordinate with them. But at this point there comes in the problem of power, that is to say, the means by which control can be maintained over the activities of those who possess or wield the largest share of the physical or other forces within the community, and of ensuring that these forces are used in directions consistent with the interests of the community as a whole, or with the ends aimed at in its co-ordinate institutions and desired by their supporters.

In the particular case we are now considering, the preaching of the Prophet Muhammad, as developed by his companions and successors, had two principal results: (1) it laid the foundation of a new order or structure of society; and (2) it created a powerful instrument of aggressive expansion, whether it was designed precisely for that purpose or not. But these two results were not simultaneous. The development of the first was a lengthy and complex process, involving the application of the doctrinal principles to social organisms and institutions over a period of several generations, and also the creation of appropriate organs and structures to express the resulting functions. The second, on the other hand, was an almost immediate development. Every creative idea generates an immense expansive energy by filling its adherents with missionary zeal; and when at the same time the idea expresses itself in a political institution—that is to say, asserts its distinctness from and opposition to other political institutions—then this expansive energy almost of necessity creates and encourages a spirit of rivalry, which finds an outlet in wars against the rival political institutions. When these aggressions are successful, and the range and size of operations constantly increase, then a tremendous instrument of power is brought into existence in a very short time.

Ideally, of course, this body of power ought to be the instrument of the ideology by which it was created. In practice, this condition is difficult to achieve, if not almost impossible, when a political institution has established itself in the early stages of the new movement. For power, once created and embodied in an institution, is a giant which cannot be controlled by its own creator, but rather controls him and follows the laws of its own being. There is only one thing that can control power, namely, an equal or superior power. It is one of the principal factors which has differentiated the history of Christendom from that of Islam that a Christian political institution began to be established only after three centuries from the foundation of Christianity, and that the political institution was from the first confronted by an ecclesiastical institution which had acquired from its leadership during the two preceding centuries a powerful authority over the wills and actions of its adherents. But in early Islamic history, so long as the expansive energies of the new ideology were flowing into its instrument of aggressive expansion, there was no internal organism of equal force to counterbalance it. Before a new society can even hope to control the instrument of force which it has itself created, some part of its expansive energies must be transferred to building up the other social institutions in which the new ideology is expressed.

But this, as already pointed out, takes time—certainly not less than a century, perhaps much more. And meanwhile the world does not stand still. This is the factor in the history of the Umayyad Caliphate so frequently misunderstood by later observers, whether misled by prejudice, or from lack of knowledge and sense of historical perspective. During the first century or so of its existence, the new ideology had not yet embodied itself in any social institutions other than that of government. Consequently there was no other institution to dispute the monopoly of power enjoyed by the institution of government. The alternative did not lie between the government's monopoly of power and its abdication of some of its power to some other institution. There was no other institution, and in any case power cannot be transferred. The only alternative lay between a monopoly of power—whether that was exercised by the Umayyads or by some other group—and anarchy. And that in practice only the Umayyads were capable of exercising it seems to be shown by the experiment during the Second Civil War of a Zubairid anti-caliphate, which degenerated into a thinly veiled anarchy.

In the next place, we have already defined the creation of the new social order as an adaptation or remolding of the pre-existing social organisms in the spirit of the new ideology. But this implies, not only that the older social organisms continue for a time to exist (as of course they do), but also—which is more important— that they still exercise a powerful social influence until they have been subjected to a long-continued and vigorous process of sapping and reconstruction by the other activities and organs of the new order. Consequently, since the instruments of power inevitably fall into the hands of the strongest, the new organization for aggressive expansion is sooner or later captured by those who represent the dominant social forces, even should those be still opposed to, or very imperfectly integrated with, the spirit of the ideology which created it.

This development began within the Islamic Community very early indeed—as early as the third caliphate. But it went even further, largely as the result of the violent reaction and reassertion of the old tribal groupings and political tendencies which shortly afterwards challenged the Islamic organization of government, with the same rapidity and suddenness with which it had been built up in the first place. This was the critical moment for the survival of the whole organized Islamic movement; the issue at stake in the First Civil War was no other than whether the new social factor and its political embodiment in the caliphate were to succeed in holding out or to be swept away. There can be little doubt that the inner impulse to the Civil War was the reassertion of tribal autonomy, but it was complicated by the personal position and aims of Ali. So far as can be glimpsed through the distortions of the later sources, Ali did not merely stand for a negation (i.e., opposition to the Umayyads or to the exploitation of the empire by the great Meccan families), but had also a positive vision of a structure of government which should embody the social and ethical values of the Islamic ideology. How in practice such a structure should be organized, and how it should control and master the disruptive tendencies displayed in the Civil War, we do not know; for the ideal was, as so often, swept under in the clash of the real forces engaged, and Ali found himself, or was compelled to become, the figurehead of the tribal reaction. Consequently, by another paradox, the victory of Ali could scarcely have led to any other conclusion than the destruction at the hands of the tribesmen of the only social institution as yet created by the Islamic ideology; whereas, by the victory of the Umayyads, that ideology was preserved, to re-emerge in time and grow in strength so mightily that ninety years later it all but exterminated its preservers.

It is evident, however, that after such a struggle the instrument of power, if it survives at all or can be refashioned, must be —in the first instance, at least—very different from the old instrument whose collapse brought about the Civil War. The ideological principle as such must emerge from the conflict weakened or shorn of much of its effective influence upon the organization of government, and the governing institution must be more consciously based upon the dominant social forces within the body politic.

I emphasize the word "consciously," because at this point the first true crisis within the movement is reached. The Civil War decided whether the Islamic movement, as an organized political force, was to continue or not; but the future of the political organization of Islam was decided by what was done after the Civil War. Muawiya might have chosen to rebuild the Arab empire upon an exclusively Arab foundation, and to give no place in his system to the Islamic principles. But he did not do so. While he was forced by the circumstances to give the main weight to Arab social traditions, he did what he could to supplement them by the moral influence of the Islamic ideology. Even when, under his successors, the Umayyad state was forced, by the instability of the Arab tribal structure and its failure to provide a solid foundation of power, to seek for new instruments and sanctions in the monarchical traditions of the empires which Islam had displaced, they still recognized the moral influences of the Islamic principles, and sought to gain and use their support. This is the essential point; this is where the Umayyads served the cause of Islam. For as long as the instrument of power recognizes the moral claims of the ideology, the creative and expansive forces inherent in the ideology remain unimpaired, and gradually take up the task of building up the other social institutions. More than that, the very fact that the power of the governing institution is largely drawn from other sources means that a large and increasing proportion of the creative energies generated by the new doctrines is transferred from the effort of external expansion to the problems of internal consolidation.

This transfer of energy does not, however, weaken the governing institution at all in the first instance. For the total sum of energy available is immense, and its transfer takes place very gradually. Moreover, we have seen that, in the case of the Umayyads, the expansive force originally called into being by the ideology had in effect become identified with the expansive force of Arab tribalism; at a later stage, as the ideological stimulus towards external expansion waned, the government was still able to rely on and to exploit the aggressive character which it had impressed upon the spirit and outlook of the tribesmen.[4] And since the aggressive spirit stirs up external opposition, it continues for some time to renew itself and to make still greater efforts to expand, in order to destroy the external enemies, or at least to weaken them to the point when they are no longer dangerous. Nevertheless, there must come a time, sooner or later, at which some rough equilibrium is reached in relation to the external forces—a point at which the impulse of expansion is either exhausted or has become too weak to overcome the opposing forces, and when the governing institution is forced back on the defensive.

This preludes the major crisis in the political development of the new society; for in the meantime, as the other social institutions take shape, and more particularly the new class structure and law are elaborated, they begin to exhibit and to illustrate, with a clarity hitherto lacking, the specific features and the general moral principles characteristic of the new society. And in so doing, they inevitably show up the fact that the principles which underlie the actions of the old established governing institution are more or less divergent from what are now coming to be accepted as the principles upon which the society is based, and may even be in certain respects opposed to them. Thus there springs up in an exaggerated form the tension which is always to be found in every society between the idealists and the realists, between those who wish to remodel the government of the society in accordance with their ethical principles, and those who hold the state to be inextricably entangled in the complex of human passions.

This conflict, however, rarely reaches a climax until what I have called a state of external equilibrium is reached, and the political institution, with the decline of its aggressive power, is moving into a defensive phase. In such an institution as the Umayyad Caliphate, the weakening of aggressive power against external enemies seems to be linked with a weakening of its power of internal compulsion—the two being in some way related, not logically but psychologically; but whether this is so or not, the whole problem still remains on the plane of power. Granted that the mere fact of the divergence between the principles of action of the state and the norms eventually recognized in the society as a whole creates a cleavage; granted further that the more the creative energy of the new ideology is diverted from the service of the governing institution into the elaboration of the other social institutions, the more intensely this cleavage is felt, and the more convinced men will be that their hopes and aspirations can be realized only by making a fresh start, and even by forcible over-throw of the existing government if it continues to resist their demands for a change of measures—granted all this, however, this moral indignation can produce effective results only in one of two ways.

Either the moral forces which have been exerting themselves in the construction of the new nonpolitical institutions become so widely and intensely active that they begin to exercise a real power of compulsion upon the governing institution, by defining their political ideals and forcing it to reshape itself into better agree-ment with these ideals and the principles now universally acknowl-edged. This is the peaceful (or what we might now call the demo-cratic) method. Or, alternatively, the opponents of the regime may seek to build up a rival aggressive power and hold it in readiness until the weakening of the government's own aggressive power offers, or seems to offer, an opportunity to overthrow the govern-ment by the method of civil war. During the reign of the Caliph Hisham both these methods were in operation. Few students of Islamic history would now doubt that the statesmen of the Umay-yad house had been profoundly influenced by the program of Umar II. But it would scarcely have needed a prophet to see that in a society in which the nomadic tradition of crude violence was still so powerful and could so easily be stimulated by appeals to atavistic instincts clothed in moral or religious terms, the chances of reaching a peaceful solution were not very high.

At the crisis of the First Civil War, as we have seen, the issue at stake was whether the political institution of Islam, the cali-phate, was to survive at all as an effective instrument of govern-ment, and its outcome was to re-establish the caliphate upon the dominant social forces of the time. In the Third Civil War, or Abbasid revolution, the issue at stake this time was not the imme-diate survival of the caliphate as such—since the existence of the caliphate was now taken for granted—but whether a new line of caliphs, whose power was based upon a new distribution of social forces, would or could bring the principles of the governing institution into line with the creative principles of the Islamic ideology.

The true significance of the Abbasid Caliphate can be assessed only from this point of view. It would be premature to attempt to answer here the questions which this raises. They involve first of all a fresh and objective assessment—which has not yet been made—of the physical and moral foundations of the power of the Abbasid caliphs, and after that an equally objective assessment of the positive relations of the caliphate to the other and rapidly developing social institutions of Islam. To what extent did the self-styled "Imamate" of the Abbasids really represent a closer adaptation of the institution and principles of government to the social principles of the Islamic ideology than the repudiated "kingship" of the Umayyads? How much of the extraordinarily rapid development, not only of material culture, but also in all the socio-religious institutions and their instruments, was due, directly or indirectly, to the changes in the bases and the attitudes of the governing institution under the early Abbasids?

I shall venture here only on one general remark, which does not prejudge the answer to the first of these questions, but indicates one respect at least by which the answer must be conditioned.

Revolutions, as history seems to show, rarely change the essential character of basic institutions, but only emphasize—with or without external change of structure—the tendencies which are already shaping them in a given direction. During the Umayyad Caliphate, among the influences which were shaping the governing institution of Islam, were, in the earlier period, the Hellenistic, and, towards its end, the Sasanian, traditions of government. In both of these traditions, the political institution was dominated by the millenial concept of the "Universal Empire" and the *Pan-basileus*. Whatever the degree of satisfaction which the Abbasid revolution may have given in its early years, and in response to other influences, to those forces in the Muslim society which had felt themselves hampered or thwarted by the Umayyads, in this respect there is no room for doubt that the Abbasid Caliphate was even more strongly influenced by the Sasanian form of the "universal empire" concept and its consequent modalities. Indeed, its influence went much further; for the later "juristic" expositions of the caliphate are reaffirmations of the principle of the "universal empire" in an Islamic guise or disguise.

But this fact does not mean that this "juristic" interpretation of the Sunni Caliphate was either a natural or a justifiable result of the application of Islamic principles to the governing institution. It means only that the Sunni jurists, *modo suo*, in seeking to justify the historical process, were forced to attempt to integrate the concept of the "universal empire" with Islam. In other words, the Abbasid Caliphate, so far from adapting its practice to the principles of the Islamic ideology, imposed on the official jurists of Islam the task of adapting their principles to its practice. To the best of my knowledge, the only authoritative voice which was raised against this tendency was that of the Hanafi chief qadi Abu Yusuf, who in the preface to his *Kitab al-Kharaj*, addressed to Harun al-Rashid, explicitly bases the principles of a truly Islamic government exclusively upon the *sunna* of the Patriarchal Caliphs and Umar b. Abd al-Aziz, and implicitly against the prevailing cult of the Sasanid traditon. But the protest, or rather the warning, went unheeded. It was a warning, because, in the ultimate analysis, what was involved in the Abbasid revolution was the continued existence of the caliphate as an effective governing institution; and that in turn depended upon its becoming a truly Muslim institution, standing in a proper relation to all the other institutions derived from the principles of the Islamic ideology. History, at least, seems to show that the Abbasids failed in this respect as signally as the Umayyads, and in their failure, only a few decades after the reign of Harun, dragged the caliphate down with them. The nemesis of the over-rapid conquests of the Arabs—and the political tragedy of Islam—was that the Islamic ideology never found its proper and articulated expression in the political institutions of the Islamic states.

NOTES

[1] Note that there is no Arabic word for "state" as a general concept. Even for Ibn Khaldun the word *dawla* often explicitly means and always implies the membership of the ruling family. Similarly, *mamlaka* combines the concepts of "kingship" and "kingdom," etc.

[2] The evidence for this is inferential, but sufficient. It is reasonably certain that, had the fiscal reorganization been the work of the early Abbasids, it would have been chronicled in their favour.

[3] See *Studia Orientalia Ioanni Pedersen dicata* (Copenhagen, 1954), pp. 105-106, and *Encyc. of Islam*, vol. 2, s. v. Abd-al-Hamid b. Yahya.

[4] I have not discovered the authority for Wellhausen's statement (*Arab. Reich*, 167) : "Den Eroberungskriegen war er [Umar II] abhold; er wusste wol, dass sie nicht für Gott, sondern um der Beute willen geführt wurden." It is clear, however, that while Umar II positively encouraged the *jihad,* he endeavored to restore and to limit it to its original ideological character: see *Arabica* II/I, pp. 3, 9.

3. Arab-Byzantine Relations under the Umayyad Caliphate

The wars between Islam and Byzantium occupy so prominent, indeed almost exclusive, a place in our history books and in
the chronicles on which they draw, that the student of medieval
history may be excused for taking the rubric "Arab-Byzantine
Relations" as a record of little more than continual warfare. The
record is not untrue, for in fact frontier warfare lasted almost
unbrokenly for a period of centuries. It is not, however, the whole
truth. The proof of this statement is not easy, for direct references
to relations of any other kind in the medieval sources, if we ex-
clude those that arise out of warfare, such as truces and embassies,
can almost be counted on the fingers. Fortunately, however, there
are, to supplement these scanty materials, a few other facts or
details that can be exploited.

In dealing with any subject of this kind there are two general
considerations to be borne in mind. Medieval chronicles, whatever
their merits (and they are many), suffer from one almost universal
defect. They present a narrowly focused view of events. Those, the
majority, written around the activities of some ruling institution,
caliphs, emperors, or sultans, concentrate on the political affairs
undertaken by or relevant to the history of that particular institution, and rarely note things that happened or activities that were
going on elsewhere. Their standard of reference is what may be
called the "official level," the level of matters that interested official
circles or affected their working, even if they might be the most
trivial news items from the capital. The affairs of the provinces are
seldom mentioned except insofar as they were reflected in events
at the capital, such as the calling to account of some too enterprising provincial taxmaster.

To compensate for this in part there survive a few local
chronicles, histories of provinces or cities, such as Egypt or Bokh-

ara, which take the political history of the caliphate or empire
for granted and concentrate on their own local affairs. But these
are even more narrowly focused, and in a certain degree even
more concentrated at the official or scholastic level. It is a local
history of Egypt, for example, that furnishes almost all our early
information about the Andalusian adventurers who captured
Crete in 827. But this information is incidental only to the trouble
which they gave to the governors of Egypt during their occupation
of Alexandria, and the local chronicler is interested neither in how
they came to be in Alexandria nor, after their departure to Crete,
in what happened to them there. Any attempt, then, to present an
over-all picture must proceed by fitting together odd bits and
pieces, and filling in the gaps by reasonable deduction.

The second general consideration links up with this. In a
society as loosely articulated as were all medieval societies, and not
least in the East, it is completely unrealistic to assume that the
interests and activities of all sections of any one society were the
same as those of the official class, or were even controlled in more
than a general fashion by the governing institution. The complex
of society was made up of a mosaic of small communities that lived
their own lives, carried on their own affairs and fended for themselves, often in isolation from the other communities, and almost
always without much notice being taken of what they were doing
or whether it was in agreement with official policy.

The major problem therefore remains—to find the data
which may serve as clues to Byzantine-Arab relations, other than
warfare, during one century of Islamic history, the century of the
Umayyad Caliphate of Damascus, 661-750.

The pre-Islamic relations of the Arabs with the Byzantine
Empire are sufficiently well known, if not yet explored in full
detail.[1] Under Islam regular or official relations, if they may be so
termed, begin with the establishment of the Umayyad Caliphate.
Before then, the Greeks, the *Rum*, are simply the enemy whom the
Arab generals drove out of Syria and Egypt, finally began to harry
at sea, in Cyprus and Rhodes, and even succeeded in defeating in
the first naval battle of an Arab fleet. With the establishment of
the Umayyads, the situation begins to alter subtly. To be sure, the
Greeks are still the enemy, and Arab armies and fleets push their

way through to the gates of Constantinople once, twice, and yet a
third time; and in between these massive culminating enterprises,
and after the failure of the last, maintain a program of annual
incursions in winter and spring. All this is the formal and indispensable public duty of the caliphs, the commanders of the faithful who are bound by the conditions of their office to pursue the
Holy War against the unbelievers, and who must justify their
claim to be the successors of the Prophet in the eyes of their
Muslim subjects by visibly striving for the extension of Islam.
At the same time, it serves to maintain the discipline and fighting
qualities of their Syrian troops, for on this depends their ability to
control the open or suppressed insubordination of the Arab tribesmen in the other provinces.

The public policy of the Umayyads, then, remains the same
as that of their predecessors. Byzantium is the enemy, and that is
all there is to it. In reality, however, the Umayyad relations with
Byzantium were by no means confined to simple national or religious hostility, but were governed by more ambivalent attitudes
of both attraction and opposition.

Since the Syrian troops were of crucial importance for the
maintenance of the Umayyads, the origins and distribution of the
Syrian army are of some significance. It was grouped in five divisions, two in the south, two in the center, and one in the north.
The southern divisions were composed mainly of southern and
western Arabian tribes, some of whom were established there well
before the Islamic conquest and in relations with the Byzantine
governors, and some of whom had come in with the Islamic armies.
The central divisions were formed almost solidly of old, established
tribes, who had in pre-Islamic days been enrolled as auxiliaries of
the Greeks in the wars with Persia, and whose chiefs had held
Byzantine titles and had long been familiar with Constantinople
and its government. The northern division, on the other hand,
was composed chiefly of north Arabian tribes who had come in at
the time of the conquests and had known no relations with Byzantium except in warfare.

It was the central divisions and tribesmen, those of Damascus
and Emesa, with which the Umayyad Caliphs were most closely
associated, both by geography and by marriage relations, and who

were their most devoted supporters. There can be little doubt that this connection played some part in familiarizing the caliphs with the former Byzantine institutions, but it must obviously not be exaggerated. Nor must even the influence of the ex-Byzantine officials who continued largely to staff the administrative services in Syria be overstressed. Nevertheless, the increasing tendency of the Umayyads to adopt Byzantine usages and to emulate the Greek emperors is a patent fact. The remarkable care shown by the caliphs for the upkeep of roads, even to the extent of imitating the Roman milestones, was certainly not inspired by Arabian custom or tradition; and the further facts that the Latin *veredus* and *millia* were transposed into Arabic as *barid* and *mil* show where the idea came from. The earliest gold coinage of the Caliph Abd al-Malik was Byzantine in design, even to the extent of bearing an effigy of the caliph, until it was withdrawn and replaced by a more orthodox Muslim design in deference to the religious feeling of his subjects. In ceremonial also, although it continued on the whole to be governed by Arab and Islamic usage (again in deference to the traditions of the subjects), there was a slow process of small adjustments to Byzantine practice; and, as is well known, the ex-Byzantine provinces retained their Byzantine systems of revenue administration.

In addition to these adaptations or adoptions of the outward usages of Byzantium, recent research has revealed a more subtle way in which the caliphs were imitating Byzantine usage, by the practice of defining legal norms by administrative rescript. Islamic law was in its first century still fluid or inchoate in detail, and left open a wide field for regulation on specific points. Although few of the Umayyad rescripts have survived in their original form, the traces of them have been discovered both positively, in a number of rulings of the later law schools, and negatively, in the declared opposition of these schools to some of the Umayyad rulings and to the principle of definition of law by rescript in general.[2]

The most striking legacy of the imperial heritage, however, is furnished by the Umayyad policy of erecting imperial religious monuments. The Byzantine inspiration of this policy is beyond doubt, and is made more unmistakable by the fact that this policy was *not* followed by the Abbasid Caliphs of Baghdad in their capital provinces, although they did enlarge the mosques of Mecca and Medina. Certain Muslim historians, of much later date, and not generally sympathetic to the Umayyads (besides being based on Iraqi traditions, and therefore ignorant of the Byzantine example), surmise that the object of the Umayyad Caliphs was to replace Mecca and Medina as religious shrines by Jerusalem and Damascus. This is a fantastic idea, even though it is still echoed by western historians, and obviously belied by the fact that the mosque of Medina was one of the three imperial monuments built or rebuilt by the Umayyads.[3] An echo—belated, but nevertheless authentic—of the native Syrian tradition has survived in the work of the tenth-century geographer al-Maqdisi, a native of Jerusalem. He cites a local tradition that the Umayyad Caliphs Abd al-Malik and al-Walid were moved to build the Dome of the Rock and the Great Mosque at Damascus by fear lest the Muslims be tempted away from their faith by the magnificence of the Church of the Holy Sepulchre and other Christian edifices in Syria.[4] The tradition may possibly reflect rather too narrowly the outlook of Jerusalem, but it very probably preserves a trace of the true motives of the Umayyads: not simply to rival the Christian edifices in Syria, but also (as the reconstruction of the Prophet's Mosque at Medina shows even more clearly) to emulate the imperial example. That this was a leading motive is made still more certain by a particular circumstance relating to the construction of at least two of the three mosques, to which most of this paper will be devoted.

The Dome of the Rock was built by Abd al-Malik about 690; the mosques of Damascus and Medina (as well as the Aqsa Mosque at Jerusalem) by his son al-Walid I, between 705 and 712. The circumstance in question is the tradition current in later Muslim sources that the caliph requested and obtained the aid of the Greek emperor for the decoration of the Prophet's Mosque at Medina and the Great Mosque at Damascus. The discussion of this tradition involves entering into somewhat complicated detail, since a fresh study of the sources has led the present writer to disagree with some of the arguments put forward by the most recent and authoritative writers on these three monuments, Professor K. A. C. Creswell, Mlle. Marguerite van Berchem, and the late French historian, Jean Sauvaget.

The tradition on which all discussion has hitherto centered is one contained in the great chronicle of al-Tabari (d. A.D. 923):

> Muhammad says: Musa b. Abu Bakr told me that Salih b. Kaisan said: "We began to pull down the mosque of the Prophet in Safar 88 (i.e. January 707). Al-Walid had sent to inform the lord of the Greeks (*Sahib al-Rum*) that he had ordered the demolition of the Mosque of the Prophet, and that he should aid him in this work. The latter sent him 100,000 *mithqals* of gold, and sent also 100 workmen, and sent him 40 loads of mosaic cubes; he gave orders also to search for mosaic cubes in ruined cities and sent them to al-Walid, who sent them to [his governor in Medina] Omar b. Abd al-Aziz."[5]

Further, in regard to the mosque of Damascus, the geographer al-Maqdisi, already cited for the Syrian tradition, says: "The implements and mosaics for the mosque were sent by the king of the Greeks."[6] The developments of this tradition in the later Arabic works, progressively elaborating the story with imaginative detail, such as al-Walid's threat to the emperor to devastate his eastern provinces if he refused the request, need not be taken into consideration. So far as is known at present, no similar statement is found in regard to the construction of the Dome of the Rock at Jerusalem. This omission may itself be significant, as an indication that the two traditions quoted are specific and independent, and do not rest upon what may be called a "general hypothesis."

In Creswell's great survey of Umayyad architecture, Mlle. van Berchem attempts to discredit the tradition cited by al-Tabari.[7] She points out first that it is not included in the earlier historical chronicle of al-Baladhuri, and proceeds to question al-Tabari's complete veracity, adding: "Moreover, Tabari was a Persian and he lived (in Persia or in Iraq) at an epoch when legends concerning the first great Khalifs had already blossomed in a very luxuriant fashion." Now this, with all due respect, is a preposterous assertion. To begin with, al-Tabari has no responsibility for the tradition beyond reporting it. Here, as in the whole of his history, he simply quotes what he regards as the most reliable sources, and there has never been any question of his veracity in quoting these sources. Any criticism must therefore be directed to the report itself and its sources.

"Muhammad says." As many other passages make clear, this

is Muhammad b. Omar al-Waqidi, who died in 823—a truly prodigious figure in Arabic historiography, the first systematic collector
of the materials for the early history of Islam. That this report was
really transmitted from him is certain from brief allusions to it in
other surviving works prior to al-Tabari,[8] even though al-Baladhuri (who also based his chronicles largely on al-Waqidi) omits it
in his summary chronicle; but in this, it should be noted, he
devotes only five lines or so to this reconstruction. Now, as Sauvaget points out, al-Tabari, in selecting from the mass of documents
at his disposal relating to this event, chose four which were *"d'une
qualité exceptionelle."* What is remarkable is that all four are
taken from materials collected from al-Waqidi, that all four relate
the statements of eyewitnesses on the evidence of *one* intermediate
link (a different one in each narrative), and that two of them (of
which this particular report is one) are statements of Salih b.
Kaisan, who was the officer actually in charge of the work of
demolition and reconstruction of the mosque. We should need to
discover extraordinarily strong arguments to disprove the authenticity of this narrative; it is indeed difficult to see any way of doing
so except by demolishing the entire foundations on which early
Islamic history rests. Sauvaget himself, as will be seen presently,
makes no attempt to deny or disprove the statement, but tries only
to change its interpretation.

To return to Mlle. van Berchem. After a long and methodi-
cally rather confused analysis of this and other texts, she is finally
compelled, in face of the formal statement quoted above from
al-Maqdisi—that the emperor sent implements and mosaics for
the work on the mosque of Damascus—to concede that the texts
are "not absolutely conclusive" on the subject of Byzantine assistance. And so she falls back on the final argument, that "political
conditions under the reigns of Abd al-Malik and al-Walid were
scarcely favourable to friendly exchanges between the court of
Byzantium and that of Damascus," adding as a final fling: "Would
not so patriotic a monarch as al-Walid have experienced some
reluctance in asking a favour from Constantinople?" (pp. 163-164).

These final arguments may be set aside for the moment with
the remark that the attitude of mind that they presuppose is too
much a modern one to be applied without a good deal of shading

to any period of medieval history. To sum up, Mlle. van Berchem's arguments on historical grounds are entirely unconvincing. When, on the other hand, she comes to the archaeological evidence from the monuments themselves, it is impossible for the layman to question her conclusions that the mosaic decorations are almost wholly Syrian in workmanship, although she explicitly adds: "without denying the possibility of one or even several master-mosaicists having come from Constantinople."

It is much more surprising, however, to find such a careful historian as was Jean Sauvaget practically accepting the whole of Mlle. van Berchem's conclusions. Indeed, he goes even further, to deny as a "tradition of legendary character" the participation of workmen from Byzantium.[9] To be sure, he cannot wave aside as airily as she does the tradition reported by al-Tabari through al-Waqidi from Salih b. Kaisan, which he has already described as a tradition "of exceptional quality." This would seem to involve him in a dilemma, but the dilemma is ingeniously resolved by a reinterpretation of the tradition. The fact that the mosaics of Damascus and Jerusalem are "more probably" (plutôt) the work of Syrian Christians gives the clue, he says, to the origin of the tradition which represents the Byzantine emperor as taking a hand in the construction of the Umayyad monuments: "the Arabic word Rum (properly "Romans") having been used indifferently to denote the Byzantines and the Christians of the Melkite [i.e., Orthodox] Greek rite who lived in Muslim territory, there has been a misunderstanding of the meaning to be given to it in historical narratives relating to the construction of these monuments." Sahib al-Rum, he explains in a footnote, may mean either the Byzantine emperor or "the head (spiritual or lay) of the Greek Melkites." The misunderstanding in the original tradition relating to the Mosque of Medina, he adds, "was no doubt perfectly innocent, and it is permissible to see in it a more or less conscious alteration of the true meaning under the influence of political afterthoughts." These, he explains, were due to the attempt, in pious or anti-Umayyad circles, to cast discredit on the Umayyads by representing al-Walid's purpose in reconstructing the mosque, "laudable in itself, as a blameworthy initiative, because it led to having the Prophet's own mosque rebuilt by infidel subjects of a monarch who was the enemy of Islam."

This last argument is even more surprising, coming from the pen of such an authority; in fact he produces little evidence to support it beyond quoting certain pietistic traditions against the decoration of mosques *in general*. If there had really been any widespread, or even factitious, resentment of al-Walid's initiative, one would expect to find it expressed in much more open terms, without having to guess at an anti-Umayyad implication. In the later elaboration, at least, the tone is clearly one rather of exultation that the emperor was in some sense contrained to do this service on behalf of the rival faith. And finally, although *Sahib al-Rum* may possibly, in certain contexts, mean "the chief of the Orthodox Melkite community," it would be desirable to find other instances of its use in this sense and in such a context. On all grounds, therefore, it is evident that the efforts to discredit or reinterpret the tradition transmitted by al-Waqidi carry no conviction. The most that might be admitted (but that readily) would be that the figures may be suspected of having grown a little even in the course of *one* transmission.

But the most surprising feature in all this discussion is that the most massive testimony of all has been entirely overlooked. A certain scholar of Medina, Ibn Zabala, composed in 814 a *History of Medina,* which is known so far to have survived only in extracts cited in later works. What Sauvaget has to say of Ibn Zabala's *History* is highly relevant here. "This work is for us of capital importance. Its interest lies (1) in the personality of the author, a disciple of the great *Medinian* doctor Malik b. Anas. . . . Ibn Zabala was in a position to assemble *on the spot,* in the best conditions for both transmission and criticism, the local tradition relating to the ancient history of the mosque; (2) in his date. This gives us the assurance that the evidence of contemporaries could have been noted down without an excessive number of intermediaries, the composition of the work being *just one century later* than the execution of the operations of al-Walid. To the extent that it is known to us, Ibn Zabala's work remains the best authority on which to support an attempt to reconstitute the Umayyad mosque."[10]

In the extracts preserved from Ibn Zabala's *History* in the historical work of al-Samhudi (d. 1506)—itself a work of extraordinary erudition[11]—there is the following statement, supported not by a single tradition, but by an imposing list of excellent authorities:

> They report: [12]Al-Walid b. Abd al-Malik wrote to the king [*N.B.*] of the Greeks: "We purpose to restore the greatest mosque of our Prophet; aid us therefore to do so by workers and mosaic cubes." And he sent him loads of mosaic cubes and some twenty-odd workmen—but some say ten workmen, adding "I have sent to you ten who are equal to a hundred"—and (sent also) 80,000 dinars as a subvention for them."[13]

In view of this statement, supplementing the statements already cited, there seems to remain no possible doubt that the Greek emperor did in fact supply some workmen in mosaics, along with mosaic cubes, for both the mosques of Medina and Damascus, and sent also money or gold for the work on the mosque of Medina at least.[14]

Nevertheless, this participation of the emperor does raise certain questions, both in itself and in its implications. How did it come about that the Umayyads, officially engaged in almost continuous warfare with the Greeks (indeed the very next item in al-Tabari's chronicle after the tradition discussed above is the report of a series of successes by Arab armies in Anatolia), were yet able to make this request, on at least two occasions, and that it was granted on each occasion? How, to begin with, were the requests transmitted? It is precisely here that the deficiencies of the chronicles—with their laconic "he wrote"—become most apparent. The chronicles were composed in Iraq, largely on the basis of Iraqi materials, more than a century later. Apart from the official public actions of the caliphs, they supply absolutely no information about Syria in the Umayyad period. For the century during which Damascus was the capital of an empire extending from Central Asia to Spain, we remain almost ignorant of its own history, except for such scraps and crumbs as can be gathered from archaeology and by fragmentary materials from other sources.

As a result of this absence of data relative to the internal conditions in Syria, it is very commonly supposed that its conquest by the Arabs brought about the complete suspension of its former commercial relations with the Greek territories. Certainly, they were severely curtailed; but it would be an anachronistic proceeding to read back into medieval life the common phenomena of

modern political relations. A state of official war did not necessarily involve the suspension of all commercial or courtesy relations. We have the indisputable evidence of the flourishing commercial intercourse between the Muslim cities of Syria and the
crusaders' ports of Tyre and Acre during the crusades,[15] which was
almost completely unaffected by the military operations between
the opposing princes and their armies.

By lucky chance, however, we are not reduced entirely to
conjecture in regard to the continuance of a certain amount of
commercial intercourse between Byzantium and Syria—and (or)
Egypt—in the Umayyad period. Several fragmentary references
survive in the Arabic sources:

1. A certain Abu Ubaid al-Qasim b. Sallam compiled, about
840, an extensive and valuable corpus of traditions relating to the
fiscal institutions of the Muslim state, which, unlike the better-
known Iraqi works on the subject, preserves a number of Syrian
traditions. On the subject of the tolls to be exacted from merchants
at the frontier, he cites a regulation ascribed to Omar I (634-644)
—whether accurately may be doubted, inasmuch as it was a commonplace of Muslim tradition to represent rules established after
the time of Muhammad as ordinances of Omar—which lays down
the rates as 2½ per cent on the merchandise of Muslim traders,
5 per cent on that of non-Muslims resident in Muslim territory
(i.e., *Dhimmis*), and 10 per cent on the merchandise of foreign
traders. As justification for the last rate it is added: "because they
were taking the same percentage from the Muslim merchants when
these entered their territory." A few lines later, the identity of
these foreign traders is defined unambiguously: "the *Rum*—they
used to come to Syria."[16]

2. In a rescript of Omar II (717-720), the caliph prohibits
the placing of obstacles in the way of those who trade by sea. This
is puzzling, since there seems to be no record of obstacles placed
by Arab governors to trading by sea in the first Islamic century,
and in fact Basra was already developing by that time a flourishing
overseas trade through the Persian Gulf. The most probable explanation, although admittedly inferential, is that this too must
refer to Syria, and to trade between the Syrian ports and the
Byzantine territories. From the very little and mostly indirect

evidence we have about such places as Antioch and Latakia, they seem to have continued to flourish after the Arab conquest, and they can hardly have done so except by commerce.[17]

3. In the Arabic traditions relating to the striking of gold dinars by Abd al-Malik, it is stated that "Papyrus used to be exported to the land of the *Rum* from the land of the Arabs, and dinars to be received from their side."[18]

4. The fourth passage is still more decisive, and throws wide open a window into the subject of this discussion. It is found in a local history of Egypt, by the ninth-century Ibn Abd al-Hakam (the same writer who transcribed, in another work, the rescript of Omar II quoted above). In dealing with the settlements of the Arabs in Fustat (Old Cairo), he relates at some length a dispute in regard to the possession of an establishment called "the Pepper House" (*Dar al-Fulful*).[19] This dispute is, of course, his main interest, but in a note he adds: "Why it was called the Pepper House was because, when Usama b. Zaid al-Tanukhi was director of taxes in Egypt, he purchased from Musa b. Wardan pepper to the value of 20,000 dinars, on instructions from [the Caliph] al-Walid, who purposed to send that as a gift to the *Sahib al-Rum*, and he stored that pepper in this house."

There can be no doubt that the *Sahib al-Rum* here has its normal significance of the emperor of Byzantium. And this little note seems to supply a clue to the whole transaction. There is no question at all of al-Walid either threatening the emperor with dire destruction, or sacrificing his patriotic feelings (whatever that may mean) to beg a favor. If such a present was made once, there is no reason to regard it as an isolated instance; it just happens that this one record has survived, and it is enough to show that, even while the two empires were at war, the continuance of commercial relations permitted the exchange of courtesies between the two courts.

To return finally to the public sphere, it has sometimes been remarked that the government of the Umayyad Caliphs was in several respects that of a "succession state" to the East Roman Empire, notwithstanding the ideological oppositions involved in the sphere of religion. At the Byzantine court, one may suspect, a formal pretence was maintained that the caliphs were just another group of barbarian invaders who had seized some of the provinces of the empire, and were disregarding their proper status as vassal princes. Hence the indignation of Justinian II when Abd al-Malik infringed the imperial privilege of striking gold coinage. The Umayyad Caliphate, however, in its attitude to the empire, was much more than a provincial succession-state. The two facets of its policy, the military assault and the administrative adaptation, point clearly to the real ambition of the first-century caliphs, which was nothing less than to establish their own imperial dynasty at Constantinople. Seen in this light, their administrative imitations and adaptations take on a different character; they are not merely the tribute paid by raw and parvenu princes to the achievements of their predecessors, but an almost deliberate effort to learn the ropes and fit themselves to assume the imperial destiny.

But after the catastrophe (or victory) of 718, there follows a sudden and complete reversal. The whole policy of the Umayyad caliphs swings decisively away from the Byzantine tradition and becomes oriented in the true sense, i.e., towards the East. This change, which has not as yet been fully appreciated by students of Arab history, is clearly marked in the reign of the Caliph Hisham (725-743), a brother of the Caliphs al-Walid and Sulaiman who mounted the last, and fatal, assault on Constantinople, but the first signs can be seen immediately after its failure, in the reforming Islamizing policies of their cousin, the pious Caliph Omar II.

It is tempting to bring this reversal into relation with the crushing disappointment of the hopes and dreams of the Umayyad Caliphs, and to see in it a kind of Freudian compensation—a deliberate rejection of the Byzantine tradition, motivated by resentment, and the search for some more compliant and attractive substitute. But it was almost certainly much more than that. After a century of Arab empire in Western Asia, the over-all structure of the empire was beginning to solidify, and the relative weight of its constituent provinces to tell. In the balance of forces, Syria still held a military preponderance, but one which became increasingly precarious, as first Iraq and then one province after another had to be held to obedience by Syrian garrisons. Ideologically, however (as we should say now), the center of Muslim culture and thought was already located in Iraq, and the imperial background and determinants of the Arabs of Iraq were not Byzantine, but Persian and hostile to Byzantium. It was the Caliph Hisham who first grasped the implications of the growing weight of Iraq and the East, and who deliberately broke away from the ambitions of his predecessors to organize the Arab empire as the future heir of Byzantium. So far as we can reconstruct, on direct or indirect evidence, the fiscal and administrative policies of Hisham, they appear consistently directed to establishing the Arab empire as the heir of the oriental tradition and the successor of the Persian Sasanid empire. It was he, too, who began the process by which the administrative center was gradually moved eastwards, a process which was continued by the last Umayyad Caliph Marwan II, and finally consolidated by the foundation of Baghdad under the succeeding Abbasid Caliphate.

NOTES

[1] Recent studies include A. A. Vasiliev, "Notes on some Episodes concerning the Relations between the Arabs and the Byzantine Empire from the fourth to the sixth Century," *Dumbarton Oaks Papers*, 9-10 (Cambridge, Mass., 1955-1956), 306-316; and I. Kawar, "The Arabs in the Peace Treaty of A.D. 561" in *Arabica*, III, fasc. 2 (Leyden, 1956), 181-213. See also M. Canard, "Quelques 'à-côté' de l'histoire des relations entre Byzance et les Arabes" in *Studi Orientalistici in onore di G. Levi della Vida*, I (Rome, 1956), 98-119, for later Arab-Byzantine relations.

[2] See J. Schacht, *The Origins of Muhammadan Jurisprudence* (Oxford, 1950).

[3] Al-Walid is said to have embellished also the Sanctuary at Mecca with mosaics.

[4] *Bibl. Geographorum Arabicorum*, III, 159. See also E. Lambert, "Les Origines de la Mosquée et l'architecture religieuse des Omeiyades" in *Studia Islamica*, VI (Paris, 1956), esp. 16.

[5] II, 1194, Musa b. Abu Bakr is again quoted as intermediate authority for a tradition from Salih b. Kaisan relating the visit of inspection of the Caliph al-Walid to the mosque at Medina in A.H. 93: II, 1232-3.

[6] *B.G.A.*, III, 158.

[7] K. A. C. Creswell, *Early Muslim Architecture*, I (Oxford, 1932), 156-157.

[8] J. Sauvaget, *La Mosquée omeyyade de Médine* (Paris, 1947), 10-11.

[9] *Op. cit.*, 111-112.

[10] *Op. cit.*, 26.

[11] See Sauvaget's remarks, *ibid.*, 27-28.

[12] Al-Samhudi, *Wafa al-Wafa*, I (Cairo, 1336h), 367 (the chain of authorities, which cites not less than seven sources, is on p. 364 *infra*). I am indebted for this reference, and for that from Ibn Abd-al-Hakam cited below, to Dr. S. A. El-Ali.

[13] This quotation is followed by several other reports collected by al-Samhudi from other sources. These give differing figures for the number of workmen, and specifically mention Syrians and Copts among them. One report adds that the Emperor sent also chains for the mosque lamps.

[14] Mr. John Parker has drawn my attention to the story of Theophanes (A.M. 6183, ed. de Boor, p. 365) which relates that Abd al-Malik, wishing to build "the temple at Mecca" was on the point of taking columns from a church at Jerusalem, but was dissuaded by local Christians who told him that they could persuade Justinian II to supply other columns, "which was done." There appears to be no confirmation of this story in the known Arabic sources.

[15] Ibn Jubair (Wright-de Goeje), 298; trans. R. J. C. Broadhurst (London, 1952), 313.

[16] Abu Ubaid ibn Sallam, *Kitab al-Amwal* (Cairo, n.d.), nos. 1651 and 1655.

[17] See H. A. R. Gibb, "The Fiscal Rescript of Umar II" in *Arabica*, II, fasc. 1 (Leiden, 1955), 6, 11.

[18] Ibn Qutaiba, *Uyun al-Akhbar*, I (Cairo, 1925), 198. Cf. J. Walker, *Catalogue of the Muhammadan Coins in the British Museum. Arab-Byzantine and Post-Reform Umaiyad Coins* (London, 1956), liv: "An exchange of letters between the emperor and caliph led to a breach of diplomatic and trade relations."

[19] Ibn Abd al-Hakam, *Futuh. Misr*, ed. C. C. Torrey (New Haven, 1922), 98-99.

4. The Social Significance of the Shuubiya

In re-examining briefly the shuubiya conflict in the second and third centuries of the Hijra, the argument of this paper is that it was not merely a conflict between two schools of literature, nor yet a conflict of political nationalisms, but a struggle to determine the destinies of the Islamic culture as a whole. The literary aspects of the shuubiya movement, analysed by Goldziher in the first volume of *Muhammedanische Studien,* can therefore be taken for granted, in order to concentrate more closely on the significance of the sociological factors which lay behind them.

If we look back at the social situation in the Arab empire in the last thirty years of the Umayyad Caliphate (720-750 A.D.), it would be extravagant to discover as yet any serious rivalry between Persian and Arab, notwithstanding the economic conflict between the Arabs and the non-Arab *mawali.* The most striking feature of the period is the division which had begun to develop within the ranks of the Arab conquerors themselves—not, however (in this context), the division between the factions of northern and southern Arabs, but the social division between those who remained *muqatila* in a real sense, actively engaged in the military forces of the empire, and those who (while still called *muqatila*) had become citizens and ceased to be soldiers, a division represented more particularly by the Arabs of Syria and those of Iraq respectively.

Already, in the former garrison cities of Kufa and Basra, Arab elements, profiting by their enforced leisure, had begun to lay the foundations of the future "Arabic humanities" by the study of the Arabic language and the traditions of the peninsula from which their ancestors had come. But one cannot yet speak of an Iraqi written literature at this time. On the other hand, there already existed the outlines of a Syrian Arabic written literature.

Its origins, objects and character were entirely divergent from all that interested the Arabs of Iraq. The great movement of Arab conquest had ended. The Umayyad Caliph Hisham, engaged in the task of maintaining and organizing the vast and still amorphous empire, was apparently interested in the methods of administration employed in the ancient empires, and his secretaries were translating for his use such books as were available to them on the subject. His chief secretary, the *mawla* Salim, translated the supposed epistles of Aristotle to Alexander,[1] and we have the explicit statement of al-Masudi that he had seen a translation made for Hisham of the histories of the kings of Persia and other Persian books.[2] The influence of these works is to be seen in the original epistles which have come down to us from Salim's successor, the *katib* Abd al-Hamid. Thus, even before the advent of the Abbasid Caliphs, there was already in existence an Arabic court literature, drawing its inspiration partly from the Persian Sasanid tradition.[3]

The secretaries of the first Abbasids were men who had begun their careers under the Umayyads, mostly as secretaries of the governors in Iraq, such as Abu Ayyub al-Muriyani, chancellor of al-Mansur, and especially the famous translator and adaptor of Persian works, Rozbih Ibn al-Muqaffa. That his writings should bear witness to a more marked Persianizing tendency was only to be expected; but it is unnecessary to look for an explanation to any supposed philo-Persian sympathies of the Abbasid Caliphs. There is nothing to indicate that al-Mansur was interested in any branch of Persian culture except astrology. The court literature was simply expanding under its own impulse, derived from its Umayyad beginnings and the general expansion of the bureaucracy, towards the re-establishment of the Sasanian traditions; and the success of Ibn al-Muqaffa's works gave at first no more than a further stimulus in this direction.

It might have been expected that after the transfer of the seat of the caliphate to Iraq, the court literature would be influenced to some extent by the developing schools of Arabic studies. The secretaries, however, were not interested in the Arabic language for its own sake; for them it was only a means, an instrument, and if they found themselves at a loss to express themselves

in it, they improvised. Let the poor pedants of Basra and Kufa
dispute over the rightness or wrongness, the *fasaha,* of such and
such a word or rule; it was all one to them. They were concerned
only with the interests of their own class and their relations with
their masters; they learned by heart the epistles of Abd al-Hamid,
the manuals of protocol (*adab*) of Ibn al-Muqaffa, and if they
needed more they sought for other Persian works. Their thought
was oriented exclusively towards the ancient culture of the Sasanid
court; what guidance for the execution of their duty could they
expect to get from the Bedouins and the traditions of desert
Arabia?

In the second century, therefore, there were in Iraq two
schools of Arabic letters, entirely distinct from one another, deriving from different sources, animated by a different spirit, serving different purposes, and almost entirely negative towards each
other. Neither the one nor the other addressed itself to the general
public, but each was confined to delimited and more or less closed
circles. At the outset there was no rivalry, whether literary or
national, between them, and their emergence into the outer world
as rivals was due to the rise of the new urban society in Iraq under
the stimulus of economic development.

This new urban society was a mixed society of Arabs and
non-Arabs—mainly Persians and Aramaeans, the latter also more
or less Persianized—who were engaged in trade and commerce,
had attained a certain degree of wealth, and showed an increasing
interest in literature. It was no longer the old Arab society, whose
manners, ideas, and poetic traditions were foreign to its life, its
habits, its interests, and even its speech. To most of its members
the subjects discussed in the circles of Arabic scholars seemed to
bear no relation to their own situation; the philologists were anti-
quaries, their disputes boring (*mumill*). They looked for something more attractive and less heavy, and they found it partly in
the new poetry and the *ghazal,*[4] and partly in the literary productions of the secretarial school.

In the latter decades of the second century the manufacture
of paper was introduced at Baghdad. For the first time in the cultural history of the West, there were cheap and abundant means
for the multiplication of books. What wonder then that the works

of Ibn al-Muqaffa and other translators from the Persian were
followed by a flood of imitations? The names of some hundreds of
these works of entertainment have been preserved in the *Fihrist*.
Since practically nothing of this output has survived it would be
risky to attempt a precise judgment on their character and value;
but we may conclude, from their titles and subjects, that most of
them were short and ephemeral works, which circulated for a time
and then disappeared. The subjects themselves, moreover, display
one capital defect. Even if account is taken of the new themes
which could be drawn from the old Persian books and legends,
they lacked diversity. All the available materials must have been
repeated over and over again, incorporated in the successive works
of a series of forgotten writers.

Against this flow of Persianizing literature the first literary
reaction of the Arabs can be seen towards the end of the second
century. If the new middle classes were not interested in anything
but entertaining works, there were elements in the Arabic tradition too which could be dressed up to suit their tastes. Out of the
ghazals of the Bedouin poets of the Umayyad age were developed
the so-called Udhri romances, the mixed prose and verse tales of
the ideal and unfortunate lovers in the nostalgically romanticized
desert. The philologists themselves did not consider it beneath
them to share in this popularization of the Arabic tradition, and
amongst the numerous authors of works on the *Ushshaq* cited in
the *Fihrist* there are found such leaders of the schools of Arabic
studies as Hisham al-Kalbi and Haitham b. Adi. Other Arab
themes also made their way into the literature of entertainment;
such were the *nawadir* or compilations of anecdotes, amongst
whose authors were the noted philologists al-Kisai of the school of
Kufa and Abu Ubaid of the school of Basra; or again the stories
of singing girls (*qiyan*) which, with similar literary bric-a-brac,
were to enter into the fourth-century *Book of Songs* of Abul-Faraj
al-Isfahani.

Whatever success these works may have had with the public
of Baghdad or Basra, they could do little to close the gap between
the "classical" tastes of the philological schools and the predilec-
tion of the secretaries for the Persian tradition; they only served
to make it more consciously felt. For the cleavage between the two

schools was itself a reflection, an external manifestation, of the division which was to be found in all aspects of the social and intellectual life of the age. A new civilization is not created in a day, and the conflict between the Arab tradition and the Persian tradition went down to the roots. The issue at stake was no superficial matter of literary modes and fashions, but the whole cultural orientation of the new Islamic society—whether it was to become a re-embodiment of the old Perso-Aramaean culture into which the Arabic and Islamic elements would be absorbed, or a culture in which the Perso-Aramaean contributions would be subordinated to the Arab tradition and the Islamic values.

The more the two parties became aware of their rivalry the more tenaciously they maintained their points of view. On both sides partisanship grew fiercer. While hitherto the secretaries had felt or shown indifference towards the schools of Arabic philology, their indifference now turned into violent hostility to the Arab tradition and to all that belonged to it, and above all to the claims put forward on behalf of Arabic culture. It seems to me entirely erroneous, however, to interpret their attack on the Arabs as in any sense a Persian nationalist movement. During the second half of the second (eighth) century, Persian resistance (if nationalism is too strong or misleading a term) had repeatedly displayed itself in Khurasan and the northern provinces of Iran in risings which were not only anti-Arab but also anti-Islamic. There is nothing to suggest that the secretaries as a class were sympathetic towards these movements; all the presumptions, indeed, are to the contrary. Their aim was not to destroy the Islamic empire, but to remold its political and social institutions and the inner spirit of Islamic culture on the model of the Sasanian institutions and values, which represented in their eyes the highest political wisdom.

The anti-Arab polemic of the secretaries reached its climax in the first half of the third century. By this time their attitude had come to be designated by the term *shuubi*, though it seems uncertain whether the name was applied to them by their partisans or their opponents. The term itself was not new; on the contrary, it was, as often happens, an older appellation which was perverted to a new use. The original *shuubiya* were the Kharijites, who on religious grounds maintained the doctrine that no race or tribe enjoyed any inherent superiority, and in particular opposed the theory of the inherent right of the Quraish to the caliphate. In rejecting any exclusive superiority attaching to the Arabs, the Kharijite *shuubis* equally rejected any superiority of the Persians; whereas the third-century *shuubis* proclaimed the superiority of the Persians (or of other non-Arab races) to the Arabs, and defended their claim by social and cultural, not religious, arguments. But there is no evidence at all that the founders and early leaders of the secretarial school, such as Abd al-Hamid or even Ibn al-Muqaffa, were *shuubis* in either sense.

Goldziher, in his study already cited, is aware of the connection between the shuubiya and the administrative officials, but seems to overlook the precise relation between the secretarial school of writers and the anti-Arab polemic, and to overemphasize the support which the shuubiya received from the Abbasid Caliphs and the Persian viziers. After giving examples of the arguments employed by them to demonstrate the superiority of the Persians to the Arabs, he stresses particularly their attacks on the Arab pride of race by dilating on the weaknesses of the tribal genealogies and the flaws in their claims to purity of descent; and finally he examines the literary activities of one of the outstanding philologists of the second century, Abu Ubaida Mamar b. al-Muthanna, whom he presents as "a typical example of the whole class of shuubi philologists and genealogists" (p. 206).

If this view of Abu Ubaida is accepted, the distinction drawn above between the secretarial and the philological schools must be abandoned, together with the sociological argument associated with it. It must, however, be pointed out in the first place that it would be difficult to discover any other philologist who could be reckoned to belong to "the whole class of shuubi philologists and genealogists," and that if Abu Ubaida were such, his case would be unique rather than typical. But even this is open to serious question. It is true that Ibn Qutaiba, two generations later, says outright that "he hated the Arabs."[5] and that later sources sometimes count him definitely as a *shuubi*.[6] Yet it would be hard to find this accusation sustained by al-Jahiz or other of his contemporaries or by any of his illustrious pupils; and by the general testimony even of those who disliked him, Abu Ubaída was the most universal scholar of his age. His services to the development of the Arabic humanities are beyond calculation; almost half of all the information about pre-Islamic Arabia that was transmitted by later authors came from him. He was, moreover, the author of one of the earliest works on *gharib al-hadith*[7] and also of the earliest extant work on *tafsir* (*Kitab majaz al-Quran*), and when Ibn Hisham re-edited the *Sira* of the Prophet by Ibn Ishaq it was to Abu Ubaida that he applied for the explanation of the Koranic texts.

That Abu Ubaida should have been, after all this, a persophile shuubi seems a contradiction in terms. If the work is applicable to him at all, it can only be in the Kharijite sense. To what, then, is due the imputation that he was a hater of the Arabs? It does not appear to me difficult to find the explanation—an explanation to which, indeed, there are not a few parallels even at the present day. The method generally adopted by the early philologists was to group their materials under categories, so that facts of the same or similar kinds were collected together in monographs, whether philological forms like *faali,* or subjects of antiquarian interest, like the works on Arab horses which have come down from Ibn al-Kalbi and from Abu Ubaida himself. Abu Ubaida, therefore, grouped many of his data relating to the Arab tribes under the headings of "virtues" (*mafakhir*) or "vices" (*mathalib*), as may be seen from all the lists of his works. At the same time, as a Kharijite,[8] he made light of the pretensions of the Arab *sharifs* of his day, such as the Muhallabids (the heroes of Azd), and publicly exposed the results of his researches into their genealogies.

It can be imagined with what alacrity the arabophobe shuubis of the third century—mostly, that is to say, after the death of Abu Ubaida—seized upon those materials in his works which served to point their satires on the Arabs. But there is nothing, so far as is known, prior to the accusations of Ibn Qutaiba, to indicate that Abu Ubaida was more interested in *mathalib* than in *mafakhir,* or was actuated by malice, or to suggest that he falsified or misrepresented the materials derived from his Arab informants in order to serve the interests of any party. In all that has come down from him he stands out as a thorough, and, in the scientific sense, disinterested scholar. But what could be more natural than that Ibn Qutaiba and the partisans of the Arabs, at grips with the increasingly bitter shuubi polemics of the third century, should have regarded him as the auxiliary, if not even the partisan, of their opponents?

By this time both the strength of the shuubi movement and the dangers implicit in it had come to be more clearly realized. Its strength lay in the appeal of its literary productions to all ranks of society, outside theological and philological circles. The most striking evidence of the extent to which the new tendencies were gaining at the expense of the old is perhaps to be seen in the recession of poetry. Up to about the year 200 it was in poetry that contending ideas found expression and fought it out; from about the year 200 poetry serves as a barometer of educated and popular taste, but was prevented by its conventions from acquiring the flexibility that so fundamental a struggle demanded. It is in such a clash of ideas and interests that a new literature is born, and it was in the new prose literature that the contending parties engaged one another.

The dangers of the shuubi movement, on the other hand, lay not so much in its crude anti-Arab propaganda (in spite of its appeal to the still lively hostility to the Arabs amongst the lower classes in Iraq and Persia) as in the more refined scepticism which it fostered among the literate classes. The old Perso-Aramaean culture of Iraq, the centre of Manichaeism, still carried the germs of that kind of free thinking which was called *zandaqa*, and which showed itself not only by the survival of dualist ideas in religion, but still more by that frivolity and cynicism in regard to all moral systems which is designated by the term *mujun*.

It was these considerations which brought increasingly effective support to the defenders of the Arab tradition. The *kuttab* were no doubt powerful at the court, but they were not all-powerful. I cannot entirely share Goldziher's view that the shuubi secretaries had the backing of the Abbasid Caliphs and the influential Persian viziers. It is very questionable whether the Abbasids were persophile or whether the Khurasani nobles of the second century were enthusiastic supporters of the Sasanid tradition.[9] The Ab-

basid state was based upon the alliance of Khurasan with Iraq, and
both these provinces were (with the exception of Kufa) strongly
orthodox. The efforts made by the Abbasid Caliphs to conciliate
the esteem and support of the orthodox leaders is well known.
It was one thing to allow the re-establishment of the Sasanid protocol at the court, but quite another to patronize the open expression
of arabophobe sentiments. By the second century the close association which had existed from the first between Koranic studies and
Arabic philology had been so strengthened by the expansion of
Arabic studies in general that the Arabic *adab*,[10] the study of the
pre-Islamic literature and culture, had become to a great extent
fused with theological learning. At the same time, the growth of
zandaqa and scepticism was already coming to be regarded as so
pernicious to the state that even al-Mahdi, who is often regarded
as persophile in the highest degree, was compelled to combat it by
executive action. The Khurasanian leaders also, at grips with the
popular *khurrami* revolt against orthodox Muslim authority, were
no less concerned. The more virulent the propaganda of the shuubis, therefore, the more their anti-Arab sentiments lent themselves to the suspicion of being anti-Islamic sentiments.

But it was necessary to find, alongside negative and repressive
measures by the public authorities, a more positive remedy which
should stop up the evil at its sources. Even though, in our present
state of knowledge, it may be hazardous to assert a definite view
on the point, it may well be that this challenge—religious, intellectual and social—to Islam called out that movement in orthodoxy, at the same time rationalizing and puritan, out of which
the Mutazilite theology emerged at a later date. Already in the
second century the Mutazilite Bishr b. al-Mutamir was attempting
to spread his instruction by means of popular forms of poetry.
Thanks to the studies of the late Michelangelo Guidi, we now
know that the first Mutazilites were the militant wing of orthodoxy against the dualist heresies; and they were compelled, in this
mission, to create for themselves dialectic weapons more powerful
than affirmations and negations based upon revelation or the
threats of the civil authorities.

These weapons they found in Greek logic and dialectic and
in the discourses of early Christian controversialists against pagan

beliefs. It was no mere accident, therefore, that the translations of Greek logical and philosophical works were multiplied at the beginning of the third century. That the Caliph al-Mamun, in instituting his academy, the *bait al-hikma,* was actuated by a purely personal interest in Greek philosophy, is hard to conceive. A more intelligible explanation of his decision is that he was persuaded to see in this work of translation the most propitious means of ridding Islam of the legacies of dualist *zandaqa.*

Nor was it accident that it was from the ranks of the Mutazila that there arose the man who, more than any other, found the reply to the literary challenge of the secretaries, and established the new Islamic literature firmly upon the foundations of the Arabic humanities. Amr b. Bahr, known as al-Jahiz, had begun his career as a writer by imitating the secretarial works, and—whether of set purpose or not—had learned the secret of their literary arts and success. Realizing how far the scholastic and rebarbative style of the philologists and their choice of subjects were from the living interests of the age, he set out to publish that inexhaustible series of epistles in sonorous, pliable and witty language, which widened the range of Arabic literature to cover all aspects of contemporary life and remain to this day the masterpieces of Arabic prose. No doubt he chose his subjects for his own pleasure, but at the same time almost all his writings were directed to specific, though often well-concealed, ends.

Three of these purposes were particularly important. In *al Bayan wal-tabyin* he displayed the rich resources of the Arabic humanities, and taught the classical philologists that their studies served a wider purpose than the mere classifying of linguistic fiches. In his "secretarial" epistles he, on the one hand, satirized the defects, the pomposities, the narrow-mindedness of the secretaries, but at the same time integrated what was of practical value in the Persian tradition with the Muslim sciences. In the third place, he produced apologetic works to combat the infidelity or cynicism of the literate classes. Even that picturesque and at times fantastic work, the *Book of Animals,* conceals a religious and homiletic end beneath its gay and whimsical loquacity.

By the breadth and vigor of his writing, al-Jahiz overwhelmed once and for all the literary frippery of the secretarial school. His successors were far from being his equals, but he had taught the new generation to widen their range and to experiment with new subjects and new methods. The secretaries found themselves confronted with a living literature, instinct with the new Hellenistic learning as well as the solid erudition of the philological schools, and avidly accepted by the general public as well as by their own patrons. For a decade or two they held out, but were finally constrained to recognize that the Arabic humanities had triumphed, and that their task henceforth would require ot them at least a passable familiarity with the Arab tradition. It was the merit of Ibn Qutaiba that, grasping this need, he furnished them with volumes of extracts and selections on the various Arabic and Muslim sciences, drawn from the original sources which, as he says, "they would be too lazy to acquire for themselves."[11] But while on the one hand he castigated their ignorance, their false values, their contempt for religion, he also (following in the path of conciliation traced by al-Jahiz) incorporated in his collections the Sasanian tradition in matters of court etiquette and administration, and thus gave it a permanent place in the complex of Muslim culture.

With this concession the shuubiya movement was in effect disembowelled. But there are, in conclusion, two consequences of this typically Islamic conciliation that deserve to be mentioned briefly. The Persian materials admitted by Ibn Qutaiba closed the canon, as it were. All later Arabic works relating to government and courtly life draw on him, directly or indirectly. Of the later Persian works, such as the *Shahnama* of Firdawsi or the *Siyasat-nama* of Nizam ul-Mulk, nothing entered into Arabic literature or the standard Islamic works on ethics. It is perhaps not difficult to explain why this was so. For the Sasanian strands which had been woven into the fabric of Muslim thought were, and remained, foreign to its native constitution. The ethical attitudes which they assumed were in open or latent opposition to the Islamic ethic, and the Sasanian tradition introduced into Islamic society a kernel of derangement, never wholly assimilated yet never wholly rejected.

NOTES

[1] *Fihrist* 117.

[2] *B.G.A.* VIII, 106.

[3] See *Encyc. of Islam*[2] s.v. Abd al-Hamid ibn Yahya. A detailed study of this subject has been made by M. H. al-Zayyat in an unpublished dissertation on Arabic court literature.

[4] Al-Jahiz, *Bayan* (Cairo, 1932), III, 235.

[5] K. al-Maarif 269; cf. K. al-Arab, in *Rasail al-Bulagha*[3] (Cairo, 1946), 346.

[6] Goldziher, *op. cit.*, I, 197.

[7] Tarikh Baghdad, XII, 405.

[8] Goldziher dismisses the statement of his Kharijite sympathies as "a superficial description" (p. 197), but it is fully sustained by the best sources (cf. Jahiz, *Bayan* I, 273-274; Ashari, *Maqalat* I, 120). Goldziher's argument is based on Umar b. Shabba's report that A. U. admired the poetry of the Shiite al-Sayyid al-Himyari (*Aghani*[2] VII, 5). The literary basis of this appreciation is well brought out by Taha al-Hagiri in his pamphlet *al-riwaya wal-naqd inda Abi Ubaida* (Cairo, 1952).

[9] Ibn Qutaiba, *K. al-Arab* 345, explicitly asserts that the Persian nobles were not shuubis; and cf. the well-known story of Abdallah b. Tahir ap. E. G. Browne, *L.H.P.* I, 346-347.

[10] May not the choice of this word itself imply a counterclaim to the *adab* works of the secretaries?

[11] *Uyun al-akhbar* (ed. Brockelmann) I, 4.

5. The Armies of Saladin

I The Egyptian Army

On Shirkuh's third expedition to Egypt, Nureddin gave him a grant of 200,000 dinars, with arms and animals, allowed him to select 2,000 troopers from his regular regiments (askar), and made a special grant to each of these of 20 dinars for the expenses incurred in preparing for the expedition.[1] With his grant Shirkuh hired 6,000 Turkmen cavalry, probably from the Yaruqi tribe, since their commander was Aineddawla Yaruqi.[2] To these 8,000 horsemen were added Shirkuh's own regiment, which he maintained as feudal lord of Hims, consisting of 500 mamluks and Kurds,[3] and perhaps an unspecified number of auxiliaries. After the occupation of Egypt he "distributed the land in fiefs to the regular troops (askaris) who had come with him,"[4] at the same time maintaining the existing rights of the Egyptian officers.[5]

Saladin's appointment as the successor of Shirkuh led to the withdrawal of the Turkmens and several of Nureddin's Turkish amirs with their troopers. On the other hand, Shirkuh's Asadiya and other Kurdish troops remained in his service, and before a year was out he had already formed a personal regiment of guards, called the Salahiya and commanded by the amir Abul-Haija.[6] In spite of the reduction in his forces, he began to displace the Egyptian officers from their fiefs in favour of the troops who had remained with him.[7] During the next five years the size of his army was continually increased by recruitment both for his own regiments and for those of his amirs, and by 1174, when Turanshah set out on his expedition to the Yemen, Saladin was able to furnish him with a contingent of 1,000 horsemen in addition to the troops from his own halqa.[8]

No details appear to be furnished in the sources at our disposal on the distribution of the fiefs (iqtaat) of the troops or of

Saladin himself, who presumably inherited the fiefs and revenues of the Egyptian wazirs.[9] Such information as we have relates only to the fiefs given to members of his family. On his father's arrival in Egypt in 565:1170 Saladin assigned to him as *iqta* Alexandria, Damietta and al-Buhaira.[10] At the same time his brother Turan-shah was assigned the southern provinces in upper Egypt (Qus, Aswan and Aidhab), the value (*ibra*) of which was 266,000 dinars, and a few months later received Bush, Giza district, and Saman-nud in addition.[11] When his nephew Taqieddin Omar arrived in 567:1172, accompanied by his personal regiment and 500 troopers, their allowances were assigned on the revenues of al-Buhaira.[12]

From a notice given by Ibn al-Athir, it appears that in Nu-reddin's feudal organization the fiefs were hereditary, and a reg-ister was kept of the men and arms that each vassal was bound to furnish.[13] Saladin's system seems to have been the same.[14] The principal amirs and officers had each an *iqta*; their mamluks re-ceived a *jamikiya* or allocation of pay, or were assigned *iqtas* or shares of an *iqta*,[15] and *nafaqat*, i.e., provisions and fodder in kind.[16] Soldiers who were not on regimental payrolls were called *battalin*.[17]

The *muqta* or fiefholder did not enjoy the whole revenue of his *iqta*, unless by special grant. Thus when Taqieddin was ap-pointed viceroy in Egypt in 579:1183, he was assigned Alexandria and Damietta as fiefs, but given in addition al-Buhaira, al-Fayyum and Bush as his *khassa*.[18] From scattered references it can be gathered that the fiefholder was responsible for seeing that the land was adequately cultivated and watered,[19] for maintaining the dikes,[20] and for seeing that the state dues (*kharaj*) in money or kind on each crop were collected.[21] At what stage he collected his own fixed revenue in money and kind is not stated, if indeed he did so at all. But unlike later fiefholders each one personally superintended the harvests in the spring. The date of the Fatimid conspiracy in April 1174 was chosen when "the *askaris* would be scattered far and wide in the regions of their *iqtas*, at the approach of the harvest, and none but a few would be left in Cairo."[22] And when the Sicilian fleet attacked Alexandria at the end of July in the same year, the defenders were rapidly reinforced by those troopers who were at their *iqtas* in the vicinity.[23]

In a brief and incomplete note appended to al-Mammati's work, the rates of pay and allowances in kind for each category of troops is listed, on the basis of the assessed value (*ibra*) of each *iqta*.[24] The assessment was made in a money of account called *dinar jundi*. Turkish, Kurdish and Turkmen regulars were paid at the full rate. The second category was composed of the Kina-niya,[25] the former troops from Ascalon (*asaqila*),[26] and similar troops on the Egyptian (Fatimid) registers; these received half rate. The third, composed of troops for naval service and "commandants" (?), received quarter rate.[27] Lastly, the Arab auxilia-ries, with some exceptions, received one-eighth of the full rate. "Full rate is a term for what is assigned to the troops as pay, *i.e.*, for each *dinar jundi* one ardabb of grain, that is two-thirds of an ardabb of wheat and one-third of barley, and the assignment on the treasury is calculated at a quarter dinar in cash for each *dinar jundi* as an agreed settlement, but some are assigned two-thirds or one-third of a dinar in cash, as may be ordered in each case."[28] It would seem from this statement that each of the regular troopers received in cash a proportion, never less than one quarter, of the assessed value of his *iqta*, and an allowance of grain at the rate of one ardabb per dinar of assessed value. The lower categories re-ceived smaller allowances of grain, but nothing certain can be deduced from this statement with regard to their pay in cash.

Al-Maqrizi has preserved two records from the diary (*al-mutajaddidat*) of al-Qadi al-Fadil which give figures for the Egyp-tian army in Saladin's time.[29] In the first, it is stated that on 8th Muharram 567 (11 September, 1171) Saladin held a review of all his troops, old and new, in the presence of Greek and Frankish envoys. The total number of *tulbs* reviewed was 174, and 20 *tulbs* were absent. "A *tulb*, in the language of the Ghuzz, is (a unit consisting of) an officer in command, who has a standard fixed on a lance (*alam maqud*) and a trumpet which is sounded, with a number of horsemen ranging from 200 to 100 or 70."[30] The total number of these horsemen was approximately 14,000, the majority being *tawashis*[31] and the rest *qaraghulams*.[32] At the same time, the Judham Arabs in the service of the Sultan were reviewed; these numbered 7,000 horsemen, "but their number was fixed at 1,300 horsemen, no more."

A military establishment of this size, however, must have strained the financial resources of Egypt, and accounts for Nureddin's complaint that he received no contribution from Egypt towards the expenses of the *jihad*, and his despatch of a commissioner to audit Saladin's accounts.[33] Saladin himself, indeed, took steps to reduce it, first by sending a large contingent to the Yemen, as already noted above, in 1174,[34] and in 1177, when "he stopped the pay of many of the Kurds" on the ground of their responsibility for the disaster at Mont Gisard.[35] Finally, in 577:1181, he reorganized the regular forces in Egypt, as related in the second extract from al-Qadi al-Fadil's diary.[36] "The number of the troops was established at 8,640, of whom 111 were amirs, 6,976 were *tawashis*, and 1,153 were *qaraghulams*. The total sum assigned to them was 3,670,600 dinars. These figures are exclusive of troops without fiefs and entered on the register of assignments from the *ushr*,[37] of the Arabs holding *iqtaat* in al-Sharqiya and al-Buhaira, of the *Kinaniyin*,[38] the Egyptian (i.e., Fatimid) troops, the jurists, qadis, sufis and the diwans, amounting to not less than 1,000,000 dinars."

This extract is followed in *al-Khitat* by a further passage from the diary containing details of the accounts in Shaban 585 (October, 1189). The total of the assignments amounted to 4,653,019 dinars, of which 1,190,923 were affected to specific purposes, and the balance of 3,462,096 was presumably assigned to the regular troops. Of the former, 728,248 dinars were affected to the *diwan* of al-Adil; 158,203 to amirs and troops whose *iqtaat* were outside the districts registered for *ibra;* 13,804 to work on the walls of Cairo; 234,296 to the Arabs; 25,412 to the Kinaniya; 7,403 to qadis and shaikhs; 12,540 to the "Qaimari, Salihi, and Egyptian troops;" and 10,725 to "the *ghazis* and Ascalon troops stationed at Damietta and Tinnis and others."

It must not be assumed, however, that Saladin was able to use the whole of the Egyptian army in his Syrian campaigns. The circumstances of his own establishment in Egypt, and the subsequent naval expeditions of the crusaders, convinced him that the Franks had never given up hope of capturing Egypt by a sudden assault. Therefore half of the Egyptian forces could not be spared from garrison duty at home. The only occasion on which Saladin

apparently led a larger proportion of the Egyptian army into Syria
was on the expedition to Ramla in 1177,[39] and the ensuing disaster
at Mont Gisard probably confirmed his decision not to run the
same risk again. During his first campaign in Syria (1175-1176),
after the occupation of Damascus, the number of his cavalry is put
at 6,000; as this figure included the askar of Damascus (see below)
and his own guard, the Egyptian contingent can be put at not
more than 4,000.[40] When he set out from Egypt at the end of 577:
1182, Imadeddin states precisely that "he took half of the askar
with him and left the other half to guard the frontiers."[41] The
numbers of the Muslim troops at Hattin, as will be seen below,
confirms this conclusion. This policy had the further advantage
also that by this means Saladin was able to maintain a supply of
fresh troops in the field and to send back those worn out by the
campaigns to rest and refit in Egypt.[42]

II   The Syrian and Mesopotamian
Contingents

To the Egyptian nucleus of his military strength Saladin
gradually added the regular askars of the Syrian and Mesopotamian princes. The next task is therefore to evaluate the strength
of these contingents.

Damascus.   The feudal forces of Nureddin's army were split
up after his death between Damascus, Aleppo, and some minor
principalities (Hims, Hamah, Harran, etc.). The total strength of
Nureddin's askar does not appear to be stated in any extant source,
but it seems probable that the larger proportion (perhaps two-
thirds, at a guess) originally joined al-Malik al-Salih in Aleppo.
Those who remained at Damascus were placed under the command of Nureddin's general Shamseddin Ibn al Muqaddam, who
was given also the fief of Baalbek.[43] During the temporary insubordination of Ibn al-Muqaddam, resulting from Turanshah's desire to obtain Baalbek for himself, Saladin appointed his nephew
Farrukhshah to command the askar of Damascus, and despatched
him with it to deal with the raiding force of the Franks under
Humphrey of Toron in 574:1178. The letter of al-Qadi al-Fadil

relating the victory gained by Farrukhshah on this occasion specifically mentions the size of his askar as "less than 1,000 men."[44]
Since Ibn al-Muqaddam's own contingent was no doubt defending
his fortress of Baalbak at the time, the total askar of Damascus can
be estimated at 1,000 or a little over.

Hims. After his first campaign in north Syria (1175-1176)
Saladin gave Hims in fief to his paternal cousin Nasireddin Muhammad, the son of Shirkuh, in addition to the fief of Rahba
which he already held.[45] On his death in 581:1186, his twelve-year-
old son Shirkuh was confirmed in possession of all Nasireddin's
fiefs, and a Kurdish amir, the *hajib* Badreddin Ibrahim al-Hak-
kari, was placed in command of the citadel.[46] No figures are quoted
in the sources for their troops, but, as already noted, the askar of
the elder Shirkuh, when he held Hims, numbered 500, and this
may be taken as the approximate figure.

Hamah. Saladin's first governor in Hamah (1176) was his
maternal uncle Shihabeddin Mahmud al-Harim,[47] who was succeeded in 574:1179 by Saladin's nephew Taqieddin Omar.[48] With
him was associated the former commander in Damascus, Ibn al-
Muqaddam, as fiefholder of Barin, Kafr Tab and Raban,[49] and
the famous Kurdish general Saifeddin al-Mashtub. Immediately
afterwards, Taqieddin and Ibn al-Muqaddam had to move north-
wards to defend Raban against the Seljuk Sultan of Rum, and
their joint forces on this expedition are given as 1,000 men.[50] This
may consequently be taken to represent the strength of the askar
of Hamah together with the forces maintained by the commanders
of the castles within the province of Hamah, including Shaizar.[51]

Aleppo. As already noted, the larger part of Nureddin's
askar probably joined al-Malik as-Salih and supported him in the
defense of Aleppo against Saladin. Under the treaty negotiated
between Saladin and al-Malik as-Salih in 1176, however, Saladin
was entitled to call on the services of the askar of Aleppo against
external enemies, and it served under his command in the operations against the Armenians in Cilicia in 576:1180.[52] The detachment of Hamah and other districts on the south, as well as of
districts on the Euphrates,[53] so greatly reduced the resources of
Aleppo that it seems unlikely to have been able to support more
than Nureddin's own regiment of guards, the *Nuriya,* and the

small forces of the remaining amirs. No precise figures are available, but if the former originally numbered, as seems to have been customary, 1,000 troopers, the total regular forces of Aleppo are not likely to have much exceeded this figure. After Saladin's occupation of Aleppo in 579:1183, he gave it first to his son az-Zahir, then to his brother al-Adil in the same year, and finally in 582: 1186 to az-Zahir again, but there is no indication of any marked increase in the number of regular troops.

Mosul and the Jazira. Ibn al-Athir, in his narrative of the Mosul expedition against Saladin in 571:1176, makes a valuable statement about the size of its forces. The askar of Mosul was accompanied in this campaign by the troops of all the vassal principalities, including Hisn Kaifa and Mardin. In a pointed refutation of Imadeddin's statement that their forces were reported to number 20,000, he says that they numbered "precisely" a little less than 6,500, and adds: "I myself inspected the register of the review and the battle distribution of the askar between right and left wings, center, and advance guard, and the officer responsible for keeping the register was my brother Majdeddin. . . . What, I should like to know, does al-Mawsil and its dependencies up to the Euphrates amount to, that it should be able to maintain for itself and in them 20,000 horsemen?"[54]

During his first campaign in the Jazira (578:1182), Saladin secured the transfer to his suzerainty of the principalities of Harran (Muzaffareddin Geukburi, together with Edessa), Hisn Kaifa and Amid (the Artuqid Nureddin b. Qara Arslan), Sinjar, Dara, Nasibin, and other minor governments. Sinjar was transferred in the following year to the Zangid Imadeddin in exchange for Aleppo. In 580:1184 Irbil and its dependencies, held by Zaineddin, the brother of Geukburi, accepted Saladin as suzerain,[55] and in 581: 1185 Mardin and Mayyafariqin also capitulated, and the whole of Diyar Bakr was given in fief to his mamluk Husameddin Sunqur al-Khilati.[56]

The total numbers of these provincial forces, which henceforth operated under the direct orders of Saladin and independently of Mosul, may be estimated in the neighbourhood of 4,000.[57] The askar of Mosul, therefore, which came under Saladin's command by the treaty of 581:1186, would number some 2,000 regular troopers.

These figures, though in part simple estimates, are confirmed in the round by the figures given in the narratives of the campaigns of 583:1187. In Muharram (March) Saladin, leaving his son al-Afdal to operate the concentration of the northern contingents at Ras al-Ma, himself led his regiment of guards into the south for a campaign there in conjunction with the Egyptian askar. On the basis of our figures, this would give him 1,000 plus 4,000 troopers, being a half of the Egyptian regular army.[58] Meanwhile there assembled at Ras al-Ma the cavalry of the Jazira, the "Easterners" (i.e., Mosul) and Diyar Bakr, led by Geukburi, the askar of Aleppo under the command of Dildirim b. Yaruq, and the askar of Damascus under Sarimeddin Qaymaz an-Najmi. During Saladin's absence these combined armies made a demonstration raid into the lands of Tabariya and overwhelmed a force of Templars at Saffuriya. The Western sources place their numbers at 7,000 horsemen.[59] Finally, Saladin returned with his troops from the south and reviewed the whole force, numbering 12,000 cavalry, at Ashtara before setting out on the march that ended at Hattin.[60] These may therefore be distributed approximately as follows: 1,000 of the guard, 4,000 of the Egyptian askar, 1,000 from Damascus, 1,000 from Aleppo and north Syria (leaving 1,000 there on guard), and 5,000 from the Jazira, Mosul and Diyar Bakr.

III   The Auxiliary Forces

In addition to the regular askars of mounted archers and spearmen, Saladin's armies included variable numbers of auxiliary troops, horse and foot.

Turkmens. As already noted, Nureddin had made much use of Turkmen auxiliaries, and Saladin continued the practice. Thus, before the final attack on the castle at Jacob's Ford in 575:1179, he "sent to the Turkmens and their tribes and to the territories for the gathering of their levies thousands of Egyptian dinars to be distributed among their hordes and paid to them as grants for their (service as) auxiliary troops, and ordered that large quantities of flour should be made ready for the Turkmens and that they should be liberally provided with all necessities."[61] The Yaruqi Turkmens, in fact, played a notable part in the Third Crusade, since it was their arrival at a critical moment and their attacks on the supply lines of the crusading forces below Jerusalem which largely contributed to Richard's withdrawal.

Kurds. There were, of course, large numbers of Kurds who, like the Ayyubid family itself, were enrolled as members of the regular askars, and received fiefs or *jamikiyat* like the Turkish mamluks. They were to be found not only in the regular forces of Nureddin, but also of the other Zangid and Artuqid princes.[62] Alongside these, however, were to be found numerous Kurdish soldiers of fortune, and more especially, it may well be supposed, in the service of the Ayyubid princes. Their presence in Egypt is attested in several passages,[63] and Imadeddin refers to the Kurdish tribesmen in the army of the Artuqid Nureddin of Hisn Kaifa.[64] During the second siege of Mosul, in 581:1185, Saladin sent Saifeddin al-Mashtub and others of his Kurdish amirs into Kurdistan to occupy the fortresses, [65] and presumably also to act as recruiting agents for his intended operations in Syria. But the protracted and extensive feud which broke out between the Kurds and Turkmens in Diyar Bakr and Mesopotamia towards the end of the same year[66] almost certainly put an end to any hopes of securing Kurdish troops from these provinces.

Arabs. The regular forces also included a number of Arab knights, of whom the most conspicuous in our sources are the Banu Munqidh of Shaizar.[67] The Bedouin tribesmen of Syria and Egypt are frequently mentioned, though not always favorably. As already related, they held certain regions of the Sharqiya and Buhaira as fiefs, and 1,300 of the Judham were enrolled in the army. In 577: 1181, however, Saladin ordered the confiscation of their lands in the Sharqiya and ordered them to remove into Buhaira, because of their inveterate smuggling of grain to the Franks,[68] and three years later an army had to be sent into al-Buhaira to put down disturbances among the Judham tribesmen.[69] The tribesmen in the south of Palestine and Transjordan were a perpetual annoyance. Saladin's expedition to Kerak in 568: 1173 was undertaken to clear them from the district and to prevent them from assisting the Franks by acting as guides,[70] and after his defeat at Mont Gisard they plundered the remnants and baggage of his forces.[71] On the credit side, however, the Bedouins of Syria supplied Saladin with auxiliary raiding forces, which he employed effectively on several occasions, notably in the operations of 574:1179: "He sent out the Arab tribesmen into the lands of Sidon and Bairut to reap the enemy's crops and remained himself at Banyas until they returned, loaded with their plunder.[72] Also during the final operations against Richard on the Jerusalem road, Arabs played a useful part as light cavalry and raiders."[73]

al-Ajnad. This term is employed in the sources in three senses. As the plural of *jundi* it is used for any soldiers, including troopers in the regular forces; and it is used collectively for the whole of the military forces of a region (both uses being naturally congenial to the rhyming-prose style affected by al-Qadi al-Fadil and Imadeddin). But there are traces of an earlier and more specialized usage to denote local or militia troops, distinguished from the *askaris* in that they were not mounted archers, but fought with spear and sword.[74] By this time, however, it is likely that the old militia organizations of Syria were falling into disuse, as a result of the increasing use of Turkish *askaris* and the suppression of the local principalities.[75] As auxiliary troops, their place was taken in Saladin's armies by volunteers, *muttawwia,* who came from far and wide to share in the Holy War. There is seldom specific reference to them in the narratives, but Imadeddin records their presence at Jacob's Ford in 575:1179, and that it was "some of the *muttawwia* fighters in the Holy War" who set the grass on fire at the battle of Hattin.[76]

Footsoldiers. The rapid movement of cavalry campaigns excluded the use of infantry troops in the ordinary course of fighting, and they appear in the sources only in connection with siege operations, either as defenders or attackers.[77] In the latter case they are classed as *sunna,* technicians, of whom three kinds are frequently mentioned: *hajjarin,* who manned the mangonels and catapults (*arradat*); *naqqabin,* who dug mines underneath walls;

and *khurasaniya,* who manned the penthouses or "cats."[78] Along
with them are mentioned the *jandariya,*[79] who seem to be, in this
context, the officers in charge of siege operations.

IV   Equipment and Supplies[80]

The regular army, as noted above, was organized in *tulbs* of
from 70 to 200 men under an amir. Before setting out on campaign, the armour and weapons stored in the arsenal *(zardkhana)*
were distributed to the troops, and a special allotment of pay was
issued to them for campaign needs. Each amir and trooper took
with him supplies of provisions and forage, out of his regular grain
allowance or purchased at his own expense. Additional supplies
were bought from merchants *(sabila),* who established themselves
at the base of operations or followed up the expedition. Imadeddin relates that when the army reached as-Sadir on the expedition
to Ramla in 573:1177 an announcement was made in the camp
that all troops should take supplies for a further ten days "for the
sake of precaution, since no provisions are to be had when we enter
the lands of the infidels." He goes on to say: "So I rode to the army
bazaar *(suq al-askar)* to buy in supplies, but prices were already
rising. So I said to my *ghulam,* "I have changed my mind... Offer
for sale all that I have in my loads and baggage and take advantage
of this enhanced price."[81] When Saladin was engaged in his first
siege of Mosul in 578:1182, the troops in Sinjar "prevented the
sabila from bringing up provisions."[82] In his account of the second
siege of Kerak, 580:1184, William of Tyre reports that "those who
acted as cooks and bakers in the enemy's army and those who
provided the market with all sorts of commodities... freely carried
on their work amidst conveniences of all kinds."[83]

During the actual campaign, the knights could not move far
from their baggage *(athqal),* where not only their provisions but
also their armour was kept. This was put on only when there was
an immediate prospect of fighting; hence the disadvantage of
being taken by surprise, which in effect meant being caught un-
armed.[84] Short expeditions were occasionally made *jaridatan,* i.e.,

without baggage, and therefore without heavy armour for the knights, and the same term is employed for light forces in winter quarters.[85]

NOTES

[1] Ibn al-Athir, *Atabegs* (*R.H.C.*, Hist. Or., II. ii) 249 f.; abridged version in *Kamil* (ed. Tornberg), XI, 222-223.

[2] On the Yaruqi Turkmens and their relations with Nureddin see C. Cahen, *La Syrie du Nord*. (Paris, 1940), p. 378.

[3] Ibn Abi Taiy ap. Abu Shama (Cairo, 1287 H.) I, 173, gives this figure as the number of the *Asadiya*, i.e., the personal regiment of Asadeddin Shirkuh in Egypt.

[4] *Atabegs* 253 (*Kamil* XI, 224). According to *Atabegs* 249 (cf. *Kamil* XI, 222) the right to do so had been promised to him by al-Adid before he set out on the expedition to Egypt.

[5] Ibn Abi Taiy ap. A. Sh. I, 172 foot.

[6] *Ibid.* 173; Imadeddin, *ib.* 178 (cf. *Kamil* XI, 229) . The only infantry troops with Saladin mentioned during this early period are the "sappers of Aleppo " (*naqqabat alhalabiya*; see n. 77 below) employed in the attack on Gaza in 1170: despatch of al-Qadi al-Fadil ap. A. Sh. I, 193.

[7] Imadeddin ap. A. Sh. I, 178; I. Athir XI, 227, adds "and his own family." The transfer (which seems to have been accompanied by a good deal of indiscipline and forcible seizure, v. I.A. Taiy ap. A.Sh.I, 197,28 and 200,10, and Imad., *ib.*, 219, 24) was one of the complaints made by the Egyptian amirs at the time of the revolt in 569:1174: I.A. Taiy ap. A. Sh. 1, 220, 8. According to *Bustan al-Jami* (ed. Cahen, in *B.E.O.* VII-VIII, p. 138) a large body of the Egyptian army was drowned in the winter of 1169-70: غرق فى تلك السنة عسكر المصريين فى بحيرة
الاشموع وهلك أكثرها وكانت آخر سعادتهم

[8] I.A. Taiy ap. A.Sh.I, 217; the last phrase is *kharijan amman sayyarahu min halqatihi*, which leaves some doubt as to whether the term *halqa* applies to Saladin's or to Turanshah's regiment. This seems to be the earliest instance of the use of this term.

[9] The revenues of *al-diwan al-khass al-sultani* were fixed in 588:1192 (i.e., at the end of Saladin's reign) at 354, 444 dinars: Maqrizi, *Suluk* I, 11.

[10] I.A. Taiy ap. A. Sh. I, 184. The value of the *iqta* of al-Buhaira was 400,000 dinars (*Suluk* I, 91, n. 3) .

[11] I.A. Taiy, ap.A.Sh. I, 184, 192. According to Maqrizi (*Suluk*, *loc. cit*) the value of Bush and its dependencies was 70,000 dinars and that of Samannud and its dependencies 60,000 dinars.

[12] *Suluk* I, 48: *taqarrarat hawalatuhum fin-nafaqati alaihim ala kuratilbuhaira*. The author of *Bustan* notes that they were immediately employed in expeditions to Barqa and the West (p. 139 f.), probably in lieu of fiefs.

[13] *Atabegs* 308.

[14] Ibn al-Muqaddam's diploma as governor of Damascus in 578:1182 required him to review the *askar wa-ilzamihim bi'iddati ajnadihim wa'uddat rijalihim*: Imadeddin, *al-Barq al-Shami*, V, fol. 47a.

[15] From the same diploma it would appear that an *iqta* or *jamikiya* might be shared between an amir and his mamluks, since the governor is enjoined "to prevent the amirs from encroaching on the *qarar or iqta* of their men"

النتحيف على رجالهم فى القرار والاقطاع (*ibid.*, 47b); and cf. al-Mammati, *Qawanin al-dawawin* (1943), 356, 1.2. Cf. also I. Athir, XI, 350, where the regular troopers are defined by the phrase *man lahul-iqtau nal-jamikiyatu.*

[16] I.A. Taiy ap. A. Sh.I, 219 ذأراه جراند الأجناد بمبالغ الطاعم وليبين جامكيتهم وراتب لقاتهم cf. also Mammati, pp. 354, 355, where 1,000 dinars is given as typical of an annual *jamikiya*, and the passages cited in n. 1 above, where for *minal-qarari-lladhi lahu* Ibn al-Athir substitutes *min jamikiyatihi.* When Maqrizi says (*Suluk* I, 65) that Saladin, after the battle at Mont Gisard, *qataa ahbaza jamaatin minal-akrad*, it is probable that *khubz* means here "allowance of pay" rather than *iqta*, as in later Mamluk usage. Cf. also I.A. Taiy ap. A. Sh. I, 196, I, 19.

[17] Ibn Abi Taiy ap. A. Shama I, 209; *anfadha maahu jamaatan min al-akrad al-battalin.* During the siege of Akka Saladin made efforts to enlist numbers of *battalin* by promises of pay (*ata*) and allowances in kind (*nafaqat*): Imadeddin, *Fath* pp. 313-314.

[18] I.A. Taiy ap. A. Shama II, 53. Maqrizi (*Suluk* I, 82) says: "Taqieddin (al-Muzaffar) took over al-Malik al-Adil's *iqta* in Egypt, which yielded an annual revenue of 700,000 dinars." But in a supplementary note (p. 91, n. 3) he says: "Al-Muzaffar's *iqta* was the whole of al-Buhaira, worth 400,000 dinars, with al-Fayyum, worth 300,000 dinars, and Qay, Qayat and Bush, worth 70,000 dinars," from which it follows that he uses the term *iqta* in the sense of *khassa*. Likewise in *Khitat* I, 87, the revenues of *al-diwan al-adili* in 585:1189 are shown as amounting to 728,248 dinars.

[19] Mammati 366.

[20] *Ibid.* 232-233.

[21] *Ibid.* 258-276.

[22] From a despatch of al-Qadi al-Fadil quoted by A. Shama, I, 221. Abu Shama says likewise of the troops of Nureddin at the time of the third Frankish invasion of Egypt: *wa-askar al-Sham mutafarriqun kullun minhum fi baladihi hafizun lima fi yadihi* (I, 154).

[23] Ibn al-Athir, *Kamil* XI, 272. In the autumn of 1175 Saladin sent the Egyptian troops home with order to return when they had collected the harvest (*idha staghalluha*): Imad. ap. A. Shama I, 252.

[24] Mammati 369.

[25] The Kinaniya were the amirs and other fiefholders from the Arab tribe of Kinana, who had emigrated from southern Palestine after the fall of Ascalon in 1153, and were settled by the wazir Talai b. Ruzzik in Damietta and its neighbourhood (Qalqashandi I, 350). At the Mont Gisard expedition al-Qadi al-Fadil was accompanied by *al-Kinaniya wal-adilla* (*Barq* III, fol. 15b; cf. A. Shama I, 273, 30), the Kinana Arabs evidently being familiar with the border regions. See also Maqrizi, *Khitat* I, 87 and *Suluk* I, 75 and for the amirs of the Kinaniyin at Damietta in the following century *Khitat* (ed. Wiet) IV, 2, p. 61. But in some passages it may be doubtful whether the word is not to read *kitabiya*, for whom see Gaudefroy-Demombynes, *La Syrie à l'époque des Mamelouks* (1923), p. xxxiii, n. 5: "young mamluks under instruction for entering the Sultan's service," and D. Ayalon in *J.A.O.S.* vol. 69, No. 3 (1949), p. 141, No. 36.

[26] From the register quoted in *Khitat* I, 87, it appears that the Asaqila also were stationed on garrison service in Damietta and Tinnis.

[27] Maqrizi, *Suluk* I, 45, states that in 567:1172 Saladin raised the rate for naval troops from five-eighths to three-quarters of the full rate; it may seem

doubtful, therefore, whether *ghuzah* in this passage has the usual meaning of naval personnel. The precise sense would probably be determined by the associated word *quwwad*, which I have been unable to identify.

[28] I am not certain of the exact sense of some of the phrases used in this passage.

[29] *Khitat* I, 86. The second is given also in a shorter form in *Suluk* I, 75.

[30] See the long note in Quatremère, *Histoire des Sultans Mamlouks*, I, i, 34-5; ii, 271-2, where he explains Ghuzz as meaning Kurds.

[31] Al-Maqrizi in this context defines *tawashi* as meaning "a trooper whose pay [*rizq*] ranges from 700 to 1,000 or 1,200 [the text has 120] [*sc.* dinars], and who has a baggage train of ten or less animals, horses, hacks, mules and camels, and a squire to carry his armour." Whatever the origin of the word may be, here, at least, it does not (as Quatremère has noted, *op. cit.* I, ii, 132) mean "eunuch." Poliak, *Feudalism*, p. 3, n. 4, equates the *tawashis* with the mamluks of the amirs; cf. also Mammati 356, l. 2. It is clear from this passage, however, that at this period *tawashi* meant a trooper belonging to the upper of the two ranks of regular troops, the lower being called *qaraghulams* (see the following note). This is confirmed by the well-known description of Saladin's army by William of Tyre, at the expedition of 1177 (xxii, cap. 23 [trans. New York, 1943] ii, 430-1): "ex quibus erant VIII milia egregiorum, quos ipsi lingua sua *Toassin* vocant, reliqua vero XVIII milia erant gregariorum, quos ipsi appellant *Caragolam*." (The translators, *ibid.*, refer to Noldeke's unfortunate explanation of the term in Roehricht, *G.K.J.*, 377, n. 1.) In the next sentence William includes Saladin's bodyguard ("a thousand of the most valiant knights") among the *tawashis*; and in fact Saladin addresses with the words *ya tawashi* the famous Sunqur al-Khilati (called by Imadeddin, ap. A. Shama II, 149, 5 from foot: *akhassu mamalik is-sultani wa-akhlasuhum wa-qad qaddamahu ala mamalikihi*); Ibn Taghribardi, *Nujum* VI (Cairo, 1936), p. 12, l. 4.

[32] *Qaraghulam* cannot mean "black slave" in the literal sense. William of Tyre (see note 31) describes the qaraghulams as "ordinary troopers," and would certainly have noted the fact if they had been Sudanis. S. Lane-Poole's interpretation (*Saladin*, p. 154): "doubtless the old heavy armed Egyptian infantry from the Sudan," is therefore doubly in error. The term, which seems to have dropped out of use during the Ayyubid period, was apparently applied either to mamluks of inferior rank or, as the numbers here would seem to indicate, to non-Mamluk horsemen. The former Egyptian regiments were, as will be seen below, on separate registers. In any case *qaraghulam* is not to be confused with the later Mongol term *qaraghul* (v. Dozy, *Supplement* s.v.).

[33] Imadeddin ap. A. Shama I, 206.

[34] In the same year the greater part of what remained of the Fatimid army was disbanded after the failure of the conspiracy (v. al-Qadi al-Fadil ap. A. Shama I, 221, 28-9, although, as will be seen below, some of its regiments were either incorporated or reconstituted in Saladin's forces.

[35] Maqrizi, *Suluk* I, 65.

[36] Maqrizi, *Khitat* I, 86; a shorter version in *Suluk* I, 75.

[37] *al-mahlulina min al-ajnad al-mawsumina (lege marsumina) bil-hawa-lati ala l-ushr.*

[38] The text of the *Khitat* has here *al-katibin*; v. n. 25 above. Al-Qadi al-Fadil estimated (in a letter to Saladin) the revenues of the Kinaniyin from iqtas and stipends as exceeding 200,000 dinars or perhaps amounting to 300,000 dinars. Abu Shama, *Uyun* (B.M. 1537, fol 146v.).

[39] This may be deduced from the statements of William of Tyre (see n. 31 above), although his figures are, at least for the *qaraghulams*, exaggerated. But Saladin was able to set out for Syria with fresh forces only three months later.

[40] Ibn al-Athir XI, 284. Imadeddin (ap. Abu Shama I, 248) says that the Egyptian forces consisted of 10 *muqaddams*, including Farrukhshah and Taqieddin.

[41] Abu Shama II, 27 foot.

[42] The first occasion seems to have been in 1179; see Imadeddin ap. Abu Shama II, 6, 28; 8, 24.

[43] "He (Saladin) assigned all its affairs to Ibn al-Muqaddam, and he stayed there, well established and, no doubt, milking its dependencies heavily": Imaddeddin ap. Abu Shama II, 2.

[44] Imadeddin, *Barq* III, fol. 117 a: *wahuwa fi iddatin min askarinal-mansuri la yablughu alfan*. In the same letter (fol. 117b) these troops are referred to as *mamalikunat-turk*. Their instructions were to shadow the Franks and send word to Saladin, who would then assemble the local troops to support them *(wanahnu najmau alaihim minal-atraf il-ajnadal-anjad).*

[45] Imadeddin, ap. Abu Shama I, 250 foot.

[46] *Ibid.,* II, 69.

[47] *Ibid.,* I, 250 foot. He and his son Takush, a nephew of Saladin, both died in Jumada, II, 573; *ibid.,* I, 275.

[48] *Ibid.,* II, 8.

[49] *Ibid.,* II, 5, 9.

[50] Most clearly in *Barq* III, fol. 138a: *wahuma fi alfin.*

[51] *Barq* III, fol. 122a: *wasahibu shaizara biaskarihi muhtatun fi mawridihi wamasdarihi*. Imadeddin adds: *waamarahum bil-istikthari minar-rijali*, apparently by enlisting Turkmens, who are referred to in the next sentence.

[52] Bahaeddin (ed. Schultens) 47; cf. Imadeddin ap. A. Sh. I, 261, and I. Athir XI, 286.

[53] Buzaa was captured after the second defeat of the Mosul armies in 571:1176, and given in fief to Izzeddin Khushtarin al-Kurdi: Ibn Abi Taiy, ap. A. Sh. I, 256. Khushtarin played a notable part in the battle of Marj Uyun (575:1179), capturing Balian the Younger (Ibn Barzan): Imadeddin, *Barq*, III, fol. 121a.

[54] XI, 284.

[55] The diploma is quoted by Imadeddin ap. A. Sh. II, 60.

[56] Imadeddin ap. A. Sh. II, 64.

[57] It may be noted that Ibn Shaddad's revenue statement for Harran in 640:1242 (quoted by C. Cahen in *R.E.I.* VIII, III) includes provisions in kind for 1,000 horsemen. But since the total annual revenues were about two million dirhams, the askar must have been much less than 1,000—probably 300 to 400 at the most. In 565:1170 the askar of al-Bira numbered 200 horsemen: I. Athir XI, 232 inf.

[58] See p. 78 above.

[59] Ergoul 146 (some mss. read 6,000); *Libellus,* quoted by S. Lane-Poole, *Saladin* p. 201 foot. For the composition of the Saracen raiding force cf. Imadeddin, *Fath* 14 and A. Sh. II, 75.

[60] Imadeddin ap. A. Sh. II, 76; cf. I. Athir XI, 350.

[61] Imadeddin, *Barq* III, fol. 139 b: *sayyara ila't-turkumani waqabailiha wa ila'l-biladi lijami rajiliha ulufan misriyatan tufarraqu fi jumuihim wahushudihi'mwatutlaqu lahum jawaida wufudihim*. During the famine of the

previous year, 573:1178, al-Qadi al-Fadil wrote to Saladin advising him against calling up the askars *wahashdi jammil-kataibi wastidai amdadilajnadi*, which I take to mean "and assembling the troops of Turkmen cavalry and summoning reinforcements from the local forces."

[62] Bahaeddin (ed. Schultens), 229, 230.

[63] See notes 16 and 35 above.

[64] *Barq* V, fol. 14a: *wamin junudihi qabailul-kurd*, adding *wal-akradu akdarul-wirdi*, which suggests their lack of discipline. They were probably hired in the same way as the Turkmen tribesmen.

[65] Imadeddin ap. A. Sh. II, 62.

[66] Michel le Syrien, tr. Chabot, III, 400-2; Bahaeddin 63; I. Athir, XI, 342.

[67] Two members of this family, Shamseddawla al-Mubarak b. Kamil and his brother Hattan (so vocalized in the mss. of *Barq*) played a prominent part among the Ayyubid troops in the Yemen: A. Sh. I, 260; II, 25-26. See also n. 51 above.

[68] Maqrizi, *Suluk* I, 71. From another notice (*ibid.* 74) it appears that they had a pirate fleet in Lake Menzala, which Saladin attempted to put down, but without success.

[69] *Ibid.* 87.

[70] Imadeddin ap. A. Sh. I, 206, confirmed by Wm. T. xx. 28 (tr. ii, 390). In the instructions issued to the governor of Damascus (*Barq* V, fol. 47 b) he is ordered to "send out the askar against the Arabs who remain in the land of the Franks and to keep on raiding them until they dispose themselves to submission."

[71] Wm. T. xxi. 24 (tr. ii, 433). In *Barq* III, fol. 70a, Imadeddin also quotes an incisive remark of al-Qadi al-Fadil. العرب كالنظل كما زيد سقيأ بالماء اطلو افرطت
مراد: غره وفرت نضارة خضره

[72] Imadeddin ap. A. Sh. II, 8 (*Barq* III, fol. 124a); cf. Wm. T. xxi. 28 (tr. ii, 440, 441). The governor of Damascus was responsible for maintaining order among the Arab tribes, making the customary payments to them (*rasmihim wa-maishatihim*) and collecting the customary dues from them (*idad*, see Quatremère, *Sultans Mamlouks* I, i, 189): *Barq* V, 47ab.

[73] Bahaeddin 215, 229, 231. In the second passage they are significantly distinguished as *arab al-islam*.

[74] See *Damascus Chronicle*, Introduction, pp. 36-37, and n. 61 above. Maqrizi (*Suluk* I, 69) uses it in this sense also in his version of the first passage quoted in this note: *kataba ila't-turkumani wa-ajnadil-biladi*, where *ajnad* replaces Imadeddin's term *rajil*. Also in the account of the second attempt at the assassination of Saladin, during the siege of Azaz in 571:1176, the assassins were disguised *fi ziyil-ajnad* (not in the rhyming position), i.e., among the auxiliary troops who were operating the siege artillery (Imadeddin ap. A. Sh. I, 258, 4; I.A. Taiy, ib., 1. 21, says *jau biziyil-ajnad wadakhalu bainal-muqatila*). It seems very unlikely that they could have passed themselves off as askaris. Likewise in I.A. Taiy's account of the expedition of Qaraqush to Barqa (ap. A. Sh. I, 260 mid.) a distinction is made between Taqieddin's *ajnad* and *mamalik*, the former probably, therefore, being Kurds and Arabs.

[75] As late as the siege of Akka, however, the contingents from Hims and Shaizar were accompanied by *jumuun minal-ajnad wal-ayan wahushudun minal-arabi wa't-turkuman*: Imadeddin, *Fath*, 241, 2-3.

[76] Abu Shama II, 11 (from *Barq* III, 143 b): *al-ghuzah al-muttawwia*, and 76: *badu muttawwiatil-mujahidin*.

[77] The infantry of Aleppo were especially noted as miners, see n. 6 above; miners from Aleppo used also by Richard at the siege of Darum: Bahaeddin 227. In the diploma for Aleppo granted to al-Adil in 1183 (*Barq* V, foll. 124a-126a), he was required to furnish a fixed number of footsoldiers, and in 1187, the askar of Aleppo was in fact accompanied by siege-troops (*Fath* 75). A contingent of moat-diggers (*jassasin*) from Mosul is mentioned in *Fath* 413.

[78] *Barq* III, fol. 142a: *jamaa alaihi as-sunnaa' n-naqqabina wa'l-hajjarina wajaal-khurasaniyatn waraal-jafati jarina waliathqaliha jarrina*. There are still fuller accounts of siege operations at Amid in *Barq* V, fol. 54a-55a, and at Tyre in *Fath* 75 sqq.

[79] *Barq* III, fol. 143a: *hadaral-jandariyatu was-sunnau*. Similarly, when Saladin attacked Tabariya before the battle of Hattin he sent for *al-jandariya wan-naqqabin wal-khurasaniya walhajjarin*: Imadeddin, ap. A. Sh. II, 76.

[80] For a full description of the armour and siege artillery of Saladin's time see C. Cahen, "Un Traité d'armurerie composé pour Saladin," in *Bull. d'Etudes Orientales*, T. XII (Beirut, 1948), pp. 108-163.

[81] A. Sh. I, 271, abridged from *Barq* III, fol. 8 b.

[82] *Barq* V, 23 b. The forage and provision train is called in a despatch of al-Qadi al-Fadil, cited A. Sh. II, 28-9, *atlab al-mira*, and was commanded by a high-ranking amir; cf. also Ibn Jubair (G.M.S., V) p. 299, 1. 1.

[83] xxii. 30 (trans., ii, 503).

[84] In a despatch of al-Qadi al-Fadil's, Saladin's defeat at Mont Gisard in 1177 is attributed chiefly to the dispersal of the troops *wakhuluwin minalaslihatillatihtajat fi libasiha ila lihaqi athqaliha* (*Barq* III, fol. 17a).

[85] A. Athir XI, 322, 7. Examples of the former usage: expedition to Beirut in 578:1182, Imadeddin ap. A. Sh. II, 29, 1.25; march to Kerak in 583: 1187, I. Athir XI, 349 (the translation in *Recueil*, Hist. Or., I, 678, is incorrect); cf. also Dozy, *Supplément aux dictionnaires arabes*, s.v.

6. The Achievement of Saladin

In the effort to penetrate behind the external history of a person whose reputation rests upon some military achievement, the modern tendency is to analyse the complex of circumstances within which he acted, with the sometimes explicit suggestion that the individual is rather the creature than the creator of his circumstances, or, more justly, that his achievement is to be explained by a harmonious adjustment of his genius to the conditions within which it operated. That this is generally true calls for no argument. But history, especially the history of the Near East, is full of conquering kings, who seem to owe nothing to their circumstances except the possession of a powerful army and the weakness of their antagonists. The question posed by the career of Saladin is whether he was just another such conqueror, or whether his career involved distinctive moral elements which gave his initial victory and subsequent struggle with the Third Crusade a quality of its own. That he fought in the cause of Islam against the crusaders is not enough to justify an affirmative answer to the second question, and might even be irrelevant. To put the matter precisely: was Saladin one of those unscrupulous, but fortunate, generals whose motive was personal ambition and lust of conquest, and who merely exploited religious catchwords and sentiments to achieve their own ends?

The problem is thus one which involves a judgment upon interior questions of personality and motive. It is rarely indeed in medieval history that we have at our disposal authentic materials from which positive conclusions, that will stand up to rigorous historical criticism, can be drawn as to the motives of prominent historical figures. Before entering on the discussion at all, therefore, it is necessary to be assured that some at least of our sources are of a kind which offers some possibility of reaching an answer. For the life and achievements of Saladin we possess, by a fortunate conjunction, five contemporary sources in Arabic, in whole or in part, besides casual references in the writings of travelers and others. Of these five, one has survived only in fragments. This is the history of Ibn Abi Taiy, who, as a Shiite of Aleppo, one would expect to be hostile to Saladin (as he clearly was to his predecessor Nur ad-Din), but in fact shows himself, in the quotations from his works by other writers, to be rather favourably disposed to him.

The three other historical sources were all written by easterners, not Syrians. The most famous is the Mosul historian Ibn al-Athir, who belonged to a feudal family in close relations with the Zangid princes of Mosul and wrote a panegyrical history of their dynasty. His presentation of Saladin fairly reflects the original hostility and later wry admiration and grudging allegiance of the Zangid partisans. But except for this psychological attitude he is not a firsthand source. All, or almost all, his narratives relating to Saladin were taken from the works of Saladin's secretary Imad ad-Din and rewritten with an occasional twist or admixture of fiction.[1] Irrespective of his personal attitude, however, it is obvious that a chronicler, even if contemporary, cannot be relied upon to solve questions of interior personality and motive; if, therefore, we had nothing but Ibn Abi Taiy's and Ibn al-Athir's chronicles to go by, we should have no means at all of discovering the real quality of Saladin's achievement.

Equally well known is the biography of Saladin by his Judge of the Army, the qadi Baha ad-Din Ibn Shaddad, also of Mosul. From 1188 Baha ad-Din was the confidant and intimate friend of Saladin, and his history, written in a simple and straightforward style, portrays Saladin for us, as no ordinary chronicle can do, in his character as a man. Baha ad-Din may perhaps be called uncritical, but he was no deluded hero-worshipper. His admiration is that of an upright and honest friend from whom nothing was concealed, and there can be no question of deliberate suppression or deflection of the truth in his narrative of the last five years of Saladin's life. To have one such source for the history of any medieval prince is rare indeed. The portrait it gives us, however, is that of Saladin at his climax of success and in the desperate conflict of the Third Crusade; it supplies, therefore, little direct evidence on the long and hard struggle to build up his power.

In these circumstances it is a piece of incredibly good fortune that our fourth source, which covers (in the original text or in reliable summaries) the whole of his active career, is almost equally close and authoritative. This source is the works of "the secretary" (*al-Katib*) Imad ad-Din, a native of Isfahan. He belonged to the relatively new class of college-trained civil servants, entered the employment first of the Seljuk Sultans and the Caliphs in Iraq, then rose to high rank at Damascus in the service of Nur ad-Din, and finally became personal secretary to Saladin in 1175. In addition to his one-volume history of the campaigns of 1187-1188 and the Third Crusade,[2] he wrote a large work in seven volumes, entitled *al-Barq al-Shami,* covering the period of his own career under Nur ad-Din and Saladin. Of this work only two volumes of the original are known to have survived, but the whole was carefully summarized by Abu Shama of Damascus (d. 1267).

Imad ad-Din was one of the most famous stylists of his age, and his works are composed in the elaborate and florid rhyming prose cultivated by the secretarial class; yet with all his display of verbal virtuosity, his actual narratives of events are invariably full, precise, and straightforward. He shows no sign of the twisting of facts, whether to cover up his own weaknesses or those of others or for the sake of a rhyme, nor of fanciful adulation, even of Saladin. To be sure he greatly admired Saladin, yet in his writings he criticizes at times his actions and judgment, and indeed seems to have done so to his face. He was on the best of terms with his official superior, the Chief Secretary al-Qadi al-Fadil, and he was clearly too conscious of his own merits and of the trust reposed in him to play the toady or to conceal the truth. His *Barq* is, one might say, almost as much an autobiography as it is a history of Saladin; and its importance is that it presents Saladin to us from the angle of a trained administrator, in close and daily contact with him, though on a less intimate footing than Baha ad-Din.

The fifth of our sources is in some respects the most valuable of all. These are the despatches and letters of his most trusted adviser and secretary of state, the Palestinian al-Qadi al-Fadil, preserved in full or in excerpts in the works of Imad ad-Din, Abu Shama, and various collections of documents. The intimacy of the relation between them can be felt in the loyal and affectionate

letters addressed by al-Qadi al-Fadil to Saladin, especially during
the Third Crusade, sustaining him in times of adversity and even
admonishing him on occasions. While, therefore, the historian will
treat with all necessary caution the more elaborate public despatches addressed by al-Qadi al-Fadil on Saladin's behalf to the
caliphs and other potentates, yet the consistency with which certain themes and ideas are expressed in them must be taken to
reflect some at least of Saladin's real purposes and ideals.

Saladin's fame, as has already been said, rests upon his mili-
ary achievement in the battle of Hattin in 1187 and subsequent
recapture of Jerusalem. Consequently, he is regarded by historical
writers, both Muslim and Christian, as, first and foremost, a
general, and secondly as the founder of a dynasty. The first is,
naturally enough, the view taken in the western sources for the
Third Crusade, and it is encouraged by Ibn al-Athir's presentation
of him as a man who used his military talents to satisfy his dynastic
ambitions and to build up a vast empire.

It is from the same angle that he is compared or contrasted
with his predecessor Nur ad-Din. Unfortunately, we do not possess
for an estimation of Nur ad-Din's personality anything comparable to the materials that exist for the study of Saladin. All the
contemporary Muslim records (save for casual anecdotes) are
chronicles, and their panegyrical tone reflects the attitude of Sunni
circles to his services not only in organizing the defense of Syria
against the Crusaders, but also (and perhaps even more) in
propagating orthodoxy by the foundation and endowment of religious institutions (mosques, madrasas, oratories, sufi convents)[3]
and by repression of the Shiites. Later chronicles, except for the
extracts preserved from the works of the Aleppo Shiite writer Ibn
Abi Taiy, are even more eulogistic. But when the judgment even
of Christian writers like William of Tyre concords with their
attitude, we can be sure that it is a faithful reflection of Nur ad-
Din's *public* life; and it would be a gratuitous assumption, in the
face of such evidence, that, inasmuch as these measures served the
political interests of Nur ad-Din, they were not motivated by
sincere personal attachment to their objects and ideals.

There are, however, some essential differences between the
circumstances in which Nur ad-Din and Saladin carried out their

tasks. Nur ad-Din operated *from within* the structure of politics of his age. Since the break-up of the Seljuk sultanate at the end of the eleventh century, Western Asia had been parceled out amongst a number of local dynasties, all of them (except a few remote baronies) founded by Turkish generals or Turcoman chiefs, and all of them characterized by two common features. One was the spirit of personal advantage and aggrandizement which determined their political actions and relationships. It seems well-nigh impossible to discover in the relations of the Turkish princes or the Turcoman chiefs with one another—even when they were members of the same family—any sense of loyalty or restraint in exploiting each other's weaknesses, let alone that solidarity shown, for example, by the Buwaihid brothers in Persia in the tenth century. The tale of plots, revolts, ephemeral alliances, treacheries, calculated perfidies, dethronements during the twelfth century is unending. In the general political demoralization even the most resolute and unscrupulous princes, a Zangi or a Takash, could scarcely keep their feet.

The other was the composition of their military forces. The foundation of each prince's power was a standing regiment of guards or *askar* of Turkish *mamluks,* consisting of Turkish slaves purchased in boyhood and trained as professional cavalrymen, freed in due course, and maintained by the grant of military fiefs, from which they drew their revenues in money and kind. The continual warfare between the principalities was carried on by these professional troops, whose intensely personal loyalty was given to their immediate commander, and who therefore followed him into rebellion or changes of allegiance with little regard to the interests of their prince. Being professional armies, they were expensive to maintain and therefore small in numbers; one of the reasons for the constant efforts of princes to seize their neighbors' territories was precisely in order to gain the means of enlarging their forces. Furthermore, they could not and would not remain on campaign longer than a certain period at a time; on the one hand, the prince could not afford a high rate of wastage, and on the other the troops themselves, as soon as their period of campaign service (called in Arabic *baikar*) was over, had no thought but to return to enjoy the proceeds of their fiefs.[4] The Turcoman troops, though nomadic irregulars, were little different; they too went on campaign only for a limited time, for so long as they could subsist on plunder or were paid for their services in money and supplies.[5]

Nur ad-Din, the son of a Turkish professional soldier, not only understood this system, but himself formed a part of it. Assuming his object to have been the creation of a centralized military power strong enough to deal with the crusaders, rather than personal aggrandizement, nevertheless his military and political action conformed almost entirely to the practice of the time (even if at a higher moral level); while on the other hand his rivals and vassals accepted him as a natural representative of the system by reason of his family connections, and respected him because of the success with which he operated it, both as a diplomatist and as a commander of armies. Even his campaign of what we may call "moral rearmament" by giving every support to the religious leaders and revivalists was not in any way unprecedented; indeed, it was on the basis and example of what had already been accomplished in this way in the Seljuk empire that Nur ad-Din founded his own policy, and the most that can be claimed for him is greater honesty and deeper sincerity than some of his predecessors in adopting it.

Nur ad-Din, in fine, both as general and administrator, displayed an insight and a capacity which rose above the average of his time but without conflicting with the established system. There can be little doubt that, had he lived, and the temporary rift between him and Saladin been closed, the counterattack on the crusaders would have been quicker and more vigorously pressed than it actually proved to be. The fact of the rift with Saladin cannot be denied, but the causes of it are clear enough to anyone who studies the sources without the bias induced by Ibn al-Athir's malicious interpretations. To Nur ad-Din the conquest of Egypt meant only an immediate and substantial accretion of military and financial resources for the war in Syria; whereas Saladin, faced with a dangerous situation in Egypt, felt that his first responsibility was to build up the local forces to hold Egypt against the threat of collusion between pro-Fatimid elements within and Frankish attacks from without. Presumably, after the failure of the Sicilian expedition to Alexandria in 1174 the general situation in Egypt would have been sufficiently stabilized to restore full understanding between Nur ad-Din and Saladin, but even before it arrived Nur ad-Din had died.

The immediate consequence of Nur ad-Din's death was that the centralized military power which he had built up fell to pieces, under the normal operation of the politico-military system. His Mosul relations seized the Jazira provinces, and his Syrian forces split up under the rivalries of the generals surrounding his minor son al-Malik as-Salih. The whole task had to be begun again, and on a very different footing. Since there was no hope of finding a true successor to Nur ad-Din among the members of the Zangid house, any attempt to revive Nur ad-Din's structure, from what-ever quarter it came, would have to begin by challenging the existing Zangid principalities; and while its leader, if he were of the right type, might eventually hope to gain the support of the "moral rearmament" movement, he would certainly be opposed by its representatives in the first instance, out of loyalty to the memory of Nur ad-Din.

As these circumstances, therefore, made the task of recon-structing a centralized military power in Syria a different, and in some respects harder, task than had been faced by Nur ad-Din, so also the methods and qualities of the man who undertook it would have to be different from those of Nur ad-Din. It might not have been done at all; but if it was to be done, there were, so far as one can judge, only two alternative methods. One was the absorption of the whole Zangid structure into a powerful military empire from outside (such as, say, an expanded Seljuk Sultanate of Ana-tolia, or a new empire in the East, had either been possible at the time). The other was to build upon the foundations of moral unity laid by Nur ad-Din, and so greatly strengthen them that the Zan-gid structure would be forced into the service of its ends. To purely outward appearances Saladin's way was the first; in reality, the secret of his success was that he adopted and carried through the second. To be sure, this involved the building up of a vast empire extending from Kurdistan and Diyar Bakr to Nubia and the Yemen; for whoso wills the end must will the means, and the circumstances of his task and time required nothing less than this.

But Saladin's personal position and qualities, the spirit in which
he approached his task, and the methods he employed were utterly
different from those possessed and displayed by the founders of
great military empires.

To begin with, Saladin was not a Turk but a Kurd. If the
Turks, because of the sense of superiority bred in them by their
military tradition and the all but universal monopolization of
political power in Eastern Islam by Turkish princes, despised all
the other Muslim races, those of Mosul and northern Syria regarded their Kurdish neighbours with special contempt.[6] The Mosul
troops, marching out against Saladin for the first time in 1175,
had[7] abused and mocked him, calling him "a dog that barks at his
master." Seventeen years later, a Mosul officer, as he watched
Saladin being assisted on to his horse during the defence of Jerusalem, is reported as saying: "Have a care, son of Ayyub, what
sort of end you will come to—you who are helped to mount by a
Seljuk prince and a descendant of Atabeg Zangi!"[8] The difference
in tone between the two taunts may fairly enough represent the
extent and the limits of the change of attitude towards him among
the more race conscious and the more resistant to the ideals for
which he stood.

Secondly, although Saladin's father, uncle, brothers, and he
himself were enrolled in Nur ad-Din's feudal forces, he was far
from outstanding as a general or a strategist. This may seem a
paradox in the victor of Hattin; but Saladin was a good tactician.
Hattin, like his two early victories against the forces of Mosul,
was won by good tactics, and these were his only successful battles
in the open field. His most remarkable feat of arms was the capture of the reputedly impregnable fortress of Amid (Diyarbakr)
in 1183 after a siege of only three weeks, an episode generally
overlooked in Western histories. It is remarkable how often lack
of confidence in his generalship was expressed by the officers in
his own armies, and not always without reason, even if valuable
opportunities were sometimes lost during the Third Crusade by
their opposition to his tactics and plans of campaign.

Nor was he a good administrator. He seems to have taken
little personal interest in details of administration beyond trying
to suppress abuses. In his own territories he leaned heavily on his

brother al-Adil Saif ad-Din and his secretary of state al-Qadi al-Fadil; the administration of the provinces was turned over entirely to their governors on two conditions, that they should follow his example in suppressing abuses and furnish him with troops (and if necessary with money) when he required them to do so for the Holy War.

The independent and concordant testimony furnished by the surviving documents of three of the men who stood closest to him, al-Qadi al-Fadil, Imad ad-Din and Baha ad-Din, supply us with the real explanation of his success. Himself neither warrior nor governor by training or inclination, he it was who inspired and gathered round himself all the elements and forces making for the unity of Islam against the invaders. And this he did, not so much by the example of his personal courage and resolution—which were undeniable—as by his unselfishness, his humility and generosity, his moral vindication of Islam against both its enemies and its professed adherents. He was no simpleton, but for all that an utterly simple and transparently honest man. He baffled his enemies, internal and external, because they expected to find him animated by the same motives as they were, and playing the political game as they played it. Guileless himself, he never expected and seldom understood guile in others—a weakness of which his own family and others sometimes took advantage, but only (as a general rule) to come up at the end against his singleminded devotion, which nobody and nothing could bend, to the service of his ideals.

The true nature of those ideals has not yet, in my opinion, been appreciated. The immediate task to which he found himself called was to drive the Franks out of Palestine and Syria. This was the part that his contemporaries saw, and that later generations assumed to have been his whole purpose. It is natural, when a men accomplishes some great work, to imagine that this was what he had set as his goal. In reality, it is more often the case that what a man achieves is only a part of what he sets out to achieve; and perhaps it is only because his eyes are fixed on some more distant goal that he succeeds in doing as much as he does.

This was, in my view, eminently true of Saladin. His wider design was one which only a man of unbounded ambition or of unbounded simplicity would have entertained. In a certain sense, Saladin was both, but his ambition arose out of the simplicity of his character and the directness of his vision. He saw clearly that the weakness of the Muslim body politic, which had permitted the establishment and continued to permit the survival of the crusading states, was the result of political demoralization. It was against this that he revolted. There was only one way to end it: to restore and revive the political fabric of Islam as a single united empire, not under his own rule, but by restoring the rule of the revealed law, under the direction of the Abbasid Caliphate. The theory of the caliph's disposal of provinces by diploma, to the other princes of the time a convenient fiction, was to him a positive and necessary reality. He saw himself as simply the adjutant and commander of the armies of the Abbasids, as he had become for a brief time the wazir and commander of the armies of the Fatimid Caliphs. That he was called *sultan* was simply the title he had inherited as wazir of the Fatimids; it had nothing to do with the theory or claims of the Seljuk sultanate, and it never appears in his protocol or on his coins. Imad ad-Din relates an incident during the siege of Acre, which is particularly instructive because it is one of the occasions on which the secretary reproaches Saladin for his simplicity.[9] At the request of an envoy from the caliphate, he had consented to transfer the region of Shahrazur in Kurdistan to the Caliph's possession; when faced with the anger and scorn of his amirs at this decision, he replied: "The Caliph is the lord of mankind and the repository of the True Faith; if he were to join us here I should give him all these lands—so what of Shahrazur?"

But the argument does not rest on an incidental episode of this kind, however authentic it may be. This objective is the explicit theme of many of his despatches to Baghdad. "These three aims—*jihad* on the path of God, the restraining of actions hurtful to the servants of God, and submission to the caliph of God—are the sole desire of this servitor from the territories in his occupation and his sole gain from the worldly power granted to him. God is his witness that... he has no desire beyond these things and no aim beyond this aim."[10] It reappears in his bewilderment at the failure of the caliph and the caliph's officers at Baghdad to understand his motives and to give him at least moral support: "For let him consider, is there anyone else of the governors of Islam whose increase distresses the infidels?"[11] in the punctiliousness with which he supplicates for the caliph's diploma of investiture before operating in new territories, and his protests against the Zangids' claims to the Jazira on grounds of "inheritance" in default of a diploma, and their seizure of Aleppo;[12] in his attribution of the speedy capture of Amid to the influence of the caliph's authority;[13] and in his forthright message to sultan Qilij Arslan of Anatolia in 1178 that "he would not permit mutual warfare among Muslim princes instead of their uniting in the *jihad*."[14]

At the same time his idealism was yoked with a strong practical sense. The clarity with which he judged each step towards his objective and each situation as it arose supplies the clue to the steady expansion of his power. Knowing that the problem which he faced was not only political, but also or still more a moral and psychological one, and that to attack it merely on the political and military plane would fail to solve it, he realized that to gain effective results it was essential to cement political allegiance by moral and psychological stimulants and deterrents. The difficulty —even the apparent hopelessness—of this task in the circumstances of the time are evident, but Saladin found ways to meet it, often to the bewilderment or astonishment of his friends and counselors.

In dealing with the princes, whether friends or enemies, his first principle was sincerity and absolute loyalty to his word. Even with the crusaders a truce was a truce. There is no instance on record in which he broke faith with them, and to those who broke faith with him he was implacable, as Reginald of Chatillon and the Templars were to learn. Towards his Muslim rivals he supplemented loyalty with generosity. After the pact with al-Malik as-Salih in 1176 (and the famous incident of the return of Azaz), he left Aleppo alone until as-Salih's death, although he held the caliph's diploma for it.[15] The siege of Amid was undertaken because he had promised it to the Artuqid prince of Hisn Kaifa as the price of his alliance, and after capturing it he turned over all its immense treasures to his ally as they stood—an act of loyalty to his pledged word so unprecedented that it created a sensation.[16]

To achieve his object, however, he had to reinforce his own actions and example by creating a moral and psychological current in his favour so strong that it could not be resisted. For this he needed allies, and especially the influential class of "college men" who were the leaders of public opinion. This was one of his most serious difficulties since, as already noted, these were precisely the sections which Nur ad-Din had mobilized in his support. Since Saladin at first appeared to be a usurper who challenged the heirs of Nur ad-Din, they, with the people of Syria generally, were in the beginning opposed, or at least reserved, towards him. The Arabic sources give us little indication of the gradual change in their attitude, but that his sincerity finally gained their respect and admiration is amply evident, both from the chronicles and from the reports of other contemporaries.[17] His patronage of the sufis, again following the example of Nur ad-Din, was probably of particular importance for this "missionary" work, if the term may be used, among the population of Syria. The most effective appeal to the general population, however, was probably made by his insistence upon the removal of wrongful dues and burdens in all territories under his government and suzerainty, even if it is by no means certain that his subordinates were always prompt to carry out his instructions on this point. Finally, it is remarkable that the turbulent Shiites of Aleppo and northern Syria, who had remained unreconciled to Nur ad-Din, not only gave Saladin no trouble (after the early Assassin attempts on his life) but positively assisted him during the reconquest.[18]

The secretary Imad ad-Din supplies a striking example of this aspect of Saladin's diplomacy,[19] on an occasion when the Zangid atabek of Mosul and his advisors attempted to take advantage of his loyalty to the caliphate, by requesting the caliph's *diwan* to send the Shaikh ash-Shuyukh of Baghdad to intercede with Saladin in 1184, "because of their knowledge that we had no thought of anything but implicit obedience to the command that should be obeyed" (i.e., of the caliphate). Although the conduct of the envoy from Mosul made an accommodation next to impossible, Saladin finally placed himself unreservedly in the hands of the Shaikh ash-Shuyukh, only to be repulsed again by the envoy, who openly threatened an alliance between Mosul and the caliph's enemy, the Seljuk sultan of Persia, Tughril II. It was this, adds Imad ad-Din, which determined Saladin, who had hitherto been lukewarm in prosecuting the conflict with Mosul, to deal with it firmly. That Imad ad-Din's account is not exaggerated is proved by the fact that Saladin's conduct on this occasion was the starting-point of his friendship with the qadi Baha ad-Din, who was himself in the suite of the Mosul envoy and in his narrative confirms the main points of this statement.[20]

Apart from the capture of Amid (and perhaps even there as well), in fact, the extension of Saladin's empire in Asia between 1182 and 1186 was due far more to the influence of these factors than to military action. His campaigns before Mosul and Aleppo were demonstrations rather than sieges. The lesser princes of the Jazira, confident in the character of the man, voluntarily placed themselves under his protection. The leaders of Nur ad-Din's regiment at Aleppo, after little more than a show of battle,[21] came over *en masse* to give him the most loyal service. Even at Mosul, as Ibn al-Athir himself conveys in his narrative,[22] Saladin found supporters among the commanders, and it was they who eventually forced the Zangid atabek to yield in 1186. The extent of the influence exerted by the *fuqaha* over the troops should not perhaps be exaggerated; but there are several examples in our sources of their decisive intervention, and they certainly counted as a contributory factor. The most remarkable case of all is that of the powerful Shah-Arman of Khilat, who had been among the most tenacious of Saladin's adversaries but who, just before the end of the Third Crusade, voluntarily offered Saladin his allegiance and his troops.[23]

How much Saladin's reputation for absolute faithfulness to his word and generosity contributed to the recovery of Palestine and inner Syria during the year and a half that followed Hattin is well known. If it had been necessary to take every castle and fortified town by regular siege, not more than a tithe of them would have fallen before the opening of the Third Crusade, and the history of that crusade would have been very different if the crusaders had had the support of garrisons in Saladin's rear.

The stability of Saladin's structure was destined to be tried to the utmost limit by the Third Crusade. It was to prove a contest of a kind which he had never anticipated and for which he had made no preparations. Instead of pursuing his noble, if idealist, dream of restoring the reign of law in the Islamic world, he was involved in a struggle of the most painful actuality; but because he had sought to realize the former by unselfishness, justice and loyalty, and only because of these moral foundations, he was able to sustain the unprecedented task now thrust upon him. No Muslim prince had for centuries been confronted with the problem of maintaining an army continuously in the field for three years against an active and enterprising enemy. The military feudal system was entirely inadequate to such a campaign, even if it was possible to organize a limited system of reliefs between the Egyptian and the Mesopotamian regiments.

The contest uncovered one by one the material and even moral weaknesses in Saladin's empire which had remained concealed during the era of victory. He had never cared for money or for prudent management of his revenues. He had "spent the revenues of Egypt to gain Syria, the revenues of Syria to gain Mesopotamia, those of Mesopotamia to conquer Palestine,"[24] and now found himself without adequate resources to meet the cost of weapons, food, forage, equipment, and the pay of the auxiliary troops. In consequence, he could do little to ease the difficulties of the feudal troops, who were either forced into debt or into pressing their cultivators.[25] Perhaps this, even more than the survival of old rancors, may explain the reluctance of some of the Eastern contingents to sustain their part in the campaign. In addition, all the military equipment from Egypt and Syria had been locked up in Acre,[26] which Saladin had refortified as his main base for future operations; the siege and loss of Acre therefore seriously crippled the offensive power of the Muslim army.

Apart from this, however, the tactics and fighting traditions of the regular troops were baffled by the fortified trenches of the crusading besiegers. In open fighting on the plain against the western knights the Turkish regulars more than held their own, although Saladin's Kurdish guards proved less stable (as again at Arsuf). But when repeated success in the open field proved to be of no effect whatsoever in relieving the pressure on Acre, it was a natural reaction to slacken effort and to grumble against Saladin. Once it had started, grumbling became a habit and developed into criticism and opposition, especially in the later period of the campaign, when the fall of Acre seemed to have proved the weakness of Saladin's military leadership.

Yet this was after all a minor matter in comparison with the damage inflicted on Saladin and on the whole cause for which he stood by his own kinsmen. Here, if anywhere, was his most vulnerable point. The scarcely concealed appetites of several of his brothers and other relatives[27] had caused him much trouble in the past, but had been brought more or less under control. But at the very climax of his struggle with the crusaders his nephew Taqi ad-Din deliberately disobeyed his orders in Diyar Bakr, and by his disobedience opened up a series of conflicts and mutinies which grievously disabled Saladin during the campaign in Palestine after the fall of Acre. Not only did they involve the absence of Taqi ad-Din's own troops and those of Diyar Bakr during the rest of the active fighting, but they led to further rifts within his family and to dissensions amongst his overstrained personal troops during the last crucial months.

These were the factors which robbed Saladin of the chance of complete victory in his struggle with Richard. But they only throw into stronger relief the most surprising and significant feature of the whole campaign—that year after year the Mosul contingents returned for active service, even if they sometimes lingered on the way. In the circumstances, there could have been no question of physical compulsion, nor could Saladin have restrained them (as the episode of Taqi ad-Din proves) from reoccupying the Jazira, as in fact they attempted to do immediately after his death. There can be no explanation of this except that the feeling of personal loyalty to Saladin, even in Mosul, was strong enough to overcome the reluctance or resistance of individuals. His own modestly-phrased remark to Baha ad-Din: "If I were to die, it is very unlikely that these *askars* would ever come together again,"[28] sums up the real nature of his achievement. For a brief but decisive moment, by sheer goodness and firmness of character, he raised Islam out of the rut of political demoralization. By standing out for a moral ideal, and expressing that ideal in his own life and action, he created around him an impulse to unity which, though never quite complete, sufficed to meet the unforeseen challenge flung down to him by destiny.

NOTES

[1] See "Arabic Sources for the Life of Saladin" in *Speculum*, xxv, no. i, pp. 58-72 (Cambridge, Mass., 1950).

[2] *Conquête de la Syrie et de la Palestine*, ed. Carlo de Landberg (Leyden, 1888) . This text has been little used so far by historians of the crusades.

[3] See N. Elisséeff, "Les Monuments de Nur ad-Din" in *Bulletin d'Études Orientales*, t. xiii (Damascus, 1951) , pp. 5-43.

[4] This practice was dictated not only by personal considerations but also by sound economic reasons. The regular forces had to maintain themselves and their retainers on campaign with supplies and forage out of their own revenues, and a prolonged campaign involved them in considerable expense and even debt (cf. Imad ad-Din in Abu Shama, i. 271 foot, and *Fath* 392-3; Baha ad-Din (ed. Schultens) 200, 221) .

[5] Cf. Ibn al-Athir (ed. Tornberg) , x. 400; Imad ad-Din, *Barq,* iii. 139b.

[6] This is expressed vividly and with typical elaboration even by Imad ad-Din, who devotes more than a page to disparaging the unmilitary qualities of the Kurds in the Artuqid armies in contrast to the virtues and sobriety of Saladin's troops: *Barq*, v. 57b sq.

[7] If Michael the Syrian is to be believed: ed. and trans. Chabot, iii. 365.

[8] Ibn al-Athir, xii. 50.

[9] *Fath* (ed. Landberg), 218-219.

[10] From Abu Shama, ii. 48, after the occupation of Amid.

[11] From Abu Shama, ii. 41, after the capture of Amid.

[12] Cf. Abu Shama, ii. 24, 31 n. It might be claimed, and with truth, that such passages could be paralleled in the artificial correspondence of other princes with the caliphate. But it would be utterly inconsistent with all that we know of the character of Saladin to regard them as equally hypocritical; and if it all meant nothing more to him than mere playing with words, why should he have kept up such a stream of entreaties and expostulations to Baghdad?

[13] Abu Shama, ii. 40-41.

[14] *Barq,* iii. fol. 123a.

[15] Abu Shama, ii. 34.

[16] So consistent was his conduct in this respect, and so frightening to his enemies, that it was necessary to invent an incident to offset it, which is duly recorded (with a great show of impartiality) by Ibn al-Athir (xi. 341; see "Arabic Sources," *Speculum*, xxv, 67-68).

[17] See Ibn Jubair, *Rihla*, pp. 297-298; Abd al-Latif al-Baghdadi in Ibn Abi Usaibia, *Uyun al-Anba*, ii. 206 (both translated in *R.H.C.Or.*, iii. 435 sqq.) .

[18] C. Cahen, *La Syrie du Nord à l'époque des croisades* (Paris, 1940) , pp. 428-429.

[19] *Barq*, v. fol. 129 sqq.

[20] Ed. Schultens, p. 57.

[21] Imad ad-Din, *Barq*. v. 79b sqq. (Abu Shama, ii. 43-44) .

[22] Ed. Tornberg, xi. 338, 340. See also the significant incident of the garrison of Harim (quoted by Grousset, ii. 720) .

[23] Baha ad-Din, 260.

[24] Al-Qadi al-Fadil in Abu Shama, ii. 177.

[25] Abu Shama, ii. 177, 178, 203; *Fath*, 207, 392-393, 443; Baha ad-Din, 200, 221, etc.

[26] Baha ad-Din, 174.

[27] Vividly portrayed by al-Qadi al-Fadil in a letter quoted by Abu Shama, ii. 178.

[28] Baha ad-Din, 218.

7. Tarikh

Ilm al-Tarikh, or historiography, as a term of Arabic literature embraces both annalistic and biographical, but not as a rule literary, history. The development of Arabic and Persian historiography is summarized here in four sections: I. from the origins to the third century of the Hijra; II. from the third to the sixth centuries; III. from the end of the sixth to the beginning of the tenth century; IV. from the tenth to the thirteenth centuries.

I From the Origins to the Third Century of the Hijra

The problem of the origins of Arabic historiography is not yet finally solved. Between the legendary and popular traditions of pre-Islamic Arabia and the relatively scientific and exact chronicles which appear in the second century of the Hijra, there lies a wide gulf, as yet unexplained. One view expressed by several modern writers would allow a decisive influence in this development to the example of the Persian *Book of Kings*. It appears more probable, however, that Arabic historiography arose from the confluence of several streams of historical and quasi-historical composition, which may for convenience be treated here separately.

Pre-Islamic historical tradition. It might have been expected that in the Yaman, the seat of a long-established civilization whose monuments are preserved in the Minean, Sabean and Himyaritic inscriptions, some form of written historical tradition would be found. All that has come down to us, however, bears the marks of an oral tradition: some few names of ancient kings, vague and exaggerated tales of the distant past, and a more accurate, but still confused, memory of the events of the last century before Islam.

During the first century of the Hijra, this oral tradition was imaginatively expanded into a vast body of legendary lore which professed to relate the ancient history of Arabia, associated with the names of Wahb b. Munabbih and Ubaid b. Sharya. Both books furnish ample proof of the lack of historical sense and perspective amongst the early Arabs, even when dealing with almost contemporary events.[1] Yet their narratives were accepted in the main by later generations and incorporated by historians and other writers in their own works. Ibn Ishaq was one of the transmitters of Ubaid, and Abd al-Malik b. Hisham edited the *Kitab al-Tijan* of Wahb in its extant form; and even in such a monument of religious scholarship as al-Tabari's Commentary on the Koran, Wahb's materials are freely drawn upon. Ibn Khaldun, it is true, points out the absurdity of some of these Yamanite legends (i. 13-14), yet goes on to quote precisely the same legends as illustrations of his theories. Thus they remained through the whole range of Arabic historiography as an irrational element, which stood in the way of the development of a critical sense and of any clear understanding of ancient history.

Amongst the northern Arabs we find a rather different situation. While each tribe possessed its own tradition, which in many cases so far transcended the tribal horizon as to include some sort of collective genealogical conceptions, there is nothing to indicate the existence of a common north Arabian tradition. The form taken by the tribal tradition is also of importance. For the most part it relates to *aiyam*, "days" in which the tribe or clan fought with another [Aiyam al-Arab], and each narrative usually includes some verse. The relation between the prose and verse elements is not always the same; in some instances the verse is a kind of *memoria technica*; in others it appears that the prose narrative is nothing more than an interpretation of the verse. In either case, however, it was the verse which maintained the currency of the tradition, and ancient traditions disappeared as the corresponding verses were forgotten, while new verses celebrated more recent episodes in the tribal history. Such a tribal tradition, while necessarily one-sided, vague in chronology and often romantically exaggerated, nevertheless reflected a reality and sometimes preserved a substantial core of truth. The Islamic conquests deflected the course of the tribal traditions without changing their character, and the new traditions preserve, against a wider background, the old association of prose and verse and the old exaggerations and inexactitude. This too was destined to influence Islamic historiography, in that tribal traditions furnished materials upon which later compilers drew for their history of the Primitive and Umayyad Caliphates [see *The history of the caliphate* §].

The other element in the tribal tradition was the preservation of the tribal genealogies. In the early Umayyad period, however, the activities of the genealogists, stimulated by the institution of the *diwan* and the partisan interests of rival Arab factions, were such as to bring the whole "science" of genealogy into confusion.[2]

In the second century of the Hijra, the fields of tribal tradition, hitherto the preserves of the *rawi* and the *nassab*, were invaded by the philologists who, in trying to recover and to elucidate all that survived of the ancient poetry, performed a valuable service to history by collecting and sorting out this mass of material. The typical figure in this activity is Abu Ubaida (110-209: 728-824), a *mawla* of Mesopotamian origin. Of the two hundred monographs credited to him not one has been transmitted under his name, although the substance of many of them passed into later works. They compass the whole range of north Arabian tradition, arranged under convenient heads such as the traditions of individual tribes and families and those relating to the "days," and extend also to the post-Islamic traditions relating to the conquests of single provinces, to important events and battles, and such groups as the *qadis* of al-Basra, the *khawarij,* and the *mawali.* He was accused of aiming to discredit the Arabs in the interests of the shuubiya, but examination of the charges brought against him suggests that they may well be regarded as proofs of impartial scholarship rather than of deliberate bias.

Somewhat similar was the work of Hisham b. Muhammad al-Kalbi (d.c. 204:819),[3] who set in order and expanded the collections made by his father (d. 146:763), Awana and Abu Mikhnaf. His monographs cover much the same ground as those of Abu Ubaida, but in particular he collected from written sources the historical information relating to the town and dynasty of al-Hira.

This work, said to be based on the archives of the churches of al-Hira and on Persian materials translated for him, thus takes a long step towards a scientific historiography, and, though it is preserved only in excerpts, its general accuracy has been confirmed by modern research. Hisham is said to have followed the same method in his other works, using such inscriptions and written materials as were available, but this did not save him from bitter attacks on the grounds of untrustworthiness and forgery by more conservative scholars.

The rise of Islam. Apart from the Hiran material utilized by Hisham al-Kalbi, the beginnings of scientific history in Arabic are associated with the study of the life and activities of the Prophet. The source of this discipline is consequently to be found in the collection of the Prophetic Tradition [hadith], and more especially of the traditions relating to the military expeditions of the Prophet (hence the general term *maghazi,* "military expeditions," applied to the early biographical works). The home of this study was al-Medina, and it was not until the second century that students of the *maghazi* were to be found in other centers. Its association with the *hadith,* which left an enduring impress on historical method in the employment of the *isnad,* explains the immense change which appears from this moment in the character and critical accuracy of historical information amongst the Arabs. For the first time we can feel that we are on firm historical ground, even while we admit the existence of some doubtful elements in the traditions relating both to the Meccan and Medinian periods of the Prophet's life.

The second generation of Muslims appear in this development as sources rather than collectors. Although two of them, Aban b. Othman and Urwa b. al-Zubair, are named as authors of "books" on the *maghazi,* no such books are quoted by later writers. In the following generation several traditionists were noted for their collection of *maghazi* traditions, especially the famous Muhammad b. Muslim Ibn Shihab al-Zuhri, who, at the request of Omar II or of Hisham, wrote down his *hadith* materials, which were deposited in the royal store-room, afterwards destroyed. He is credited with having been the first to combine traditions from several sources into a single narrative (*e. g.,* the *hadith al-ifk*), which marks an advance in historical presentation, though one open to abuse by less scrupulous traditionists.

Al-Zuhri's traditions formed the basis for books on the *maghazi* compiled by three writers of the next generation. Two of these, as well as two other independent works, are lost, or preserved only in fragments. The third, however, the famous *Sira* of Muhammad Ibn Ishaq b. Yasar (d. 151:768), was the fruit of a wider conception than that of his predecessors and contemporaries, in that it aimed at giving not only a history of the Prophet, but a history of Prophecy. In its original form it was apparently composed of three sections: *al-Mubtada*, dealing with pre-Islamic history from the creation, and drawn largely from Wahb b. Munabbih and Jewish sources; *al-Mabath*, relating the life of the Prophet down to the first year of the Hijra; and *al-Maghazi*, to the death of the Prophet. The book, though severely criticized for its inclusion of many worthless and forged traditions and poetical citations, became the principal authority for both pre-Islamic and early Islamic history. Several recensions are known to have existed; unfortunately, all those which were utilized by the later Iraqi compilers (and were therefore, presumably, the best [cf. al-Khatib al-Baghdadi, i. 221, 6-8]) have been lost, and have left the field to the somewhat distorted epitome produced by the Egyptian compiler Abd al-Malik Ibn Hisham (d. c. 218:833).

It is worthy of note that all these writers on the *maghazi* were *mawali*. Although the term did not necessarily imply, even at that time, non-Arab origin, Ibn Ishaq was certainly of Mesopotamian origin, his grandfather Yasar having been captured in al-Iraq in the year 12:633. But it would be absurd to look for any but the most indirect Persian influences in the conception of Ibn Ishaq's work; the relations between it and the work of Wahb b. Munabbih, on the one hand, and the Medinian school of Tradition on the other, show it to have been of true Arabian inspiration, and disciplined by the truly Arabian science of *hadith*.

With the next generation the scope of historical study and writing widens. Ibn Ishaq is indeed credited with a *History of the Caliphs,* but it seems to have been a short and summary work. His most famous successor, Muhammad b. Omar al-Waqidi (130-207: 747-823), wrote not only on the expeditions of the Prophet but also on several episodes of later Islamic history, as well as a *Large History* down to the reign of Harun. Thus the historical science which derived from the *hadith* was approaching the historical materials collected by the philologists, while retaining its own method of traditional presentation. Al-Waqidi's history of the *maghazi* has alone survived in its original shape; but much of his material was utilized by his "secretary," Muhammad Ibn Sad (d. 230:844-845), in his biographical dictionary of the Prophet, his Companions, and the *tabiun*, known as the *Book of Classes*. The conception of such a biographical dictionary itself marks a fresh development in the art of history, and illustrates its still close connection with the science of *hadith*, since it was chiefly for purposes of *hadith* criticism that these materials were assembled.

That part of Ibn Sad's work which he himself put into final shape, namely his history of the Prophet (vols. i. and ii. of the printed edition), has a double importance. The history of the *maghazi* is supplemented by the Prophet's edicts and letters, for which (following al-Waqidi) Ibn Sad utilized such written documents as were available. Still more significant are the sections now added on the habits and characteristics of the Prophet (*sifat akhlaq al-nabi*) and on the "tokens of the Prophetic Mission" (*alamat al-nubuwa*), the precursors of the later *shamail* and *dalail* literature respectively. This development carries one stage farther the fusion of the genuine *hadith* elements with a second current of tradition (already seen in Ibn Ishaq), which is to be sought in the art of the *kussas* or popular preachers, and represents a throwback to a type of popular literature akin to the productions of Wahb b. Munabbih. With this new direction of the *sira*, which was followed by all later biographers of the Prophet, it is evident that its contribution to the development of historical method has come to an end.

The history of the caliphate. The beginnings of a monographic treatment of episodes subsequent to the death of Muhammed have been described in the preceding sections. It is noteworthy that this activity was confined to al-Iraq; no similar treatises are recorded of any scholar in Syria, Arabia or Egypt during the first two centuries of the Hijra. The result of this was to give al-Iraq and its tradition a dominant place in later historical works.

For the history of the Primitive Caliphate, however, the tradition of al-Medina also supplied material which was utilized by writers (such as al-Wakidi) who were associated with the Medinian school of *hadith*. Whether there were written archives available at al-Medina is open to doubt, although the accuracy of the chronological data in the Medinian tradition suggests that some materials of this kind existed. For the Umayyad period the existence of archives both in Damascus and al-Iraq is confirmed by numerous references.[4] It is probable that it was from such materials that the later compilers obtained their exact chronological framework, with its lists of governors, leaders of the pilgrimage, etc., for each year.

In order to fill up this framework, however, recourse was had to materials in the collection of which were combined the methods of the traditionists and the philologists. Prominent amongst these were the traditions of the Arab tribes in al-Iraq. One was that of Azd, collected (along with other traditions) by Abu Mikhnaf (d. 157:774) and handed down by Hisham al-Kalbi, which presents the pro-Alid and anti-Syrian tradition of al-Kufa. The Kalbite tradition, represented by Awana b. al-Hakam (d. 147:764 or 158: 775) and also handed down by Hisham al-Kalbi, shows an anti-Alid and rather pro-Syrian tendency.[5] A third tradition, that of Tamim, was propagated by Saif b. Omar (d. c. 180:796) in the form of an historical romance on the conquests, based largely on poetical materials, whose relation to the narrative is much the same as in the *aiyam* literature. Fragments of other tribal traditions also appear, e. g., the tradition of Bahila in connection with the wars of Kutaiba b. Muslim. By their vivid detail and their bold handling of episodes the tribal traditions offer a marked contrast to the annalistic of their own and later times. Though partial and one-sided, their historical value is by no means negligible, more especially in the insight which they give into the inner factors of the first century of Islamic history. It must again be noted that on the formal side, by their careful observance of the rule of the *isnad*, the collections link up with the science of tradition (the beginnings of this activity are, indeed, associated with al-Shabi (d. c. 110:728), the leading traditionist of al-Kufa), and show no trace of foreign influence in either manner or content.

At the beginning of the third century a fresh impetus towards literary activities in general was given by the increasing standards of material culture and by the introduction of paper, the first factory for which at Baghdad was set up in 178:794-795. It is from this period that the earliest written redactions of literary works have come down to us, but this practice did not at once supersede the custom of transmitting collections of material through *rawis,* which continued until the end of the century. It is consequently uncertain how many of the 230 monographs credited to the Basrian Ali b. Muhammad al-Madaini (d. 225:840) were actually written down in his lifetime. Many of these were probably little more than recensions of Abu Ubaida's collections. More important, however, were his large works on the history of the caliphate and his monographs on the history of al-Basra and of Khurasan. By applying to the mass of Iraqi traditions the sound methods of criticism associated with the Medinian school, he gained for his work such a reputation for trustworthiness that it became the principal source for the compilations of the succeeding period, and one whose general accuracy has been confirmed by modern investigation.

In summing up these developments, the outstanding fact is that, in spite of the hostility of a section of early theologians to historical studies, the Islamic community had become history conscious. The historical arguments contained in the Koran, the natural pride taken in the extensive conquests and the rivalries of the Arab tribes no doubt contributed to this. But the remarkable feature that, apart from the philologists, the collectors of the historical tradition were almost exclusively theologians and *muhaddiths* suggests that a deeper reason existed. For in the theological view history was the manifestation of a divine plan for the government of mankind; and while the historical outlook of the earlier generations might be limited to tracing it through the succession of prophets which culminated in Muhammad, all Islamic schools were agreed that it did not end there. In the Sunni doctrine, it was the Islamic community, the *ummat Allah,* with which the continuation of the divine plan on earth was bound up; consequently the study of its history was a necessary supplement to the study of the divine revelation in Koran and *hadith.* More-

over, the doctrine of historical continuity was one of the bases of
Sunni politico-religious thought. To the Shia, the divine government was continued in the line of the Imams, and the solitary
Shiite collector amongst those already mentioned, Abu Mikhnaf,
shows the influence of this religious preoccupation in his concentration on the history of the Shiite movements at al-Kufa. It bears
still stronger testimony to the place of history in religious thought
that mistaken piety and religious controversy were already opening
the door not only to partisan and apologetic, but also to irenical
falsifications, of which a striking example was given by Saif b.
Omar in his second work, on the assassination of Othman. Henceforward historiography is an inseparable part of Islamic culture.
In the lands of the Mediterranean the ancient historical traditions
are replaced or remolded in the Islamic spirit; and both in those
cultured eastern lands where no written history existed, and in
primitive Africa, where there was no literature at all, the establishment of Islam is followed by the rise of an historical literature.

    Connected historical narrative. The beginnings of historical
composition in the wider sense, i.e., the combination of materials
derived from the *sira,* the monographs already mentioned and
other sources into connected historical narrative, belong to the
middle of the third century. The earliest compiler, Ahmad b.
Yahya al-Baladhuri (d. 279:892), carries on the "classical" tradition; he studied under both Ibn Sad and al-Madaini, and his two
extant works show the influence of these teachers as well as the
critical taste of his age at its best. The characteristic composition
of this stage is, however, the *Universal History,* which, beginning
with the creation, offers a summary of world history on a larger or
smaller scale by way of introduction to Islamic history proper.
This conception is not new; it is rather an expansion of the idea
underlying the work of Ibn Ishaq, by the addition of the history
of the Islamic Community and a wider range of pre-Islamic history.
The *Universal History,* therefore, is not a world history in the
truest sense; from the moment of the rise of Islam, the history of
other nations has no farther interest for the writer.

    It is at this point that, for the first time (excepting only in
the work of Hisham al-Kalbi), the Persian tradition enters into
the mainstream of Arabic historiography, although the Persian

Book of Kings (*Khuday-nama*) had been rendered into Arabic more than a century before by Ibn al-Mukaffa (d. c. 139:756). As has been shown above, materials derived from Jewish and Christian legend had long since found a way, under cover of Koranic exposition, into Arabic history, not entirely to its advantage. The influence of the Persian tradition was equally unfavorable. For, during its apprenticeship to the science of *hadith,* the native credulousness and romanticism of Arabic memories of the past had been schooled by a certain empiricism and respect for critical standards which are the essential conditions for any genuine historiography. As soon as history passed outside the Islamic field the old difficulty of distinguishing between legendary, semi-legendary and historical elements reappeared, and with it the tendency to take on trust whatever materials were available. It was this tendency which was now reinforced by the character of the sources from which the Arabic compilers drew their materials for the ancient history of Persia and other lands. The *Khuday-nama* itself in its earlier sections consisted of tales of mythical personages, priestly speculations, Avestic legends, and reminiscences of the Alexander romance, and even in the narrative of the Sasanid kingdom genuine tradition was frequently overlaid by epic and rhetorical elements.[6] At the same time, the revival of Greek studies through Syriac translations maintained an interest in Judaeo-Christian and Greek antiquities which had to satisfy itself from sources not always superior to the *Khuday-nama,* amongst them, for example, being the Syriac work known as the *Treasure-Cave (Mearat gazze).*

From these sources were drawn the materials now taken up into the corpus of Islamic historiography by such compilers as Abu Hanifa al-Dinawari (d. 282:895) and Ibn Wadih al-Yaqubi (d. 284:897). The range of the latter, however, is so wide (embracing even the northern peoples and the Chinese) that his work is to be described rather as an historical encyclopedia than as a universal history. To the same class belong the historical "note-book" (*Kitab al-Maarif*) of the traditionist Ibn Qutaiba (d. 276:889), and, in the next century, the surviving historical works of Hamza al-Isfahani (d. c. 360:970) and al-Masudi (d. c. 345:956). Al-Masudi is, indeed, entitled to be reckoned amongst the major Arabic histo-

rians, but the loss of the larger compositions, of which his surviving works are an abstract, renders it difficult to reach an exact idea
of his methods.

It is evident from such works as these that a fresh intellectual
element had entered into Arabic historiography, an element which
we may define as the desire of knowledge for its own sake. It is
significant that writers like al-Yaqubi and al-Masudi were not
only historians but also geographers, whose geographical information was gained chiefly by wide travels. In this development we
can doubtless trace the working of that legacy of Hellenistic culture which was penetrating into all branches of intellectual activity in Islam during the second and third centuries. In historiography, indeed, it went little farther; but the link thus created
between history and geography was maintained by a succession of
writers down into the Ottoman period.

These intrusive elements, however, are absent (except for
the Persian history) from the work in which the classical historical
tradition reaches its culmination, the celebrated *History of the
Prophets and Kings* of Muhammad b. Jarir al-Tabari (d. 310:
923). For al-Tabari was primarily a traditionist, and in his *History*
aimed to supplement his *Commentary* on the Koran, by presenting
the historical traditions of Islam with the same fullness and critical
guarantees as he had done in his earlier work. The book, as it has
come down to us, is apparently reduced from the elaborate scale
on which it was originally planned; and whereas in the *Commentary* the author's criticism is explicit, in the *History* it is implicit. Its weaknesses are such as were to be expected from a
traditionist—the preference given to the pseudo-historical compilation of Saif, for example, as against al-Waqidi, because of the
suspicion attaching to al-Waqidi amongst the *muhaddiths*. But
against these weaknesses must be set the positive excellence of the
rest, which by its authority and comprehensiveness marked the
close of an epoch. No later compiler ever set himself to collect and
investigate afresh the materials for the early history of Islam, but
either abstracted them from al-Tabari (sometimes supplemented
from al-Baladhuri), or else began where al-Tabari left off.

At the same time, the poverty of the latter part of al-Tabari's
work gave warning that the purely traditionalist approach to

history was no longer sufficient. The bureaucratic organization of government brought the class of officials and courtiers to the fore as authorities for political history, and relegated the men of religion to the second place. For this reason also, the third century marks the end of a stage in Arabic historiography.

II   From the Third to the Sixth Centuries

With the recognition of history as a science in its own right, it entered on a period of rapid expansion, and the output of historical works between the third and the sixth centuries grew to such proportions that it is impossible to do more than summarize the main tendencies.

Already in the third century provincial scholars had begun to collect the local historical traditions. Apart from a history of Mecca by al-Azraqi, which belongs essentially to the *sira* cycle, the earliest provincial history is that of Egypt and the conquests in the west compiled by Abd al-Rahman b. Abd Allah Ibn Abd al-Hakam (d. 257:871). It is noteworthy that this work contains the same characteristic materials as the general histories already described, but lacks their element of critical handling. The conquests are related on the basis of the Medinian and the far from trustworthy local traditions; the prefatory section is derived, not from genuine Egyptian materials, but chiefly from Jewish sources and Arabian traditions, mediated through the school of al-Medina. The same uncritical combination of legend with more or less genuine tradition is to be seen in the early history of Muslim Spain fathered upon Abd al-Malik Ibn Habib (d. 238:853) and in the encyclopedia of south Arabian antiquities (*al-Iklil*) composed by al-Hamdani (d. 334:945-946). More sober and matter-of-fact, probably, were the local histories of various cities compiled during the third century, all of them now lost except for one volume of the *History of Baghdad* (Ibn Abi Tahir Taifur). In the following centuries there was a prolific output of such local chronicles, which usually took one or other of two forms, according to whether the main interest was biographical or in the historical events. Those of the latter class which have survived, though not always devoid of romantic elements, preserve much valuable material which was excluded from the larger histories, and are often of considerable importance on that account [e. g., al-Narshakhi, Ibn al-Qutiya, Omara, Ibn Isfandiyar]. As in style and methods of treatment they conform as a rule to the general practice of their region and time, they may be excluded from farther consideration here, but it should be remembered that they constitute a by no means insignificant part of Islamic historiography, both in Arabic and in Persian.

After the middle of the fourth century, however, the distinction between general history and provincial history becomes difficult to maintain. Henceforward the main type of strictly historical composition is contemporary annalistic, frequently prefaced by a summary of universal history. In such annals the interest and information of the writer can no longer be "universal"; each is limited by the boundaries of the political structure within which he lives, and is rarely able to deal with events in distant regions. How far this limitation can be regarded as the counterpart in intellectual life of the loss of Islamic political unity may remain open to discussion. The more important factor for us is that the recording of political history passed mainly into the hands of officials and courtiers. This change affected form, content, and spirit alike. For practised clerks and secretaries it was an easy and congenial task to compose a running chronicle. The sources from which they drew their information were official documents and the personal contacts and gossip of official and court circles; formally, therefore, the *isnad* was reduced to a brief indication of the source, and later compilers frequently dispensed with it altogether. But it was inevitable that their presentation of events should reflect the bias and narrow outlook—social, political and religious—of their class. The old theological conception which had given breadth and dignity to history was discarded, and annalistic tended to concentrate more and more upon the activities of the ruler and the court. On the other hand, the information which these secretarial works give in regard to the external political events of their age is generally trustworthy, granted the limitations of the individual writers. The contemporary annals of an Ibn Miskawaih (d. 421:1030) or a Hilal al-Sabi (d. 448:1056) show

the influence of an exacting standard of accuracy and relative
freedom from political bias; and that this standard was universally recognized is proved by what remains of the histories of Egypt
and of Andalusia written by Ubaid Allah b. Ahmad al-Musabbihi
(d. 420:1029) and Ibn Haiyan al-Qurtubi (d. 469:1076-1077), to
mention only the most prominent names.

The secularization of history had another serious consequence. In place of its earlier theological justification, the historians now pleaded the moral value of its study: history perpetuates
the record of virtuous and evil actions and offers them as examples
for the edification of future generations.[7] Such a plea was highly
acceptable to the host of moralists and dilettantes; if history were
merely a branch of ethics, not a science, they need not scruple to
adapt their so-called historical examples to their own ends. The
adab-books and *Mirrors of Princes,* full of such perversions, went
far towards vitiating public taste and judgment, and even historians and chroniclers themselves were not always immune from
the infection.

In this connection mention may be made here of the numerous historical forgeries put into circulation during this period or
at a later date. Like the works of Saif b. Omar already mentioned,
the majority of these falsifications are not pure inventions, but
contain a basis of genuine tradition worked up with all manner
of popular traditions, romantic legends, and partisan or propa-
gandist material, usually with a definite political or religious interest in view (for example, Ibn Qutaiba, al-Sharif al Murtada,
al-Waqidi).

Although the scholar and traditionist had yielded place to
the official in political historiography, there still remained in their
hands the even more extensive field of biography. This too, as has
been shown above, was a branch of the classical tradition; indeed,
after the diversion of political history to dynastic annals, it preserved more faithfully the ancient conception. For the lives of the
ulama, "the heirs of the Prophet," represented in the eyes of the
learned the real history of the *ummat Allah* on earth much more
truly than the ephemeral (and sometimes ungodly) political organizations. Alongside the classified lists (*tabaqat*) of *muhaddiths*
and jurists of one or other school, which served in the main a

technical function and are scarcely biographical in the strict sense, the materials relating to prominent individuals formed from an early date the subject of separate collections. Amongst the earliest of these works now extant is the biography of the Caliph Omar (II) b. Abd al-Aziz, compiled by the brother of the above mentioned Ibn Abd al-Hakam, and professedly based in part upon written documents, in part upon the tradition of pietist circles, chiefly at al-Medina. More usually, however, these compilations embrace a whole group or category of persons. In mystical circles, for example, several works were devoted to lives of the saints, notably the extensive *Hilyat al-Awliya* of Abu Nuaim al-Isfahani (d. 430:1038), while amongst the Shia there circulated not only books devoted to Shiite scholars and their works, but also a considerable literature of Alid martyrology. A characteristic product of this period is the biographical dictionary of scholars and famous men connected with a single city or province, compiled by local *ulama* and often of enormous bulk—that of al-Khatib al-Baghdadi (d. 463:1071), for instance, filling fourteen printed volumes. Most of these works have perished, but the vast *History* of Damascus by Ibn Asakir (d. 571:1176), probably the most catholic work of its kind in Arabic literature, is still extant, as also are a series of Andalusian biographies (Ibn al-Faradi, Ibn Bashkuwal, and Ibn al-Abbar) and some shorter dictionaries.

Biographical literature was alimented also from other sources. A prolific one, as might be expected, derived from philology, both in its narrower and its more humanist branches. The former produced *tabaqat* of grammarians and biographies of prominent philologists, the latter created an extensive literature on poets and men of letters (Ibn Qutaiba and al-Thaalibi). Similar volumes were devoted to other professions, such as physicians and astronomers, and the art of music supplied the stimulus for the compilation of the greatest Arabic biographical work in the early centuries, the *Kitab al-Aghani* of Abu l-Faraj al-Isfahani (d. 356: 967).

Autobiography, on the other hand, appears to have been little cultivated, and only two memoirs of this period have survived, those of al-Muaiyad fi l-Din (d. 470:1087) and of Usama b. Murshid b. Munqidh (d. 584:1188).

The whole of this biographical literature, as well as all later Islamic biography, shows certain common characteristics. The discipline of the *isnad* is usually carefully observed. The chronological data, especially the death date, are fixed with the greatest precision, and the main events of the subject's life are briefly related. The shorter notices are limited to these, together with lists of works in the case of writers and fragments of verse in the case of poets. In the more extended biographies, however, the greater part of the matter consists of anecdotes, in which no sort of arrangement, whether of chronology or of subject, seems to be observed. The impression of character so produced is often vivid but sometimes confusing, especially when there is no guarantee of the reliability of the stories. Yet with all its looseness and its gossipy tendencies this kind of literature, by its nearness to the life of the people, supplies a valuable supplement and corrective to the political annals.

At an early date, history and biography were combined in what may be called biographical chronicles. This form was eminently suitable for histories of wazirs, such as those compiled by Muhammad b. Abdus al-Jahshiyari (d. 331:942-943), the above-mentioned Hilal al-Sabi (d. 448:1056), and Ali b. Munjib al-Sairafi (d. 542:1147-1148) —the last-named dealing with the wazirs of the Fatimid Caliphs—, and of qadis, of which the earliest examples are those on the qadis of Egypt by Muhammad b. Yusuf al-Kindi (d. 350:961) and on the qadis of Cordova by Muhammad b. Harith al-Khushani (d. 360:970-971). A peculiar combination of political and literary biography is offered by the Abbasid history *(Kitab al-Awrak)* of al-Suli (d. 335:946). On the rise of local dynasties the same method was applied to them, until, indeed, during the fifth and sixth centuries dynastic histories practically supplanted the traditional annals, at least in the eastern provinces. This was a disastrous step, for the enhancement of the personal element gave fuller play to personal factors, especially when the rulers themselves began to command and to supervise the writing of the chronicles of their own times. History becomes a work of artifice, and the rhetorical and involved style of secretarial dispatches *(Saj)* replaces simple narrative. The new fashion was apparently set by Ibrahim al-Sabi (d. 384:994) in his lost work *al-Taji* on the history of the Buwaihids, and was popularized by its counterpart *al-Yamini,* composed by al-Utbi (d. c. 427:1035) on the history of Sabuktigin and Mahmud of Ghazna. It may possibly be connected with the revival of Persian and of the Persian historical tradition in the east, and may even have been influenced by the Persian epic poetry which was simultaneously coming into existence (Daqiqi and Firdawsi). Even when the writers of such "official histories" may be acquitted of deliberate untruthfulness, or of the more common vices of servility and *suppressio veri,* their bombast and lack of judgment make the most unfavorable impression. Unfortunately, the high reputation in literary circles of several of these works and their all too numerous progeny have often caused them to be regarded as representative of Islamic history in general; but this view does less than justice to the science which had been patiently built up by the early generations of Muslim scholars.

It was at this unfavorable juncture that historical works began to be written again in Persian. It is noteworthy that many of the earliest were translations and abridgments of Arabic works, beginning with the somewhat arbitrary abridgment of the classical chronicle of al-Tabari made in 352:963 by the wazir Abu Ali al-Balami, but often with important additional materials (e. g., Gardizi). Few, however, of the local and dynastic histories written in Persian during this period have survived, and these have little to distinguish them from the contemporary Arabic production in the eastern provinces. Several writers, such as al-Nasawi, seem to have used now Arabic and now Persian according to circumstances. One outstanding exception to the general run of such compositions is furnished by the full and impartial "diaries" of Abu l-Fadl Baihaqi (d. 470:1077), a work which is unique in extant pre-Mongol literature.

The revival of Persian as a literary vehicle, begun under the Persian dynasties of the fourth (tenth) century, also owed a good deal to the Turkish rulers of the following centuries, who were generally ignorant of Arabic. As their conquests extended westwards into Anatolia and south-eastwards into India they carried the Persian language with them, and already by the close of the sixth (twelfth) century Persian chronicles began to be written in these regions also: in Asia Minor by Muhammad b. Ali al-Rawandi (c. 600:1203) and in India by Fakhr al-Din Mubarakshah (d. after 602:1206), the ancestor of the long line of Indo-Persian chroniclers.

Before passing to the next period a brief reference should be made to two other branches of literary activity associated with history. The application of mathematical and astronomical science to the determination of chronology, of which traces are to be seen in several early works, left one outstanding monument in *al-Athar al-baqiya* of Abu Raihan al-Biruni (d. 440:1048). The second group of works, of an antiquarian rather than strictly historical tendency, was devoted to the settlements of the Arab tribes in their new territories. This topographical or *khitat*-literature apparently arose in al-Irak, the principal work, now lost, being that of Haitham b. Adi (d. 207:822-823), but was cultivated with particular attention in Egypt.

Finally, the spread of Arabic among the oriental Christian communities led to the compilation of Arabic works relating to the history of the Christian churches, sometimes combined with Arab and Byzantine history, notably by the Melkite Patriarch Eutychius and the Jacobite bishop Severus Ibn al-Mukaffa. A curiosity in this field is the history of the Christian monasteries in Egypt and Western Asia compiled by a Muslim writer, Ali b. Muhammad al-Shabushti (d. c. 388:998).

III   From the End of the Sixth to the Beginning of the Tenth Century

From the sixth (twelfth) century, Arabic and Persian historiography begin to diverge more widely. As the conquests of the Mongols completed the process by which Persian supplanted Arabic as the literary medium in the zone of Perso-Turkish culture, while the latter was simultaneously extended by the Islamic expansion in India, an immense impetus was given to Persian historical composition in all these regions. Arabic historiography too, however, shows a still increasing volume of output, and with such a vast range of material it is necessary to deal separately with historical literature in Arabic and in Persian.

Arabic. The Arabic historiography of this period, while following in the main the lines already marked out for it, is distinguished by a number of fresh combinations. Of these changes the most marked are in the relations between biography and political chronicle and in the constituents of the compilations devoted to general history. The underlying factors in these developments were, for the first, the re-emergence of the scholar-historian alongside the official-historian, and for the second, the displacement of the center of Arabic historiography from al-Iraq to Syria and later to Egypt.

The principal feature with which the new period opens in annalistic is the revival of the *Universal Chronicle* (beginning with the creation) or more frequently the *General Chronicle* (beginning with the rise of Islam). The older and more humanistic view of history as the annals of the community is thus recovered, although no fresh investigation is made into the history of the early centuries. The outlook of the scholar is, moreover, revealed in the effort to combine political and biographical annals, as had indeed already been done in some of the earlier local chronicles, such as the Damascus chronicle of Ibn al-Qalanisi (d. 555:1160). The relative proportion of the two elements, of course, varies with the interests of the writer; in some chronicles (Ibn al-Jawzi, al-Dhahabi, Ibn Duqmaq) the obituary notices so overshadow the political events that the latter are often reduced to a few abrupt sentences, while in the famous *Kamil* of Izz al-Din Ibn al-Athir (d. 630:1233) these proportions are reversed. This chronicle is remarkable also far the author's attempt to give a less static presentation of history, by means of grouping the events into episodes within an annalistic framework. While close examination reveals some defects in his handling of his materials, the elegance and vivacity of his work acquired for it almost immediate celebrity, and it became the standard source for later compilers.

It may plausibly be conjectured that this universal outlook was inspired in part by the revived conception of a universal caliphate. But the example thus set was imitated, even to excess, by a host of later chroniclers, the majority of whom lean heavily upon Ibn al-Athir (Ibn Wasil, Sibt Ibn al-Jawzi, Barhebraeus, Abul -Fida, Baibars al-Mansuri, Ibn Kathir, al-Yafii), though supple-

menting their borrowings with local and later materials. Somewhat more independence is shown in the annals of the Egyptian
encyclopedist Shihab al-Din al-Nuwairi (d. 732:1332) and of Ibn
al-Furat (d. 807:1405), while the Christian Jirjs al-Makin (d. 672:
1273) is in the line of Eutychius. Of these later general histories
in Arabic, however, the most interesting historiographically were
written in Spain and the Maghrib. Compared with their contemporaries in the East, the western writers frequently show a
somewhat broader conception of history and a less partisan vision.
Of the many historical works of Ibn Said al-Maghribi (d. 673:
1274)—an indefatigable traveler and researcher, who had the
audacity even to seek an interview with the redoubtable Hulagu—
only fragments remain, but enough to prove that they were based
on extensive and accurate transcripts of many earlier books. With
the world-famous history of Abd al-Rahman Ibn Khaldun (d.
808:1406) it is impossible to deal adequately here. As a chronicler
his work is sometimes disappointing, but on his significance as an
historical philosopher the last word has certainly not yet been
said, though much has been written. From the point of view of
Islamic historiography, it remains an unsolved problem that, in
spite of the brilliant school of Egyptian historians in the following
centuries and the vigorous cultivation of history in Turkey (where
a translation of the *Muqaddima* was made in the twelfth [eight-
eenth] century), there is no indication that the principles which
he put forward were even studied, much less applied, by any of
his successors.

Alongside the general chronicles, and often cultivated by the
same writers, there was a prolific output of regional, dynastic and
biographical chronicles. In Persia and al-Iraq, Arabic culture, all
but overwhelmed by the Mongol invasions, has little to show,
after the lost Abbasid history of Taj al-Din Ibn al-Sai (d. 674:
1275), but some minor chronicles and compendiums [Ibn al-Tiq-
taqa]. Even before this, however, the center of Arabic historiography had shifted to Syria, where the rise of the Zengid and
Aiyubid dynasties gave an impulse to the composition of a series of
chronicles. Amongst those who were attracted into this field was
Imad al-Din al-Isfahani (d. 597:1201), one of the last representatives af the rhyming-prose school of Persia and al-Iraq. But the

Syrians rejected this ornate style in favour of a more straightforward and natural prose, to the great advantage of subsequent Arabic history; and the biographical works of Baha al-Din Ibn Shaddad (d. 632:1234) and Abu Shama (d. 665:1268) rank far above those of Imad al-Din on the same subject.

From time to time, it is true, the ornate chronicle reappears, and the Egyptian secretary Ibn Abd al-Zahir (d. 692:1293) even set a fashion by composing his chronicle on Sultan Baibars in verse. This development, like the employment of *saj* in the chronicle of the stylist Badr al-Din Ibn Habib (d. 779:1377), is not apparently to be ascribed to outside influences; but the famous rhyming-prose biography (in this instance defamatory) of Timur by the Damascene Ibn Arabshah (d. 854:1450) is undoubtedly influenced by contemporary Persian writings (see below). On the other hand, the rhetorical history of the Fatimid dynasty entitled *Uyun al-Akhbar* and compiled by the Yamanite *dai* Imad al-Din Idris b. al-Hasan (d. 862:1467) reads curiously like a belated echo of the old Sasanid tradition.

The patronage accorded by the Aiyubids to historical writing was continued by their Mamluk successors. Damascus, and to a lesser extent Aleppo, remained seats of a very active tradition which, though interconnected to some extent with that of Cairo, displayed a certain individuality, especially in the field of biography (see below). It was not until the last century of Mamluk rule that there emerged a distinctively Egyptian school of historians, which, after producing a remarkable pleiad, as suddenly collapsed again. The series begins with the prolific Taqi al-Din al-Maqrizi (d. 845:1442) and his rival al-Aini (d. 855:1451); it is continued by al-Maqrizi's disciple Abu l-Mahasin Ibn Taghri (Tanri)-Birdi (d. 874:1469), his rival Ali b. Daud al-Jawhari (d. 900:1494-1495), Shams al-Din al-Sakhawi (d. 902:1497), the polymath Jalal al-Din al-Suyuti (d. 911:1505) and his disciple Ibn Iyas (d. c. 930:1524). In the next generation, the other chronicler of the Ottoman conquest, Ahmad b. Zunbul (d. after 951:1544), already belongs to a different tradition. Although these writers share many of the defects of the earlier political annalists, the alternation of scholar and courtier among them makes for a wider outlook and judgment, and they are by no means wholly eulogistic.

The marked feature of their work is its concentration upon Egypt, to such an extent that even those who cast their composition in the form of a general chronicle set it in an exclusively Egyptian framework. The outstanding figure is, however, al-Maqrizi, not so much for his accuracy (which is not unimpeachable) as for his industry, the wide range of his interests, and the attention which he gives also to the more social and demographic aspects of history.

The writings of the other provincial chroniclers differ from these more in respect of scale than of method or personality. Such Yamanite works as those of Ibn Wahhas al-Khazraji (d. 812:1409) or Ibn al-Daiba (d. 944:1537) present very similar material to the Egyptian chronicles, though in a narrower frame, and the same may be said of the local and dynastic chronicles written in the Maghrib and Spain. Certain writers—an Abd al-Wahid al-Marrakushi in the seventh (thirteenth) century or an Ibn Abi Zar in the eighth (fourteenth)—may rise superior to other western chroniclers in regard to their materials or method of treatment, but only one, the Granadan wazir Lisan al-Din Ibn al-Khatib (d. 776: 1374), is distinguished by a virtuosity which amounts to genius. As a critical historian he was probably equalled, however, if not surpassed, by his contemporary Ibn Idhari, so far as can be judged from the extant and available works of both.

In spite of this intensive cultivation of political history, the true genius of Arabic historiography shows itself rather in biography than in chronicle. The combination of biography with political annals, both general and local, is an all but universal practice amongst Arabic historians of this period, as has been seen, but it remains to deal with that large body of literature which was devoted explicitly to other than political biography.

During the first half of the seventh (thirteenth) century the specializing tendencies of the previous period culminate in a group of biographical collections of special importance. Six centuries of Arabic literature are surveyed in the *Irshad al-Arib* of the Greek Yakut al-Rumi (d. 626:1229); and the whole of early Islamic scientific and medical activity is mirrored in the dictionaries of the Egyptian Ibn al-Qifti (d. 646:1248) and the Damascene Ibn Abi Usaibia (d. 668:1270). Regional biographical "history" is continued in the history of Aleppo of the qadi Kamal al-Din Ibn

al-Adim (d. 660:1262), that of Gharnata by Ibn al-Khatib, and
other collections, usually supplementing earlier works. In addition
to these there are the usual *tabakat* of jurists and others, and the
antiquarian researches exemplified by the *Dictionary of the Companions* (*Usd al-Ghaba*) of the historian Ibn al-Athir.

Alongside such specialized works two new types of comprehensive biographical dictionary were now evolved and cultivated
especially in Syria. The creator of the first or universal type was
Ibn Khallikan (d. 681:1282), the high reputation of whose work
is justified by its taste and accuracy. Nevertheless, even with the
supplement of Ibn Shakir al-Kutubi (d. 764:1363), it is far surpassed in range and extent by that of Khalil b. Aibak al-Safadi
(d. 764:1363), the very bulk of which has prevented its publication
hitherto. This in turn was supplemented by the historian Abul
-Mahasin in *al-Manhal al-Safi*. The second new type of biographical dictionary also casts its net widely, but within a limited period
of time. This method is probably to be linked up with the general
chronicle of al-Dhahabi, in which the biographical materials are
arranged in decades down to the end of the seventh century, and
can be abstracted from the chronicle proper as an independent
work. The idea of arranging them in blocks of centuries may possibly be traced to al-Dhahabi's contemporary al-Birzali (d. 739:
1339). With the *Durar al-Kamina* of Ibn Hajar al-Asqalani (d.
852:1449) the new system is fairly launched: all the notable men
and women of the eighth century are included in alphabetical
order, a final trace of the obituary system being preserved in that
each person is reckoned to the century in which he died. The
corresponding dictionary of the ninth century was compiled by
Ibn Hajar's disciple, the above-mentioned al-Sakhawi (d. 902:
1497), under the title of *al-Daw al-lami*, and the series was carried
on by later generations down to the twelfth century.

Persian. Amidst all the diversities of Persian schools of
historiography from the seventh to the tenth centuries, a common
substratum is found in the traditional structure of general Islamic
history. But it is only in so far as they build independently upon
this basis that the Persian works acquire significance and individuality. The numerous general histories, whether written in Persia
or in India, which merely reproduce extracts from earlier sources

with additional materials down to their own time, are as imitative
and secondary as those in Arabic, and often show even less critical
sense. Such works as, for example, that of Minhaj al-Din Juzjani
(d. after 664:1265), have a certain value as local chronicles, but
are of little interest from the historiographical point of view. Our
attention will therefore be directed mainly to the productions of
the various "schools" which flourished from time to time in different parts of Persia and India and which created a distinctive
historical literature.

The rise of the Mongol empire in Western Asia gave the
first stimulus to such a distinctive series of works, preluded by the
isolated and original chronicle of Ala al-Din Ata Malik Juwaini
(d. 681:1283), which itself, however, is to be linked rather with the
type of "secretarial history" already described above. The Mongol
"school" proper begins with the celebrated *Collection* of the wazir
Fadl Allah Rashid al-Din Tabib (d. 718:1318), and was the direct
outcome of the conversion of the Ilkhans to Islam. Rashid al-Din's
work was composed piecemeal in both Persian and Arabic. The
first part is a dynastic chronicle based largely on the Mongol tradition, and subsequently supplemented by a history of Oljaitu.
The second is allied to the long-neglected encyclopedic branch of
Arabic historiography, in that it includes also notices on the history of India, China and Europe; it differs from its predecessors
by drawing the materials from contemporary informants, but like
them remains better in conception than in achievement, though
even that is not to be belittled. The book is remarkable, moreover,
for the sobriety of its prose style and its pursuit of detail and
accuracy rather than of aesthetic satisfaction. Whether the credit
for it is really due to Rashid al-Din or to Abd Allah b. Ali Kashani
matters little from our point of view. The significant thing is that,
in spite of its immense reputation, it at once fell out of circulation, and that all the other writers of this school, although they
were protégés of Rashid al-Din, decisively rejected his method,
except for the epitomizers Banakiti (d. 730:1329-1330) and Hamd
Allah Mustawfi Kazwini (d. after 750:1349). Most of them, in fact,
Kazwini included, attempted instead to outrival Firdawsi by the
composition of long epic chronicles in the identical metre which
he had employed. The only other outstanding prose work, the

highflown chronicle of Abd Allah b. Fadl Allah, called Wassaf (d.
after 712:1312), reverted to the old type of "official history," and
likewise became a classic destined to lure generations of future
Persian historians into the wastes of rhetoric.

History languished during the interval between the extinction of the Mongol school and the rise of Timur, who carried a
staff of secretaries in his train to compose the history of his campaigns and had their finished works read before him. Thus his
reign was commemorated by a Turki chronicle in verse (*Tarikh-i
Khani*) and in Persian by Nizam al-Din Shami, who was expressly
bidden "to avoid bombast and rhetoric." Nevertheless, his *Zafar-
nama* was all but forgotten in favor of the similarly-named but
much more ornate work of Sharaf al-Din Ali Yazdi (d. 858:1454),
which has ever since enjoyed the reputation of a model of elegance.
It was under Timur's successors, however, that this historical activity reached its height, more especially in the "school of Harat"
which, under their patronage, revived the tradition of Rashid al-
Din. Shah-rukh himself commissioned Hafiz-i Abru (d. 833:1430)
to re-edit and supplement the *Djami al-Tawarikh,* and the same
historian compiled another universal history, of little originality
but simple and sober in style, for Shah-rukh's son Baisonghor. The
same sobriety is observed in the *Mujmal* of Fasih al-Khwafi (written about 845:1441) and probably also in the *History of the Four
Ulus* of the learned and versatile Sultan Ulugh-Beg (d. 853:1449),
apparently preserved only in an abridgment. But the flowery elegance cultivated by such contemporary writers as Husain Kashifi
could not be kept out of history-writing. The generality of Timu-
rid authors succumbed to it, and the later works of the Harat
school sink ever more deeply into bombast and rhetoric. The
relatively restrained style of Abd al-Razzaq Samarqandi (d. 887:
1482) failed to compete in popular favor with the florid *Rawdat
al-Safa* of Mir Khwand (d. 903:1498), whose grandson Khwandamir (d. 942:1535-1536) carried the tradition of Harat in this later
form into India, where it found an equally congenial soil.

The beginnings of Persian historical composition in India,
as a result of the Ghorid conquest and rise of the sultanate of
Dihli, have already been noticed, and the main line of Indo-
Persian annalistic in the following centuries links up with this

tradition. The principal work, after the *Taj al-Maathir* of Hasan Nizami (c. 614:1217), is the continuation of Juzjani's chronicle by Diya al-Din Barani (d. after 758:1357), besides which there is little but florid and eulogistic biographical chronicles. In the province of Sind, however, there are indications of an indigenous tradition going back to the period of the Arab conquest in the first (eighth) century, which probably lies behind the historical romance put into circulation in the seventh (thirteenth) century, under the name of *Chach-name*, while in Gujarat and the south the local historiography is apparently to be connected rather with that of Fars.

During the whole of this period the Persian literary tradition still held the field in the Turkish and Ottoman dominions. From the literary point of view, neither the prose works nor the epics relating to the Anatolian Saljuks (Ibn Bibi) are in any way remarkable, but they are of interest in so far as they supplied models to the nascent Turkish historiography. Here again simple narrative, though not entirely driven out, found in the end less favor than ornate composition, which was brought to a climax of artifice and bombast in the prose work entitled *Hasht Bihisht*, written by Idris b. Ali Bidlisi (d. 926:1520) to the order of Bayezid II. At the same time, it would be a superficial view to equate bombast with triviality, and Bidlisi's work, like the history of Wassaf and several other ornate compositions, conceals beneath its verbiage a serious chronicle of great historical value.

One of the most marked differences between Arabic and Persian historiography is the relative absence of historical biography in Persian. Literary biography, of course, is very extensively cultivated, and a number of the general histories include obituary notices of the familiar pattern, or a section devoted to notable persons, especially ministers, poets and writers. Next to these come biographies of saints and mystics—both of individuals, notably the biography of Shaikh Safi al-Din by Tawakkul b. Bazzaz (written in 750:1349), and of general or special groups (Attar, Jami, Mawlawi). Two biographical works relating to wazirs were written by writers of the "school of Harat," *Athar al-Wuzara* by Saif al-Din Fadli (written in 883:1478) and *Dastur al-Wuzara* by Khwandamir (written in 915:1509). But it is not until the fol-

lowing period that there are written in Persian works which can
be compared to the contemporary biographical dictionaries in
Arabic. The reason for this is evidently to be sought in the close
association between biography and theological studies. If it is
remembered that until the Safawid period Arabic remained, even
in Iran and India, the language of theology and science, and that
Persian was used almost exclusively for poetry, belles-lettres and
court chronicles, the absence of Persian biographical works becomes intelligible. It is less easy to explain why no biographical
works relating to the Persian and Turkish areas were written even
in Arabic.

IV   From the Tenth to the Thirteenth
Centuries

The first quarter of the tenth (fifteenth) century witnessed
a redistribution of political forces almost from end to end of the
Islamic world. The Ottoman Turks established their authority
over Western Asia and North Africa as far as the borders of Morocco; the Safawids created a self-contained Shiite state in Iran;
the Shaibanids set up Uzbek states in Central Asia; the Mughal
dynasty was founded in India; a new Sharifian dynasty led the
offensive in Morocco against Spanish and Portuguese pressure; and
the Negrolands on the Niger acquired a more definitely Islamic
organization under the Songhoy. These movements were inevitably accompanied by cultural regroupings and reorientations, which
left their mark on all forms of literature and more especially
on history. Arabic historiography was the most seriously affected,
but Persian historiography also suffered from the sectarian isolation of Persia itself. On the other hand, a new and vigorous historical literature now sprang into existence in Turkish, which, while
linked to its predecessors, developed to some extent upon original
lines.

The subjection of the central Arabic provinces to Ottoman
rule, by depriving Arabic historiography of the local stimuli which
had hitherto sustained it, brought about its all but complete collapse. A few poor general chronicles (al-Bakri, al-Diyarbakri, al-

Jannabi) and some local chronicles or biographical histories of varying worth constitute the whole of the strictly historical output of Egypt, Syria, al-Iraq and Arabia down to the opening of the thirteenth (nineteenth) century, when the old Arabic historical tradition comes to an end with two more considerable writers, Abd al-Rahman al-Jabarti (d. 1237:1822) in Egypt, and Haidar Ahmad al-Shihabi (d. 1251:1835) in the Lebanon. In central, east and south Arabia it survived to the end of the century; in the Maghrib it produced a last worthy representative in al-Nasiri al-Slawi (d. 1315:1897), after a similar series of minor chroniclers (al-Wafrani, al-Zaiyani), broken only by the outstanding figure of al-Maqqari (d. 1041:1632) of Tilimsan, whose *Analects* on the history of Andalusia and biography of Ibn al-Khatib are a fitting epilogue to the brilliant tradition of Spanish Islam.

The decline of the Arabic historical tradition in its homelands was, however, offset to some extent by a limited cultivation in Turkey itself, including the valuable general chronicle of Munajjim Bashi (d. 1113:1702), and by its extension to several of the more recently converted outlying Islamic regions, notably in West Africa. Here a number of local chronicles were written, among the most important being the Songhoy chronicle of Abd al-Rahman al-Sadi (d. after 1066:1656) and the chronicles of Mai Idris of Bornu (reigned 910-932:1504-1526) by the Imam Ahmad. In East Africa, there has survived an early history of Kilwa and a chronicle of the wars of Ahmad Gran in Abyssinia, written about 950:1543 by Shihab al-Din Arabfaqih, in addition to later offshoots from the Ibadite school of Oman. The close relations between Arabia and the west coast of India led to the adoption of Arabic as an official language there also, especially in the south,[8] and it is not surprising therefore to find an Arabic history of the Portuguese wars written by Zain al-Din al-Mabari (d. 987:1579). Farther north, however, it came into competition with Persian, and only one Arabic chronicle of any extent has survived, written by Muhammad b. Omar Ulughkhani of Gujarat (d. after 1014:1605), who derived much of his material from Persian works. In Persia itself only one or two brief chronicles were written in Arabic.

In contrast to the historical tradition, the biographical tradition, less dependent upon political changes, maintained its vitality, especially in Syria. Damascene scholars continued the series of dictionaries of notable persons of the tenth, eleventh and twelfth centuries (al-Burini, al-Muhibbi, al-Muradi), and other works commemorate the scholars of single towns and districts. Alongside these there flourished also in Egypt and Syria a type of ornate and involved biography in rhyming prose, bearing much the same relation to the preceding works as the rhyming prose history to the plain chronicle. Of this school, the principal representative is the Egyptian Shihab al-Din al-Khafaji (d. 1069: 1659); the popularity of his work may be judged from the fact that a supplement was composed in India in 1082:1671 by Ali Khan Ibn Masum, which is in turn quoted by the above-mentioned al-Muhibbi (d. 1111:1699), who himself wrote a second supplement.

Even in the Turkish and Persian zones important biographical works were written in Arabic. *Al-Shaqaiq al-Numaniya* of Ahmad b. Mustafa Tashkopruzade (d. 968:1561), qadi of Istanbul, is a fundamental work for the history of Turkish Islam, afterwards supplemented in both Arabic and Turkish. The relations maintained between the Arabic Shiite communities and the Shiites in Persia and India are reflected in several Shiite dictionaries, amongst the authors of which are not only Arabs (al-Hurr al-Amili) but also the Persian Muhammad Bakir Musawi (Khwansari) and his Indian contemporary Saiyid Idjaz Husain al-Kanturi (d. 1286: 1869). Several Sunni biographical works also were written in India.

From the Maghrib, where it continued to be cultivated (al-Wafrani), the Arabic biographical tradition spread into the Western Sudan and found a notable disciple in Ahmad Baba of Timbuktu (d. 1036:1627). In the Eastern Sudan also, the pious and learned men of the Funj kingdom were commemorated in the *Tabaqat* of Muhammad wad Daif Allah (d. 1224:1809-1810).

NOTES

[1] See F. Krenkow, "The Two Oldest Books on Arabic Folklore," in *Islamic Culture*, vol. ii.

[2] See Goldziher, *Muhammedanische Studien*, i, 177-189.

[3] See E. Sachau in Introduction to Ibn Sad's *Tabaat*, vol. iii., xxi-xxiii.

[4] See especially A. Grohmann, *Allgemeine Einführung in die arabischen Papyri* (Vienna, 1924), p. 27-30.

[5] See on these sources Wellhausen, *Das arabische Reich*, Einleitung.

[6] See Th. Nöldeke, *Das iranische Nationalepos*, 2nd ed., 1920.

[7] Cf. the introductions to Ibn Miskawaih's *Tajarib al-Umam* and Hilal al-Sabi's *Kitab al-Wuzara*.

[8] Cf. the documents published by João de Sousa (Lisbon, 1790).

BIBLIOGRAPHY

C. Brockelmann, *Geschichte der arabischen Litteratur* (i.: Weimar, 1898; ii.: Berlin, 1902; Supplement: Leyden, 1936 sq.).

F. Wüstenfeld, *Die Geschichtsschreiber der Araber* (Göttingen, 1882).

D. S. Margoliouth, *Lectures on Arabic Historians* (Calcutta, 1930).

Pons Boigues, *Ensayo Bio-bibliográfico su los Historiadores y Geógrafos Arábigo-Españoles* (Madrid, 1898).

C. A. Storey, *Persian Literature, A Bio-bibliographical Survey*, section ii. (London, 1935 sq.).

E. G. Browne, *A Literary History of Persia* (Cambridge, 1930).

Sir H. Elliot and J. Dowson, *The History of India as told by its own Historians* (London, 1867-1877).

The *Catalogues* of the principal collections of Oriental Manuscripts.

J. Horovitz, "The Earliest Biographies of the Prophet" in *Islamic Culture* (Hyderabad, 1928).

E. Lévi-Provençal, *Les historiens des Chorfa* (Paris, 1922).

Part Two   Islamic Institutions,
Philosophy and Religion

8. Some Considerations on the Sunni Theory of the Caliphate

The object of this paper is to draw attention to four points, most of which are not in any sense new, but which have been given less than their due weight in the various modern expositions of the theory of the caliphate, whether by eastern or by western scholars.

I

The first point relates to the now classic work of the qadi al-Mawardi. In all discussions on the caliphate, it seems to be generally assumed that al-Mawardi codified, as it were, the orthodox Sunni doctrine on the subject, and laid down once and for all the authoritative Sunni theory of the caliphate. This view I hold to be mistaken on two grounds. The first I shall deal with more fully later, as it is my fourth point; but for the second it is necessary to say a few words here by way of preface. It is of the essence of Sunni doctrine that the *Umma*, the historic community, is based upon the Sharia, that its historical development is divinely guided, and its continuity guaranteed by the infallible authority of *ijma*. This being so, it was one of the duties of the jurists, as keepers of the public conscience, to demonstrate afresh for each generation the legality of its political constitution. This question was in their view bound up with that of the caliphate, which, as an institution, is essentially the symbol of the supremacy of the Sharia. That these two questions were so connected was due largely to the polemics of the rival groups, Shia and Khawarij, whose main contention was precisely that the Sunni community, by giving allegiance to false caliphs, had diverged from the true line of Islam and was consequently living in sin. To meet this attack, the efforts of the jurists were necessarily directed to justifying the actual situation. But it did not follow that all the defenders of orthodoxy should take up the same position. The theory which lies at the base of al-Mawardi's exposition is, in fact, the theory of one school only, that of al-Ashari; and it shares two of the characteristics of Asharite theory in general, namely that it forces the argument a little too far, and formulates the conclusions too rigidly. In this case, it was the Asharite insistence on the historic continuity of the caliphate that lies at the root of their difficulties.

We now come to al-Mawardi. Granting that his work is in the Asharite tradition, is it to be accepted as the final and definitive exposition of Asharite political doctrine? On the contrary, as I have tried to show elsewhere.[1] So far from being an objective exposition of an established theory, it is in reality an apologia or adaptation inspired and shaped by the circumstances of his own time. And, what is more important, by the arguments with which al-Mawardi endeavoured to accommodate the Asharite theory to these rather unhappy circumstances (for it will be remembered that it was written during the Buwaihid regime) , he took the first steps on the downward slope which was to lead to the collapse of the whole theory.

The violent changes which followed in the political structure of Islam accelerated the breakdown by forcing al-Mawardi's successors to move ever further along the path of compromise. I cannot say how the Asharite theory was modified in the next generation by al-Juwaini, the Imam al-Haramain, since his book Ghiyath al-Imam[2] is unfortunately not yet accessible to me. But in his Irshad, recently published by M. Luciani, one can already see a tendency to thrust the embarrassing problem of the Imama into the background. Indeed, in the field of contemporary politics, the old sectarian quarrels were losing much of their reality, while the emergence of the temporal sultanate was raising new and graver issues. The same tendency is seen, another generation later, in the attitude of al-Ghazali,[3] who, however, in a later passage,[4] shows almost startlingly the rate at which the Asharite doctrine was collapsing: "We consider that the function of the caliphate is contractually assumed by that person of the Abbasid house who is charged with it, and that the function of government in the various lands is carried out by means of sultans, who owe allegiance to the caliphate. Government in these days is a consequence solely of military power, and whosoever he may be to whom the possessor of military power gives his allegiance, that person is the caliph."

From this passage it is clear that the caliphate, as represented by the Abbasid family, was no longer regarded as conferring authority, but merely as legitimating rights acquired by force, provided that the holder of military power, by giving allegiance to the caliph, recognized the supremacy of the Sharia. When the caliphate of Baghdad was extinguished by the Mongols in 1258, it remained only to take the last step and to declare that rights acquired by force were legitimate in themselves, and that military power constituted a valid Imama. The nominal "shadow-caliphate" set up at Cairo made no difference, since it receives no recognition in the works of any authoritative jurist. It was indeed a chief qadi of Cairo under the Mamluks who gave the final consecration to secular absolutism. The relevant passage of Ibn Jamaa's *Tahrir al-Ahkam* is too well known to need quotation again here,[5] but one sentence is particularly significant: "When the Imama is thus contractually assumed by one person by means of force and military supremacy, and thereafter there arises another who overcomes the first by his might and his armies, then the first is deposed and the second becomes Imam, for the reasons of the well-being and unity of the Muslims."

So, step by step, in logical development from the principles of al-Ashari and the political apologia of al-Mawardi, the Asharite theory ends up by divorcing the Imamate from the Sharia and the complete negation of the rule of law. This was clearly an absurdity which could not be accepted by the mass of Muslims. But the rejection of the conclusion involved also the rejection of the argument which had led up to it, and made it necessary to seek for a new basis of political theory which would at least safeguard the principle of the supremacy of the Sharia and the function of the caliph as its upholder. It would seem that this need was felt more especially in the Persian and Perso-Turkish lands of eastern Islam, which had been severed from the old tradition by the conquest of the heathen Mongols, and where a long struggle had to be waged for the restoration of the supremacy of the Sharia over the Mongol code, the Yasaq.

II

In this difficulty it was natural for the jurists to turn back to other theories which had been obscured by the Asharite doctrine. One of these was that the only real caliphs were the first four, and that the rule of the Umayyads and Abbasids was a fictitious caliphate. This had been rejected by the Asharites, because it had not only a Mutazilite but still more a heretical tinge. But it was taken up into Maturidite doctrine, which then met the demand of the Sunni community for a present and visible representative of the Sharia by distinguishing between the caliphate, which had ceased, and the Imama, which continued to exist.[6] But as there was no present and visible authority except the temporal power, the practical conclusion of this theory seemed to be much the same as that reached by Ibn Jamaa. This dilemma is reflected, for instance, in the *Aqida* of Adud ad-Din al-Iji, who expressly limits the caliphate to the four Rashidin, but omits all reference to the Imama. But this was an obvious evasion of the issue. The dilemma was finally resolved by recourse to another theory, which had arisen in philosophical and semi-Shiite circles, and so had not hitherto found much favor among the theologians. This was the adaptation of the Platonic ideal of the philosopher-king to the Islamic Imam, administering the Sharia under the guidance of divine Wisdom. As Sir Thomas Arnold has already shown the development of this theory in Arabic and Persian literature,[7] there is no need to discuss it afresh in detail. What we are chiefly concerned with is that, when stripped of its theosophical elements and brought into line with orthodox views, it supplied the later Sunni jurists with a practical and satisfactory basis for the politico-religious structure of the community. It had, moreover, the merit of rationalizing the practice, which had already become customary in the eastern Muslim lands, of the assuming of caliphial titles by local Muslim princes. By the end of the fourteenth century we find it explicitly stated by the Maliki qadi Ibn Khaldun: "Government and kingship are a caliphate of God amongst men, for the execution of His ordinances amongst them."[8] But it was not till a century later that it was given final and acceptable expression in the *Akhlaq-i Jalali* of the Persian Shafii qadi Jalal ud-Din Dawwani, through his personal reputation and the widespread influence of his writings throughout the East.

From this time onwards one may say that the recognized doctrine of the caliphate is that the caliphate lasted for thirty years only, and that thereafter there was only an Imama to which the caliphial titles were attached as it were by courtesy.[9] But, unlike Ibn Jamaa's theory, the Imama is not simply delivered into the hands of every military usurper. There is a vital difference. Both Ibn Khaldun and Dawwani make it perfectly clear that there is a distinction between secular kingship and the caliphate, and that it is only the righteous ruler who governs with justice and who enforces the Sharia as the law of the community that is entitled to the style of caliph or Imam. Thus, in contrast to the later developments of the Asharite theory, the caliphate remains explicitly linked with the supremacy of the Sharia.

III

It is undoubtedly this theory and not the Asharite theory in any of its formulations, which underlies the use of the terms caliph and Imam in both the Ottoman and Mughal empires. The story of the transference of the caliphate to Selim I by the last pseudo-caliph of Cairo is admitted to be a falsehood; but that fact does not invalidate the perfectly justified claim of the Ottoman sultans to be Imams within their own dominions. Its general acceptance is shown (for example) by the regular use of the terms "dar ul-khilafa" and "dar ul-imama" (alongside dar us-saltana) for the Ottoman court; and when Nadir Shah in 1741 attempted to persuade the sultan to recognize the Shia as a fifth (Jafari) "madhhab," he even went so far as to call the Ottoman sultan "khalife-i Islam."[10] Yet in the same century the Tripolitan chronicler Ibn Ghalbun applies the terms "Shadow of God" and "Khalifa" to the local Qaramanli prince, and sees no inconsistency in affirming the suzerainty of the Ottoman sultan in the same breath.

Nevertheless, the later caliphate is juridically only an Imama, and it is noteworthy that neither in their formal protocols nor in their official documents are the Ottoman sultans accorded the title of "Amir al-Muminin." A fairly thorough search through the Turkish and Arabic literature of the eighteenth century has not yielded a single example of the application of this title to an Ottoman sultan, and as late as 1813, we find in al-Jabarti the formula of the "hutba" after the recovery of Mecca and al-Madina given as: "The Sultan son of the Sultan son of the Sultan, Mahmud Khan, son of the Sultan Abd ul-Hamid Khan, son of the Sultan Ahmed Khan, the Warrior for the Faith, Servitor of the Two Noble Sanctuaries."

It seems, however, to be in contradiction with the statement made in the last paragraph that the term "Amir al-Muminin" is in fact occasionally applied in official formulae to several of the earlier Ottoman sultans. Three such cases are known to me, and there may possibly be others. The latest and least remarkable is an inscription in the citadel of Jerusalem, in which Sulaiman I is so entitled.[11] This in itself gives no indication as to the sense in which the term is to be understood, but it is most probably to be connected with the two earlier examples. More surprising is a recently published inscription from the Masjid al-Juma at al-Madina, which reads: "amara bibina-i hadhal-masjidil-mubaraki ... mawlana amirul-muminina s-sultanul-malikul-muzaffaru Bayezid."[12] This is Bayezid II, the predecessor of Selim I, and the inscription therefore dates from a time when al-Madina still acknowledged the suzerainty of the Mamluk sultans. It is evident that we have to do here with a conception of the person of the "Amir al-Muminin" which fits in with none of the theories discussed so far. That it should be merely an empty compliment seems unlikely in view of two considerations: first, that so remarkable a compliment should be publicly paid in the dominions of a rival sultanate; and second, that whereas compliments usually take a common form, the extreme rarity of this title implies that some special meaning was attached to it.

With the third and earliest instance, we get the hint of a clue to this meaning. It occurs in the protocol of a "waqfnama" of Sultan Muhammad Fatih, recently published at Istanbul,[13] where the sultan is called "Amirul-muminin wa-imamul-muslimin, say-yidul-ghuzat wal-mujahidin, al-muayyad bi-tayidi rabbil-alamin, . . . shamsu samais-saltana wal-khilafa wad-dawla wad-dunya wad-din, abul-fath wan-nasr, as-Sultan Muhammad Khan." In this collocation of phrases two points stand out. On the one hand there is the sharp contrast between the colourless conjunction of "sal-tana" and "khilafa" in the set phraseology typical of contemporary "juristic" and later Ottoman usage, and the vigorous epithets with which the series opens. The title "Amir al-Muminin" stands in no relationship to "the firmament of sultanate and caliphate." But, on the other hand, it finds its natural complement and counter-part in the second group of epithets, the title by which the early Ottoman sultans set most store, "Lord of the Ghazis and Warriors for the Faith."[14]

The hint contained in this document is expanded and con-firmed by a much later instance. This, perhaps the most remark-able of all, is a passage in the biographical dictionary *(Silkud-Durar)* of Shaikh Muhammad al-Muradi (d. 1206:1791).[15] It should be borne in mind that al-Muradi was chief Hanafi mufti of Damascus, a man of great influence in religious circles, and in personal relations with both Sultan Abdul-Hamid I and the Turkish ulema. In his work (which includes biographical notices of the Ottoman sultans) the term "Amir al-Muminin" occurs once, and once only, and then not of an Ottoman sultan but of a Grand Mughal of India: "Awrangzeb, Sultan of India in our time, Commander and Imam of the Faithful, Stay and Support of the Musulmans, and Warrior on the Path of God . . ., Who has destroyed the infidels in his land and brought them low, and pul-led down their temples and humbled their polytheism, who has given strength to Islam and lifted up its beacon in India, and has made the Cause of God to be uppermost, and secured the victory of the Faith . . .[16] In fine, he has no equal among the kings of Islam in his age in uprightness of conduct, fear of God and zeal in performance of religious duty."[17] This is to me one of those flashes of self-revelation which compensate for many hours of tedious reading. The motive of flattery cannot enter in here, for Awrangzeb had long been dead when these words were written.[18] This can be no other than the free expression of an inner conviction that breaks through the formal doctrine of the caliphate of the righteous Sultan. In its light the latter stands revealed, not indeed as a fiction, but as a mere juristic device to satisfy a point of politico-theological doctrine. The passive representative of a "pacific" Sharia is but the pale simulacrum of a caliph; only he is "Amir al-Muminin" who scorns the path of inactivity and compromise, and by word and deed vindicates the claims of a "dynamic" Sharia against its enemies.[19] It is the same voice, pointing the same contrast, which we have seen in the roll of Sultan Muhammad's titles, a contrast which had lost none of its vitality in the intervening centuries.

IV

We have seen that even in the Sunni community there was no one universally accepted doctrine of the caliphate. The assumption that any such general acceptance existed finds little to support it either in the writings of the jurists themselves, or in the psychology of Sunni Islam. It is true that al-Mawardi's work was accepted by later generations as an exposition of an ideal of government and administration, but that is a very different matter from accepting it as an exposition of the only recognized Sunni doctrine. The very basis of Sunni thought, in fact, excludes the acceptance of any one theory as definitive and final. What it does lay down is a principle: that the caliphate is that form of government which safeguards the ordinances of the Sharia and sees that they are put into practice. So long as that principle is applied, there may be infinite diversity in the manner of its application.

But this is not all. Our brief survey of the development of Sunni political theory furnishes a striking example of the truth which we are beginning to realize more and more fully. As is so often the case in Islam, the inner reality is quite other than would appear from the external formulations of the jurists. Between the real content of Muslim thought and its juristic expression there is a certain dislocation, so that it is seldom possible to infer the reality from the outer form. Only when both are known can the relation between them be discerned; and the formula is then seen to be an attempt, not so much to express the inner principle as it is, as to compress it within a rigid mold in order to serve a legal argument and a partial end. But at the same time our survey furnishes an equally striking example of the converse truth, that Muslim thought refuses to be bound by the outward formulae. It exerts a constant pressure, whose influence is to be seen in the unobtrusive reshaping of theory which, beneath an outward inflexibility, characterizes all branches of speculative activity in Islam, where Islam has remained a living organism. And if necessary, it does not hesitate to overstep the limits of theory and to give independent expression to its sense of realities.

Lastly, not less significant is the further conclusion to be derived from our argument: that the "Amir al-Muminin"-concept which we have disengaged is not narrowly Sunni, but Islamic in the widest sense. It cannot be coincidence that the same principle which finds expression in the "dynamic" caliphate of Muhammad Fatih and Awrangzeb is clearly recognizable in both Zaidi Shiite and Ibadi Kharijite doctrine—even if we leave aside altogether its relationship to the Mahdi-conception.[20] The heterodox groups have narrowed down the ideal by sectarian restrictions; the Sunni jurists have gone to the other extreme, and have emptied it of its real content by excessive concessions. But beneath the complex forms into which the simple principle has been twisted to serve the ends of rival schools, there lies a common Islamic conviction that overrides all superficial differences of creed.

NOTES

Revised from a paper read at the XXth International Congress of Orientalists, Brussels, September 1938.

[1] *Al-Mawardi's Theory of the Caliphate,* chapter 9.
[2] See Brockelmann, *G.A.L.,* Suppl., I 673.
[3] See the final section of his *K. al-Iqtisad-fil-Itiqad.*
[4] *Ihya* II 124 (Cairo, 1352).
[5] See the edition of the text by H. Kofler in *Islamica,* VI, 4, 355 sqq.; also D. Santillana, *Instituzioni di Diritto Musulmano,* I 24.
[6] See, for instance, the *Aqida* of an-Nasafi.
[7] *The Caliphate* (Oxford, 1924), chap. X.

[8] *Muqaddima*, Bk. II, c. 20. Note the unusual indefinite construction: *kihilafatun lillah.*

[9] See, e.g., at-Taftazani on the relevant section of *al-Aqaid an-Nasafiya.*

[10] Muhammad Mahdi, *Tarih-i Nadiri* (Bombay, 1849), p. 231.

[11] I am indebted to Dr. L. A. Mayer for this reference.

[12] *Revue des Études Islamiques*, 1936, p. 109.

[13] *Zwei Stiftungsurkunden des Sultans Mehmed II. Fatih,* hg. von Tahsin Öz (Istanbul, 1935), pp. 7-8. I owe this and the following reference to the kindness of Dr. Paul Wittek.

[14] See P. Wittek, in *Ann. de l'Institut de Philologie et d'Histoire orientales et slaves,* t. VI (Brussels, 1938). Similarly, in *Tarikhi-i Abul-Fath* of Tursun Beg (Istanbul, 1930), p. 30, the phrase "Amir ul-muminin" is included in the titles of Muhammed II, whereas it is omitted from those of Bayezid II (pp. 14, 179), in whose reign the book was written.

[15] Brockelmann, *G.A.L.* II, 294; *Suppl.* II, 404.

[16] "Sultanul-hindi fi asrina, wa-amirul-muminina wa-imamuhum, waruknul-muslimina wa-nizamuhum, al-mujahidu fi sabilillahi . . . alladi abadalkuffara fi ardihi wa-qaharahum," etc.

[17] *Silkud-Durar* IV, 113-114.

[18] Awrangzeb died in 1118:1707.

[19] In this sense the term may even be applied to a person other than a sultan. Dr. Wittek draws my attention to the (probably apocryphal) firman of Murad I to Ghazi Evrenos, *malikul-ghuzat wal-mujahidin,* where the latter is entitled also *amirul-muminin* (Feridun[2] I, 87). In *Hilyat al-Awliya,* VII, 144, 15, it is applied to a scholar (*amirul-muminin fir-riwaya*).

[20] There is a further and independent example in the usage of Spanish-Arabic writers of the fourth (tenth) century, who frequently refer to Abdar-Rahman I and his successors as *khulafa,* but apply the term *amir ul-muminin* exclusively to Abdar-Rahman III.

9. Al-Mawardi's Theory
of the Caliphate

Al-Mawardi's work on the Ordinances of Goverment, *al-Ahkam as-Sultaniyah,* is too well known among Islamic scholars and in Muslim political circles to require any introduction.[1] Since the revival of interest in the caliphate it has been generally accepted as the most authoritative exposition of the Sunni Islamic political theory,[2] and indeed the existence of other works on the subject is frequently ignored. Yet in spite of its reputation, no attempt has been made to situate the work in its own setting. This task involves an investigation into three things: the reasons for its compilation, al-Mawardi's sources and the use which he makes of them, and the reception of his work by the scholars of his own and succeeding generations. To discuss the subject fully would outrun the limits of an essay, and I propose only to treat in outline the first and second questions, with reference to the chapter on the caliphate and to the section of the third chapter which deals with the "Amirate by Seizure."

I The Reasons for the Composition of
Al-Ahkam as-Sultaniyah

It might seem, in the first place, unnecessary to postulate any special reasons. Almost every comprehensive work on *fiqh* included a section, long or short, on the Imama, and a jurist who aspired to cover the whole field had of necessity to give his attention to this among other questions, so that it might well be made the subject of a special study. Since the list of al-Mawardi's surviving works shows him to have taken an interest in matters of political conduct,[3] it might have been assumed without question that the reason lay in his personal preferences had not he related otherwise. For his introduction, after the usual exordium, opens with the words: "Since the ordinances of government have a special claim upon [the attention of] those who are set in authority, and since their admixture with all [manner of other] ordinances debars these persons from making a thorough study of them—not to speak of their preoccupation with policy and administration— I have devoted a book exclusively to this subject. In so doing I have complied with the command of one to whom it is obligatory to render obedience, in order that he may know the views of the jurists as to those ordinances which define his rights, that he may exact them in full, and his duties, that he may perform them in full, with the object of showing equity in his execution and judgment, and from a desire to respect the rights of others in his taking and giving."[4]

To whom do these expressions refer? None of the biographers directly answer this question, but a brief survey of the political situation during the period to which the book must be ascribed enables us to give a reasonably definite reply. Since 334: 946 the caliphs of Baghdad had been kept under strict control by the Buwaihid amirs, but from the beginning of the fifth century the authority of the Buwaihid house was undermined by internal dissensions and military revolts. Simultaneously, Sultan Mahmud of Ghazna was engaged in the creation of a vast empire in Iran and the adjacent lands, with many professions of loyalty to the Abbasid house. These circumstances encouraged the Caliphs al-Qadir billah (d. 422:1031) and his son and successor al-Qaim bi-amrillah to hope for a restoration of Abbasid rule and even to take some tentative steps to reassert their claims.[5] It is well known that al-Mawardi, who had been honored with the novel title of *aqdal-qudah*,[6] was the emissary and mouthpiece of the caliphs in their negotiations with the Buwaihid amirs. There can be little doubt, therefore, that it was at the wish of one or other of these caliphs that his book was composed. This is confirmed by the language of the introduction itself, since, while "one to whom it is obligatory to render obedience" could, in the jurists' view, be applied to any civil authority, it applied more especially to the caliph, and it is only the rights and duties of the caliphs that are discussed by the earlier jurists.

If this view is accepted, it remains to ask whether the caliph's motive, in moving al-Mawardi to the compilation of such a work, was simply a desire for knowledge, or whether it was intended to serve a political end in his struggle with the Buwaihid amirs. From various indications, some of which will appear in the sequel, it would seem that the second is the more plausible alternative. Three generations had passed since the caliphate was accepted without question as the supreme authority in temporal affairs, and the first step towards its rehabilitation was an authoritative exposition of its neglected and all but forgotten rights. Against this supposition, however, must be set the statement, related by Ibn Khallikan,[7] that al-Mawardi's works were not collected and published until after his death. But Ibn Khallikan himself does not vouch for the truth of the assertion, and though there seems to be no reason for rejecting it as regards his general treatises, it can hardly be true of a work written to the command and for the use of the caliph.[8]

This view of the reasons for the compilation of al-Mawardi's book would also absolve him from two charges frequently brought against him. Several writers comment on the irony of the fact that a work which centralizes every function of the state upon the caliphate should have been written during the period of its greatest degradation, and regard it as a striking example of mis-directed ingenuity. Others[9] have suggested that what al-Mawardi set out to do was to describe the ideal state, a sort of Islamic counterpart to Plato's *Republic* or More's *Utopia,* but specula-tively derived from the basic principles of Islamic law. In reality, as we shall see, he was no philosopher, and legal speculation plays but a small part in his work; he was a jurist who built upon and to some extent systematized and expanded the views of his pred-ecessors, and who exercised his own judgment[10] only to adapt these views to the situation in his own day. It is, indeed, precisely in these two aspects—his avoidance of mere speculation, and the application of the classical juristic theory to contemporary facts—that the chief significance of his work lies.

At the same time, it would be unjust to regard him as merely a commentator or interpreter of earlier works, and equally unjust to accuse him of twisting their theories to suit a case. He does not hesitate to express his own views, even when they are in some contradiction to those of earlier authorities; and though he shows a tendency to put the best face on things, his independence can be seen in his assertion of several points of doctrine which cannot have been wholly to the liking of his Abbasid patron.[11] Whether or not we agree with all the arguments which he puts forward, we have every reason to respect them as the sincere and honest beliefs of a strong supporter of the Abbasid cause.

II   Analysis of al-Mawardi's Doctrine

Before examining in detail the views expressed by al-Mawardi, it would be well to summarize briefly the main factors in the development of political thought among the Sunni jurists. As in other fields of juristic activity, the original basis was given by the injunctions found in the Koran and the Sunnah. Consequently, the early doctrine of the duties and functions of rulers was exclusively ethical, as may be seen from the introduction addressed by the qadi Abu Yusuf to Harun al-Rashid in his *Kitab al-Kharaj*. The rationalization of this doctrine and the working-out of practical detail was a gradual process, which followed point by point upon the doctrinal disputes of the first three centuries. It will be recalled that it was precisely on questions relatng to the caliphate that a large part of the early struggles between Sunnis, Khawarij and Shiites centered. And since the gravamen of the charges brought against the Sunnis by their opponents was that they had erred upon given occasions, as, for example, in recognizing the election of Abu Bakr or in acknowledging Muawiya, the Sunni jurists were inevitably forced into arguments in defence or condonation of the actual historical process. They obviously could not admit any principle which might lead to the conclusion that the *Jamaa,* the community in being, had fallen into sin, with the corollary that all its religious and judicial activities were void.

The fully developed political theory of the Sunni jurists was thus—in contrast to the theories of the Shia and the Khawarij—not speculatively derived from the sources of Revelation, but rather based upon an interpretation of these sources in the light of later political developments, and reinforced by the dogma of the divine guidance of the community and the infallibility of its *ijma* ("My community will never agree upon an error"). Almost every succeeding generation left its mark upon political doctrine, as fresh precedents were created and the theory was accommodated to them. This close dependence upon historical fact is clearly seen in (and serves to explain) yet another feature of Sunni theory, namely its refusal to lay down rules for cases which had not yet arisen in practice, beyond vague generalities and some casuistical deductions.

All these features are mirrored in al-Mawardi's exposition. But, whether deliberately or not, he often omits all but a brief reference to the disputes out of which the actual decisions arose, and thus gives to his statements (in spite of their framework of scholastic discussion) a somewhat final and assertive air, as if they merely recapitulated what always was, is now, and ever should be. So far, however, as the traditional doctrines are concerned, they can readily be interpreted through the materials to hand in the work of an equally authoritative contemporary, the *Usul ad-Din* of Abu Mansur Abd al-Qahir b. Tahir al-Baghdadi.[12] In the thirteenth chapter of this work, the author sums up the doctrine of the Imama, together with the arguments on each question, in a form which is in some respects more satisfactory than that of al-Mawardi. But the points on which the latter expands or departs from the doctrine of his predecessors are more interesting for our purpose, for, as in so many medieval writings, the real significance of the work is to be found not so much in the external and obvious statements as in the apparently casual remarks and the concealed implications.

We shall now take one by one the heads of al-Mawardi's exposition, and endeavor to suggest their relations to the old dogmatic disputes and to the contemporary political situation.

(i) The Imama is obligatory by revelation, not by reason. The arguments coincide generally with those summarized by al-Baghdadi (*Usul* 271), who represents this as the view of al-Ashari in opposition to the Mutazila.

(ii) The office is filled by election, carried out by qualified electors. So also al-Baghdadi (279-281), against the Shiite doctrine of designation. But al-Mawardi omits the explicit statement of al-Baghdadi that if the contract is made by an evildoer the Imama is invalid, though it is implied in his stipulation of *adala*. For it might well be doubted whether some of the Buwaihid caliph-makers possessed *adala* "in its most rigorous acceptation."

(iii) The qualifications of candidates for election, including descent from Quraish. Al-Baghdadi's discussion is fuller on the latter point (*Usul* 275-277), but al-Mawardi's detailed recapitulation of the Sunni arguments suggests that there was at this time a certain body of opinion which held that a non-Quraishite might validly be elected to the office.[13]

(iv) The election of the Imam is valid even if made by a single qualified elector. This is again the doctrine of al-Ashari (Baghdadi 280-281). It is difficult to determine the precise bearing of this decision, since it does not in itself justify, as is often assumed, the practice of nominating a successor (this being discussed and justified separately below), but it may be a preliminary step towards it. No actual historical precedent is quoted,[14] and though al-Mawardi may have had in mind the "elections" made by the Buwaihid amirs, the phrasing of the argument suggests that it is merely a matter of juristic casuistry.

(v) Preferences between equally qualified candidates, apparently based on juristic deduction. Not in al-Baghdadi.

(vi) Solicitation of the office of Imam does not debar a candidate from election. This is evidently directed against the argument that since the solicitation of other offices of delegated authority (*walaya*) is forbidden, the same principle should apply to the caliphate—an argument which the Sunni doctors could not accept for obvious historical reasons.

(vii) A duly elected Imam cannot be displaced in favor of a worthier candidate. Although professedly directed against al-Jahiz and other Mutazilites (and possibly also by implication against the Shia[15]), it at the same time condones many historical examples of unworthy caliphs.

(viii) Election cannot be dispensed with, even if there is only a single qualified candidate. This also is apparently directed against the Shia.

(ix) There cannot be two Imams at one and the same time.

On this point al-Mawardi shortly but definitely rejects the Asharite view, expounded by al-Baghdadi (*Usul* 274), which deprecates the coexistence of two Imams but permits it in widely separated lands. Al-Mawardi's fresh insistence upon the illegality of two caliphs probably therefore reflects the refusal of the Abbasids and their partisans to admit the claims of their dangerous rivals, the Fatimids,[16] and excludes also the Umayyads of al-Andalus.

(x) Methods to be applied in the settlement of disputes between rival claimants. This is a lengthy and casuistical expansion of the Asharite doctrine (Baghdadi 281).

(xi) The assumption of the Imama in virtue of nomination by the preceding Imam is legal, and a reigning Imam may on his sole authority confer a valid contract for the succession. So also al-Baghdadi (284). It is noteworthy, however, that on the disputed point whether a contract so made in favor of a son is valid—a point which can be answered in the affirmative only by a downright assertion that executive power is superior to legal principles—al-Mawardi abstains from recording his view. His silence is significant of the dilemma in which the Sunni apologists were placed by this practice; for while no legal arguments could be adduced for its validity, historical reasons made it impossible for them to declare it invalid.

(xii) The nomination of a successor is not valid until accepted by the nominee; when once validated, it cannot be revoked by the nominating Imam, nor can the nominee resign, except under specific conditions. These all appear to be theoretical deductions from legal principles, since no certain historical precedents can be quoted. The same conclusion applies to the further conditions regarding the nomination of an absent person and the limitation of the powers of the nominee.

(xiii) The Imam may limit the choice of the electors after his death to certain persons, and may also designate the electoral conclave, on the precedent set by Umar b. al-Khattab.

(xiv) The Imam may nominate two or more persons and prescribe the order of their succession. Support for this rule is sought in a weak analogy with the instructions given by the Prophet for the command of the army at Mutah and in a still

weaker legal argument; so that al-Mawardi himself finds it necessary to cite the historical precedents as constituting a proof by
ijma.

(xv) A prior successor may, after becoming Imam, set aside
the eventual successors nominated by his predecessor in favor of
his own nominee. This is expressly given as a Shafiite view "held
by the majority of jurists," in contrast to the earlier view that he
was not at liberty to do so. Here the historical precedents were
against al-Mawardi, and though he tries to explain away al-
Mansur's action in the case of Isa b. Musa, he neglects entirely
Umar II's refusal to set aside Yazid b. Abd al-Malik and al-Amin's
attempt to set aside al-Mamun. It is very curious that he should
have chosen in this instance to have followed legal *taqlid,* and the
reasons for his doing so are obscure, since it seems unlikely that
he had any special contingency in view. The further discussion
relating to the establishment of an order of succession is certainly
based purely on legal speculation.

(xvi) It is not necessary that all members of the community
should know the caliph in person and by name. This is explicitly
directed against a Zaidi doctrine.

(xvii) The designation of the caliph as *Khalifat Allah* is
illegal and impious.[17]

(xviii) A detailed statement under ten heads of the public
duties of the Imam. The religious, legal and military duties agree
in principle with the brief statements of al-Baghdadi (*Usul* 272),
but with some juristic expansion. The administrative duties summarize the main points in early writings on the art of government.
Note especially the insistence on the personal duty and responsibility of the Imam to supervise all public functions, even when
the actual carrying-out of them is delegated to others. Later
writers[18] sometimes regard the first two duties mentioned in this
statement, that is the maintenance of the faith and the execution
of justice, as the principal functions of the caliphate. But the
emphasis laid by al-Mawardi on its administrative duties is clearly
directed against any conception of the caliphate as a purely or
mainly religious and judicial office, such as it was in fact tending
to become. This is indeed central in al-Mawardi's theory and the
basis of his entire work, since almost all his remaining chapters

consist precisely of detailed expositions of these administrative duties. And, of course, this was the point at issue between the caliphs and the Buwaihid amirs, since the latter, even if their view was never explicitly formulated, implied, by their disregard of the caliphate in matters of administration, that these lay outside its competence.

(xix) Finally, al-Mawardi enters on a long and legalistic discussion of the conditions and circumstances leading to forfeiture of the Imama. These are:

1. Loss of probity by reason of evil conduct or heresy.[19] He admits, however, that "many of the doctors of al-Basra" (mindful no doubt of al-Mamun and his successors) deny that errors of interpretation debar from holding the caliphate. His own stricter view, besides being the more logical,[20] might perhaps have been influenced by the fear of seeing a Shiite caliph installed at Baghdad—a contingency by no means impossible at the time when he composed his treatise.

2. Infirmity of mind or body such that it affects the capacity of the Imam to carry out the duties of his office.

3. Curtailment or loss of liberty. This touches very closely the contemporary problem of the caliphate, and his exposition was probably worded, in consequence, with special care, especially if (as we have suggested) his book had a political significance. It may therefore repay us to examine this section in rather fuller detail. All possible combinations are discussed in turn, following the usual system of the author, but of these some are rather theoretical and need not detain us.

The first category of curtailments of liberty comprises the cases which may arise when the caliph is placed under restraint, "control over him having been seized by one of his auxiliaries, who arrogates to himself the executive authority"—words which exactly describe the situation of the Abbasids as it had been for about a century.[21] Can a person in this position be the Imam? It is difficult to see how this can logically be reconciled with the duties just enumerated (in section xviii); but al-Mawardi, acutely conscious that a negative answer meant the rejection of al-Mutilillah and all his successors, briefly asserts that he can be and is, and then adroitly turns the discussion to the relations between the caliph and the usurper, that is to say, the Buwaihid amirs. If they act conformably to the ordinances of the faith and the requirements of justice, the anomalous situation may be allowed to stand for fear of prejudice to the *Jamaa*; but if not, "it becomes the duty of the Imam to call to his aid those who will restrain the usurper's hand and put an end to his domination." This can scarcely be construed as other than a threat to the Buwaihids, should they continue to make themselves objectionable. If the book was composed before 421:1030, the covert reference is possibly to Sultan Mahmud of Ghazna; that on the establishment of the Saljuqids in Khurasan a few years later the threat was in fact carried out is a matter of history.

The second category is that of captivity. The provisions relating to a caliph who is taken prisoner by infidels are theoretical, but if the captors are "rebel Muslims" a delicate situation arises. It is, of course, "the duty of the whole community to seek his liberation," and al-Mawardi seems to be unconscious of the ironical implications of his next assumption, that "the whole community" may be unable to do so. In this case, the effect may be much the same as when the caliph is "placed under restraint," except that a substitute should be appointed to act on his behalf. This again seems to be theoretical. But it might happen that the rebels "have already set up an Imam for themselves"—in plain language, were partisans of the Fatimid Caliphs. Then, says al-Mawardi, the captive Imam automatically forfeits the Imama. But he will not admit that the Imam of the "rebels" is thereby substituted for him; on the contrary, the electors in the "domain of loyalty" have the duty of choosing a new Imam. In effect, his argument is that the conquest of Baghdad by the Fatimids would not automatically result in the termination of the Abbasid caliphate, but he prudently leaves it to the "electors" either to recognize the Fatimids or to continue the line of the Abbasids elsewhere. That this would reduce the Abbasids to a position rather like that of the Umayyads of al-Andalus is eloquent of the embarrassments into which the apologists for the Abbasid caliphate were being forced by the facts of the contemporary situation.

This concludes al-Mawardi's exposition of the caliphate in the chapter specifically devoted to it. But there remains the very important and significant section in his third chapter, dealing with the "Amirate by Seizure," *imarat al-istila*. Before passing on to this, however, some note should be taken of two omissions in the chapter just analyzed.

Unlike some of the most authoritative exponents of the law, he does not explicitly deny the right of the subjects to refuse obedience to an impious Imam. It is true that in the first section he asserts that submission to those set in command is "imposed upon us," and supports this with a Tradition from Abu Hurara. But the unemphatic terms of his own statement and the Tradition (which seems to have been deliberately chosen instead of the better known and more vigorously phrased tradition of al-Hasan al-Basri)[22] stand in marked contrast to al-Ashari's downright statement: "We maintain the error of those who hold it right to rise against the Imams whensoever there may be apparent in them a falling-away from right. We are opposed to armed rebellion against them and civil war."[23] Further, it has already been seen that he definitely asserts evil conduct and heresy to be causes of forfeiture of the Imama. His position is thus intermediate between the positive Kharijite doctrine of the duty of insurrection and the negative Sunni doctrine of the duty of submission, but he is prudently content to leave this too with these rather vague indications.

The second omission is the complement of the first. For though he speaks of forfeiture of the Imama, he is careful not to lay down any procedure by which an Imam may be deposed. In this he remains faithful to the principles of Sunni political thought, having neither an authoritative view nor precedents to fall back upon. Many caliphs had indeed been deposed, but al-Mawardi was well aware that one and all had been deposed by force. It is true that a forcible deposition may have been accompanied by a formal *fatwa* authorizing it on various moral or religious grounds, but he was too honest to accept at its face value the transparent pretence of legality. The forcible measures discussed in his final section are expressly qualified as proceeding from "rebel Muslims." Hence it appears that while a caliph may legally be deposed, there is no legal means of deposing him.

This dilemma is characteristic not of al-Mawardi alone, but

of all Sunni political thought up to his time. It thus reinforces the argument outlined at the beginning of this section, that Sunni political theory was, in fact, only the rationalization of the history of the community. Without precedents, no theory;[24] and all the imposing fabric of interpretation of the sources is merely the *post eventum* justification of the precedents which have been ratified by *ijma*.

III   The Significance of the "Amirate by Seizure"

Let us return now to the *imarat al-istila*. It is clear that, on the accepted juristic principles, an irregular situation is created when the governor of a province, instead of being appointed and revocable by the caliphs, imposes his rule by force. It becomes even more anomalous when it is impossible to qualify the usurper as a rebel, even technically. At no period during the establishment of his authority in Ghazna and Khurasan did Mahmud, for example, take any action which could be construed as opposition to the caliph or to any of the governors in the name of the caliph. At the same time it was no new thing; the situation had been in existence for well-nigh two centuries, ever since, in fact, Harun had recognized the hereditary amirate of the Banul-Aghlab in Ifriqiya. There were thus ample precedents, and the adaptive genius of the Sunni community had saved the principle of unity by the device of a sort of concordat, the caliph recognizing the governor's sole control of policy and civil administration, in return for recognition of his own dignity and right of administration of religious affairs.[25]

Even in this case, therefore, the solution was already provided by a sort of practical *ijma*, but the difficulty remained of giving it legal form and validity. Al-Mawardi's predecessors seem to have shirked the task and closed their eyes to the apparent illegality, but it is characteristic of his honesty that he rejected this easy way out. Besides, if our reading of his work is justified, it was not enough for him merely to find a legal justification for what had happened in the past, but he was even more concerned to regularize the contemporary situation and to provide for what might well happen in the near future. Since the complete restoration of the old Abbasid empire was obviously an impossible dream, it was of importance for his purpose to regulate the present and future relations of the caliphate with such independent Sunni rulers as Sultan Mahmud. At the same time the difficulty remained that his formulation must not conflict either with legal principles or with the exposition which he had already given of the functions of the caliphate.

The second was the easier task, and it is partly for this reason that the subject is not discussed in the chapter on the caliphate but in that on the government of the provinces. Certain concessions might be made to the governors of outlying regions, without prejudice to the rights of the caliph as effective ruler of the central provinces. It is to be observed that al-Mawardi implicitly excludes such an arrangement at the center. In his brief and embarrassed discussion of "curtailment of liberty" he has already said all that he has to say about that. Consequently, the present paragraph has no relevance either to the Buwaihid amirs of al-Iraq nor to the later Saljuqid Sultanate, when a new situation arose which he had probably not foreseen. By thus limiting the concession to the outer provinces, he avoids formal contradiction of his previous statements. This itself is not sufficient to safeguard the principle, however; and he goes on to explain that the concession is permissible only subject to stringent stipulations, intended to guarantee that the concordat is a genuine agreement and not merely an outward formality. The governor must undertake to preserve the dignity of the caliphate and show such respect to it as will preclude any idea of insubordination on his part; further, he must undertake to govern according to the Sharia and to maintain the Faith in word and deed. The caliph on his part validates all such religious appointments and decisions as may hitherto have been irregular, and both parties must make a pact of friendship and mutual assistance. If these conditions are fulfilled, al-Mawardi goes so far as to say that the caliph *must* grant the conqueror this recognition and authorization, in order to forestall the danger of driving him into rebellion; and even if they are not fulfilled, the caliph may do so in order to induce him to make submission, though in the latter case he should also appoint a representative as the valid executive authority.

But what were the legal principles upon which the validity of such sweeping concessions could be based? One resource alone was open to al-Mawardi, and he frankly admits it. Necessity dispenses with stipulations which are impossible to fulfill. To this he adds another, derived not so much from legal principles as from current political maxims: that fear of injury to public interests justifies a relaxation of conditions.[26] It must be supposed that in his zeal to find some arguments by which at least the show of legality could be maintained, al-Mawardi did not realize that he had undermined the foundations of all law. Necessity and expediency may indeed be respectable principles, but only when they are not invoked to justify disregard of the law.[27] It is true that he seeks to limit them to this one case, but to admit them at all was the thin end of the wedge. Already the whole structure of the juristic theory of the caliphate was beginning to crumble, and it was not long before the continued application of these principles brought it crashing to the ground.

NOTES

[1] The only edition of the text which makes any approach to accuracy is that of Enger. published at Bonn in 1853. All Cairo editions which I have seen are disfigured by such serious misprints and omissions as to be totally unreliable.

[2] It was not, however, regarded with favor in Turkey during the reign of Sultan Abd-al-Hamid II, and Count Leon Ostrorog's translation was in fact banned at Istanbul (see M. Hartmann, *Unpolitische Briefe aus der Türkei*, 1910, p. 242) .

[3] Brockelmann I, 386, or his article in the *Encyc. of Islam*.

[4] The text of the second sentence translated above runs:

انثلت فيه أمر من ازمت طاعته ليعلم مناصب الفقهاء في اليه منها فيستوثيه وما عليه فيوفيه توفيا العدل فى تنفيذه و فنالة وتعرى النصفة فى أخذه وعطائه

[5] See on this subject generally Dr. A. H. Siddiqi's thesis "Caliphate and Kingship in Medieval Persia," in *Islamic Culture* X, 1 (Jan. 1936) , 109 ff. Al-Mawardi's work is touched on in pp. 121-122.

[6] See Yaqut, *Irshad al-Arib* V, 407, where it is remarked that in spite of the Arabic superlative, the rank of the holder of this title was below that of the *qadi'l-qudah*.

[7] Trans. de Slane II, 225.

[8] Note in this connection that his treatise *Al-Iqna*, on the Shafii *madhhab*

is also said to have been written at the request of al-Qadir billah and to have been presented to him (Yaqut V, 408).

[9] Including the writer of the present article in his survey of *Arabic Literature*, p. 67.

[10] Note that he claimed to be a *mujtahid* in law: Yaqut V, 409.

[11] As, for example, point xvii in the following section.

[12] Published at Istanbul 1346:1928. For the author (d. 439:1027) see Ibn Khallikan No. 365 (de Slane II, 149-150); Brockelmann I, 385.

[13] But it may be intended as a covert counterblast to the claims of the Fatimids, whose descent from Quraish was denied by the partisans of the Abbasids.

[14] The Tradition inserted by al-M. concerning al-Abbas and Ali relates to the period following the death of the Prophet, not to the election of Ali as caliph after the death of Othman.

[15] The controversial background of this discussion may be seen in the arguments as to the relative "worthiness" of the four Orthodox caliphs, summed up by al-Ashari in *Maqalat al-Islamiyin* II, 458-459 (Istanbul, 1930).

[16] It will be recalled that this problem, previously rather an academic one, took on a new urgency and actuality after the Fatimid conquest of Egypt in 358:969.

[17] See on this Goldziher, *Muhammedanische Studien* II, 61.

[18] See Ostrorog's note to his translation of this chapter (*Le Droit du Califat*, p. 144, n. 2).

[19] This is the only cause of forfeiture mentioned by al-Baghdadi (*Usul* 278).

[20] But it is doubtful whether it is the more orthodox, since it approaches very closely to the Kharijite heresy. See below.

[21] The further definition, "but without outward show of insubordination," can hardly be applied without qualification to some of the Buwaihids, but are inserted in order to distinguish "restraint" from "captivity."

[22] See Abu Yusuf, *Kitab al-Kharaj* (Cairo, 1346), p. 11.

[23] Translation by D. B. Macdonald, *Development of Muslim Theology*, p. 298.

[24] Although, as several of al-Mawardi's arguments show, the theory may be speculatively expanded by deduction from, or on the lines indicated by, a given precedent.

[25] This is frequently called a fiction, but it was not a fiction at all in the first instances, though the relationship undoubtedly became more symbolic as time went on.

[26] The text is in some disorder, but this is unquestionably the meaning of the passage. The same principle is invoked in his discussion of "curtailment of liberty" above, and underlies the Sunni doctrine which forbids rebellion against an evil-doing caliph.

[27] The legally recognized "necessity" which permits, for example, the eating of carrion to escape death by starvation is of a totally different order, and to adduce it in this instance (although al-Mawardi himself does not do so) is a flagrantly false analogy.

10.   The Islamic Background of
         Ibn Khaldun's Political Theory

It seems an odd coincidence that from 1930 to 1932 there should have appeared four different studies devoted to the work of Ibn Khaldun, considering that in the half century following the issue of de Slane's translation of the *Muqaddima*,[1] apart from von Kremer's study[2] and a few short articles drawing the attention of a wider circle of students in various countries to its significance, it was not until 1917 that the first monograph on the subject was published by Dr. Taha Husain.[3] This work, like most of the earlier articles, dealt primarily with the sociological aspects of Ibn Khaldun's historical theory, and the same interest predominates in all but one of the three or four articles published since 1917. Of the latest studies it may be said that, though still giving prominence to the social aspect, they cover as a whole a rather wider ground. Dr. Gaston Bouthoul, indeed, limits himself in his title[4] to Ibn Khaldun's "Social Philosophy," but the contents of his essay overlap these bounds, especially the first thirty pages, devoted to a very suggestive analysis of the personality and intellectual outlook of the historian. Professor Schmidt's tractate[5] is in the nature of a survey of the field; he assembles and examines the views of earlier writers on different aspects of Ibn Khaldun's work, but does not put forward any synthesis of his own. Lastly, the two recent German works of Drs. Kamil Ayad[6] and Erwin Rosenthal[7] mark a return towards the more strictly historical thought of the *Muqaddima,* and the latter in particular is the first monograph to be devoted exclusively to Ibn Khaldun's political theory.[8] The two books differ considerably in plan. Dr. Ayad, after a long and philosophical introduction on the general trends of Islamic cultural and intellectual development, displays a remarkable critical faculty and acuteness of observation in the analysis of Ibn Khaldun's historical method, and concludes by examining in outline his social theory. Dr. Rosenthal on the other hand prefers to let Ibn Khaldun explain himself, and describes his own work as "a modest attempt to present the historian with the material from which to construct a picture of Ibn Khaldun's view of the state, by means of as accurate a translation as possible of the most important passages in his *Muqaddima* in which he analyses the theory of the state, together with an historical interpretation limited strictly to the text."[9]

In view of these admirable and very serviceable books it would be an unnecessary task to attempt to traverse the whole field of Ibn Khaldun's political thought here. The object of the following remarks is solely to draw attention to a point which appears to the writer to be fundamental for any critical study of Ibn Khaldun's thought, but which has been consistently overlooked or even misrepresented in most, if not all, of the works already cited. (For purposes of discussion it will be convenient to illustrate the argument more especially from the two last-named German works.) The general explanation of the deficiency referred to is to be sought in a certain tendency to exaggerate the independence and originality of Ibn Khaldun's thought, which in turn arises from a misapprehension of his outlook, especially in its relation to religious questions.

The true originality of Ibn Khaldun's work is to be found in his detailed and objective analysis of the political, social, and economic factors underlying the establishment of political units and the evolution of the State, and it is the results of this detailed analysis that constitute the "new science" which he claims to have founded. The materials on which his analysis is based were derived partly from his own experience—a point rightly emphasized in all these works—and partly also from the historical sources to his hand relating to the history of Islam, which he interpreted with a striking disregard of established prejudices. But the axioms or principles on which his study rests are those of practically all the earlier Sunni jurists and social philosophers. Dr. Ayad is at some pains to argue that a fundamental difference exists between Ibn Khaldun's first principles as to the origins of society and those of his predecessors (pp. 165-166); the latter start from a global conception of "human society" *(al-mujtama al-insani)*, whereas he starts from a dynamic conception of "human association" (al-ijtima). But apart from the evidence against this assumption to be found in the typical passage which will be quoted shortly, Dr. Ayad has almost immediately to admit (p. 168) that Ibn Khaldun simply took over their "utilitarian" arguments, "although his conception does not wholly agree at bottom with their views." This admission is fully borne out by Ibn Khaldun's own explanation, that the difference between the subject of his book and the observations of his predecessors lies in the fact that their statements were "not argued out as we have argued them out, but simply touched on by way of exhortation in a belletristic style," and served only as general introducton to works of an ethical character.[10] While they in pursuance of their objects have been content to summarize the historical process in general terms, he has made it his business to explain the mechanism in detail, since his object, which he admits is of subsidiary importance (thamara-tuha ... daifa), is solely to establish criteria for the "rectification of historical narratives." In doing so, of course, he introduces many conceptions which find no place in their outline sketches, but are not in any way in contradiction to them.

Yet both Dr. Rosenthal and Dr. Ayad assert the contrary. The former remarks (p. 9) that it should be particularly emphasized that Ibn Khaldun "on the basis of his own observations" recognizes that kingship can come about without any divine investiture or aid, and regards this (p. 12) as "an indication of independent thought, free of all theological restraint." Dr. Ayad is even more emphatic. Noting that Ibn Khaldun does not make prophecy a prerequisite for human association, he adds (p. 114), "This proposition of Ibn Khaldun's is openly directed against the Muslim theologians, who describe any human life as impossible without prophetic guidance," and repeats the observation (p. 169) in reference to Ibn Khaldun's argument against the exaggerated postulates of the "philosophers."[11]

If, however, we examine the actual phraseology of the Muslim theologians, we shall find that it does not bear out these assumptions. To take an extreme case I shall quote the relevant passage from a work of the kind referred to by Ibn Khaldun and written by one of the protagonists of the strictest orthodox views,

Ibn Taimiya (d. 728:1328), two generations before him. This passage, which forms part of the general introduction to his treatise on the censorship,[12] runs as follows:

> None of mankind can attain to complete welfare, either in this world or in the next, except by association (*ijtima!*), cooperation, and mutual aid. Their cooperation and mutual aid is for the purpose of acquiring things of benefit to them, and their mutual aid is also for the purpose of warding off things injurious to them. For this reason it is said that "Man is a political being by nature." But when they unite together (*jama'u*) there must of necessity be certain things which they do to secure their welfare and certain other things which they avoid because of the mischief which lies in them, and they will render obedience to the one who commands them to the attainment of those objects and restrains them from those actions of evil consequence. Moreover, all mankind must of necessity render obedience to a commander and restrainer. Those who are not possessed of divine books or who are not followers of any religion (*man lam yakun min ahlil-kutubil-ilahiyati wala min ahli dinin*) yet obey their kings in regard to those matters wherein they believe that their worldly interests lie, sometimes rightly, sometimes wrongly.

If this passage is compared with the Introduction to Book i, section I, of the *Muqaddima,* or such a restatement as Book iii, chapter 23,[13] or the still more illuminating passage in Book v, chapter 6,[14] it will be seen that Ibn Khaldun does little more than expand these ideas and give them greater precision by introducing his conception of *asabiya*.

This example leads up to the second question—how far Ibn Khaldun deserves to be credited with the freedom from religious bias or preoccupations which both these writers ascribe to him. Granted at the outset that he aims at describing the phenomena of political life as he sees them to exist, and that on the basis of these empirical observations he does in fact describe them objectively and dispassionately, with a remarkable grasp of the essential characteristics of political power, the stages of its evolution, and the intricate interrelations of the State with all aspects of human civilization. His "materialism," "pessimism" or "fatalism" has been remarked by all his commentators, on the ground that he never puts forward suggestions for the reform of the institutions which he describes so minutely, nor considers the possibility that they may be modified as the result of human effort and thought, but accepts the facts as they are and presents the cycle of states and dynasties as an inevitable and almost mechanical process. Dr. Ayad remarks, for example (p. 163), that he makes no attempt to justify history, that his principles are not theocentric (p. 97), and that he holds, "in blunt opposition to the Muslim theological view," to the doctrine of causality and natural law in history (p. 143). Further, he emphasizes (pp. 51-53) his treatment of religion "simply as a weighty cultural phenomenon and an important socio-psychological factor in the historical process," while admitting that he remained a sincerely convinced Muslim. Similarly, Dr. Rosenthal insists more than once that Ibn Khaldun holds firmly to the doctrines of the *Sharia,* and that by religion he has in view the religion of Islam exclusively, yet it is one of the outstanding features of his theory that he treats religion (p. 58) "as no more than one factor, however important it may be."

"Religion [he proceeds] is an important factor also in the autarchic State, but it does not alone give its content to the State, not even to the Islamic State. It is, like every phenomenon, liable to changes, at least so far as its degree of intensity and the realization of its demands are concerned. . . . The law of the State is derived from religion, but the State abstracts itself in practice from the whole compass of its validity and follows its own aims. These, however, are determined by power and lordship and extend to the well-being of the citizens, primarily in this world, within the body of the State. . . . Human need and human effort have founded the State as a necessity, and it exists for man. The help of God lightened his work, the divine ordinance directed him to the best way, the word of God urged him on and supported his impulse towards conquest and power. But it is not *ad maiorem Dei gloriam* that the State exists, but rather for the protection of men and the ensuring of order" (pp. 59-60). At the same time "for Islamic thought, the formulation of the Religious law are ideal demands, and recognized as such also by Ibn Khaldun."

These two views, according to Dr. Rosenthal, exist side by side in his work, but it is the former which is at the center of his conceptions.

It seems to me that, in spite of the efforts made by both doctors to reconcile such a view of religion and the State with the orthodox standpoint of Ibn Khaldun, there is an unresolved contradiction between these two statements. Ibn Khaldun was not only a Muslim, but as almost every page of the *Muqaddima* bears witness, a Muslim jurist and theologian, of the strict Maliki school. For him religion was far and away the most important thing in life—we have seen that he expressly calls his study a thing of subsidiary value—and the *Sharia* the only true guide. This means not just that Ibn Khaldun was careful to safeguard himself in his arguments from the suspicion of unorthodoxy—still less that, as Dr. Ayad would have us believe, he "shows great adroitness in interpreting the Islamic law in accordance with his view, and so seeks to subordinate religion to his own scientific theories" (p. 173)—but that he did not and could not introduce into his system anything that was logically incompatible with the Islamic standpoint. He was all the less likely to do so since, as M. Bouthoul (p. 17) points out, and as we shall have occasion to recall further on, he was by early training and inclination strongly attracted to logic and the rational sciences. Amongst his early works cited by Dr. Ayad (p. 17)) was a treatise on logic, and it is this logical bent of his mind which supplies the key to the whole conception of the *Muqaddima*. Indeed, as Dr. Ayad shows more than once (pp. 57-58, 135, 159), in spite of his rejection of the logical systems of the metaphysicians, based as they were on abstract *a priori* ideas, his own insistence on the absolute validity of his deductions leads him at times into premature generalizations.

The explanation of his apparent reduction of religion to a secondary place in his exposition is that in his work he is not concerned with religion, i.e., Islam, as such, but only with the part played by religion in the outward course of history. The state occupies the central place, because it is the subject of his study. But a careful examination of the chapters which constitute the first three books of the *Muqaddima* will show that he uses the term religion in two different senses. On the one hand is religion in the true or absolute sense, when the whole will of man is governed by his religious conviction and his animal nature is held in check. Opposed to this is "acquired religion," a secondhand and relatively feeble thing, which saps his manhood and fails to control his animal impulses.[15] This distinction underlies also the chapter,[16] "That a religious rising *(dawa)* unsupported by *asabiya* is doomed to failure," upon which so much weight is placed by these investigators, for Ibn Khaldun makes it quite clear that he is speaking of religious movements which have no divine commission behind them, and thus are religious only in the outward sense.

The ethical and Islamic basis of Ibn Khaldun's thought is, however, implicit throughout his exposition, quite apart from his constant appeal to texts from Koran and Tradition. His doctrine of causality and natural law, which in Dr. Ayad's view stands in such sharp opposition to Muslim theological views, is simply that of the *sunnat Allah* so often appealed to in the Koran. Although for theological purposes it was found necessary to insist that cause and effect are not integrally connected, in so far as both the apparent cause and the apparent effect are in reality separate divine creations, yet it was accepted that God did in fact, by eternal "custom," create the appropriate "effect" after creating the "cause"; indeed, without this presupposition, the further doctrine of the special power bestowed upon prophets of "violation of natural order" *(kharq al-ada)* would have no meaning. It may, however, be allowed that Ibn Khaldun lays much greater stress than most Muslim writers upon the inevitable working of cause and effect as "natural law."

A similar conclusion emerges from his historical theory in the strict sense. The association of men for mutual assistance "fulfils the wise purpose of God for their survival and preservation of the species," and without it there would not be perfected "what God has willed for the population of the world by them and His establishment of them as His viceregents."[17] The institution of kingship is likewise ordained by God, whether it be good or evil,[18] and the *asabiya* which furnishes the mechanism whereby it is attained is itself due to the aid of God.[19] Thus even the civil state exists as part of the divine purpose. Ibn Khaldun then goes on to recognize several varieties of states, classified according to their laws.[20] This passage is particularly worth attention, in view of the express statements of Dr. Rosenthal that Ibn Khaldun "passes no judgments of value and prefers no form of state over another"

(p. 47), and of Dr. Ayad that "he refrains *on principle* from judgments of value" (p. 123).

> The state [says Ibn Khaldun] whose law is based upon violence and superior force and giving full play to the irascible nature is tyranny and injustice and in the eyes of the law blameworthy, a judgment in which also political wisdom concurs. Further, the state whose law is based upon rational government and its principles, without the authority of the *Sharia*,[21] is likewise blameworthy, since it is the product of speculation without the light of God . . . and the principles of rational government aim solely at worldly interests.

Opposed to both of these stands the caliphate as the only perfect state, being based on the true practice of the *Sharia*, which furthers both the temporal and spiritual interests of its subjects.[22]

The central position which the caliphate or ideal state occupies in Ibn Khaldun's thought may be supported by another argument. It has been remarked above that Ibn Khaldun develops his thesis along strictly logical lines, and a glance at the sequence of his chapters shows that they lead up to and culminate in the caliphate.[23] Having reached this point he halts to discuss in elaborate detail the organization associated with the caliphate,[24] before passing on to investigate the causes of the decay of the state and its final destruction. It is in the course of this discussion that he explains the gradual transformation of the historical Arab caliphate into an ordinary kingship,[25] as due to the force of *asabiya* amongst the Umayyad family (though not, in his view, amongst the early Umayyad rulers themselves) regaining an ascendency over the religious enthusiasm which had restrained it in the time of the early caliphs.

Thus it is impossible to avoid the impression that Ibn Khaldun, besides setting out to analyze the evolution of the state, was, like the other Muslim jurists of his time, concerned with the problem of reconciling the ideal demands of the *Sharia* with the facts of history. The careful reader will note how he drives home the lesson, over and over again, that the course of history is what it is because of the infraction of the *Sharia* by the sin of pride, the sin of luxury, the sin of greed.[26] Even in economic life it is only when the ordinances of the *Sharia* are observed that prosperity follows.[27]

Since mankind will not follow the Sharia it is condemned to an empty and unending cycle of rise and fall, conditioned by the "natural" and inevitable consequences of the predominance of its animal instincts. In this sense Ibn Khaldun may be a "pessimist" or "determinist," but his pessimism has a moral and religious, not a sociological, basis.

NOTES

[1] *Les Prolegomènes historiques* (Paris, 1863-1868) .

[2] A. von Kremer, *Ibn Chaldun und seine Kulturgeschichte der islamischen Reiche*, S.-B. Ak. (Wien, 1878). Full bibliographies of the other articles will be found in any of the works mentioned below.

[3] Taha Hussain, *Étude analytique et critique de la philosophie sociale d'Ibn Khaldoun* (Paris, 1917) .

[4] Gaston Bouthoul, *Ibn Khaldoun, Sa Philosophie sociale* (Paris, 1930) , p. 95.

[5] Nathaniel Schmidt, *Ibn Shaldun, historian, sociologist, and philosopher* (New York, 1930), p. 68.

[6] Kamil Ayad, *Die Geschichts- und Gesellschaftslehre Ibn Halduns*, 2tes. Heft der "Forschungen zur Geschichts- und Gesellschaftslehre" hrsg. v. Kurt Breysig (Stuttgart and Berlin, 1930) , pp. x + 209.

[7] Erwin Rosenthal, *Ibn Khalduns Gedanken über den Staat*, Beiheft 25 der Historischen Zeitschrift (Munich and Berlin, 1932), pp. x + 118.

[8] Mention may also be made here of the Special Number issued by the Arabic journal *al-Hadith* of Aleppo in Sept., 1932, to celebrate the sexcentenary of Ibn Khaldun's birth. The articles, which are all from the hands of leading Arabic scholars of the present day, are somewhat unequal in value, but demonstrate the very keen interest shown in his work in modern Arabic circles. A note of dissidence is, however, introduced by the encyclopadist Farid Wagdi, who in a brief and rather unsatisfactory article argues that the *Muqaddima* is a work neither of sociology nor of the philosophy of history.

[9] The necessity for a revision of de Slane's somewhat loose translation (indispensable as it still is) has long been known to orientalists, and it is one of the merits of R.'s book that, with some assistance from Professor Bergsträsser, he provides a much more literal and accurate version of the passages translated, so far as I have tested it. Some errors remain, however; e.g. p. 41: "... hat den Namen Königtum, und es ist sein Sein, das sie beherrscht" (*tusamma l-malakata wahiya kawnuhu yamlukuhum*) ; p. 97: "und auf jede einzelne von ihnen (diesen Künsten) grosse Sorgfalt zu verwenden" (*litta annuqi fi kulli wahidin sanaiu kathiratun*). Doubtful words or readings are responsible for some errors; p. 23: I suspect the word "*umumiyatun*" rendered as "die Bevölkerung (?) " to mean something like "complex of tribal relationships"; a few lines further on "unterstützen sie," which makes nonsense in the context, is due to an apparent error of *ma'unatun* for *ma'unatun* ("source of expense"); p. 57: "einen Genuss aus dem Streit machen (?) " has arisen from a misreading *bilkhilafi* for *bilkhalaqi* ("enjoyment of worldly happiness") .

[10] Muqaddima to Bk. i (Quatremère i, 65) .

[11] First Muqaddima to Bk. i, section 1 (Q. i, 72).

[12] *Al-Hisba fil-Islam* (Cairo, 1318 H.) , p. 3.

[13] Q. i, 337-338; translated in Rosenthal, p. 39.

[14] Q. ii, 290, ll. 9-18.

[15] Cf. esp. Bk. ii, chap. 6, translated in R., pp. 68-69 (Q. i, 230-232) , and ii, 27 (Q. i, 275) .

[16] Bk. iii, chap. 6 (Q. i, 286-290) , translated in R., p. 54.

[17] Bk. i, ch. 1, 1st Muqaddima (Q. i, 70-71) .

[18] Bk. ii, ch. 20 (Q. i, 259-60).

[19] Bk. iii, ch. 4 (Q. i, 284) .

[20] Bk. iii, ch. 25, translated in R., 61-2 (Q. i, 342-3) .

[21] De Slane's translation misses the point of the phrase *min ghairi nazari' shshari* inserted in Q. after *bi-muqtadas-siyasati wa ahkamiha.*

[22] The same judgment is expressed in a slightly different fashion in Bk. ii, ch. 20 (Q. i, 259-60), from which it is clear that Ibn Khaldun's connotation of the term caliphate is general and not restricted to the historical caliphate.

[23] It is the chief defect of Dr. Rosenthal's otherwise admirable survey of Ibn Khaldun's political thought that he has overlooked the logical sequence of his exposition, and by shuffling about his chapters unwittingly distorts his point of view. For example, in the section headed "The evolution of the State" the order of the passages which he has selected is as follows:—Bk. ii, ch. 15; iii, 14; iii, 17; ii, 16; iii, 15; ii, 18; iii, 11; iii, 12; iii, 16; ii, 22; iii, 2; iii, 3; ii, 4; ii, 5; ii, 23; iii, 7; iii, 8; iii, 18; iii, 10; iii, 13; iii, 47; iii, 46.

[24] Dr. Ayad points out that Ibn Khaldun denies that the caliphate (or Imamate) is one of the "pillars of the faith," but fails to observe that it is the *Shiite* doctrine that he rejects, and that in his arguments against the rational necessity of the caliphate (iii, 26; Q. i, 345-346) he is in complete agreement with the classical doctrine expounded by al-Mawardi (p. 4).

[25] Bk. iii, ch. 28 (Q. i, 367 ff.) ; note especially *walam yazhari ttaghayyuru illa fil-wazii lladhi kana dinan thumma'nqalaba asabiyatan wa-saifan* (Q. 375, 9-10) . This instance brings out clearly that what Ibn Khaldun means by "natural" development in social and political life is very different from the mechanical doctrine which Dr. Ayad regards as the outstanding feature of his theory.

[26] M. Bouthoul's accusation (p. 88) that Ibn Khaldun's outlook is governed by a kind of intellectual sadism, characteristic of "medieval mentality," appears to me very wide of the mark. Cf. again Bk. v., ch. 6 (Q. ii, 290) .

[27] Bk. iii, ch. 38 (Q. ii, 79) .

11. Structure of Religious Thought in Islam

I The Animistic Substrate

The object of this and the three following essays in this series is to analyze the religious attitudes of Muslims, the sources from which they derive and the concepts which determine what they think in general about God, and how they view the relation between the unseen and the visible world. The ideas so disengaged may not and need not be exclusively Muslim—many or most of them are, indeed, paralleled in other faiths—but Muslim religious thought derives its distinctive character from their combination or formulation. Details of history and doctrine will not be included, except for such brief historical introductions and notes as are needed by way of explanation.

"Formulation" does not mean exclusively theological definition in terms of an organized system. From the outset it is important to draw a distinction between the verbal expression of religious feeling or intuition and its formal rationalization in logical or philosophical terms, although the latter may in turn influence or canalize modes of thought and verbalization of religious experience. Even in regard to the Koran a similar distinction must be drawn. Its definitions and expressions, though in one sense the starting point of specifically Muslim thought and belief and therefore of their systematic formulation, are themselves not systematic in the theological sense, but a direct verbal statement of certain immediate attitudes and intuitively grasped ideas. These attitudes and statements, having then been stabilized by the Koran and invested with supreme authority, serve as basic determinants of religious thought for Muslims in general.

Such sources or determinants of Muslim religious thought may be classified under four heads: (i) primitive attitudes and beliefs which survived in the Muslim community; (ii) the teaching and influence of the Koran, supplemented by the Prophetic Tradition; (iii) the systematization of Islamic belief and ethics by the dogmatic theologians; (iv) the influence of the Sufi brotherhoods. It is not always possible to draw sharp lines of division, but the classification is useful for the purposes of analysis and discussion; and it can be applied to the religious attitudes of any particular Muslim community, all of which differ from one another in the relative influence of these four factors, not perhaps in theory, but certainly in practice.

As any discussion of this kind must necessarily be colored by personal attitudes and approaches, some generalized reflections have been introduced from time to time into these papers. However absolutely expressed, they are not to be regarded as dogmatic statements, but as prolegomena by means of which the reader may be made aware of the writer's point of view and may evaluate and criticize the opinions he expresses.

The term Islam in these essays refers primarily and fundamentally to a religious conception of life. Whatever secondary elements and factors may enter into religious and social usages, the kernel or factor of synthesis is the inner sense of the meaning and ultimate end of life in this world, whatever may be the forms in which it finds expression.

No one who has attempted it will underestimate the difficulty of grasping the religious attitudes of men whose outlook upon the world differs widely from our own and has been molded, wholly or in part, by a different tradition. But it is peculiarly difficult for the modern western mind to do so. Religion, wherever it exists as a concrete and spiritually effective force, requires the exercise of the faculty of intuitive perception, the leap of the mind across and beyond all the data and methods of rational and logical analysis to grasp directly and in concrete experience some element in the nature of things which reason cannot describe or identify. Faith is the substance of things hoped for, the evidence of things not seen. In the typical western man, who has inherited English rationalist thought and values of the eighteenth and nineteenth centuries, and who has become mentally conditioned by it or by German thought and values of the last century and a half, the intuitive faculty has been so starved and neglected that he has the greatest reluctance to admit even its existence and cannot imagine how it operates. Our religious judgment has become in consequence seriously unbalanced.

But essential as intuition is in the religious life, it too is unbalanced unless the substance of its vision is correlated with a rational understanding of things in general. This relation is partly a negative one. The rational understanding of nature prevents the intuitive imagination from following capricious fantasies, and, being progressively enlarged, releases it from certain types of secondary error arising from ignorance of natural processes, such as a belief in astrology and the significance of eclipses. On its side, the intuitive perception constantly asserts the incompleteness of the data with which the rational intelligence operates. But this in turn issues in a positive interplay of religious and ethical with philosophical ideals. The religious imagination constantly sets new objectives to philosophy, which undertakes to define them and to integrate them with the rational world. This is the function and essence of theology, which defines for a time the horizon of the intuitive vision, until sooner or later it ventures out again in search of new experience.

In the great religious systems this conflict and interaction of intuition and reason, emotion and intelligence, or (as the Orientals and Pascal have termed it) heart and mind, is to a certain extent concealed by becoming standardized or formalized. Both elements, which together make up the religious life and attitude, are guided into specific channels, expressed in terms of a given symbolism, and issue in certain established patterns of thought and worship. This complex gives rise in time to a theology which seeks to explain the significance of the symbols and patterns in rational terms. But it is the symbols and patterns themselves, not the theology, that stimulate the emotions and imagination of the worshiper; and no religion can survive unless its symbolism remains adequate to its function, not merely of inspiring the devotion and governing the will and action of its members, but of enlarging their perception beyond the limits of the seen and material world.

In no religious community, however, is the significance of its symbols and the emotional response which they evoke the same for all its members. On the contrary, wide differences in this respect are to be found between group and group, almost between individual and individual. The larger the community, and the more widely divergent its component groups are in ways of life, geographical situation, economic occupations, levels of culture or education, historical background and social traditions, the greater are the differences between them in their emotional, imaginative, and intellectual attitudes to its religious symbolism. And this difference persists from generation to generation in spite of all the efforts of the hierarchy or the professional religious leaders to organize, unify, or consolidate the community in a common pattern of outlook, thought, and action. Examples within every Christian community are too familiar to require citation here.

In no great religious community, probably, has this duality of religious intuition and theological reason been more fundamental or more openly visible than it is in Islam. It is to be seen in Islam also at the widest diversity of levels, from magical animistic interpretations to the most spiritualized conceptions, according as each reflects, in Robertson Smith's phrase, "habits of thought characteristic of very diverse stages of intellectual and moral development." Indeed, not only does the conflict between these interpretations form the historical drama of Muslim religious development, but it also characterizes the internal situation of Islam as a religion today.

It is a fact of basic importance in the history of Islam that it originated in the midst of a particular kind of animistic society, that of ancient Arabia. It did not, of course, originate in or develop out of that society; on the contrary, it was essentially a revolt against Arabian animism; yet it could not help reflecting in some degree the colour of its surroundings.

The general features of Arabian animism have been described in several well-known works. It shared the distinctive characteristics of animism everywhere: that the range of the supernatural is extremely wide, that in all the affairs of daily life man is in continual contact with it and constantly exposed to its influences and action, and that a great variety of natural objects or events are regarded with fear or awe as manifestations of supernatural power or as its locus. So the Arabs believed in magical powers which were inherent in or which haunted such objects as stone fetishes, sacred trees, or wells, or which were possessed by certain persons, some of them human, such as sorcerers, sooth-sayers, and even poets, but the majority of them non-human. These latter were the jinn, for the belief in whose demoniac nature and powers anthropologists have suggested different origins. This argument is irrelevant in the present context, where it is sufficient to note that it was connected with what Westermarck describes as "strange and mysterious phenomena which suggest a volitional cause, especially such as inspire men with fear."[1]

The magical power emanating from all these objects or beings might be either beneficent, when it was called *baraka* or "blessing," or maleficent, as, for example, the evil eye. In its crudest form, the old Arabian religion might be summed up as the endeavor to find and to use the most powerful conveyors of *baraka* against the ever-present malevolence of evil spirits. But there is no evidence for the existence in Arabia of ritual cere-monies corresponding to those of African medicine-men, even although the Arabic word for medicine (*tibb*) seems primarily to mean incantation. The culminating ritual of Arab paganism was the tribal pilgrimage to a sacred stone at specified times, the worshipers being obliged to observe certain rules in respect of clothing, shaving the head, etc., and certain taboos, the whole ceremony ending with ritual processions round the shrine, the sacrifice of an animal or animals upon the sacred stone, and a communal sacrificial meal.

In a world so closely besieged by the supernatural, the divine was very near and familiar. At first sight, this would seem to be contradicted by the stark realism imposed upon the Arabs by the physical conditions of their life and reflected in their poetry. As D. B. Macdonald has said "The Arabs show themselves not as especially easy of belief, but as hard-headed, materialistic, ques-tioning, doubting, scoffing at their own superstitions and usages, fond of tests of the supernatural—and all this in a curiously light-minded, almost childish fashion."[2] Yet the contradiction is only formal; scepticism and superstition, as many examples in our day have clearly demonstrated, are the obverse and reverse sides of the same medal.

And even this scepticism had its limits. It was particular, not general. The Arab might question whether this or that sooth-sayer was not a fraud, or might take the risk of daring to violate a certain taboo, but he never doubted that behind all visible phenomena there was an unseen world. I am convinced that a great part of the success of Muhammad's preaching was due to the fact that among many of his hearers the level of rational under-standing had risen to a point at which the old symbols and rituals had lost their meaning and value, and no longer satisfied their craving for an explanation of what lay behind the external phe-nomena.

The new channels opened up by the Koran to the emotional and imaginative outlook of the Arabs and its influence in Muslim religious attitudes will be discussed in the second of these essays. In the present context we are concerned rather with that general body of pagan Arabs who accepted the dogmas of the Koran with-out completely giving up their old beliefs. What Muhammad did for them was to superimpose upon the deposit of Arabian ani-mism a supreme controlling power in the personality and activity of an all-powerful God. But under this supreme disposer the Arabian legacy persisted. The belief in magic, in the superhuman and mostly malevolent powers of the jinn, in the *qarina* or familiar spirit attached to each individual—these and similar beliefs sur-vived with more or less of an Islamic veneer, to play a very large part in the ideas of Muslims about the world, especially (though not exclusively) amongst the unlettered popular masses. The whole subject has been illuminatingly analyzed by D. B. Mac-donald in his lectures on *The Religious Attitude and Life in Islam*.

When, however, Islam and the Arabs issued out of Arabia and spread over Western Asia and Persia, it might have been expected that, as a result of the contacts and conflicts with their peoples of ancient culture and the heritage of Zoroastrian, Chris-tian and Hellenistic beliefs, the influence of Arabian animism would have diminished. This is a subject which has not yet been thoroughly studied, and any conclusions that may be expressed here have only the value of personal impressions. But certain facts seem to be clear. Among these peoples also, in spite of the official cults and religions, there was still a very large substratum of ancient rituals and practices and of popular beliefs of animistic origin. Where these beliefs and practices ran counter to the complex of Muslim and Arab ideas (as, for example, some of the ancient fertility rituals of the agricultural peoples) the Arab-Muslim impact practically drove them out, at least among those who were converted to Islam. But where they were easily reconcilable with Arab animism, as, for example, the belief in astrology, the two currents combined and strengthened one another.

After the end of the Arab-Muslim conquests there was a period of three centuries during which the territorial spread of Islam, though vast indeed, remained practically stable. This gave time and opportunity for a thorough interpenetration of the religious attitudes and beliefs of the original Arab immigrants and of the peoples with whom they mixed to form the medieval Muslim nation. In the course of these centuries, after a long stage of theological disputes, a certain equilibrium was reached. The theology of Islam was established in logical and rational terms, and this achievement did something to counteract the influence of the grosser superstitions.

At the same time, however, it weighted the intellectual as against the emotional side of religion. Those who were opposed to the rationalism of the theologians therefore formed congregations to emphasize and to induce personal intuitive experience of the unseen divine component of things. In the beginnings these Sufi brotherhoods or religious orders confined themselves to the horizons set by the Koran and Islamic orthodoxy. But as they stressed more and more strongly the all-surrounding nearness of the supernatural, they began to draw upon other sources, including older pre-Islamic beliefs and practices. Already in the eleventh and twelfth centuries the term Sufism covers a vast range of religious attitudes, from an exalted spiritual integrity which measures up to that attained in any other religion, to something not far removed from a pure thaumaturgy with an external dressing of Islam.

It was at this point that the second great wave of Islamic expansion in Central Asia, India, Indonesia and Africa brought into Islam peoples of a very different religious and cultural background from those of the ancient cultural centers of Western Asia and Egypt, peoples whose former religions were either wholly animistic, like the Negroes and the Turks, or else animistic with an overlay of Hinduism, as in India, Sumatra and Java. The inevitable result was to reinforce very powerfully the heritage of animism which still survived in popular Islam. It is evident that among the Negroes of West Africa, for example, the tenacious pagan cults would not and could not be easily uprooted, as they have not been entirely uprooted even among the old, established Negro communities in America. And since much of the work of conversion was carried on not by the orthodox theologians but by the Sufi brotherhoods, it often ended in a kind of compromise which left much of the old animistic ideas still effective in the life and thought of the new converts.

The eventual situation was, however, much more complex than this, as will be seen when the activities of some of the Sufi orders are discussed in a later essay. It would be entirely wrong to assume that Islam simply supplied a screen for old animistic beliefs. At the very bottom of the scale, possibly, this may be largely true, and examples are still to be found among the remoter peoples. But alongside these there is a whole series of gradations corresponding to the more effective penetration and influence of Muslim doctrine and education.

At this point it is necessary to draw a distinction between animistic beliefs and animistic symbols. All living religions preserve (and perhaps must preserve) a certain number of symbols which were originally related to animistic rites and beliefs. In the course of religious development great religious teachers have been careful not to destroy a symbolism which served to stimulate the imaginative complex out of which the intuitive religious vision emerges; but they have given to these symbols a new interpretation that entirely transforms their spiritual and intellectual significance and lifts them clear out of their animistic heritage. The working distinction is therefore between those for whom an animistic symbol still carries its animistic associations, and those for whom it has acquired a new and higher significance. It is the crudest materialism to suppose that any symbol always and necessarily carries its primitive associations with it. Thus in Islam reverence for the Black Stone, originally an animistic symbol, was transposed by Muhammad into a rite associated with the worship of the One God, just as the Christian Eucharist transposed the Temple sacrifices and pagan sacrificial meal.

Nevertheless, it is undeniable that in the structure of religious thought amongst all Muslim peoples there still subsists something of the attitudes and beliefs derived from primitive animism. The numerous works on folk-beliefs of the Muslims of North Africa, Egypt, Syria and Indonesia supply ample confirmation of this statement. It will be enough here to quote some unpublished notes on Islam in India written about thirty years ago by Sir Thomas Arnold, a scholar whose long and familiar acquaintance with the Muslims of India, sympathy with Islam, and accuracy of statement are not open to question, though it is possible, of course, that some of the customs he relates have since died out.

Muhammadan India is full of such survivals, in spite of the constant efforts of the orthodox teachers of Islam to root them out. First, there are those survivals of local cults, where some shrine has continued to be a centre of religious worship, though the name of the god or the saint has been changed, as the earlier faith has disappeared before the triumphant advance of the other. This has frequently happened in the case of Buddhist shrines in the North West of India, and still more so in Kashmir.

But apart from such cults, there are survivals where no attempt is made to conceal the real character of the Hindu observance or belief. In Western India, for example, there are Muhammadans of the working classes, such as brick-layers, stone-masons, gardeners, butchers and others, who openly visit and offer vows to Hindu gods; they seldom visit a mosque, and rarely perform any Muslim rite, except circumcision; they wear the same dress as their old Hindu caste-fellows—and this in a country in which distinctions of creed usually express themselves in some characteristically different costume. Most of them believe in the goddess Satvai, the goddess who registers the destiny of a child on the sixth night after birth; they believe also in the goddess Mariai (i.e., Mother Death), who is worshipped to save them from cholera,—in Mahasoba, the guardian deity of the field, to whom husbandmen offer a fowl or a goat at harvest time or when the new ploughing season begins.

The worship of Sitala, the dreaded goddess of smallpox, is widespread amongst the poorer classes all over India; her cult is kept up especially by women; and in the villages of the Eastern Punjab, for example, a Muhammadan mother in such a class who had not sacrificed to Sitala would feel that she had wantonly endangered the life of her child.

In Bengal there are even Muhammadans who join in the worship

of the Sun and offer libations as Hindus do, and Muhammadan cultivators who make offerings to the tutelary deity of the village, before sowing
their rice. The Bengali Hindus and Muhammadans sometimes meet at
the same shrine, invoking the same object of worship, though under
different names: thus, the Satya Narain of the Hindu is the Satya Pir
of the Bengali Musalman. In one district of Bengal, the Sonthal Parganas,
Muhammadans are often seen carrying sacred water to the shrine of the
god Baidyanath, and, as they are not allowed to enter the temple, they
pour it as a libation outside. It is remarkable too how many of the low-
caste Muhammadans join in the national festival of the Bengali Hindus
—the Durga Puja, and Muhammadan poets have even composed hymns
in honour of this goddess.

The persistence of such superstitions carries implications
which are often forgotten, or insufficiently appreciated, in Western
Europe and North America. It is easy for those, both within Islam
and outside it, who have attained to a more rational understanding of natural processes to despise them. But merely to despise
them is to overlook their effects and potentialities. In the first
place, there is an obvious kinship between these attitudes and
ideas and the animism of the pagan Arabs. Face to face with them,
the position and function of Islam today is practically what it was
in the time of Muhammad. There is nothing new or unusual in
this situation; it merely furnishes a contemporary and striking
illustration of the continuity and uniformity of the problems
which have confronted Muslim teachers throughout the centuries.
The facts of history and geography decreed that both in its origins
and in its later development Islam has had to grapple more
immediately and more consistently with the irrationality of simple animism than with the skepticism and refined infidelities of a
self-confident reason which have confronted Christianity.

But such superstitions are by no means the only, nor the
most dangerous, legacies of animism. It scarcely needs to be
stressed at this time that the animistic substrate is not peculiar to
the peoples who profess Islam. Animism, with its fears, its irrationality, and its imaginative powers, lies in the subconsciousness of
every historic faith, because it is part of the inescapable heritage
of mankind, the legacy of those 500,000 years which lie behind the
5,000 years of religious development. It is a prime function of
religion to discipline and to control these primitive survivals

which haunt the background of our conscious existence. Their impulses, which without religious direction remain subjective and anarchical, are governed and directed in and through religion towards less egocentric ends; and the irrational fears which loom so large in animistic attitudes are transformed into ethical and religious reverence. The "higher" a religion, that is to say, the more universal its terms of thought, the more it directs the imagination from the self-regarding interests, in which animistic survivals are strongest, to universal objectives.

But this can be achieved by religion only because religion itself springs from and remains essentially a part of the imaginative life. Reason may and does reinforce the controls exerted by religion over these impulses, but cannot itself control, and still less transform, them, because the life of the imagination is independent of the reason. When reason has attempted to take over sole control, all experience hitherto has shown that the imaginative impulses, no longer channeled in fertilizing streams by the forces and insights of religion, break out, among all peoples, in violent and capricious forms and cling, in spite of all that reason can do, to the most irrational symbols.

No truly living religion has ever lost sight of these facts, or disregarded its function of sublimating the subliminal. Christianity affirmed and affirms still the doctrine of original sin. Although Islam officially rejects it as a dogma, the theme of *al-nafs al-ammara*, the uncontrolled appetitive soul, runs through all its religious and ethical literature. And since Islam, during the whole of its existence, has been closely engaged in the struggle with simple animism, the persistence of this conflict has continuously oriented the main axes of its religious life and outlook in directions which differ, sometimes widely, from those of Christianity.

At the same time, this struggle itself, and the constant absorption of converts from animistic environments, have contributed to maintain in it an intense conviction of the nearness and reality of the unseen world. The imaginative powers, released from the tyranny of irrational fears and earth-bound egocentrism by the willing acceptance of its controls, have gained within Islam a new dimension of intuitive insight and illumination. Not only so, but this in turn, through the effort to reach a fuller comprehension of the truths thus intuitively visualized, has laid the foundations for a parallel expansion of the intellectual powers.

II · Muhammad and the Koran

In the section just preceding it was suggested that, already before the beginning of Muhammad's preaching, the old Arabian religions with their tribal fetishes no longer satisfied the religious emotions and insights of many of the Arabs. There is a clear indication of this in the abandonment of local shrines and the growing practice of pilgrimage to central shrines venerated by groups of tribes (of which the Kaba at Mecca was one of the most important). At these common shrines, the presence of multitudes engaged in common rituals of worship seems to have generated a feeling of religious exaltation which reflected still more unfavorably on the tribal religions. Although the rites of pilgrimage appear to have retained their animistic character and associations, the existence of a common shrine implies the recognition of some common divinity. It is evident from many indications that—whether owing to the influence of Jewish and Christian infiltrations or to other causes—there was already in Arabia a general recognition of a supreme God, called vaguely Al-Ilah (or in shortened form, Allah), "The God."

This is important as showing that Muhammad's preaching was preceded (as might be expected on grounds of historical analogy) by an evolution of ideas, a kind of *praeparatio evangelica*. But it is clear also that the conception of a supreme God was still vague and confused, entangled with animistic superstitions, and unrelated to any ethical or teleological concepts or to ideas of a future life. The revolution wrought by Muhammad was to lift the conception of Allah clear of all naturalistic entanglements, to present Him not only as the Supreme God, but as the Only God, and moreover as Creator of the heavens and the earth and all that is in and between them, including mankind and jinn, as well as final Judge, to whom mankind and jinn must render account of all their actions.

Thus, at one stroke, the religious horizon of the Arabs was

elevated above all visible, earth-bound, or personal objects to one unseen, all-powerful, and transcendent Being. But this was clearly not enough. In order to sustain the conception of God at this new height, so immensely above everything that the Arab mind had hitherto imagined, it had to be supported, as it were, by a scaffolding of congruent religious ideas and attitudes. This was, indeed, the main problem faced by Muhammad, as by every great original thinker. The whole of the religious life and thought of a people had to be reconstructed. And it was not only for the other Arabs that this reconstruction was needed; it was also, and primarily, for Muhammad himself. In his case, however, the reconstruction was from above downwards; starting from the vision of Allah as Judge Supreme and Omnipotent Creator, he intuitively deduced step by step the necessary stages through which they, in their upward ascent, could attain at length to share his conviction.

The Koran is the record and instrument of this process of reconstruction of religious thought. There were two sides to it; one, the negative side, which involved the rooting out of all animistic associations from worship and belief; the other, the substitution of a positive monotheistic interpretation of the universe and everything in it. To a certain extent these two aspects could be separated out in the teaching of the Koran. The prohibition of "dedicating" certain categories of animals or of playing with divining-arrows are pure examples of the first; the emphatic assertion of God's creation of the world is an almost pure example of the second.

But for the most part the two aspects are interconnected. In view of the argument put forward in the first section of this chapter, this was not only the natural process, but the only truly effective one. Like other religious teachers, Muhammad, so far from attempting to impose on the minds of his fellow countrymen a new and strange complex of ideas, preserved the religious symbolism of his people, with all its inherited power to stimulate their imaginative faculties, but transposed it from an animistic to a monotheistic frame of reference.

The treatment of the concept of *baraka* in the Koran is particularly enlightening. The noun is never employed in the singular, but in the plural only, and God Himself is the sole and

direct source of all *barakat*. The same applies to all its cognates;
the frequent use of *tabaraka* in glorifying God; the active *baraka*
to express God's conferring *baraka* upon persons or things; and
the participle *mubarak* to describe persons or things upon whom
God has conferred *baraka* or the power to confer *baraka*. There
is no need to deny formally the existence of any kind of *baraka*
which derives from any source but God; once the concept *baraka*
has been identified in thought and feeling with the concept *Allah*,
any other association of ideas becomes unthinkable.

With this goes a reinterpretation of the jinn. Neither their
existence nor their malevolence is denied. But they are no longer
self-determining, irrational forces; they are the creatures of God,
and work His will, however strange and inexplicable their actions
may seem to men. By their identification with the *shayatin* or
devils, they are, so to speak, rationalized, and serve in their turn
to rationalize the mysterious evils and misfortunes that befall
men, by linking them up somehow with the all-disposing decree of
God.

The most familiar and obvious example of this rededication
of religious symbolism is, however, the Meccan Pilgrimage. It
might also be called the most successful example. Belief in the
animistic *baraka* and in the irrationality of the jinn maintained
themselves in spite of the teaching and influence of the Koran,
but the universal testimony seems to confirm that in all its rites
the pilgrimage is performed with a single-minded devotion to
Allah on the part of all participants. No doubt, as the traveler Ibn
Jubair already pointed out, there are differences of understanding
and differences of conduct among the worshippers, but these do
not affect the true unity of purpose.

These examples are typical of the method of the Koran
throughout. The mercantile ideas and institutions of the Meccans
and the processes of agriculture are, like the dominant ideas of
animism, captured and transformed into instruments for driving
home the conviction of a supreme controlling power. But in order
that the impact of this conviction might not be weakened, it was
equally important to leave no loophole for confusion or controversy on the nature of the supreme power. The scientific mind,
whose attitudes are determined by the heritage of Greek thought,

finds such a controlling power in natural law, which is then equated by the religious intuition with the Law of God. Muhammad, whose intuitive vision was not circumscribed by Greek thought, implicitly rejected any concept of natural law and envisaged the controlling power in the personality of an all-powerful God, *la sharika lahu,* sole and unrestricted by any kind of association. That this was to Muhammad himself a crucial point is obvious from the prominence which the Koran gives to denouncing *shirk,* the sin of imagining any kind of association with God, not merely of Christian trinitarianism; and rightly so, since, once the teaching is accepted, all other conceivable forms of worship, such as star-worship for example, simply wither away.

But this is only a beginning. Belief in a controlling personal God may well be fortified by rededication of ritual and by providing new frames of reference for familiar concepts. They provide the scaffolding of congruent ideas; it remains to build a scaffolding of congruent attitudes. The fears which seem to lie at the heart of animistic religion may possibly be transformed into religious awe, but between awe and the reverence which issues in true piety there is a transition which it is not easy to make. It is difficult even to put it into words, but it may be roughly defined by saying that reverence requires, in addition to awe, two things: a sense of the goodness of God, and a sense of personal relation to God.

Here again Muhammad boldly took over the old animistic terms and reinterpreted them. *Taqwa* meant originally the guarding of oneself against the wrath of the divinity by taking steps to propitiate it, and its verb *ittaqa* is still employed in the Koran in that sense. The prior evolution of these words as technical religious terms is still unknown; but the occurrence of *taqwa* as early as Sura 96, v.12, suggests an established usage. Possibly, therefore, *taqwa* had already acquired the sense of religious awe. For Muhammad himself its foundation was fear of the Judgment Day and of hell fire, and his insistence upon this as fundamental in the religious life is reflected in the dominant place which it held in the thought of later generations. But while *taqwa* never lost this association with fear of hell, by the later suras of the Koran it has clearly come to mean also reverence in the wider sense, and in two particularly significant passages (5, 3 and 58, 10) it is conjoined with *birr* to denote that relationship to God which issues in willing obedience and motivates all good works.

The stress laid by the Koran on the goodness of God, linked up explicitly or implicitly with the familiar term *barakat,* is too obvious to require exposition. Mere intellectual assent, however, is not enough. God's goodness must be felt with such intensity that it calls out the emotion of gratitude. If the feeling of awe and the sense of gratitude to God are to become real influences in the believer's life, they must be inseparable from all his thinking; hence the insistent and reiterated summons to *dhikr,* the recollection of God, in all conjunctions and at all seasons. And since, for the mass of men, *dhikr* is facilitated by, and possibly even requires, the stimulus of regular bodily exercises at set times, both *taqwa* and *birr* involve the punctual performance of the ritual prayers, *salat.*

The disciplinary value of the prostrations has often been remarked, and is not to be overlooked; but discipline is valuable not so much for itself as for what it leads to. It is not improbable that the most important part of the *salat* is precisely that part which is so often neglected in descriptions of the ritual, the few moments of quiet meditation and supplication that follow after the end of the prostrations. The latter are, so to speak, the exercises which, by impressing a spirit of humility and devotion upon the mind of the worshipper, allow him to enter into communion with God, and so to attain to that personal relation which transfigures all thought and governs all action.

The attitude or character which results from this relationship is called *birr,* one of the most striking of Muhammad's revaluations of terms. In its secular use, the root indicates the paternal and filial relation, with its attitudes of affection, obedience, and loyalty. To Muhammad, as to all other prophetic teachers, the test of true belief lay in character and works. If the repeated insistence of the Koran upon good works were not enough, it would be conclusively proved by the comprehensive definition of *birr* in the noble verse, Sura 2, 172: not only belief in God, the Last Day, the angels, the Scripture and the prophets, but charity to all for the love of God, steadfastness in prayers, loyalty to the plighted word, and patience under all afflictions—these are the qualities that mark out the truly believing and the truly God-fearing. *Birr* is thus the crown of true belief, when the believer at last realizes and responds to the ever-presence of God in all his thoughts and conduct.

This, then, is the message which the Koran conveyed to the first generation of Muslims and has conveyed to all generations ever since. It is a record of direct living experience of God, both absolutely and in relation to the common affairs of life, and a summons so to order one's life as to be able to share it. By following its precepts, by striving to grasp, not with his intelligence only but with his heart and soul, the spirit of its teaching, the Muslim seeks to recapture something of the intuitive vision and of the experience of the beloved Prophet. The significance of its every phrase is enhanced for him by his belief that it is the literal Word of God, yet even if this were not an article of doctrine its value to him as a living source of religious inspiration and insight would scarcely be affected.

From this point of view (which is the essential one) the question of the sources of Muhammad's doctrines, which so greatly interests Christian and Jewish scholars in the west, is entirely irrelevant. Learned Jewish scholars have demonstrated that many or most of the sayings attributed to Jesus in the Gospels are recorded in Hebrew writings as the sayings of one or other of the great rabbis, but this does not alter the fact that the structure of even primitive Christian thought is entirely distinct from that of Judaism. Similarly, whatever Islam may have incorporated of earlier religious ideas does not alter the fact that the religious attitudes expressed in and mediated by the Koran constitute a new and distinctive religious structure.

It is essential to bear in mind also that the Koran is not a work of theology, in the sense that theology is a rational philosophic interpretation of the universe based upon or harmonized with the data of religious intuition. To be sure, intuition itself implies an interpretation of the universe, but it is the direct vision of a seer, to whom the principles of world order (which the Koran calls *al-hikma*) present themselves in a series of concrete images or symbols, and their application is linked up with concrete events. The intuitive mind does not ask, like the philosopher, "What is goodness, truth, or beauty?" It asserts "This particular action in these particular circumstances is good, that is evil; this is just, that is unjust." The Koran appeals therefore primarily to the religious imagination and only afterwards to the intellect. But, as was pointed out in the first section, it remains true that, in spite of the development of a systematic Islamic theology by later scholars, the great body of the Muslim community was composed of peoples among whom such an intuitive approach to the truths of religion exerted a far stronger and more immediate influence than any quantity or subtlety of rational argument.

Since, however, all religion remains at bottom linked up with the imaginative life, it cannot touch the soul without some kind of appeal to the senses and emotions. If the senses are not alert and its rituals and symbols evoke no emotional response, religion may exist as a body of dogmatic and ethical teachings, but it will lack soul and vision. Art is not only the handmaid of religion, but the doorkeeper of its inmost shrine.

So too with the Muslim. What gives the Koran its power to move men's hearts and mold their lives is not its bare content of doctrine and exhortation, but its vivid frame of words. Like the prophetic books of the Old Testament, it speaks in the language of poetry, though not tied to the external yokes of meter and rhyme. If by poetry one means the almost magical disposition of words so that they echo and re-echo in the mind, opening up long vistas to the inner eye and creating in the spirit an exaltation that lifts it clear above the material world and illuminates it with a sudden radiance, that is just what the Koran means to the Muslim. That this is no mere speculation is proved not only by personal experience, but by the fact that the dogma of *ijaz*, the incomparability or miracle of the Koran, rests as much on its artistic and aesthetic qualities as on its substantial contents.

I have tried elsewhere to analyze the roots of this Muslim susceptibility to linguistic artistry, and need not repeat the argument here. One further point may be added, however. Just as the Christian Church invoked the aid of music to heighten the emotional tension of its religious services, so too Islam developed the art of musical recitation of the Koran to intensify its imaginative and emotional appeal. The difference between the musical

arts of the two religions is so striking that it might well furnish the
theme of an interesting analysis; but it ought not to obscure the
fact that the ultimate end is the same in both.

It is not surprising that the Muslim cannot find in any other
sacred book anything of this poetical and emotional quality, this
power to sustain and strengthen the faculty of intuitive vision,
the upward leap of the mind and spirit to grasp in concrete experience the reality behind the fleeting phenomena of the material
world. Yet even this is not all. Indissolubly linked with the Koran,
and supplementing the rational appeal of its teachings and the
imaginative appeal of its language by the warmer emotions of
human affection, stands the figure of Muhammad himself.

It would be difficult to exaggerate the strength and the effects
of the Muslim attitude toward Muhammad. Veneration for the
Prophet was a natural and inevitable feeling, both in his own day
and later, but this is more than veneration. The personal relationships of admiration and love which he inspired in his associates
have echoed down the centuries, thanks to the instruments which
the community created in order to evoke them afresh in each
generation.

The earliest of these instruments was the narration of
hadith. So much has been written about the legal and theological
functions of the *hadith* that its more personal and religious aspects
have been almost overlooked. It is true, to be sure, that the necessity of finding an authoritative source which would supplement
the legal and ethical prescriptions contained in the Koran led to
a search for examples set by Muhammad in his daily life and
practice. One could be certain that if he had said this or that, done
this or that, approved this or that action, one had an absolutely
reliable guide to the right course to adopt in any similar situation.
And it is equally true that this search went far beyond the limits
of credibility or simple rectitude, and that it was in due course
theologically rationalized by the doctrine of implicit inspiration.

But in its origins it was the natural outgrowth of simple
piety and personal loyalty, and it has always remained so outside
theological and legal circles—and within them also. Indeed, the
existence of this attitude among the members of the community
in general is the necessary presupposition of the rise of the legal

and theological attitudes. It began, in all probability, in Muhammad's own lifetime, and one of its purposes (possibly even its primary purpose) was to preserve and pass on to later generations the portrait and personality of the man Muhammad. Without the *hadith* he would in course of time have become, if not a distant, at least a generalized figure in their historical and religious background. The *hadith*, presenting his human existence in an exuberant mass of living and concrete detail, not only set before Muslims a minute picture of human life as it should be lived, but, still more, linked them to him in the same close personal relationship as that enjoyed by the first companions, a relationship which, so far from weakening, has grown with the centuries. The figure of Muhammad has never become formalized and institutionalized; and it is hardly an exaggeration to say that the warmth of this personal feeling for the beloved Prophet has long been the most vital element in the religion of the Muslim masses, at least among the Sunnis.

The force of this current in Muslim religious thought can be seen by the variety of forms in which it found expression. In the early centuries it swelled the mass of Tradition by transferring to the Prophet many elements from the religious heritage of Christianity and even of Buddhism (as distinct from the multiplication of legal and theological *hadiths*). But later, Muslim piety found other and freer means of expression than the *hadith*, with its somewhat rigid and scholastic framework, could supply. On the purely literary side there were the many *siras* or biographies, of which those written in our own time by several eminent Muslim writers are not the least remarkable; works on the evidences of Muhammad's prophethood (*dalail*) and his personality (*shamail*); and a multitude of other works in both prose and verse, particularly the *qasidas* or panegyrical odes, of which the *Burdah* of al-Busiri is the most famous.

Popular as many of these were and are, however, their circulation and influence were far outranged amongst all sections and classes by the hymns and chants composed by sufis in honor of the Prophet, and especially those which entered into sufi devotions on public occasions. The ecstatic beauty of many of these sufi hymns[3] grips the heart and mind with a power comparable to that of the Koran itself; but even much more mediocre compositions could, in an atmosphere of collective enthusiasm, generate similar effects and emotions. The ceremonial veneration of Muhammad, initiated and popularized throughout the Muslim world by the sufis, corresponded so exactly to the feelings and devotional needs of Muslims that they have survived even among the classes which are no longer attracted to Sufism. Formal family festivals continue to be rounded off with ceremonies and recitations in honor of the Prophet, and they are enthusiastically observed by the whole community on the day celebrated as the birthday of the Prophet (*mawlid annabi*, 12th Rabi al-awwal). Modernists and traditionalists, sufis, Salafis, ulama and Muslims of no label at all meet together here on common ground. In their intellectual attitudes there may be the widest diversity, but in devotion and affection to Muhammad they are one.

III　Law and Theology

The Koran, as the previous section sought to show, is the record of the intuitive experience of Muhammad on the one hand, and on the other, the fountain to which the Muslim returns again and again to refresh his spiritual vision. From the historical angle, no doubt, it is to be regarded as the source from which all subsequent Islamic ethics and theology were drawn. But true though this statement is, it is rather a simplification of the truth. In matters of faith and belief the Koran contains no philosophic or organized exposition. What it does is to transform religious thinking by setting new ideals before it and supplying for its contemplation new realities and new symbols, and to redirect the religious life by setting new objectives before it and supplying new channels for its practical activities. But the end still remains the intuitive experience to which the Koran bears witness, and the relations of that experience to the data of the practical intelligence or reason is not yet a problem.

It was some time, in fact, before it became a problem. The first questions and difficulties with which the growing Muslim community was faced as it began to absorb numbers of adherents of widely differing spiritual and intellectual capacities (a process which, it must be remembered, began already in Medina) were not dogmatic and theological, but practical. They were problems of personal relationships within the newly organized society, which was gaining and continued to gain what was, from the religious point of view, an even embarrassing success. They were, in a word, ethical problems.

It was now that the rituals and "acts of devotion" which were prescribed in the Koran proved their value. By their rigid and compulsory character they provided a social, as well as religious, steel frame. Their observance was the external sign of membership of the Muslim community, and to observe them called for not only social discipline, but also self-discipline. During its first century the Muslim religious community presents, in general, the features of an ethical society; it is little troubled with theological questions, and its saints are ascetics, not seers. It is remarkable to observe how much of this has survived as a permanent element in Islam and remains to this day characteristic of Muslim societies, particularly those whose Muslim consciousness is heightened by contrast with neighboring non-Muslim societies.

The term "ethical society" must not, however, be misunderstood. Its ethics are still revealed ethics, not the product of rational speculations or of social experience. Their authority and validity are derived from the belief that they conform to the will of an all-controlling personal God, the motive behind them is ideally one of religious devotion, their sanctions are supernatural and eschatological. It was only gradually, and rather sporadically, that the influence of social pressures came in to reinforce them against the lax or the non-conforming.

The fact that the source of Muslim ethics was religious intuition, transmitting a divine revelation to mankind, was all-important also for the structure of Muslim society. Viewed in the light of the ultimate principle which regulates human existence, all human institutions take on a new significance. They are not immaterial to the religious life; they either express or do not express the Will of God for men, and they either conduce or do not conduce to a life of true submission to God.

The priority of these practical ethical questions over the

problems presented by the speculative reason is shown already by the Koran, which lays down rules, sometimes in great detail, for the fundamental institutions of society, such as marriage, kinship, inheritance, economic activity, warfare. Since the Koranic precepts fell far short of sufficing for all the problems which arose in community life, the need to supplement them from some authoritative source was met, as is well known, by recourse to the *hadith*. The demands which the social problems of an ethical society made upon the example of its founder were, indeed, almost inexhaustible, and led to the expansion, multiplication and production of traditions on a wide scale. But there was no escape from this. It was felt to be indispensable that the public life of the Muslim community—in so far as it was, or was to be made, truly Muslim—should rest upon the Koran, as interpreted through and expanded by the sayings credibly attributed to the Prophet. So deep and strong was this conviction that to define explicitly the ethics, norms and usages of public life became, after the salvation of their own souls, the chief occupation of the religious leaders of the community, and it was the product of their insight (*fiqh*) that furnished the materials of Islamic law.

Islamic law is the typical product of an ethical society. In principle—and in practice also at the outset—it is not distinguished from doctrine. It is only at a later stage that they diverge, the one, as theology, to set out the logical and philosophical arguments for monotheism, the other, as law, to define or lay down its practical consequences in the way of *duties*. This is a first characteristic feature of Islamic law, that it is a doctrine of duties and that the duties of which it takes cognizance are of two kinds: duties towards God (right belief and the observance of the acts of religious obligation) and duties towards one's fellow men. But since the latter also are laid down by God, either explicitly or implicitly, there is no real distinction between them.

Again, it is characteristic of the practical function and non-speculative origin of Islamic law that the jurists are little interested in general principles. The foundation of the law was the body of concrete obligations declared in the Koran. On this foundation and with the aid of the materials incorporated in the *hadith*, the business of the legist was to draw out the rules of conduct, public and private (as we should say), but exclusively in similar concrete terms. After examination of each specific case, its ethical category was determined in terms of the five-degree scale of ethico-religious values: obligatory, recommended, permitted or neutral, disapproved, forbidden.

A third significant feature is that for the first three centuries this task of legal definition and classification absorbed the intellectual energies of the Muslim community to an unparalleled degree. Not only theologians, traditionists and practical administrators, but also philologists, historians, men of letters, contributed their quota to the corpus of legal literature and the discussion of legal issues. Seldom, if ever, has law penetrated so deeply into the life and thought of a community as it did in the early Muslim civilization.

So intense a concentration of thought inevitably produced disputes over details and sometimes over major issues that were bitter and prolonged. But through all this the Koran exerted a steadying and moderating influence; face to face with its authority no private opinion could be maintained as absolutely valid. All were plainly subordinate to a supreme power, and the fact of common allegiance to that power made all but extreme fanatics conscious of their community. Even sectarian divisions arising out of political and theological differences did not disturb the basic unity of legal attitudes and methods. Although at a later stage Shiite law diverged from Sunni norms to some extent, Sunni and Shiite jurists are scarcely to be distinguished in the early centuries. It was this sense of unity, based upon the Koran, in all the things that mattered most which led the great majority of Muslims first to that remarkable compromise, the toleration of differences in matters of detail, and finally to the realization that where a community is united on the main issues, the existence of differences is an enrichment of community life, to be accepted with gratitude as one of God's *barakat*. And conversely, it was the rejection of this community consciousness which led the Shia into sterile opposition.

It is almost impossible to overestimate the influence on Muslim religious thought of this legal activity. Once the science and structure of law were established, they not only supplied a rigid frame for the Muslim ideals of ethical duty and human relations (with the slight element of flexibility allowed by the four schools), but the law itself, the Sharia, defined once and for all the constitution of the Muslim Community. The Sharia to the Muslim stands for all that the Constitution stands for to the United States of America and more. It established norms for all Muslim institutions and societies, which have ever since remained the sheet-anchor of Muslim culture through the many and terrible vicissitudes of later centuries; it expressed and went far to creating a united Muslim community, in spite of political fragmentation and conflict; and it is still, notwithstanding all the criticisms of Muslim modernists and reformers, the sole embodiment of what would otherwise be a merely formal unity of faith among all Muslims.

The very immensity of this task of creating and establishing such a unity of law and community of culture required the dedication to it of a large proportion of the vital energies of the community. It constituted, without doubt, the greatest challenge to the Muslim civilization, and also its greatest achievement, however incomplete. It involved its leaders in a long and severe struggle to eliminate all conflicting legal systems and customary usages amongst the wide range of peoples who entered the *Dar al-Islam*, a struggle in which they enjoyed only limited support from their temporal rulers and not even always the support of their religious organizations, as we shall see in the next section. It was a task never fully accomplished. From the very first, the Sharia, as administered in the Muslim states, was modified (or, in the eyes of the pious, adulterated) by the addition or substitution of administrative rulings, and at the present day it is menaced by the growth and expansion of Western codes and courts of law. Yet, just as the peoples of Western Christendom always acknowledged a moral law, though they might not always observe it, so all orthodox Muslims regard the Sharia as setting the perfect standard for human society, although their own practice may fall short of it.

To reject the Sharia *in principle* is therefore in some sense apostasy, a fact which explains the shock felt by Muslims all over the world by the action of the Turkish Republic in abolishing the Sharia outright. And it is probably a true conviction, if still an

intuitive one, that respect for the Sharia (which need not necessarily imply respect for each and every one of the medieval interpretations and constructions) remains the core of Muslim social
thinking, and that with the maintenance of the Sharia is linked
the survival or disappearance of Islam as an organized system.

The same practical outlook and dislike or suspicion of intellectual subtlety characterized the evolution of orthodox theology. But again one must be on one's guard against misconcep-
tions. The danger of intellectual subtlety lies not in the use of the
intelligence, but in the abuse of it; more especially it may lead to
self-confidence or to simple surrender to the pleasure of intellectual exercise, and both are forms of infidelity. The one is irreconcilable with the Muslim duty of humility before God, the second
converts thinking about God into a kind of sport.

These dangers were brought home to the orthodox leaders
in a peculiarly vivid and direct way during the first and second
centuries. Professor Tritton's chapter on the early sects in his
work on *Muslim Theology* gives a striking picture of the incredible confusion, multiplicity, and often absurdity of the ideas
which were ventilated when Islam emerged into the clamor of the
Hellenistic world and found itself enveloped in an atmosphere of
theological controversy. The only way to keep one's feet and one's
faith was to fall back on the Koran and reject all intellectual constructions with a *bila kaif*. Nothing perhaps demonstrates more
decisively the degree to which the Koran had already gripped and
molded the Muslim mind than the observation that throughout
this critical period the great body of the community never seems
to have wavered. There is a saying quoted by Professor Tritton
and attributed to Amir ash-Shabi which sums up, with deep feeling and insight, the position and duty of the true Muslim: "Love
an upright Muslim and an upright man of the Banu Hashim, but
be not a Shii; hope for what you do not know, but be not a Murji;
know that good comes from God and evil from the self, but be not
a Qadari; love all whom you see doing good, even a slit-eared
Sindi."

Moreover, the time was not yet ripe for theology. It is the
simple truth that the intuitive type of mind is incapable of rational theologizing. Before a Muslim theology, in the strict sense,

could be elaborated, it was necessary for some Muslims, at least, to learn logic and philosophy; and the habit of philosophical discourse is not learned in one day or one generation. Orthodox theology therefore began, as one would expect, by simple protest against or negation of heretical views, or simple statement of orthodox views on disputed questions, without adducing any arguments at all. Indeed, the earliest compendium of orthodox positions explicitly asserts the intuitive as against the theological approach: "Insight (*fiqh*) in matters of religion is better than insight in matters of knowledge and law."[4]

But this position was radically altered by the sweeping movement of Aristotelianism which is associated with the rise of Mutazilite theology. The story of the refusal of the orthodox at first to enter the lists, and of their subsequent change of attitude and the victory of their Asharite and Maturidite champions, is too well known to need repetition. I suspect that it was not quite so simple an affair as it is often represented; there was a whole century of hard thinking behind it, though, even so, the victory was won not by the side that had the strongest philosophical position, but by the side whose logical arguments reflected the overwhelming mass of public opinion.

From this evolution of orthodox theology followed several important consequences, whose effects were felt through the whole range of Islamic thought, religious and non-religious, and persist in Islam down to the present day. The first arises from the fact that theology is, in its own field, a scientific discipline, working with rational concepts and using scientific tools, namely logic and physics. This in itself put an end to all that swarming of fantastic ideas which had preceded the formulation of the orthodox theology. It was not that the orthodox theology killed them; it was the discipline of thought behind it that drove them out and made it impossible for such fantasies ever to appear again in Muslim religious thinking. The intuitive imagination was at last balanced and corrected by a rational understanding of the universe and, as I have pointed out elsewhere, Islam came to terms with scientific method and modes of thought.

In the second place, and most significantly for the future of Islam, this rationalization of thought in matters of religion (which was only one aspect of a general rationalization of thought in all departments of Muslim culture) was based upon Aristotelian foundations. This meant that intellectual life in Islam came to rest upon the same foundations as the intellectual life of the Western world, as distinct from the foundations of Indian or Chinese thought. The fact of Koranic monotheism and its relations to Jewish and Christian monotheism had, no doubt, given Islam a certain bias in this direction, but this in itself would not have been enough to create an identity of logical reasoning. As important, however, as the fact of the original Aristotelian impact is the further fact that its incorporation in Islamic theology maintained a rational core of thought in face of this reaction and through the succeeding period of cultural decay. Consequently, it is largely due to the labors of Muslim theologians that in its basic reasoning processes Islam as a whole stands on the same side of the watershed as the West. There is no need to point out how greatly this has facilitated the interchange of ideas between the two civilizations both in the Middle Ages and in modern times.

A third consequence was that the theological system formulated with the aid of Aristotelian logic, because it was founded on a scientific discipline, remained remarkably stable and showed itself capable of withstanding all the pressures of sufistic and animistic impulses in later centuries. If the Koran was and is the living heart of Islam, the theology of the scholastics, backed by Islamic law, constituted its backbone. However weakened it seemed to be at times by compromise with sufistic and pantheistic tendencies, it never abandoned its central positions and always in the end reasserted the supremacy of its transcendentalist doctrine. It is probable, for example, that it was only the firm opposition of theology that prevented the universal devotion to Muhammad from passing into adoration and worship. It is certain that it was only because of the clear and firm limits set by theology that the emotional and imaginative exuberance of later Sufism was disciplined and furnished with a positive religious content. When one looks back at the fantasies of early sectarian thinking and imagines what might have happened had the Sufi movement arisen directly out of that stage of thought, one can measure what Islam and the world owe to the Mutazila and al-Ashari.

Important, however, as were these historical consequences, it is perhaps more relevant to the subject of this paper to appreciate the effects upon Islamic theology itself, and upon its function in the living structure of Muslim religious thought, of the principles upon which the system was elaborated. The central doctrine of the Koran is, of course, an uncompromising unitarianism. At the same time that it rejects the animism of the Arabs, the Koran rejects the conception of mediators between God and man, at least in this world. "In thus setting man as it were face to face with God, without any mediating spiritual or personal elements, Islam necessarily emphasized the contrast between God and man. In spite of the passages of mystical intuition in the Koran, the dogmatic derived from it could not but start from the postulate of the opposition between God and man, and (as a necessary corollary) the equality of all men in their creaturely relation to God. In this stark contrast lies, indeed, the religious tension which is the characteristic original feature of Islam."[5]

But the contrast might have become less absolute in Islamic theology had not Muslim Aristotelianism stopped short at logic and physics. *Arabic* Aristotelianism went on into metaphysics, but not *Muslim* rationalism. This is not difficult to understand. Monotheism of any kind raises grave philosophical difficulties, and the more absolute the monotheism, the more difficult they become to resolve. Perhaps, indeed, the structure of philosophical thought which Islam and Europe alike inherited from the Greeks can never supply a completely adequate or even consistent metaphysical explanation of monotheism. But leaving that aside, it seems clear that the Muslim theologians, as soon as they realized where philosophy, in the strict sense, might lead them, drew back. Consequently, Muslim scholasticism is almost exclusively logical; it never attacks the real philosophical problems; and, lacking that leaven of philosophic skepticism which restrains an excessive reliance upon logic, developed the doctrine of "difference" to the limits of negation.

On the philosophical level there would always have remained some doubts as to the absolute sufficiency of any given postulate. In more modern expression we should recognize that in every verbalization of an idea there is an element of metaphor or symbolism which, when dragged this way and that by the permutations and combinations of syllogistic reasoning, may ultimately lead to absurd conclusions. But a theologian is, almost by definition, a person who accepts as positive realities the symbols in which any religious experience has been verbalized. And for the Muslim theologians this tendency was strengthened by the doctrine that the Koran was the very Word of God, and hence exempt from the limitations attaching to human speech. Given then the Koranic conception of God as absolute will in activity, and the Koranic statements as absolute postulates, the theology worked out with the aid of Greek logic and physics could not but stress the unimaginable transcendence of God. The slightly more philosophical Mutazila had attempted to introduce a moderating element of Greek rationalism, but in reaction against them the orthodox refused to admit of any limitations whatsoever upon the power and will of God, or that terms derived from human experience were applicable to Him.

Islamic theology is thus always forced into extreme positions. There can be no agent of any kind in the universe except God, since the existence of an agent implies the possibility of an action independent of God, and therefore a theoretical limitation on the absolute power of God. Nothing is therefore positively related to any other thing; all relationships are momentary and fleeting creations. There can be no stable universe of matter, only a multitude of atoms of space and of time, ceaselessly created and annihilated by the Will of God. There can be no causation in the strict sense, no necessary relation between something that goes before and another thing that comes after. As for ethics, nothing is incumbent upon God; our concepts are quite irrelevant to Him. He rewards and punishes as He wills and cannot be called to account.

This is not the place to attempt an analysis of Islamic theology; in any case, no simplified outlines could do any sort of justice to the voluminous, learned, and acute Muslim theological literature of the Middle Ages or of more recent times. But in attempting to estimate its function in the living religious thought of Muslims, we are faced with the problem of the relations between outer formulation and inner function or reality in the Islamic system. Since the two are seldom identical, we are constantly involved in a search for the clues which will allow us to penetrate even a little way below the first to the second, and to discover how they complement or correct one another.

Nowhere is this more necessary than in the field of doctrinal formulations. Sometimes, however, the theologians themselves supply the positive correction to their fundamentally negative dogmas. In the matter of causation, for example, they qualify the negation of necessary causation by asserting that in the manifestations of God's creative will there is a certain order and regularity. The Koran appeals frequently to God's "custom" (*sunna*) and asserts that there is no change to be found in it. Consequently, man is enabled to forecast the normal sequences of events which follow upon given actions, even if they may not strictly be called consequences.

Similarly, the doctrine of "acquisition" (*kasb*) looks very like an attempt to sidestep the dilemma which resulted from pressing the doctrine of predestination to its "logical conclusion." What it means, if I have understood it correctly, is that although everything *is* predestined and man has no power of action, yet psychologically he feels in himself a power of choice and so "acquires" the responsibility. Such an argument suggests that the theologians themselves were uneasy at times about the positions to which they were committed by their own methods of reasoning.

If these examples may be used to draw a general conclusion, the relationship between formulation and function would appear to be somewhat as follows. The orthodox doctrine, in its theological formulation, is the conclusion of a purely logical argument from the theoretical premise that no limitation can be placed upon the power of God. But it is not in itself the determinant of Muslim belief. It only gives a theoretical and rigid expression to the already existing *dominant* tendency both in those passages of the Koran which refer to the subject under discussion and in the intuitive apprehension of Muslims; that is to say, it is itself determined by the prevailing trend of Muslim feeling.

At the same time, however, the attempt to rationalize this feeling or belief not only exaggerates it, but ultimately even deforms it, because it leaves out of sight or discards altogether certain elements which, in the Koran or in the intuitive apprehension of the community, are simultaneously present, although subordinate. The dogma of predestination, for example, has to override the quite explicit affirmations of free will in the Koran, which, although definitely subordinated to the prevalent assertion of predestination, yet represent a valid element in religious experience. Hence the theological doctrine in general represents and sustains a dominant intellectual or intuitive attitude, which in the practice of the community is modified by the survival of the submerged idea and its continued influence.

The conclusion so derived from the analysis of particular statements of dogma may be applied in fine to the whole structure of dogmatic theology. Logically and syntactically unassailable, it remains a fixed and permanent element in the Muslim religious consciousness, sustaining, reinforcing, and, if need be, enforcing the conviction of the oneness and absolute power of God. To be sure, its direct effect, as in every theological system, is greater upon the thought of the religious leaders than upon the thought of the general community, but its influence, mediated through ulama, preachers, and teachers, affects and directs the religious attitudes of all faithful Muslims.

Yet, because of its ruthless logical development of the doctrine of "difference," it stood opposed to the spirit and meaning of those passages in the Koran which speak of the mystic indwelling of God in the universe and in man. The religious attitudes which it fostered were characterized more by dogmatism and intellectual conformity than by inner conviction sustained by the intuitive vision of the unseen called out by the Koran in the hearts of pious Muslims. By eliminating any relation between God and man, it dammed up the springs of religious experience. So monstrous an exaggeration, for all the rightness of its postulates, could not but evoke protest. The personal intuitive experience, fortified by the Koran, refused to be crushed out of existence and maintained, with steadily increasing vigor, the validity of the intuitive as against the rational and logical interpretation of religion. From this protest arose the sufi movement.

IV Sufism

The efficient principle of Sufism is the organized cultivation of religious experience. Like theology, it arises at an advanced stage in religious development. In the first century of Islam, when the Muslim religious community constituted a kind of ethical society based upon the concrete doctrines about God and the Last Judgment and the concrete religious duties laid down in the Koran, there were neither theologians nor sufis. But as the increasing range of intellectual activity and the introduction of philosophical discussion produced first an organized system of law and eventually a systematic theology, so by parallel stages and by a natural, and indeed necessary, reaction against the external rationalization of Islam, the intuitive religious perception became increasingly sensitive and self-conscious. The effort of the earlier ascetics to attain to ethical perfection was not indeed given up, but was gradually refined and transformed. The ethical ideal proclaimed in the injunction *takhallaqu biakhlaqillah*[6] could no longer be satisfied by mere acceptance of a rule imposed from without, but demanded conformity with the content of a deep and real spiritual experience, the external rule becoming as it were imposed on oneself by one's own higher nature and insight into a true relationship with God.

The parallel with the development of theology can be pursued even further. As theology was stimulated by contact with Greek philosophy and rationalism, so Sufism was stimulated by contact with Christian mysticism and Gnosticism. Since the spirit and expression of Koranic piety had from the first been closely related to the mystical-ascetic attitudes of the Eastern Christian church, there were in this case even fewer barriers to intercommunication. But as it is demonstrably false to say that Islamic theology was simply Greek philosophy in an Islamic dress, so also it is false to assume that Sufism was simply Christian or Gnostic mysticism in an Islamic dress. Islamic theology utilized Greek philosophy and logic to elaborate its rational system on the basis of Koranic postulates; in the same way Sufism, basing itself firmly upon the intuitive insights of the Koran, admitted so much of Christian experience and Gnostic imagery into its forms of expression as could be accommodated to its fundamental religious attitudes.

In this function Sufism served as the complement of orthodox *tawhid*. When the sufis accepted the scholastic theology and law as defining the rational and moral imperatives of Islam in external terms and set themselves to seek out and to practise their inner content, they raised the whole level of religious thought and action in Islam to a higher plane of consciousness and purpose. The combination of the intuitive reason with the speculative reason is at all times difficult to achieve and few, even in Sufism, achieved it fully; but it cannot be denied that in some sufis the religious life and thought attained some of their highest manifestations.

At first, then, between orthodox theology and Sufism there was a divergence of emphasis rather than of content, theology emphasizing rational knowledge and appealing to the head, Sufism stressing intuitive perception and experience and appealing to the heart. But the rift was bound to widen, since theology, being a rational and scientific discipline, produced a stable and uniform structure of ideas, whereas Sufism was an attitude rather than a doctrine. Its personal, imaginative and experiential character meant that, in contrast to theology, it could not remain one and the same thing, finding expression at all times and in all places in the same formulas. On the contrary, it was bound to differ even from individual to individual, and to express the widest variety of reactions to stimuli of widely differing kinds.

Later Sufism, in particular, with its endless range of emotional manifestations and imaginative attitudes, eludes every attempt to tie it down by classifications and definitions. Everything is relative and personal, and one would be as hard put to it to find a professed sufi in whose thought there was not some antinomian or gnostic elements, as to find one whose thought was completely divorced from the Koranic system of ideas.

With these limitations, however, we may distinguish three main tendencies. One is "orthodox" Sufism, a mystical-ascetic attitude in which contemplation and the pursuit of religious experience is controlled by the acceptance of Koranic transcendental monotheism and the Koranic doctrine of duties. Thus Sari as-Saqati defined *tasawwuf* as "a name including three ideas. The sufi is he whose light of divine knowledge does not extinguish the light of his piety; he does not utter esoteric doctrine which is contradicted by the exterior sense of the Koran and the Sunna; and the miracles vouchsafed to him do not cause him to violate the holy ordinances of God."

As this quotation itself shows, however, Sufism, being essentially the affirmation of a direct relation between God and man, had already encouraged a tendency to brush aside the intermediate authority of the established religious institution. There were those who regarded it as an obstacle to be got around by reinterpretation, or even by more or less overt opposition to its formulas. This sense of opposition, perhaps sharpened by the inevitable conflict with the ulama, threw certain groups into attitudes dictated by emotional rejection of the demand for external conformity to the Sharia on the one hand, and of the intellectual categories of *tawhid* on the other.

The former tendency is seen among those who practised and preached a doctrine of "blame" (*malama*), setting themselves to the external performance of acts which were legally disapproved, or which even violated the law, in the belief that by incurring the censure of those whom they called "the vulgar" they could become independent of them and devote themselves wholly to God. More profound and more serious was the reaction against the absoluteness with which the theologians had formulated the logical consequences of the doctrine of "difference," so separating man entirely from God.

In its extreme form this protest was voiced by al-Hallaj, whose execution made of him a symbol of self-sacrifice and death for the love of God, and for whose followers, in consequence, the "mullas" became impious ministers of evil. It may only have been small groups who maintained an extreme Hallajism, combining with it in some cases theosophical and incarnational doctrines; and the inner contradictions between such exaggerated reactions and the fundamental positions of Islam rendered them sterile in the long run, in spite of some literary remains of undeniable beauty. Yet some of these elements, like those of *malamism*, survived into sufi thought of later times, and fostered a tendency to relegate the formulas of the orthodox institution to a secondary place. In addition, they opened up channels through which older beliefs which had been opposed or inhibited by orthodoxy were able to gain entrance into the Muslim community, and some of these, like the hermetic "sciences," penetrated its imaginative universe to an extent which baffles the modern student.

The sufi movement, therefore, so far from presenting a common body of doctrine, formed a complex association of imaginative and emotional attitudes, which are still very far from having been studied and analyzed at all fully. At bottom, it asserted the rights of the imaginative reason in religion and the claim of the intuitive aesthetic impulse to seek an outlet in the face of its repression by the orthodox system. In all other religions these demands have found satisfaction in religious art. In Islam, denied this visual expression, they took their revenge 'by assuming characteristic forms of behavior and discourse. It is not a coincidence that, at a time when the formal literatures of the Arabs and Persians had become completely dissociated from the popular literary arts, precisely these, and particularly the wine song, the short story and the romance, were taken up and recast as the main vehicles of sufi experience. Rumi's *Mathnawi* may justly be called a religious picture book.

This aesthetic element in Sufism plays a part which can hardly be overemphasized in its later expansion. Indeed, the nearest western parallel for the inner development of later Sufism is to be found not in the development of the Christian monastic orders, but rather in the history of western painting. With widening range and expanding powers it seemed to release the imaginative faculties from almost all controls and to allow them free play within the religious field, until at last the strength of the natural imaginative impulses and popular religious appetites exerted a pull on the whole range of religious attitudes in Islam.

In the higher levels of the movement, the revival of naturalism found expression in the two sufi philosophies, the illuminationist deriving from the ancient Asiatic beliefs, and the monist deriving from Hellenistic popular philosophy. In spite of the popularity of these, either individually or in combination with one another or with the hermetic "sciences," and of the great mystical poetry which they inspired, their importance lies less in themselves than in their influence and effects. Viewed as philosophies, they offer only a convincing proof of the incoherence of the religious imagination when it is not disciplined either by the vision of a prophet or the logic of the reasoning faculty. Their chief attraction lay not in their reasonableness, but in that they allowed unlimited scope to immanentist feeling and expression, and above all to the marked tendency towards pantheism which is to be found in all the greater poetical exponents of Sufism.

In my view, this quasi-Islamic pantheism attempts the very opposite of what Muhammad set out to do. He, faced with Arab animism, attempted to destroy it by setting a transcendental God over against the material world which He had created and by prohibiting the worship of any creature. At the same time, from his own mystical experience he knew that in some mysterious and inexpressible way God was also *in* His world. The orthodox theology, exaggerating the first aspect, repressed the second. Sufism began by asserting the truth also of the second, and in its philosophies attempted to find a formulation of this dual truth. But gradually, and especially in its popular forms, it came more and more to equate God's indwelling in the world with the animistic idea of divine powers and qualities inherent in material objects and persons; then, it attempted to square this with the existence of a transcendent Creator God by substituting for the indwelling of God in the world the indwelling of the world in God and by asserting that all material things are manifestations of Him.

The extremism of the orthodox denial of the immanence of God thus led in Sufism to an equal extremism in its assertion. But just as the great body of Muslims respected the theological dogmas without allowing them to affect very greatly their ordinary working beliefs, so these pantheistic or panentheistic speculations, though they were read and admired by the educated and produced a deeply affecting poetry, were not taken very seriously by the large body of affiliates to the sufi orders. The great majority succeeded somehow or other in maintaining alongside the vaguely pantheistic ideas of Ibn al-Arabi the fundamental positions of Koranic monotheism, in a kind of syncretism without assimilation.

This had both good and bad results. Whereas orthodox theology numbered no outstanding original thinkers after the fifth century, except perhaps Ibn Taimiya, the problem of reconciling orthodox transcendentalism and rigidity with sufi immanentism and experience exercised the minds of sufi leaders and thinkers generation after generation. In their writings, consequently, is most faithfully reflected the continuing effort of Muslim religious thought in the later centuries.

On the other side, these doctrines threw open the door to a number of ideas and practices which were destructive of the religious values of orthodox Islam. Sufism, as a religious movement, showed many faces, and it is impossible to separate these from one another. If it is to be judged partly by the spiritual and ethical insights which were attained by its highest exponents, and partly by its success in setting and maintaining high general standards of religious living in the Muslim community, yet its virtues cannot be viewed in isolation from the exaggerations and eccentricities in religious thought which the sufis patronized, or from the exploitation of human weaknesses, not only by the minor and irregular orders and by a host of charlatans, but also at times by some of the major orders.

The same circumstances which released the imaginative powers of the elites also released, at a second remove, the inherited religious instincts of the masses, when Sufism became a mass movement and its adherents organized themselves in corporations and orders. The instrument by which this was affected, and the root cause of the deviations, exaggerations and social weaknesses which became increasingly prominent in the new popular Sufism, was the revival of saint worship, the veneration accorded by devotees to men who displayed outstanding gifts as seers and teachers, and their canonization as saints, whose blessed power (*baraka*) continued to be effective even after death.

The system of *piri-muridi* offers a striking example of the way in which a principle entirely natural and healthy in its original setting can be perverted by changing conditions. No criticism can be pressed against the sufis for accepting the authority of men of marked spiritual character and insight. In its original function the system served to train the imaginative and intuitive powers of the neophyte and to restrain him from the dangers of excessive self-reliance. But it also perpetuated erratic tendencies, and while these were relatively unimportant so long as sufis were found only in small dispersed groups, they were of necessity intensified as Sufism developed on a mass scale. In the long run it undermined the structure of sufi ethics, both through its excessive assertion of spiritual authority, rationalized by a doctrine of secret knowledge possessed and transmitted only by the *pir*, and through the spiritual presumption which it fostered in the *pir* himself.

A system of this kind constitutes an open invitation to the instincts which predispose the ordinary man to attach himself to persons rather than to doctrines and ideas. Its chief effect was to relax the hold of Islamic orthodoxy on the inner circle of adepts, by binding them to follow implicitly the precept and example of a single individual wherever it might lead, even in such matters as observance of the canonical prayers and other doctrines and practices of Islam. "Blessing" could be acquired only through obedience to the directions of the *pir*; salvation in the future life could be assured only through the *pir's* intercession for his faithful disciples; and the service of the preceptor usurped the term *ibada*, properly applied to the worship of God alone.

Not only, then, did the later institutional Sufism reintroduce that intermediate authority between God and man which early Sufism had protested against and repudiated, but reintroduced it on a lower level. For now both worship and authority were no longer concentrated on a universal and rationally intelligible object. Instead of this they were thrown into confusion at the dictates of a vast number of individuals of an enthusiastic or ecstatic nature, whose teachings, based upon an unstable and subjective intuitionism, often differed widely from one another and from the affirmations of the Koran.

What constitutes sainthood? How can the true be distinguished from the false, the genuinely God-intoxicated from the sanctimonious swindler? Since everything depended upon the character and attainments of the men who set themselves up, or were regarded by the people as *pirs*, these were the crucial questions for later Islam. But they were burked. Or rather, because Sufism was swept on by a great tide breaking through the dikes that had held back the flood of animism still contained in the subconsciousness, a tide that the orthodox sufis themselves were unable to control, the answer was taken out of their hands.

By a fatal reversion, the great body of Muslims found it in the doctrine of saintly miracles (*karamat*). The greatest saints, it is true, might and did disavow for themselves any power to work miracles; but their very acceptance of the fact that such miracles were wrought through other saints by the power and grace of God confirmed the popular belief, and their very disclaimers strengthened the evil consequences of that belief. For if all *karamat* are the gifts of God to His elect, then any person of whom *karamat* were credibly reported could not but be one of the elect, no matter how much his teachings might challenge or be challenged by the orthodox, no matter what his personal conduct might seem outwardly to be.

Thus, under cover of Sufism, saint worship reintroduced into Islam the old association of religion with magic. Once re-established, it could not be prevented from penetrating to ever lower levels, until divination, charms, and all the other paraphernalia of imposture provided a means of livelihood for vast numbers of darwishes, self-deceived or consciously deceiving. It is sometimes difficult to see, indeed, wherein later popular darwishism differs from pre-Islamic animism except in mere externals.

Yet the ideals of the more reputable sufi orders were not entirely swept under by the flood. Though forced into grave compromises, they still clung to the Koran and its ordinances, and still served their object of stimulating and enriching the spiritual life of their adherents within the framework of the orthodox institutions. Some of them may have overdone the whipping-up of emotional excitement but it would go against most of the evidence at our disposal to assert that their effect upon the main body of their members was morally or spiritually injurious. On the contrary, the encouragement which the regular orders gave to charity, compassion, honesty, and the other social virtues left an enduring impress on Muslim society.

As often happens, the general sobriety of the major orders attracts the eye of the student less than the vast range of superstitions that flourished in every region of the Muslim world and every level of Muslim society. But superstition is the fringe of the garment of belief, or the pulp that surrounds its self-renewing kernel. Every living faith—and not only religious faiths, but political, economic and scientific faiths as well—creates around its nucleus an outer ring of superstitions, broader or narrower according to its intensity and the range of its influence. Sufism spread too rapidly, over too vast an area and too great a variety of peoples, to escape from illustrating this general tendency of the human mind in an extreme degree.

But however many and confusing the superstitions that linked themselves up with Sufism, the important thing is that it prepared the soil for the living seed of faith. In all the territories under Muslim dominion, their peoples, whether Muslims by profession or converts brought within the fold of Islam by the labors of the sufis, were led, through the attraction of the sufi appeal to their instinctive religious attitudes, into the range of influence of the orthodox institution, with its mosques, preachers and madrasas. Side by side with their still superstitious practices and beliefs, the doctrines of the Koran were slowly taking root over the centuries.

The slowness of this process, especially among the remoter and rural populations, was due not so much, as it might be supposed, to their ignorance as to the static structure of Muslim society during this period. The greatest achievement of Sufism was that the orders succeeded, deliberately or not, in creating a religious organization parallel to, and identified with, the units of which Muslim society was composed. Each village community, each guild association in the towns, each regiment of troops, in India even each caste group, had its sufi "lodge," which linked its members together in a common religious allegiance, and gave to its religious ceremonies a fraternal and communal appeal.

To this organic integration of the sufi orders with the basic units of society saint worship added a still closer sense of intimacy. As the lodge system took root, the need began to be felt of having "saints," alive or dead, within reach of every village community and in every quarter of the towns. Tombs and shrines and the mawlids associated with them not only constituted the self-renewing link between the orders and the people, but also preserved a permanent revivalist element in popular religion. The ever-felt and almost physical presence of the supernatural in close relation to the activities and circumstances of daily life maintained, even if in crude and rudimentary forms, the conviction of the unseen life; and the sense of personal relationship with the saint endowed the rites and practices of such communal religion with a warmth and intensity which was lacking in the rituals of the official institution.

In this, then, lay the ultimate justification of the sufi movement. At a time when the orthodox institution had, partly because of its rigidity, partly also because of its uneasy alliance with the secular authorities, lost much of its power to touch the hearts and wills of the ordinary Muslim, the sufis offered not only the warmth of personal participation in communal worship, but also gave power and depth to Islamic teachings which, without this, would too often have remained inert and external. One might assert, with every justification from the historical angle, that outside of a relatively narrow circle the survival of official Islam as a religion in any true sense between the thirteenth and eighteenth centuries was due to the nourishment which it drew from the sufi brotherhoods.

The orthodox ulama, in fact, must bear much of the responsibility for the weaknesses of which advantage was taken by the extremer and more antinomian practitioners of Sufism. In the measure of their aloofness they threw the strain of holding the balance between orthodoxy and the popular religious appetites upon the leaders of the regular orders. The latter, indeed, served their generations with a loyalty and zeal which have never received their due appreciation from the modern Muslim world; but the task was beyond the range of anything they could have expected to achieve unaided.

The reaction in the last century was salutary up to a point. But it was swelled by the confluence of two currents. One was represented chiefly by the puritan reformers, shocked into action by a realization of the gulf between the principles of orthodoxy and the practices of the great body of professed Muslims. The other arose in the military class and the new urban middle classes who by training and inclination were gradually divorced from the Muslim tradition, and through whom the process of inner dryingup, already far advanced in the West, began to spread to the Muslim world.

The former aimed at a reformation which would maintain the Islamic religious values intact; the latter resented the survival of superstitions which seemed to be a mark of cultural backwardness. In these, the inability to distinguish superstitions from religious values can be understood; but in those, a literalist dogmatism and narrowness of outlook, neglectful both of the precious heritage of early orthodox Sufism and of the lessons of history, seemed bent on eliminating the expression of authentic religious experience. Both, in ploughing up good and bad together, have cooperated to clear the field for the seed of a secular culture which has only, alas, produced a crop of new and deadlier superstitions. Herein lies the danger; for if, in uprooting the rituals and practices of Sufism, the reformers destroy on the one hand the sufi vision of the Love of God and on the other dry up the springs of religion itself, what will it profit Islam and the religious life of mankind?

NOTES

[1] *Ritual and Belief in Morocco*, I, 387.

[2] *Religious Attitude and Life in Islam*, p. 4.

[3] Rumi's poem in R. A. Nicholson's selections from the *Divani Shamsi Tabriz*, no. IX, may serve as an example.

[4] Wensinck, *The Muslim Creed*, p. 104.

[5] Quoted from the volume on *Mohammedanism* in the Home University Library.

[6] "Pattern yourselves upon the nature of God."

12.   Reflections on Arabic Literature

12. خواطِرُ في الأدبِ العَربيّ
I. بَدءُ التَأليفِ النَثريّ

ان في اطلاقنا على الملاحظات التي نعرضها للقراء في هذا المقال اسم (خواطر) لا (بحوث) اشارة الى تفرقة هامة بين الاسمين . فإن كلمة (بحوث) يقصد البحث والتنقيب في كل المواد التي لها علاقة بالموضوع المنتخب ، يتبعه اختبار ونقد مفصل لتلك المواد وكل ما كتبه عنها العلماء الحديثون والاقدمون . وهذه الطريقة العلمية لازمة بنوع خاص عند محاولة الوصول الى نتائج راسخة عن اية معضلة او قضية لم يتم بعد اكتشاف كل ما يتعلق بها، ومنها القضية المذكورة عند رأس هذا المقال . بيد ان هذا ليس ما ننوي تسجيله هنا والا لما تناسب المقال مع صفة هذه المجلة. فسنتبع طريقة اشبه شيء بطريقة الرسام او المصور الذي ينتخب من بين مجموعة كبيرة من التفاصيل التي تظهر امام عينيه نخبة لها اهمية خاصة في نظره هو نفسه ثم يشكلها في اطار من صنعه كذلك . فقيمة التلوين والتصوير ، اذا كانا ناجحين ، ان تجعل في قدرة الناظر او المشاهد ان يدرك بطريقة مباشرة وبوضوح شيئاً عن جوهر الموضوع الذي يقدمه له الرسام . اما القياس على ذلك النجاح فيتوقف على مدى اظهار المصور لجوهر الموضوع عن طريق اختياره للتفاصيل وعرضها للمشاهد . بيد انه ليس للمصور حق الحكم على نجاحه او فشله لان هذا الحكم انما هو من حق الآخرين .

والآن لنعد الى الموضوع ، لقد اكد البعض انه كان للعرب بالفعل آداب نثرية في العصر الجاهلي . وهنا نسأل ، هل من الممكن ان نصدر

بياناً قاطعاً في هذا الصدد سواء أكان بالتأييد ام بالدحض؟ انني اعتقد انه لم يقم برهان حتى الآن على وجود اي آداب نثرية مدونة بين العرب الذين سبكنوا جزيرة العرب. ويزعم من ناحية انه ربما انه وجدت كتب مدونة في (الحيرة) ، وانه وجدت بالفعل بعض المقيدات التاريخية هناك فهذا لا مراء فيه ولكن ما بعد ذلك لا يعدو ان يكون مجرد افتراض .

والبرهان على هذا البيان السلبي هو بحكم الضرورة غير مباشر وهذا امر طبيعي لانه يندر ان يثبت على قضية سلبية بطريقة مباشرة . ففي حالة اي بيان ايجابي لا يستدعي الامر سوى التقدم بالبراهين الواضحة او المباشرة حتى يثبت صحة البيان بينما لا يثبت البيان السلبي لمجرد غياب هذه البراهين المباشرة او الواضحة . ومع كل ، فلو انه وجدت كتب مدونة من الادب المنثور في جزيرة العرب في العصر الجاهلي لعد عجيباً اختفاء آثارها هذا الاختفاء الكلي حتى من احاديث العرب المنقولة . اذ ما هي الذكريات التي صانتها لنا احاديث العرب المنقولة عن النشاط الادبي ،في زمن الجاهلية ؟ نجد انه الى جانب الشعر وبعض الامثال والحكم قـد صانت ايضاً بضعة امثلة من البلاغة والبيان وبعضاً من القصص ؛ ثم لا شيء . هذه المنتجات قد وجدت بلا شك كما تؤكد لنا الاحاديث المنقولة ولكن مما يستحق الاعتبار ان هذه كلها من انواع الادب التي قد تناقلتها الالسن شفوياً لا كتابياً ، مثل الشعر القديم . بل اننا لنشك فيما اذا كان الجاهليون قد اعتبروها كمنتجات فنية اعتبارهم للشعر كما نشك فيما اذا كانت هذه المنتجات قد تنوقلت لأكثر من جيل او جيلين ، الاّ اذا اتفق انها اتصلت اتصالاً وثيقاً بقصيدة عصماء . ولكن مع اننا نعترف بل ونؤكد وجودها الاّ ان احاديث العرب المنقولة ذاتها لم تدع مطلقاً انها وجدت على صورة تأليف مدون ، ويتفق العلماء بالاجماع على ان الامثلة التي قد تنتخب كنموذج لقصص الجاهلية تنسب ولا ريب ، بمراعاة اسس النقد الادبي البينة ، الى عصر متأخر . والذي تجدر ملاحظته فوق ما تقدم انه عندما بدئ في اثبات مؤلفات النثر العربي كتابياً بعد الهجرة لم تكن الكتب التي دونت اولاً هي كتب الحكم ولا البلاغة او القصص ،

ولو ان الجاهليين زاولوا كتابة مثل تلك الكتب بالفعل في جزيرة العرب لكان من المنتظر ان يوالوا كتابتها بعد الهجرة ، كما تبع شعراء القصيد في عهد بني امية نموذج القصيد في العصر الجاهلي .

بل اننا لنجد من البراهين غير المباشرة ما يكون اشد قوة عند تأملنا في تطورات آداب النثر العربي في عصر بني امية واوائل العصر العباسي . فكما يعرف الجميع لقد كان العرب يملكون حينذاك مدوناً ، الا وهو القرآن . وعلى الرغم مما كان للقرآن ، كما سنرى ، من اثر كبير على نهوض التأليف النثري المدون الآ ان القرآن في نفسه لم يجعل فكرة كتابة الادب امراً مألوفاً لدى العرب وهذا يرجع الى ان القرآن في حد ذاته يعد كتاباً فريداً ، هذا من ناحية ، ومن ناحية اخرى ــ انه مع وجود عدد من نسخ القرآن ــ فان اغلبية القراء لم يقرأوا القرآن بل كانوا يتلونه غيابياً .

وعلى هذا فان العوامل التي ادت الى تداول الكتب المدونة كانت من نوع آخر وكان بعض هذه العوامل مادية والبعض الآخر عوامل نفسانية . فاول العوامل المادية هو توطيد دعائم اسلوب او طراز موحد للكتابة العربية ولا شك ان تعدد نسخ القرآن كان اكبر عون على توطيد ذلك الاسلوب ولكن المرجح ان استخدام اللغة العربية في الشؤون الادارية كان وسيلة كبرى على نشر العلم بطراز معهود في الكتابة العربية ، ومن الثابت ايضاً ان هذا الطراز لم يتم تطوره الكامل بتحقيق حروف الهجاء حتى اواخر القرن الاول بعد الهجرة . وهناك عامل آخر كان له بعض التأثير (وان لم يجب ان نبالغ فيه) ذلك هو انتشار المواد التي يكتب عليها ، ففي خلال القرن الاول كان ورق البردي هو المستخدم في العادة ولكن ورق البردي مثل الرق ــ نوع من الجلد الابيض ــ غالي الثمن ولذلك كان يقتصد في استخدامه ، حتى في الدواوين الادارية ؛ وعندما ندقق النظر في الوثائق المحفوظة في المتاحف الاثرية نرى ان وثائق هامة مذيلة بامضاء الحكام قد دونت على قصاصات من ذلك البردي ، فليس من المحتمل ان يمتلك الافراد العاديون كميات كبيرة من ورق البردي لتصرفهم الخاص ؛ وفي الواقع لقد انتشرت الكتابة بسهولة بين عامة

الافراد لاول مرة عقب اختراع الورق المصنوع من الخرق ومن الثابت حدوث هذا في اواسط القرن الثاني . وقد اسس اول مصنع للورق في بغداد في عهد هارون الرشيد وما حل اواخر القرن الثاني حتى وجد الورق بوفرة ورخص الثمن .

مثل تلك العوامل المادية قد هيأت الظروف الصالحة التي فيهـا ترعرعت العوامل النفسانية . من اهم تلك العوامل بكل تأكيد كان انتشار الاسلام بين شعوب سوريا والعراق وبلاد الفرس وامتزاجهم الكلي بالعرب ، ومن الاقوال التي اعتاد الانسان سماعها ان العرب مدينون للفرس في معظم التطورات الحديثة التي جدت على الثقافة الاسلامية . حقيقة لقد عمل الفرس كثيرًا على النهوض بمستوى الحضارة الاسلامية في العصور الوسطى وعلى الاخص في مستوى الجمال الذوقي .

ولكن الارجح ان اكتتابهم الاصلي في ناحية الآداب المدونة كان يقل عن اكتتاب الشعوب المتكلمة باللغة الآرامية لان الآداب المقيدة في بلاد الفرس في العهد الساساني كانت قليلة نسبياً وما وجد منها كان في اكثره اما آداب البلاط (مثل كتاب الملوك وكليلة ودمنة) او آداب دينية ويرجع السبب في هذا الى العوامل المادية السابق ذكرها كما كان الاسلوب الكتابي المستعمل بين الفرس في هذا العهد اسلوباً ثقيلاً غير مهذب لا يصلح لنشر ثقافة ادبية عامة هذا الى جانب ندورة ادوات الكتابة وارتفاع اثمانها ، اما في اللغة الآرامية فكانت هناك حضارة ادبية ذائعة الصيت واسعة الانتشار موروثة في اغلبها من الحضارة اليونانية كما انهم امتلكوا كتباً آلت اليهم من اجيال سبقتهم .

ولما كانت مدينة (البصرة) في واقع الامر هي المركز الرئيسي لدراسات الادب العربي في مبدأ الامر فهذا يشير الى ان احد العوامل التي عملت على تشجيع تلك الدراسات كانت (اكاديمية) جندي شابور ومع ان تلك الاكاديمية وجدت في الاراضي الفارسية فلم تكن مركزًا للدراسات الفارسية بقدر ما كانت مركزًا للدراسات الآرامية وكان اغلبية قوادها من العلماء من النسطوريين ، بيد انهـا كانت في الوقت نفسه مكاناً عاماً

لاجتماع الثقافات ــ الفارسية والهندية واليونانية والآرامية ايضاً ــ ومــا ناولته للعرب كان مزيجاً من كل هذه الثقافات .

وعلاوة على ما تقدم فلكي ينهض اي نوع من الثقافات الادبية يجب ان يتوفر عدد كاف من الاشخاص الذين يميلون الى الادب من جهة ويتوفر لديهم فراغ من الوقت ليعتنوا به ، وتوفر وقت الفراغ لدى طبقة من الناس لا يكفي في حد ذاته لخلق ثقافة ادبية على اي حال كما يدلنا التاريخ مراراً ، بل يقيناً لقد وضح لنا التاريخ ذلك مرة اخرى في تلك الفترة نفسها من تاريخ العرب اذ لقد وجدت مثل تلك الطبقة العاطلة في الواقع في مكة في القرن الاول ومع انها قد اخرجت لنا مجموعة فائقة من الشعراء الاّ انها لم تخلف آداباً نثرية من اي نوع كان . وهذا بكل تأكيد من اقوى الادلة على انه لم توجد تقاليد خاصة بتدوين الآداب حتى في مكة في العصر الجاهلي . ولكن طائفة اخرى من الافراد العاطلين اي من توفرت لديهم اوقات الفراغ قد ازدهرت في العراق في اواخر عهد الخلفاء من بني امية واوائل عهد الخلفاء العباسيين نتيجة نمو حياة الاستقرار والحياة التجارية وبين هؤلاء اخصبت البذور بالطريقة السالفة الذكر وانتجت اول ثمار الادب .

ان العوامل التي لخصناها حتى الآن ــ تطور ادوات الكتابة والامثلة والنفوذ الذي كان للحضارات السالفة في غربي آسيا ونهوض طبقة من الشعب يتوفر لديها وقت الفراغ ــ كافية في حد نفسها لتعلل اول بزوغ للآداب العربية المدونة وقد اخرجت هذه العوامل ، مستقلة عن العامل الذي سوف نناقشه الآن ، ذلك النوع من الآداب العربية الصميمة الذي يطلق عليه اسم (الادب) وقد تتوفر لدينا الفرصة مرة اخرى للكتابة عن هذا الموضوع وسنكتفي بهذا القدر الآن .

اما ذلك العامل الآخر الذي ، بالاضافة الى الاسباب السالف ذكرها ، يدخل في فاتحة الانشاء العربي فله ايضاً اصلان احدهما مادي والثاني نفساني . واما الاصل المادي فهو الاضطرار الى ارشاد المنتمين الى دين الاسلام بلغة القرآن لا من بين الجاليات غير العربية فحسب بل

الاجيال العربية ايضاً التي كانت تزداد نمواً في الامصار . وكان الاصل النفساني هو ما امتاز به العرب من شعورهم القوي نحو لغتهم واعجابهم الشديد بوفرة تلك اللغة وتراكيبها ولو كان هذا الفخر باللغة العربية والاعجاب بها قوياً الى هذه الدرجة حتى في ايام الجاهلية فما بالك به وقد نزل القرآن بتلك اللغة ونزح العرب على اثر ذلك الى خارج شبه جزيرة العرب ليحكموا اوطاناً جديدة !

وهكذا فقد كان امراً طبيعياً ، نظراً لشعور العرب هذا نحو لغتهم والرغبة في المحافظة عليها من الفساد ، ان تكون اللغة العربية اول موضوع دراساتهم الادبية حتى ولو كان عنصر الادب (والمقصود هنا الادب المكتوب) لم يعد ان يكون مجرد بذرة . وهذه هي الحقيقة التي تميز الادب العربي عن معظم الآداب الاخرى ان لم يكن عنها جميعها ، اذ في الشعوب الاخرى جاء تطور دراسة اللغة من الناحية العلمية متأخراً نسبياً ولم يكن للطرق الفنية في قواعد النحو والتحاليل اللغوية نفوذ كبير على انواع وصفات ادبهم ولكن في اللغة العربية — سواء أكان نتيجة هذا خيراً ام شراً — كانت التطورات التالية في الادب العربي تقع تحت تأثير الدراسات اللغوية التي تمت في عصور التكوين .

لما كان موضوع هذا المقال هو فواتح تدوين كتب النثر فلست انوي ان اتصدى لموضوع فاتحة الدراسات النحوية في اللغة العربية اذ كل ما يهمنا هو الشواهد او الحجج التي امد بها تاريخ الدراسات النحوية موضوع هذا المقال . وتاريخ تلك الدراسات ، اي النحوية ، يناسب موضوعنا بنوع خاص لان معلوماتنا المتعلقة بها ، على الرغم من وقوع كثير من الالتباسات في مراحلها الاولى ، تفوق معلوماتنا في اية دراسات اخرى ولانه لما كانت الدراسات النحوية قد تحولت الى دراسة علمية منظمة منذ وقت مبكر فانها ترينا بوضوح النشوء والتقدم التدريجي الذي مرّ به الادب المسطر .

ولو بدأنا بفحص الفهرست لابن النديم وهو من اهم المصادر التي تحت ايدينا لاستقاء المعلومات المتعلقة بفاتحة الادب لرأينا تفاصيل وحقائق

تهمنا كثيرًا ، فيخبرنا هذا الكاتب مثلًا ان اقدم مجلد رآه عن النحو كان يحتوي على اربع صفحات مدونة على ورق صيني ترجمتها (هذه فيها كلام في الفاعل والمفعول من ابي الاسود رحمة الله عليه بخط يحيى بن يعمر) .

هذه الجملة كما هو واضح تدل على ان محتويات هذه الورقات الاربع كانت عبارة عن مذكرات عن تدريس شفوي (كلام) وقد دونها احد تلامذة ابي الاسود ، وفي الواقع تتكرر عبارة (روى عنه فلان وفلان) في ما يحكي ابن النديم عن تدريس ابي الاسود . وعند ما نتحول الى ادباء الجيل الذي يتلوه لا نجد تغيرًا يذكر في الموقف ، فيقول ابن النديم عن عيسى بن عمر الثقفي «وله من الكتب كتاب الجامع (و) كتاب المكمل » ولكنه يضيف مباشرة ((وقد فقد الناس هذين الكتابين مذ المدة الطويلة ولم تقع الى احد علمناه ولا خبر احد انه رآهما)) واذ يروي لنا ابن النديم ان عيسى بن عمر كان ضريرًا فان لدينا كل عذر في ان نشك فيما اذا كانت هذه الكتب قد دونت على الاطلاق او تعدت ان تكون مواد منظمة درسها شفويًا فتداولتها السنة بعض تلاميذه . بيد ان ما يروى لنا عن (ابي عمرو بن العلاء المازني) لما يستلفت النظر حقيقة اذ يقول ان هذا الاديب كان نساخًا لا يمل ولا يكل وان اكوام كتبه قد ملأت حجرة حتى لامست سقفها الآ انه اتلفها كلها في نوبة من الحماس الديني . وجلي واضح هنا ايضًا ان كلمة «كتب » انما يقصد منها كتابات او على الاكثر مذكرات ومع كل فان القصة ولو تحال مبالغًا فيها الآ انها تشير الى زيادة انتشار ادوات الكتابة بين فئة الادباء وان كان ابو عمرو نفسه قد علم تلميذه الاصمعي كلاميًا وليس كتابيًا .

من هذه العبارات وغيرها مما يشابهها تتوفر لدينا ادلة كافية للاشارة الى انه في دوائر العلوم اللغوية الاولى كانت الدراسات كلها شفوية وعلى الرغم من ان الاساتذة والتلاميذ ربما دونوا كتابيًا بعض المذكرات الآ ان هذا الشيء يخالف التأليف او تداول كتب كاملة التسطير . بل وحتى عندما نصل الى الكتب الشهيرة مثل كتاب العبن للخليل بن احمد وكتاب سيبويه يظل موضوع التأليف مضطربًا مشكوكًا في امره ، فانظر مثلًا

ما يقوله مؤلف الفهرست عن كتاب العين . « قال ابو بكر بن دريد وقع بالبصرة كتاب العين سنة ثمان واربعين [ومائتين] قدم به وراق من خراسان وكان وكان في ثمانية واربعين جزءًا فباعه بخمسين دينارًا وكان سمع بهذا الكتاب انه بخراسان في خزائن الطاهرية حتى قدم به هذا الوراق وقيل ان الخليل عمل كتاب العين وحج وخلف الكتاب بخراسان فوجه به الى العراق من خزائن الطاهرية ولم يرو هذا الكتاب عن الخليل احد ولا روى في شيء من الاخبار انه عمل هذا البتة وقيل ان الليث من ولد نصر بن سيار صحب الخليل مدة يسيرة وان الخليل عمله له واحذاه طريقته وعاجلت المنية الخليل فتممه الليث » .

اما عن كتاب سيبويه فهذا ما يقول « والطريق الى كتاب سيبويه الاخفش [المجاشعي] وذلك ان كتاب سيبويه لا يعلم ان احدًا قرأه عليه ولا قرأه سيبويه ولكنه لما مات قرئ الكتاب على الاخفش » .

وهكذا فن تاريخ. هذه الكتب الهامة وكثير غيرها مثل الموطأ لمالك ابن أنس والسيرة لمحمد بن اسحق نرى انه حتى النصف الثاني من القرن الثاني لم تعلق اهمية لفكرة انتساب التأليف لمؤلف معين فكان « المؤلف » هو عبارة عن الاديب الذي ينظم مادة الكتاب او ينظم محتوياتها وهذه المواد كانت تتداولها تلامذة المؤلف شفوياً ولا تدون في صورة مقرر كامل الّا بعد وفاته بعدة سنوات وقد حدث كثيرًا انها دونت في صور كتابية مختلفة كما هو معلوم في حالة كتاب « الموطأ » ، ولا تتكون فكرة التأليف كما يفهمها الادباء الّا بعد ان تستقر سنة تسطير الكتب والذي نراه واضحاً في نشاط القرن الثاني ليس سنة ادب مسطر بل سنة التدريس الشفوي ينقل عن طريق رواة ، ولا يناقض هذا كون هؤلاء الرواة قد دونوا في بعض المناسبات مذكرات عن دروس من سبقوهم .

وتزداد هذه النتيجة وضوحاً عندما نختبر ما وصل الينا من تلك الاعمال التي تنسب الى الجيل التالي من الادباء اللغويين ، ولا ينسب لهؤلاء في الغالب مؤلفات كبيرة شاملة مثل كتاب سيبويه مثلاً بل تقرن اسماؤهم بعدد كبير من الرسائل القصيرة عن موضوعات معينة تتعلق باللغة او

الشعر العربي ، ومن اشهر هؤلاء العلماء الاصمعي الذي توفي في سنة ٢١٦ هجرية والذي قيل انه كتب او املى عدداً من الرسائل في مواضيع شتى مثل الابل والخيل والنبات والاحوال الجوية وغيرها . وقد يتخيل لنا من هذه البيانات اننا قد وصلنا عندئذٍ الى عهد من التأليف الادبي في الصورة التي نفهمها اليوم من هذا التعبير فلنتوجه ببصرنا الى الكتب ذاتها كما ورثناها .

والكتاب الذي يمكننا ان نستدل منه على اوضح صورة للعملية الادبية هو كتاب « فحولة الشعراء » وهاكم فاتحة الكتاب .

«قال ابو بكر محمد بن الحسن بن دريد الازدي قال ابو حاتم سهل ابن محمد بن عثمان السجزي سمعت الاصمعي عبد الملك بن قريب غير مرة يفضل النابغة الذبياني على سائر شعراء الجاهلية وسألته آخر ما سألته قبيل موته من اول الفحول قال النابغة الذبياني ثم قال ما ارى في الدنيا لأحد مثل قول امرئ القيس (وقاهم جدهم ببني ابيهم وبالاشقين ما كان العقاب) قال ابو حاتم فلما رآني اكتب كلامه فكر ثم قال بل اولهم كلهم في الجودة امروٌ القيس له الحظوة والسبق وكلهم اخـــذوا من قوله واتبعوا مذهبه » .

ومن هذه العبارات نفهم انه من غير الممكن بأية صورة من الصور ان يقال ان الاصمعي قد سطر كتاباً عن فحولة الشعراء فنستطيع ان نقول ان مهمة الاصمعي كانت ايجاد فكرة الكتاب ولكنه قبل ان يصبح قطعة من التأليف الادبي قد مرّ بمرحلتين اخريين فنقل عن طريق الرواية لا طريق الكتابة بواسطة ابي حاتم السجزي وفي النهاية نسقه وسطره ابن دريد او شخص آخر املاه عليه ابن دريد . وان امعنا النظر في الكتب الاخرى الباقية التي تنسب الى الاصمعي مباشرة لوجدنا ان اسانيدها تدلنا على امثال تلك الاحوال بعينها فمثلاً كتاب الدارات يستهل هكذا « قال ابو حاتم سهل بن محمد السجستاني حدثني ابو سعيد عبد الملك بن قريب الاصمعي » ويختم هكذا « تم كتاب الدارات والحمد لله اولاً وآخراً وهو عن ابي سعيد الاصمعي رواية ابي حاتم السجستاني » .

الاّ اننا في هذه المرة لا نخبر عن الشخص الذي سطر الكتاب في
آخر الامر ، ولكن في مقدمة كتاب النبات والشجر يوضح الاسناد هذا
الامر وضوحاً لا غبار عليه اذ ينتهي هكذا « اخبرنا ابو بكر محمد بن
الحسن بن دريد قراءة عليه وانا اسمع في ذي الحجة سنة ست وثلاثمائة
قال اخبرنا ابو حاتم سهل بن محمد السجستاني عن ابي سعيد عبد الملك
ابن قريب الاصمعي ».

وهكذا فان كتاب الكرم ايضاً الذي يقتبس جزئياً من تدريس
الاصمعي قد نقله السجستاني الى ابي سعيد الحسن بن الحسن السكري .
وهذه الظاهرة بعينها تبدو في كل المدونات الاولى التي خلفت لنا وهي
تامة الاسناد ، بيد انه يحدث ان تخلف لنا هذه الكتب في نسخ متأخرة
حيث اغفل اسناد الكتاب .

وسنسرد هنا مثلاً واحداً اخيراً لانه يزيد موضوع اسناد التأليف
الى مؤلف نوراً ووضوحاً ، هذا هو كتاب طبقات الشعراء لابن سلام
الجمحي المتوفى سنة ٢٣١ هجرية الذي يستهل هكذا « قال ابو محمد
انا (اي اخبرنا) ابو طاهر محمد بن احمد بن عبد الله بن نصر بن بجير
القاضي انا ابو خليفة الفضل بن الحباب الجمحي قال انا عبد الله محمد
ابن سلام الجمحي ».

في هذا المثل نجد ناقلين هما ابو خليفة وابو طاهر القاضي وعندنا
بعض التفاصيل من موارد اخرى بان هذا الكتاب قد نقله غيرهما من
تلامذة محمد بن سلام . وفي الفهرست ، كما لاحظ البروفسور هل المصدر
الاول لكتاب طبقات الشعراء ، ذكر ابن النديم كتاباً يطلق عليه ذلك
العنوان نفسه منسوباً لا الى محمد بن سلام فقط بل الى ابي خليفة وغيره من
الناقلين ايضاً . ومن هنا يقال ان كتاب طبقات الشعراء قد ألفه ثلاثة
مؤلفين ولكنه هو نفس الكتاب الذي ينسب الى الجميع ، فاذا لاحظ
القارئ هذه النقطة دعه بعد ذلك يفحص في الفهرست قائمة الكتب
المنسوبة الى الاصمعي وابي حاتم وابي دريد ومن هنا يصل الى النتيجة
التي يراها هو . وانني متأكد باننا لو كنا نملك بعضاً من مئات الكتب

التي تذكر في كتاب الفهرست وغيره من الكتب عن الكتب والتي تنسب
الى ادباء القرن الثاني لوجدنا الظاهرة نفسها تتكرر مرات عديدة .

وبناء على ذلك نتوصل من كل هذا الى ان النشاط اللغوي كافة في
القرن الثاني والنصف الاول من القرن الثالث لم يكن معيناً ولا محدداً او
ثابتاً وكان يتلاءم في ابرز مميزاته الى غيره من النشاط الادبي والدراسات
الادبية المعاصرة ، وبالاخص ان المؤلفات اللغوية المعينة ، بما يفهم
من هذه العبارة اليوم ، والتي تنسب الى مؤلفين بالذات لا يمكن ان
تؤرخ الى ما قبل اوائل القرن الثالث بعد الهجرة .

II. نشأة الإنشاء الأدبي

الأدب ، كما هو معروف لكل انسان ، كلمة اصطلاحية تدل على إنتاج إنشائي من طراز خاص باللغة العربية ؛ غير ان الكتابات التي تندرج تحت هذه الكلمة تتنوع تنوعاً كبيراً في موضوعاتها ، وأساليبها ، وأغراضها ، بحيث يصعب ان نجد عبارة تشملها جميعاً . ويترجم الكتاب الأوروبيون عادة كلمة أدب ، بهذا المعنى ، بالعبارة « belles-lettres » او الأدب الجميل ، او الكتابة الرفيعة ، وهي عبارة تكاد تكون في صعوبة اللفظ العربي تحديداً . والأيسر لنا ان نعرف الأدب تعريفاً سلبياً فنحدد ما لا يدخل تحته ، بأن نميزه من الكتابات التي في فقه اللغة ، والفلسفة ، والتاريخ ، والجغرافية ، وما الى ذلك ؛ على اننا سنرى ان الخط الفاصل بينه وبينها ليس واضحاً بحال من الاحوال .

ولعل اقرب تعريف يتسنى لنا ان نقول ان كتاباً في الأدب هو كتاب يكتبه مؤلفه وهو يشعر بغرض أدبي او إنشائي ، سواء أكان يعالج موضوعاً في فقه اللغة ، ام التاريخ ، ام الأخلاق ، ام التسلية المحضة . فالكاتب في فقه اللغة او التاريخ مثلاً يرمي في كتابته الى هدف واحد هو تزويد القارئ بمعلومات او تنظيم بعض الحقائق وتبويبها لتزود القارئ بمعلومات ، على حين ان كاتب الأدب يدخل في موضوعه ، أياً كان ذلك الموضوع ، عنصر الخيال او الابتكار بما يضفي عليه ثوب الجمال او الفن فيجعله سائغاً شائقاً للقراء الذين يشاكلونه في ميولهم وأذواقهم العقلية . ويحدث هذا طبعاً بدرجات مختلفة في مستوياتها ، من حاسة

الجمال المرهفة المثقفة التي تتميز بها الدوائر الأدبية الواسعة الاطلاع الى الفجاجة والفظاظة التي تتمثل في دهماء الشوارع . فسنجد عناصر من جميع هذه المستويات ممثلة في الانشاء الأدبي ؛ وانه من أجل ذلك كانت تلك الكتابة الأدبية ، اذا فهمت فهماً صحيحاً ، هي المصدر الذي نجد فيه أصدق صورة للمجتمع الاسلامي ، في القرنين التاسع والعاشر ، ذلك المجتمع الذي كان مدهشاً في حيويته ، وبحثه ، وقوته ، وتشعب نواحيه .

ومن الطبيعي ان يكون اول موضوع نبحثه — مهما يكن بحثنا له موجزاً — هو كيفية نشأة هذا الضرب من الانشاء في اللغة العربية والعصر الذي استحدث فيه ، وانا أرمي الى تناول هذا البحث في هذه المقالة . ولا يجوز لنا ان نفترض بادئ ذي بدء ان لفظ الأدب كان له دائماً هذا المعنى الاصطلاحي ، اذ ان مثل هذا التصور الانشائي المتمايز لم يكن من الممكن ان ينشأ إلاّ في مجتمع يدرك في كتابته الأدبية مستويات وأساليب خاصة . على ان الفحص عن تاريخ الكلمة نفسها قد يسفر لنا عن بعض النواحي المفيدة .

ويظهر ان العبارات الاولى التي استعمل فيها هذا اللفظ تدل على ان عرب شبه الجزيرة كانوا يفهمون من الأدب . « ما تلقيته او اكتسبته عن التعليم او القدوة » ، وعلى الاخص « الآداب » ، لا من حيث هي سلوك خارجي بحت ، بل بالأحرى من حيث هي دليل على نوع من الأخلاق . فمن ذلك ١ ، يقول الشاعر، أعشى ميمون :

> « جروا على أدب مني بلا نزق »

وفي حديث مشهور يروى عن عمر بن الخطاب انه يقول : « طفق نساؤنا يأخذن من أدب نساء الأنصار » . وفي هذا المجال نفسه من الافكار يستعمل لفظ التأديب بمعنى التعليم كتعليم الأولاد مثلاً ، وان لم يكن المعنى مقصوراً على الأولاد ، كما يتضح من حديث مشهور آخر هو : « أدبني ربي فأحسن تأديبي » .

وظل للأدب هذا المجال المعنوي في عهد الدولة الأموية . ومن أمثلة ذلك ما قاله الحجاج في خطبته المشهورة في الكوفة : « أسلّم عليكم امير

المؤمنين فلم تردوا عليه شيئاً ! هذا أدب ابن نهية ، اما والله لأوّدبنكم غير هذا الأدب »؛ وكذلك ما كتبه عبد الحميد الكاتب في رسالته الى عبد الله بن مروان سنة ١٢٧ هـ. حيث يقول : « أحب (امير المؤمنين) ان يعهد اليك ... عهداً يحملك فيه أدبه ، ويشرع لك عظته » .

من اجل ذلك ، اذا كان لنا ان نعتبر الأدب اصطلاحاً انشائياً على أية صورة حتى نهاية العصر الأموي ، كان اللفظ ينطبق ليس على الصفة الانشائية بل على محتويات رسائل من طراز رسالة عبد الحميد الكاتب . اي اننا نجد رسائل وعظية تشتمل على ارشادات اخلاقية وعملية بأقلام كتاب كانت الكتابة مهنتهم . غير ان رسائل الكتاب هذه لا بد ان تكون بالطبع قد نسجت على منوال ما من الأساليب الأدبية . فلا يمكن ان تكون مبتكرة ابتكاراً سواء في وظيفتها او صورتها ، بل لا بد ان تكون مرتبطة ببعض الأساليب والصور السابقة للكلام ، ان لم يكن للكتابة .

ويبدو ان الأدلة التي يمكن الوصول اليها تجمع على ان البلاغة هي المصدر الذي استقت منه هذه الرسائل الالهام . وليس ثمة شك في ان استخدام البلاغة يرجع الى ما قبل الاسلام ، وان كانت بعض الأمثلة التي تساق احياناً على ما يسمى بلاغة جاهلية لا يمكن اعتبارها اصلية دون ان تخيم عليها الشكوك القوية . والرأي الذي ينادي احياناً بأنه كان في عصر الجاهلية إنشاء بلاغي مكتوب في بلاد العرب رأي لا يقبله إلا عدد قليل من العلماء (إن كان فيهم من يقبله) ، رأي بطبيعته بعيد الاحتمال . بل ان البلاغة باعتبارها فناً مدروساً ، اي التحليل العلمي للوسائل والأساليب البلاغية، ليست من علوم العصر الجاهلي، وانما هي دراسة علمية متأخرة في نشأتها ، وتقابل علم البديع . على انه لا شك في انه كان هناك في كل من العصر الجاهلي وعصر صدر الاسلام بعض الخصائص والأساليب البلاغية المتعارف عليها ؛ ومن الميسور كل اليسر ان نحصل على فكرة عن مزاياها العامة من مصادر متعددة ، ولا سيما القرآن الكريم ، وعلى الأخص السور المكية الأولى ، ومن النماذج التي وصلت الينا من القرن الاول للهجرة .

ويمكننا ان نلخص الخصائص العامة لهذا الأسلوب البلاغي فيما يلي :
(١) إثارة خيال السامع باستعمال المجازات القوية ؛ (٢) السيطرة على
وجدان السامع وعواطفه وميله الى الموسيقى الصوتية باستعمال الألفاظ
الطنانة البالغة التأثير ؛ (٣) التحدث الى عقل السامع ، لا عن طريق
الدقة في التعبير فحسب ؛ بل كذلك عن طريق ترصيص التعبيرات
والمجازات ومزجها بعضها ببعض ؛ (٤) تفريع الصور العقلية والمعاني
وتنويعها باستخدام الازدواج في الفواصل استخداماً قـد يزيده قوة
استعمال السجع او ما يشبه السجع من الفواصل . غير ان التزام السجع
في الكلام كان متجنباً ، إمّا لأنه كان يشعر بشيء من التكلف ، وإمّا
لأن التقفية كانت ميزة خاصة بالشعر ، وسجع الكهان وما اشبه ذلك من
الانتاج الأدبي .

ونجد في خطبة الحجاج ، التي سبق اقتباسها ، مثالاً من أحسن
الأمثلة . ولنلاحظ على الخصوص أنه ، بينما يتجنب السجع ، يستخدم
التلميحات الشعرية والاقتباسات ويكثر من استعمال المجاز، كما نرى في
الجملة الآتية مثلاً :

« إني ، والله يأهل العراق ، ما يقعقع لي بالشنان، ولا يغمز جانبي
كتغماز التين ؛ ولقد فررت عن ذكاء ، وفتشت عن تجربة ؛ وان امير
المؤمنين — اطال الله بقاءه — نثر كنانته بين يديه ، فعجم عيدانها ،
فوجدني أمرها عودًا ، وأصلبها مكسرًا ، فرماكم بي ، لأنكم طالما أوضعتم
في الفتنة ، واضطجعتم في مراقد الضلال ... »

ولنقارن الآن بين تلك الجملة والجمل الآتية من رسالة عبد الحميد
الكاتب : « واعلم ان كل اعدائك لك عدو يحاول هلكتك ، ويعترض
غفلتك ، لأنهـــا خدع إبليس ، وجبائل مكره ، ومصايد مكيدته ؛
فاحذرها مجانباً ، وتوقها محترساً منها ، واستعذ بالله من شرها ، وجاهدها اذا
تناصرت عليك بعزم صادق لا ونية فيه ، وحزم نافذ لا مثنوية لرأيك
بعد إصداره عليك ، وصدق غالب لا مطمع في تكذيبه ، ومضاءة صارمة
لا أناة معها ، ونية صحيحة لا خلجة شك فيها ... » فمن المؤكد ان ليس

ثمة صعوبة في ان ندرك ان في القطعة السابقة نفس الخصائص الأساسية التي في خطبة الحجاج ، ولكنها ذللها وعبدتها الطلاقة التي يمتاز بها الكاتب المحترف للكتابة ــ وهي في الحقيقة تلك الصفة التي وصف بها مؤلف كتاب « الفهرست » عبد الحميد حينما قال : « هو الذي سهل سبيل البلاغة في الرسل » .

بيد انه ما دام لفظ الأدب كاد يؤدي هذا المعنى العام للتعليم وما يكتسب من التعليم ، لم يكن من الغريب قط ان نجده مستعملاً في بعض الدوائر الخاصة بمعنى مقيد محصور في معان خاصة تهم هذه الدوائر . فمثلاً يبدو انه بين السابقين من العلماء المشتغلين باللغة العربية ، كانت دراسة اللغة وتقسيم مميزاتها تسمى ادباً . ولست واقفاً على كثير من الأمثلة التي وصلت الينا عن هـــذا الاستعمال ، ولكن هذا الاستعمال صريح في رسالة مبكرة تسمى « الأدب الصغير » ، وهي كثيراً ما تنسب الى ابن المقفّع ، ولكنها ربما كانت من نتاج عصر متأخر بعض الشيء عن عصر ابن المقفع . واليكم المثـــال الذي أعنيه من تلك الرسالة : « جل الأدب بالمنطق ، وكل المنطق بالتعلم ، ليس حرف من حروف معجمه ، ولا اسم من انواع اسمائه ، إلاّ وهو مروي متعلم مأخوذ من إمام سابق ، من كلام او كتاب » .

ومثل هذا الاستعمال الخاص للفظ الأدب هو ما نجده في عنوان الرسالة التي اقتبست منها العبارة السابقة ــ « الأدب الصغير » ــ وفي عنوان رسالة أخرى اكثر شهرة ، لابن المقفع ، هي « كتاب الأدب الكبير » . على اننا ، قبل محاولة تحديد المعنى الخاص للفظ الأدب في هذين المثالين ، يجب علينا ان ننتقل الى البحث في التطورات الجديدة في الانشاء العربي ــ تلك التطورات التي يرتبط بها اسم ابن المقفع ، والتي يعد هو في الحقيقة اول ممثل لها ، بحسب ما وصلت اليه معلوماتنا .

وانا في غنى عن تذكير قرائي بما حدث في النصف الأول للقرن الثاني للهجرة ، من ان الحياة الاجتماعية والعقلية للعرب ، وخاصة حياة العرب في العراق ، كان يعتورها التغيير في كل ناحية من نواحيها . فسياسة

الشدة التي كان يتبعها حكام الدولة الأموية كانت ، بقضائها على
الروح الحربي لأهل القبائل ، قد مهدت السبيل الى الانقلاب بتأسيس
حياة مستقرة ونمو جماعة متحضرة ، تشتغل بأعمال سلمية ، وتعنى في
طبقاتها العليا بالبحوث العقلية . ولم يجد مثل هذا المجتمع في الأفكار
القديمة وأساليب التعبير السابقة ما كان يجده فيها من القوة والسلطان عرب
الأجيال السابقة . فقد أصبح هذا المجتمع يبحث عن مواد جديدة وصور
للتعبير جديدة ، تكون اكثر ملاءمة لأحواله الجديدة وما فيها من مجالات
عقلية ابعد شأواً . وقد زاد هذه الميول قوة زيادة امتزاج العناصر الفارسية
والآرامية وغيرها بالحياة العربية ، الاجتماعية والأدبية . والواقع ان الأدب
العربي كان يدنو من عصر انتقالي شبيه بتلك العصور الانتقالية التي
مرّت بها أمم أخرى في مراحلها الأدبية الأولى . وحتى لو ظلّت الخلافة
الأموية تحكم الامبراطورية العربية من دمشق ، لكان من الميسور ان
نتنبأ بأن هذا التطور الاجتماعي في العراق كان من شأنه ان يستحدث
عدة تغيرات . غير ان قيام الخلافة العباسية منح الحركة نشاطاً قوياً
وعجّل تطورها ، لأنه جلب معه تحولاً نهائياً في النفوذ السياسي والاجتماعي
من عناصر الحياة البدوية الى عناصر الحياة الحضرية .

وقد سلك ممثلو التيارات الجديدة للتفكير العربي ، في تلك الظروف ،
المسلك نفسه ، كما انتحلوا الخطى نفسها، التي سلكتها وانتحلتها من قبلهم
ومن بعدهم الأمم التي اجتازت مثل تلك الظروف. فكما ان الادب المسرحي
الروماني قام على أسس المسرحيات الهزلية الاغريقية ، وكما ان كتاب
الأدب الأوروبيين في القرون الوسطى ترجموا او استعاروا من كتب العرب ،
كذلك كان الشأن مع الكتاب المحدثين في اللغة العربية : سدوا خاجتهم
في اول الأمر بالاستعارة او الترجمة من الآداب السابقة . على انه كان
هناك ايضاً ، في الوقت الذي بدأ فيه هذا الأدب النثري المكتوب ، أدب
شفوي ذو كمية عظيمة وصبغة مخالفة كل المخالفة للصبغة الكتابية ــ أدب
كان بالتدريج ينتظم ويتبوب ، كما انه بعد تشكل الأدب الكتابي بشكل
مستقر تدفق ذلك الأدب الشفوي وازدهر بكمية شاسعة وصور متنوعة .

ومن الطبيعي ان مجرى الترجمة الى اللغـة العربية كان يرجع الى شخصية المترجمين والى الكتب والوسائل التي كانت في متناول أيديهم . لذلك كان من الطبيعي ان ابن المقفّع ، وهو فارسي الأصل (وكان يسمى في الأصل روزبيه بن دادويه) ، ترجم كتباً فارسية قديمة . على انه ان كان اول من أفسح مجال الأدب العربي بالترجمة من الآداب القديمة ، فليس من الجائز ان نظن انه فعل ذلك تلبية لرغبة عامة . فسترى ان تلك الرغبة العامة انما نشأت بعد ذلك بقليل . وانما كان ابن المقفع ، كعبد الحميد الكاتب ، من كتّاب الدواوين ، وكان في خدمة أمراء من بني العباس ، عيسى بن علي وسليمان بن علي . وكل ما ترجمه من الكتب — اي «كتاب كليلة ودمنة » و « سير ملوك العجم » ، (وهذا كان ترجمة للكتاب الفارسي «خداي نامة » او كتاب الملوك)، وكتاب «الآئينات» او كتب الآداب والطقوس الرسمية — كل ذلك يرجع الى ادب البلاط الملكي للدولة الساسانية، وكانت ترجمتها مقصودة لتوؤدي في بلاط بني العباس غرضاً شبيهاً بغرضها الأصلي . وينطبق هذا ايضاً على كتابه الآخر الذي ليس ترجمة بل هو تأليف أصلي، وهو «كتاب الأدب » (الذي غلب عليه فيما بعد اسم « الأدب الكبير » او « الدرة اليتيمية » تمييزاً له من كتاب متأخر عنه ينسب الى ابن المقفع ويسمى «الأدب الصغير »). فهذا الكتاب كذلك مؤلف في آداب الأمراء وحاشيتهم ، قد صيغ في قالب نصائح في السلوك وما اليه .

ويسهل علينا من هذا ان نستنتج ما كان يفهمه ابن المقفع من لفظ الأدب . واذا سلمنا بأن ابن المقفع كان اول مؤلف للانشاء الأدبي في اللغة العربية — وأرى من الحق ان نسلم بأنه كان — وجب علينا ألاّ نغفل عن ان جميع أدبه كان ، كالأدب الذي سبقه ، يرمي الى غرض تهذيبي . ولو انه اقتصر فيما كتب على « الأدب الكبير » لما كان في كتابته شيء كثير يميزه عن كتاب المواعظ والوصايا المتعلقة بالآداب وحسن السلوك . اما ما كان جديداً في مؤلفاته فهو ان كتبه المترجمة قد أعربت عن هذه المواعظ والوصايا بطريق غير مباشر في صورة

تاريخ او خرافة على ألسنة الحيوانات . و «كتاب الملوك» في نصه الفارسي لم يكن كتاباً تاريخياً بقدر ما كان رسالة بلاغية في آداب الملوك ، نسيجها سداه الاقاصيص ولحمته التاريخ . (ولو ان اللاحقين من مؤرخي العرب والفرس كانوا قد أدركوا هذه الحقيقة لتجنبوا كثيراً من الجهود المضيعة والآراء الجامحة !) اما في «كليلة ودمنة» فقد كان عنصر الوعظ معسول اللفظ بما صيغ فيه مستوراً على ألسنة الحيوانات ، بحيث يسوغ لنا ان نعتبره اول خطوة في سبيل نقل الأدب من الرسائل الوعظية او التدريبات اللغوية الى الأدب الجميل او الكتابة الرفيعة ذات التسلية السامية .

وليس مما يدخل في موضوعنا الحاضر ان نتعرض للاراء الالحادية التي تعزى الى ابن المقفع ، والتي أعدم من أجلها سنة ١٣٩ هـ. غير انه يجدر بنا قبل الانتقال الى البحث ، فيما طرأ على الانشاء الأدبي من التطور ، ان نتمعن قليلاً في موضوعين آخرين يتصلان بكتاباته ويرتبطان ارتباطاً وثيقاً بمادة بحثنا : وهما أسلوبه ، والصورة التي انتقلت فيها مؤلفاته الى الأجيال التي تلته .

ومن المحقق ان عمل ابن المقفع لم يكن قط ترجمة حرفية . فقد لاحظ الاستاذ كبريلي (Gabrieli) — الذي ندين لدراسته العميقة عن ابن المقفع باصلاح كثير من الأخطاء القديمة — ان جميع نصوص كتاب «كليلة ودمنة» تنم بوضوح عن جهد بذله المترجم في تحوير الخصائص الهندية الصميمة التي للكتاب الأصلي «بنتشا تنترا» ليجعله ملائماً لذوق المجتمع الاسلامي، ولكن من غير ان يصبه في قالب اسلامي بحت . كذلك أضيفت الى الكتاب فصول جديدة في مواضع مختلفة كما ان المقدمة تناولها التعديل ، ولو أن من الممكن ان بعض هذه التعديلات كان موجوداً من قبل في النصوص الفارسية . ومهما يكن لأمر فان ابن المقفع شعر بأنه حر في اصطناع المواد التي في الكتاب على وفق أسلوبه هو ، دون ان يلتزم اسلوب النص الفارسي . وفي حدود ما يجوز لنا الاستدلال به من العبارات التي وصلت الينا مقتبسة من مؤلفه «كتاب

التاج » ، نستطيع القول بأنه اتبع الطريقة نفسها في ترجمة ذلك الكتاب أيضاً ؛ اما في كتابه « سير ملوك العجم » فمن المرجح انه كان اكثر التزاماً في ترجمته للنص الأصلي « خداي نامه » .

على اننا حين ننظر في الاسلوب الانشائي ، ذلك الأسلوب الذي اشتهر به ابن المقفع تلك الشهرة الواسعة ، والذي سن سنّة جديدة لمن جاء فما بعد من كتاب الأدب ، يروعنا ان نجد من المستحيل ان نبدي رأياً قاطعاً بالاستناد الى نص كتاب « كليلة ودمنة » . فجميع المخطوطات التي وصلت الى ايدينا من هذا الكتاب ترجع الى عهد متأخر بعض الشيء فأقدمها يرجع الى القرن السابع او الثامن الهجري ، وهي كلها شديدة الاختلاف بعضها عن بعض . بل ان من العسير غالباً التحقق من ترتيب فصول الكتاب بمضاهاة المخطوطات المختلفة ، وما لا سبيل اليه البتة ان تساعدنا هذه المخطوطات في إعادة تكوين العبارات العربية الأصلية التي استعملها ابن المقفع . ويؤيد هذا ان الاقتباسات المأخوذة عن « كليلة ودمنة » والتي نجدها حتى في الكتب العربية المكتوبة في القرن الثالث تدل على ان النص كان قد لحقه تحريف بالغ في ذلك القرن ؛ ويقرر المؤرخ حمزة الأصفهاني ان مثل ذلك التحريف اصاب النسخ الأولى لكتاب « سير ملوك العجم » .

ومع ذلك يكاد لا يكون هناك شك في ان ابن المقفع كتب فعلاً ترجماته على رق او بردي . فلماذا حدث انه بعد ذلك بقليل وجد ذلك العدد الكبير من النصوص المتباينة ؟ هذه مسألة عويصة ، وليس من الميسور بعد ان نحلها حلاً مرضياً . وربما كان من عادة النساخ ان يخولوا انفسهم حرية التغيير والمراجعة في النصوص على مثال ما كان يفعل تلامذة علماء اللغة عند نشرهم كتب اساتذتهم ، كما أوضحناه في مقالة سابقة . ومهما يكن الأمر فمن الجلي ان النصوص الأصلية التي سطرها ابن المقفع لا بدّ ان تكون قد اختفت من التداول منذ عهد مبكر ، قبل ان تنتشر انتشاراً كبيراً في عدد من النسخ .

فاذا انتقلنا الى « كتاب الأدب » انتقلنا الى اساس أوطد : فليس

له إلاّ نص واحد كامل ، فيه اختلافات طفيفة ، وهذا النص تؤيده الاقتباسات الواردة في كتب أخرى متقدمة التاريخ . ومن ثم كان من الممكن ان نقف على خصائص الأسلوب الانشائي لابن المقفع ، من نص هذا الكتاب ، بصورة أدق كثيراً مما يتسنى لنا من النصوص التي وصلتنا لكتاب « كليلة ودمنة » .

ومع ان ابن المقفع كان فارسي المولد ، انه يرئس ثبت العشرة الذين يعدون بلغاء الناس — وهو غير ثبت البلغاء — كما ذكره مؤلف كتاب « الفهرست » ، وكان دائماً معدوداً من أساطين الفصاحة العربية . على ان هناك فوارق واضحة بين أسلوبه وأسلوب من قبله من الخطباء . فلغته وتركيب جمله كلاهما أدنى الى البساطة ، وأسلوبه اكثر مباشرة واستقامة وأقل تلميحاً وإشارة ، والالتجاء الى ما في القارئ من القوة الخيالية والمقدرة اللغوية يصل في كتابته الى مـــا يقرب من العدم ، كما ان ازدواج الفواصل يكاد لا يكون له وجود . وبدلاً من التصوير اللفظي القوي والألفاظ الطنانة ، يعتمد ابن المقفع في استحداث روعة أسلوبه على استخدام العبارات المصقولة الجلية (التي ما زالت تشتمل على قدر من معناها المهجور) ، غير انه يعاني في بعض الأحيان شيئاً من الصعوبة في العثور على العبارة الدقيقة التي تؤدي المعنى الذي يقصده وبذلك يصبح غامضاً نتيجة التساهل في التعبير .

فانه على الرغم من ان ابن المقفع كان يبني على الأساس الذي وضعه الكتاب ، لم يكن أسلوب النثر العربي قد تطور بعد تطوراً كاملاً ، وحينما كان يعالج موضوعات جديدة ويعبر عن المعاني المجردة التي لم يكن لها بعد اصطلاحات ثابتة في اللغة المتداولة كان مضطراً الى ابتكار ألفاظ ومصطلحات من عنده لتؤدي تلك المعاني ، على مثال ما يفعل كثير من كتابنا المعاصرين اذ يحاولون التعبير عن الأفكار الحديثة باستخدام تراكيب جديدة. ويدل تاريخ جميع الآداب على ان ابتكار أسلوب نثري متصرف قوي التعبير أصعب كثيراً من ابتكار أسلوب شعري ، وان الاول يحتاج الى وقت طويل من التطور والمارسة في الانشاء .

وقد سبق ان رأينا ، في مقال سالف ، انه في ذلك العهد لم يكن
من المألوف تقييد الكتب بالكتابة . ومع انه يجوز لنا ان نفترض بشيء
من الطمأنينة ان ابن المقفع كان في الواقع قد سطر كتبه ، بالمعنى المفهوم
عادة من تقييد الكتب بالكتابة ، ان تاريخ نصوصها المختلفة يدل على
ان فكرة الكتب ذات النصوص والمحتويات المقيدة ــ مما يصح ان نسميه
الحقوق الأدبية للمؤلف ــ لم تكن بعد مألوفة . ولا يجوز لنا ان ننخدع
بما كتبه ابن المقفع نفسه ، في مقدمة « كتاب الأدب » متحدثاً عن
الكتب بقوله مثلاً : « وجدنا الناس قبلنا... كتبوا الكتب الباقية » ، اذ ان
من الواضح انه يشير هنا الى كتب الفرس ولعله كان يشير ايضاً الى كتب
الاغريق . والحق ان أغرب التطورات التي كان لها مساس بكتب ابن
المقفع نفسه هو ان نصاً شعرياً لكتاب « كليلة ودمنة » نظم من بحر الرجز
لغرض تداوله بين الجماهير . وكان مؤلف هذا النص هو أبان بن عبد
الحميد اللاحقي (المتوفى سنة ٢٠٠ هـ.) ،الذي نظم كذلك كتباً أخرى
مترجمة عن الفارسية . وليس ثمة دليل أسطع من هذا على إيضاح الدرجة
التي كان ينظر بها الى الأدب في الدوائر العربية باعتباره شعراً اكثر منه
نثراً ، وعلى انه كانت ما تزال هناك مرحلة لا بد للادب العربي من
قطعها قبل ان يترسخ نثره ويستقر .

Part Three   Contemporary
Intellectual Currents

13. Studies in Contemparary Arabic Literature

I The Nineteenth Century

Of the modern literatures of the East, that of the Arabic-speaking peoples has received singularly little attention in Europe. The most probable explanation is that the small body of Europeans who read Arabic with any ease are so occupied with researches into the rich historic past of Islam and the Islamic peoples that the present holds no interest, or possibly no attraction, for them. But the fact, whatever its cause, is regrettable. It creates a misunderstanding in the minds of less qualified but more interested persons, a misunderstanding which even years of residence in the east may do nothing to remove. There is prevalent, indeed, in France and Germany, no less than in England, a markedly negative attitude towards neo-Arabic literature, which reaches its absolute point in the dictum of a recent writer that "Modern Egypt has no language, no literature, no legends of its own."[1] As it stands the statement is untrue; but for the tag it would be grotesque. Modern Egypt has not yet indeed severed its connection with the Arabic and the Islamic world. Yet in the same work it is recorded[2] that "Cairo has two hundred and seventeen printing presses, which turn out on an average one book or brochure a day." Even granting the addendum that "Much of this is translation into Arabic of western fiction," there is a substantial residue, to some part of which no unbiased critic would deny without examination the status of literature.

In face of this no apology is required for some attempt to describe the character and tendencies of a number of works by recent and contemporary writers in Egypt and Syria.[3] It is obvious that no study of the social phenomena of any country can possibly be complete without some understanding of the literature produced and read in it. In the case of the Arabic-speaking countries their present literature serves with special force as a criterion of the intellectual movements now agitating them; indeed there is no other by which the real can be distinguished from the artificial so clearly and decisively. The field is already so large that it can be covered only by long and intensive study, and the present study must be confined in the first instance to modern prose writing. Modern Arabic poetry, like classical, is a subject *sui generis*. A still more promising field of study which awaits investigation is modern Arabic drama,[4] especially the plays written in the colloquial speech of Egypt; but such a study, if it is to be anything but a theoretical exercise, demands a wider acquaintance with the Egyptian stage than falls to the lot of most European students. Even within the sphere of prose literature certain limits must be fixed. It is fully justifiable to include in a "classical" literature technical and scientific works, since it is only as books that they survive. In dealing with recent and contemporary literature, on the other hand, all considerations demand the exclusion of technical matter, unless, indeed, it possesses a literary value by reason either of its style or of the influence it exerts. Nevertheless in a young literature, standing often in close dependence on foreign models, these limits must not be enforced so strictly as where a definite tradition has been established. Arabic literature in particular must take into account much that would not come within the scope of literature, as it is understood in Western Europe.

It may be asked at this point by what right Arabic literature is called a young literature. To all appearances it is entitled to claim a history of thirteen centuries, a longer period of continuous literary activity than any living European language can boast. But beneath the apparent linguistic continuity Arabic literature is undergoing an evolution comparable in some respects to the substitution of Patristic for Classical Greek literature and idiom. Neo-Arabic literature is only to a limited extent the heir of the old "classical" Arabic literature, and even shows a tendency to repudiate its inheritance entirely. Its leaders are for the most part men who have drunk from other springs and look at the world with different eyes. Yet the past still plays a part in their intellectual background, and there is a section among them upon whom that past retains a hold scarcely shaken by newer influences. For many decades the partisans of the "old" and the "new" have engaged in a struggle for the soul of the Arabic world, a struggle in which the victory of one side over the other is even yet not assured. The protagonists are (to classify them roughly for practical purposes) the European-educated classes of Egyptians and Syrians on the one hand, and those in Egypt and the less advanced Arabic lands whose education has followed traditional lines on the other. Whatever the ultimate result may be, however, there can be no question that the conflict has torn the Arabic world from its ancient moorings, and that the contemporary literature of Egypt and Syria breathes, in its more recent developments, a spirit foreign to the old traditions.

It is indispensable to examine in some detail the genesis of these modern movements. During the nineteenth century, which found, at its opening, the Arabic world still slowly recovering from the nervous exhaustion that followed its brilliant medieval career, and still closely tied to its old traditions, there was a progressive infiltration of Western ideas.[5] While the literary activities of the early part of the century were thus merely a continuation of those of the preceding centuries, a steady current of European, and more particularly French, thought was being simultaneously injected into the minds of two different sections of the community, in two different centers, and from two sources differing widely in their aims and methods.

In Egypt the principal sources from which European thought was radiated were the technical schools founded by Muhammad (Mehemet) Ali, and the educational missions which he despatched to Europe. These schools, modeled on European lines, often under European supervision, had as their first aim the training of doctors, administrators, lawyers and technical experts of all kinds, who were necessary for the carrying out of the Pasha's ambitious projects. It was inevitable that many of the graduates should be attracted towards other sides of Western culture than those which they were primarily studying, more especially towards French literature. Particularly was this the case in the School of Languages, under the guidance of the gifted Rifaah Bey at-Tahtawi (1801-1873),[6] whose students translated in all more than two

thousand works into Arabic and Turkish. The effect on Arabic
literature in Egypt was not immediate, but bore fruit in the second
wave of Occidentalism under Khedive Ismail. As a typical product
of the advanced wing of this movement we may take Rifaah Bey's
pupil, Osman Galal (1829-1898).[7] His principal literary works
were all translations of famous French books, *Paul et Virginie*, the
fables of La Fontaine, and a few of Molière's comedies. The remarkable feature of his work, however, was not the fact of the
translations, but their modernist spirit. La Fontaine he translated
into simple, unaffected Arabic verse, but Molière into colloquial
Egyptian. The time was scarcely ripe for a step so decisive, but the
complete breach with the past which it illustrated was an indication of the spirit of the age. "Egypt," said her Khedive, "has become a part of Europe"; Egyptian literature should show its independence of Asiatic and African traditions.

In Syria the Westernizing movement was more rapid and
thorough among the Christian communities, particularly of the
Lebanon. Its agents were the missionaries and their schools, where
the younger generation came under direct European influence,
strengthened in many cases by subsequent study in the West,
chiefly in France. In its early stages the movement went rather too
far in the direction of westernization, and tended to produce a loss
of balance.[8] The most remarkable Syrian figure of this early period
was the celebrated (Ahmad) Faris ash-Shidyaq (1804-1887).[9] Only
his early education was obtained in Syria, and it is probable that
a stronger influence was exerted on him by the Westernizing movement in Egypt, where he worked for a time on the staff of the
Official Gazette, afterwards spending several years in various European countries. He was converted to Islam in the fifties, while in
the service of the Bey of Tunis, and settled finally in Constantinople, where the erstwhile modernist became one of the champions
of Islamic orthodoxy.

The break thus suddenly created between the old and the
new in both the principal centers of Arabic literature seemed to
be complete. The Arabic literary world was split into two hostile
camps, each bitterly contemptuous of the other. On both sides,
indeed, the protagonists were in an artificial position. The adherents of the old tradition were out of touch with the develop-

ments which were revolutionizing contemporary thought; they appealed only to a narrowing circle of kindred spirits, and in so far as they remained tenaciously conservative they were fighting a losing battle. The protagonists of the new movement, on the other hand, as is often the way with small groups, had run or been thrust too far ahead, and in cutting themselves adrift from the past they were hacking at their own roots. At this stage no original literary creation could be expected of them; they were still suffering from the bewilderment and lack of mental adjustment caused by the suddenness of the revolution. Western ideas had been too rapidly acquired to have penetrated more than skin-deep.

After the Reformation, the Counter-Reformation. The more farseeing conservatives realized that simple immobility meant ultimate defeat, and that if their old traditions were to count for anything in the lives of their people, the past must be restudied at its sources, and its values reaffirmed in living terms, adequate to the needs of the age. The cobwebs spun by generations of imitative writers during the last few centuries of stagnation and decay must be cleared away. This revivalist movement also showed itself in both Syria and Egypt, but again in different fashions. In Syria it took the form of an Arab revival—a throw-back to the historic *Weltanschauung* and methods of the first Arab centuries. This school is linked with the name of Nasif al-Yaziji (1800-1871),[10] its founder and inspiration. The purpose to which he dedicated his life was to restore pure classical Arabic to its old status, and sweep out all disfiguring modernisms in style and thought. He stands out as indisputably the greatest Arabic scholar of his time, and his influence extended far beyond the limits of Syria. Nevertheless his work was a *tour de force* in so far as he rejected all accommodation to the circumstances of his age, and his school, continued after his death by many of his pupils, notably his son Ibrahim (1847-1906),[11] was unable to maintain a standard henceforth impracticable. Nasif was indeed one of the "pillars" of the modern Arabic renaissance, but not in the sense that he determined the direction which it was to follow; rather that it was largely due to his life work that the Syrian school, which played so great a part in the following decades, was saved from the danger that threatened it of declining into a pale reflection of a culture foreign to its nature and traditions and recalled to a better appreciation of its own history and literature.

While Yaziji was thus striving to stem the tide of modernism, there was growing around him in Beirut itself another school of writers, whose influence eventually outweighed his and gave to Syria the predominant position in Arabic letters which it enjoyed in the latter half of the century. While associating itself with his aim of reviving the ancient learning of the Arabs, it sought also to assimilate the elements of value in Western literature and literary technique.[12] The principal leader of this school was Butrus al-Bustani (1819-1883),[13] a pioneer in many branches of literary activity, and founder of the first Syrian "National School." The breadth of his interests, visible even in his comphehensive (and clearly-arranged) dictionary of classical and modern usage,[14] found a field of expression in his encyclopedia *(Dairat almaarif),* the first of its kind in Arabic. It was left unfinished at his death, four additional volumes, bringing the total up to eleven, being afterwards added by his literary heirs and executors, his son Salim (1848-1884),[15] and distant cousin Sulayman (1856-1925).[16] Sulayman al-Bustani is the outstanding representative of the Christian Syrian community in the last decades of the century, with all its eager, many-sided activities and restless wanderings.[17] A successful journalist, merchant, statesman (he was for a time Minister of Commerce in the Turkish Government), poet, and inventor, his supreme service to Arabic literature was the translation of the *Iliad* from the original into Arabic verse—the first sustained attempt to present a masterpiece of classical literature in a form which the Arabic world could assimilate.[18]

Yet another great service to Arabic, perhaps the greatest of all, was rendered by the Syrians of this intermediate period. While Egypt had had its *Journal Officiel (alwaqai almisriya)* since 1828, it could boast of no non-official journal until 1866, when Shaikh Abus-Saud founded the bi-weekly *Wadin-Nil* at Cairo. The earliest newspapers due to private enterprise appear to have been a number of ephemeral journals which appeared in Syria between 1855 and 1860,[19] but the distinction of being the first regular non-official journal of standing issued in the Arabic language belongs to *al-Jawaib,* founded at Constantinople in 1860 by Ahmad Faris.

The example once set was not long in finding imitators. Under the favorable conditions of Ismail's reign a host of journals sprang up in Egypt, most of them doomed to early extinction. With few exceptions the proprietors and editors of these journals were Syrian Christians, graduates of the schools of Beirut.[20] The part played by journalism in the development of modern Arabic literature is almost impossible to overestimate. The journals not only supplied a school for the training of young writers, but impelled Arabic style along a line of evolution to meet the daily needs of the press. The old literary style, the creation of a small elite, involved, periphrastic, and laden with obscurities, was out of touch with modern needs and expression, and unfitted to serve as a medium for organs whose existence depended on obtaining the widest possible range of readers. Even the less stilted, but still severely academic style of Bustani and his school, was impossible. Something else was needed. By tradition and all the inherited instincts of the Arab writer, the colloquial was ruled out; moreover it would have placed a fatal obstacle to the expansion of their area of influence outside the narrowest local zone. The task which lay before the journalists was not an easy one, and their problem could not be solved in a day. In its earlier stages the language of the journals was, in the eyes of Arabic critics, a very model of poverty (*rakakah*). Syrian writers showed a tendency to cultivate fluency at the expense of style, and incurred the reproach (still laid at their door) of using unduly European turns of phrase. But as the press developed it began to acquire a power of expression and a flexibility that Arabic has scarcely known in its long literary history. For this gradual improvement journalism was greatly indebted to the growing strength of the new literary movement in Egypt, to which we must now turn.

The revivalist activities of the conservative leaders in Egypt were timid and hesitating when compared with the bold antiquarianism of Yaziji. The principal reason for this was undoubtedly that, whereas the Syrian movement was almost entirely the work of Christians stressing the *Arab* element in their history,[21] the Egyptian movement was the work of *Muslims*. The former could throw off the incubus of five or (if they liked) ten centuries with light hearts; to their Muslim contemporaries there were theological reasons for walking more warily. When *taqlid* is erected into a dogma, only the boldest spirits dare pry into what lies behind. The classical revival found its most prominent representatives in the field of education. The analogue of Nasif al-Yaziji was Shaikh Hamza Fathallah (1849-1918),[22] for many years chief inspector of Arabic in the government schools, who "loved the Arabs and the Arabic tongue, and considered that God had endowed it with every distinction (*maziyah*), that every form of modern civilization which was now being revived had been anticipated by the Arabs, and that its name had a synonym in their language." He was one of the delegates from the Egyptian government to the congress of orientalists at Stockholm in 1888.[23] The delegation was headed by Abdallah Pasha Fikri (1834-1890),[24] the Egyptian Minister of Education, whose literary style is sufficiently indicated by a current saying comparing him with the famous Badi az-Zaman of Hamadhan, the popularizer of rhymed prose.[25] Nevertheless, Fikri Pasha was a man of more enlightened views than Shaikh Hamza, and ranks justly as one of the "pillars" of the revival, together with his colleague and successor in office, the more famous Ali Pasha Mubarak (1823-1893).[26] The reputation of both ministers rests, in fact, less on their literary works than on their activities as educational reformers. By their joint efforts the Khedivial Library was brought into being, while Ali Pasha Mubarak was the founder of the *Dar al-ulum,* the first higher training college in Egypt outside al-Azhar. It is not a little due to the influence of these three scholars that the teaching of Arabic in the government schools has retained to this day a strongly conservative character, in striking contrast to the curricula in other departments.[27] A very considerable part of their work, however, would not have been possible without the aid of the printing presses, which from the time of Ismail began to publish the great medieval dictionaries and to broadcast the works of medieval Arabic writers.[28]

The movement of revival found its way even into al-Azhar,[29] where it was to gain a strong adherent in the person of Muhammad Abduh (1849-1905),[30] freshly up from his village of Mahallet Nasr in the Delta. The young shaikh would probably have been a notable personality even if he had gone no farther, but the course of his life and interests was radically changed by his contact with the fiery-spirited Jamal ad-Din "al-Afghani."[31] Under his influence Muhammad Abduh began to study modern European works, and the mystic in him gave place to the reformer. He combined in himself, as none of his predecessors had done for many centuries, the Muslim and the rationalist; the aim which he set before his eyes was to restate the truths of Islam in terms of modern thought, and to recharge the moral, social, and intellectual life of Egypt with fresh energy, derived not from vain efforts to uproot the past, still less from attempts to restore the past, but by fully accepting the past as the foundation of national life and thought, and building upon it by the aid of the vivifying elements in the rationalistic and progressive culture of the West. These ideas he expounded in a long series of treatises and articles, the language and style of which sounded a new note in journalism by their masterly blend of the strength and colour of the old idiom with the flexibility of the new.

Another factor which contributed greatly to the elevation and modernizing of Arabic style was the establishment of learned and literary societies, both in Syria and in Egypt,[32] followed in Egypt by the establishment of political societies, as a result of the impetus given by Jamal ad-Din to the movement for "freedom." The political societies especially, in accordance with their founder's methods, served as training grounds for journalism and public speaking. Their members not only took leading parts in the constitutional agitation which accompanied the Arabist movement between 1880 and 1882, but also introduced into Arabic journalism a new and fruitful principle. This principle was to appeal to and stir up the masses, in order to enlist their support for the aims of the agitators. The outstanding figures were the Christian Adib Ishaq of Damascus (1856-1885)[33] and the Muslim Abdallah Nadim (1833-4–1896),[34] both disciples of Jamal ad-Din. The former in his journals *Misr* and *At-taqaddum* created a style based on French rather than on Arabic models (he had received his early education at the famous Lazarist school in Damascus), which by its vigor, simplicity, and avoidance of all affectation, speedily gained an admiring audience. Nadim was more remarkable for his talents as an orator and poet. He was the Tyrtaeus of the movement. Yet he too made his mark as a journalist, both in the humorous journal *At-tankit wat-tabkit* ("Raillery and Reproof") of the Arabi days and the short-lived *Al-ustadh* in 1892-1893. In these, as in his orations, he relied not so much on a simplified literary style as on the ordinary colloquial language.[35] No further evidence is needed for the influence and efficacy of this new weapon than the abrupt termination of both journals by the arrest and expulsion of their editor.

The thirty years which followed the British occupation were marked by an amazingly rapid development of the material basis of literature. The restoration and expansion of its commercial prosperity and the relative freedom of expression which Egypt enjoyed, contrasted with the increasingly repressive regime in Syria, gave to Egypt an uncontested primacy in the Arabic world. Scholars, men of letters, journalists—all flocked out of Syria into Egypt; and with the union of the two parent stocks thus consummated, there is no cause for wonder that a plentiful progeny of journals, societies, and printing presses should have sprung up everywhere, and have everywhere found material to keep them in constant activity. The British connection, moreover, introduced a new element into the ferment of ideas. The study of English literature, both in the higher schools and by students in Egypt, did much to widen the Egyptian outlook, and has had in particular a marked influence on several outstanding figures in contemporary letters.

Of the many scores of writers of this period there are few who need detain us by reason of their services to Arabic literature or the influence which they exerted on their contemporaries or their successors. The first decade, in the literary as in the political field, formed a period of recovery and stocktaking after the fevers of the preceding years. In the second there was a renewal of energy and of controversy. The third was marked by the rise of a new generation, with whom begins contemporary Arabic literature in the strict sense. There was not at first any change in the relative positions and activities of the parties. The uncompromising conservatives had their Shaikh Hamza, with his Azhar-trained shaikhs or Dar al-ulum graduates supporting, by conviction or opportunism, his educational policy. The reform movement, though led by Shaikh Muhammad Abduh, had to face the bitter opposition of the "orthodox," who were supported by the Khedive,[36] and the *Muayyad* under the editorship of Shaikh Ali Yusuf (1863-1913),[37] an attempt to organize world-wide Muslim opinion in support of the religious and political aims of its promoters.[38]

The name of Shaikh Muhammad Abduh has acquired among the present generation a prestige so great that it is of some importance to gain a precise idea of the results of his life work. In his own view, as we have seen, the principal object of his endeavours was to modernize Muslim religious thought.[39] In so far as Muslim religious thought is to be judged by the teachings of its authoritative representatives, the body of Azhar-trained shaikhs, it must be admitted that as yet (for things may be vastly changed in a few years) there is little sign of his success. His real disciples were found among the laymen, more especially the European-educated classes, and that in two directions. In the first place he and his writings formed, and still form, a shield, a support, and a weapon for those social and political reformers of whom Qasim Bey Amin was the chief. By the authority of his name "they were able to gain acceptance among the people for those of the new principles for which they could not have gained a hearing before."[40] In the second place he bridged, at least temporarily, the widening gap between the traditional learning and the new rationalism introduced from the West, and made it possible for the Muslim graduate of the Western universities to prosecute his studies without being conscious of a fear, or incurring the reproach, that he had abjured his faith. With the removal of this inhibition Muslim Egypt seemed to win a release of energy. Between the opposition parties of modernists and conservatives there came into existence a new third party, to which the majority of present-day writers of standing belong. All of them are in varying degrees the heirs of Muhammad Abduh; he, more than any other single man, gave modern Egyptian thought a center of gravity, and created, in place of a mass of disconnected writings, a literature inspired by definite ideals of progress within an Islamic framework.

The Muslim community produced in the nineties two other reformers whose work was destined to have a great influence on

Egyptian thought. It is a melancholy reflection that political intrigue, by setting these two men in antagonism, did much to weaken the force they might have exerted on their contemporaries. The Kurd Qasim Bey Amin (1865-1908),[41] the champion of women's rights, seemed to have accomplished but little at his death, but his work has lived after him. Mustafa Pasha Kamil (1874-1908),[42] the reorganizer of Egyptian nationalism, gained a greater immediate success, though the movement eventually flowed into other channels than those he dug. Both earned a place in literature as the continuators of the direct style, initiated by the journalists of the Arabist movement. The influence of Mustafa Kamil's "tearing prose,"[43] in his journal *al-Liwa*, can still be traced in the Egyptian press. Qasim Amin has a stronger claim still. His limpid, effortless style has all the simplicity of great art. He sought solely to convey his feelings and descriptions to the reader's mind in the most natural and appropriate terms, without sacrificing elegance and grace, and there are passages in his works that take their place among the masterpieces of modern Arabic writing.

Side by side with these movements the old activity in the work of translation continued with redoubled vigour, strengthening the hands of the reformers by carrying the new ideas of Europe ever deeper into the mind of Egypt. Of the many translators of this period the one whose work was most effective in opening up new vistas to the Arabic world was Fathi Pasha Zaghlul (1863-1914).[44] Himself a lawyer, his earliest translation was Bentham's *Principles of Legislation*, followed in later years by translations of the sociological works of Desmoulins and le Bon, to each of which he added a preface applying their principles to Egyptian conditions and urging his fellow countrymen to measures of reform.

Meanwhile the Syrian colony too continued to exercise a considerable influence, especially on journalism. The services rendered to scientific education in Egypt by Yaqub Sarruf (1852-1927) through his journal *al-Muqtataf* received universal recognition on the jubilee celebrations of that journal in 1926.[45] As a formative influence on Egyptian thought and literature, however, he yields to his fellow countryman Gurgi Zaydan (1861-1914).[46] A self-made man, Gurgi Zaydan represents the inexhaustible capacity of the Syrian for study and assimilation at its best. The list of his works, and the variety of subjects of which they treated, is not likely to find a match in any modern literature. He did more than any other writer to spread a knowledge of Western ideas and history, but was withal a devoted student and admirer of old Arabic history and literature. However superficial some of his works may appear to specialists, they cannot but admire his general grasp and wide knowledge, and must admit that none was better fitted to present it in a form acceptable to a society so constituted as that of Egypt, Syrian though he was. By his score of historical romances,[47] his five-volume history of Islamic civilization,[48] his four-volume history of Arabic literature[49] (to mention but the principal of his many works), above all by his monthly journal *al-Hilal*,[50] he was Egypt's schoolmaster out of school. Coinciding with the third, and most intense, period of national awakening and assimilation, it is fully open to question whether his activity was not even more effectual than Muhammad Abduh's in leading contemporary Egyptian literature along the path which it has followed.

While the Syrians in Egypt thus continued to play a decisive part in the molding of neo-Arabic literature, in Syria itself the creative impulse was all but extinguished. The later years of Sultan Abd al-Hamid and the rule of the "Committee of Union and Progress" allowed no scope for independence of thought and kept all publication under a remorseless censorship.[51] Egypt's gain is the measure of Syria's loss.

Yet Syria was still to enrich Arabic literature from a direction entirely new and unexpected. Egypt was not the only, nor even the principal, center of the Syrian diaspora. For the hundreds of Lebanese emigrants that settled in Europe and the thousands in Egypt, tens of thousands settled in the United States and in Brazil.[52] In the New World too, Arabic newspapers and Arabic literary circles were founded. The new conditions of life inevitably roused new interests and aptitudes, which endeavoured to find expression in new literary forms. It was not until the early years of the twentieth century that the Syro-American school found itself, and began a literary activity that could not fail, in view of the close relations maintained between the emigrants and their native land, to attract attention and find an echo in both Syria and

Egypt. In their case the break with the past was complete and irrevocable, and they and their followers form the most distinctive school in contemporary Arabic letters.

II   Manfaluti and the "New Style"

In the preceding survey of Arabic literature during the nineteenth century, special emphasis was deliberately laid on two aspects of the subject, the struggle between the old and the new conceptions and ideals, and the gradual emergence of a simplified Arabic prose style. If it is asked why a point of view apparently so narrow and exclusive should have been adopted, to the prejudice of a more detailed investigation of the personal and literary characteristics of the individual writers, the answer is twofold. These two questions in fact overshadowed the literature of the time, as indeed every aspect of life in the Arabic East was overshadowed by the similar conflict of old and new ideals and the problem of a new technique. In the second place, it must be admitted that the literary productions of the century were of little merit in themselves, and important only for the influence which they exerted in one or the other direction. There are few young men in Egypt and Syria today who know even the names of the writers of the seventies and eighties, and practically none to whom their works would make any appeal. With the single exception of Nasif al-Yaziji, who was in reality a belated representative of medieval Arabic literature, the writers of the nineteenth century faithfully reflect the ideas, conditions, and problems of their own day and community, and with the gradual change which these have undergone have lost all but a historical value.

It is desirable therefore to pause at the threshold of the twentieth century, and inquire into the exact nature of the problem which, in its literary bearings, lay before the writers of the new generation, and how far the experience of their predecessors had guided them to a solution.

To this problem there are two sides, one psychological, the other stylistic. The former is the more fundamental, but to deal with it fully would far outrun the limits of this study. Its roots lie in the methods of education adopted in Egypt and elsewhere, the twist so given to the minds of the literate classes and their consequent capacity, or lack of capacity, either to adhere to the orthodox Muslim world-view or to assimilate the intellectual basis of Western thought and literature. It is obvious that the imitation of Western models initiated by the violent impact of Western life on the East remained and must remain sterile until such assimilation can issue in a community of intellectual method and aim. The earlier literature of the nineteenth century, swaying between a lifeless reproduction of medieval Arabic models, and an imitation of Western models without sufficient intellectual preparation, could not but be feeble and unfruitful. The whole intellectual life of the people was thrown into confusion by the contradiction in principle between the old system of thought with its dogmatic basis and the intellectual freedom of Western scientific methods.

In Egypt, at all events, this duality of method and the resulting confusion continued throughout the century, and has even yet not been eradicated. Its seeds are sown in the school, where shaikhs from the theological colleges and graduates of European universities teach side by side,[53] and its vitiating effects are only too obvious in the prevalence amongst educated Egyptians of cynicism, the inevitable companion of intellectual instability. Down to 1914, at least, only a small proportion of serious students succeeded in overcoming the handicap imposed upon them by their early training. It is largely owing to this that Syrian writers, educated from the outset on consistent Western lines, became the leaders of the movement of emancipation in the last decades of the century.

Literature of necessity followed a parallel course. The medieval and the modern views rested upon opposite conceptions which admitted of no reconciliation. For the medieval view of literature made of it privilege confined to the few. It was a mystery, in which only the scholastically educated might participate, and its aim was to supply not only intellectual recreation but also intellectual exercise. The medieval writer scorned simplicity, and repelled the simple by adopting a recondite style, strewn with obscurities and graced with literary allusions and erudite wit. But the spread of education and the increasing literacy of the population itself created a demand for simple, intelligible and interesting books. The problem was in essentials the same as—though more complicated than—that which confronted English writers at the beginning of the eighteenth century, when Defoe, Addison and Steele led the way in breaking up the stately periods of Caroline prose. The very efforts of the teachers of Arabic in the schools to stem the tide furthered the reaction. "The student who begins the study of Arabic and a foreign language simultaneously finds that he makes more progress with the latter, and consequently embraces its cultural heritage and neglects Arabic. . . . In Western literature he sees vigour of thought and congruence with the present, and a spirit, a life, an activity which he cannot find in Arabic. For where are the Arabic novels which portray our social life? Where is the Arabic poetry that represents our modern feelings? Where are the elegant and attractive Arabic books which we can place in the hands of our boys and girls for their education, where the pleasing illustrated stories which we can present to our babes?"[54] Another teacher, Dr. Taha Husain, has frequently stressed the result of this contrast in creating a dislike of Arabic literature in the minds of the students and in strengthening their preference for Western literature. To which might be added that a desire so stimulated is not likely to seek satisfaction in the best Western literature.

It was into this widening breach that the Syrian writers of the eighties and nineties stepped. Under the leadership of Gurgi Zaydan they set out to write new and interesting articles in language intelligible to all readers, "preferring," in the apt phrase of Manfaluti,[55] "that the ignorant should learn of them than that pedants should approve of them." But great as were the services of the Syrian school to neo-Arabic literature, they did not, and could not, solve the problem in either of its aspects. They could not solve the psychological problem because they were Christians, and whether Arabic literature was to have any future must of necessity rest with the overwhelming Muslim majority. Nor, for similar reasons, could they solve the stylistic problem. In the whole history of classical Arabic literature, there is only one Christian who stands out as a master of his craft, the poet al-Akhtal. The canons of Arabic literary style were laid down by Muslims on

Islamic literary models, above all on the Koran and the Traditions. It was neither possible, nor was it desirable, that modern
Arabic literature should completely sever itself from the Islamic
past, however far it might proceed on the path of adaptation to
new conditions. It might well throw off the accumulated rubbish
of centuries, but only to drink yet more deeply of the mainsprings
of its existence. And from those mainsprings the Christian, in the
impressionable years of education, was debarred.

Among the older generation of Muslim writers, as we have
seen, religious conservatism was too deeply bound up with the
entire heritage of Arabic literature to allow of any kind of simplification. But here too the reform movement led by Muhammad
Abduh brought about a profound change. In returning to the
writings of the early centuries, the new generation discovered
afresh an Arabic literary style which was simple and direct, not yet
tainted with the erudite "refinements" of the Silver Age. The ease
and lucidity of Ibn al-Muqaffa were contrasted with the labored
pedantry of the school of al-Hariri. Now that the religious inhibition was removed, there was no further reason for timidity; indeed,
religious radicalism supplied a strong incentive to literary radicalism as well. A little later this was to lead to a widespread interest
in and study of all the early productions of Arabic literature, but
in the first decade of the century the movement was still in its
infancy.[56] The writers of the Syro-American school, however, had
brought into prominence the poetry of Abul-Ala al-Maarri,[57]
whose rationalism and pessimism not only appealed to the spirit
of the age, but also supplied a point of contact between Arabic
and European thought. But for the present, the chief lesson which
was deduced from the study of the early writers was that Arabic
stylists were not tied to the wheels of a decadent scholasticism,
but free, not so much to recover the simplicity of the primitives,
but to create anew for this age, as they had created for theirs, and
by acknowledging a common inspiration, to preserve the continuity of Arabic tradition through an epoch of destruction and
rebuilding.

There remained a subsidiary problem. Classical Arabic literature offered practically no models for prose works of entertainment in the modern style. What form was the new type of belles-

lettres to adopt? The answer was dictated by various considerations. In the first place the intellectual instability on the part of
both writers and readers militated against the production of works
of any length. The necessary power of concentration was lacking,
except amongst the Syrians. Thus the only long original productions of the turn of the century were novels, and of these the
rambling and unfinished *Hadith Isa bni Hisham* of the younger
Muwaylhi (though itself possibly the most living and original
work in the whole Arabic literature of the time) alone bore the
signature of an Egyptian author.[58] More decisive, however, were
the facilities for publication within reach of the ordinary writer.
With so limited a public, publishers were naturally reluctant to
spend money on experiments, and writers to embark on the risky,
and at best ill-rewarded task of producing books. The expansion
of the daily and periodical press furnished the opportunity of
making a livelihood and a name, but at the same time limited the
field to the short essay. Most of the books issued by Egyptian
writers consist in consequence of essays on various subjects, reprinted from journals with or without alteration. In this moreover they were but following their Syrian predecessors. The activities of the Syrians were almost entirely journalistic, and their
writing had to accommodate itself to their needs. Even their novels
came out originally as serials. All these influences led Egyptian
writers to turn to the essay form, and having once acquired that
fatally convenient style, it was seldom that they roused themselves
to experiment in more elaborate and less profitable genres.

The first years of the century, however, saw one forward step.
The Syrian writers had hitherto pursued, sometimes openly, sometimes indirectly, an aim which was primarily educational and
directed to the widest possible public. For their purposes the first
essentials were clarity and simplicity, and literary polish was a
secondary, if desirable, adjunct. The newer generation of Syrians,
while retaining the essay form, began to infuse into it a more
definitely literary content. On the one hand Farah Antun (1874-
1922) kept the simple style but used the essay and the novel to
express his own philosophy of life.[59] He was at this time strongly
attracted towards Rousseau and the French Romanticists, and in
spite of, or because of, his pessimism and anti-religious bias, his

work exerted a formative influence on the more thoughtful section of readers. But he was ahead of his time, and financial difficulties drove him to attempt more popular work. On the other hand, the brilliant writers of the young Syro-American school[60] were engaged in the creation of a new literary art, the "prose poem" (*shir manthur*), which owed its inspiration to Walt Whitman and English free verse.

It has already been shown that in this revival of literary activity, Egyptian writers had begun to contest the primacy enjoyed by the Syrians. In journalism the new Muslim and nationalist press was able to touch whole classes of the population to whom the Syrian press made no appeal, at the same time striving to reinterpret the new ideas, introduced by Western education and interpreted by the Syrians, into some sort of harmony with the intellectual basis of Islamic culture. It was not yet time for radical measures, though the pace of reform was to quicken at a rate which none could then have foreseen, but a time of stirring, when political nationalism, pan-Islamic aspirations, religious reform, and Western culture fought with the forces of conservatism for the soul of Egypt, in confused rivalry and dubious alliance.

The inquiet, struggling, groping spirit of the age found characteristic literary expression in the work of Sayyid Mustafa Lutfi al-Manfaluti (1876-1924). Of half-Turkish, half-Arab stock, Manfaluti received the usual theological training in the college of al-Azhar. After distinguishing himself as a poet he began his career as a prose writer under Shaikh Ali Yusuf's wing in the *Muayyad*. From the very first he was distinguished by a width of interests foreign to the conservative theologian. His writings show how deeply he had been influenced by the work on the one hand of the Syrian school, and even of Farah Antun (for he knew no European languages), and by the religious reform movement, pan-Islamism, and the rise of Egyptian nationalism on the other. He seemed to epitomize all the half-articulate and contradictory tendencies of his time, and his essays, republished as *an-Nazarat* (1910) and supplemented in subsequent editions, have survived the furious attacks of both conservatives and modernists, and remain down to the present the most widely read work in modern Arabic literature.[61]

It is not difficult to explain the attraction of the *Nazarat* for Egyptian readers. Nothing like these racy and sparkling essays and sermonettes had ever appeared before in Arabic literature. The style, the subject, the manner of presentation, all possessed an immediate appeal to an Egyptian audience. For this Manfaluti was indebted to no superior power of psychological insight, nor even to a carefully chosen literary art; he looked within himself, and put down on paper, with native Egyptian wit, in the style and language of a trained scholar, heedless of inconsistencies and with perfect sincerity, the contents of that microcosm of pre-war Egypt, his own mind.

As a religious reformer, he attacked conservatism and its sanctuary, the college of al-Azhar, and condemned saint worship, the darwish orders, etc., yet went out of his way to insult his master Muhammad Abduh,[62] and having blamed him for introducing modern interpretations of the Koran, went on in the very next paragraph to make drastic interpretations himself. Together with a fervent Islamic patriotism, which led him at one time to condemn all Western studies and at another to protest against Armenian massacres,[63] he betrayed on almost every page of his work the influence of Western currents of thought. No more striking proof of the permeation of the Arabic world by such European currents could be given than this fact, that a man entirely cut off as he was from direct contact with the West should yet have been so completely under the influence of Rousseau and Victor Hugo. Equally eloquent of Western influences is his attraction towards Abul-Ala, whose verses he quoted, and whose *Risalat al-Ghufran* he not only summarized in one essay, but imitated in another.[64] At the same time his Islamic patriotism had to admit a growing rival in Egyptian national pride, which claimed to be the heir of Thebes no less than of Baghdad, but with characteristic candor he acknowledged the deep debt of gratitude which Egypt owes to the Syrians.[65]

His social outlook was dominated by the idealistic and doctrinaire naturalism of the eighteenth century and the French Romanticists, mediated through Farah Antun. "The City of Happiness"[66] represents an early attempt to systematize his vague socialism, but for the most part their ideas hover sentimentally above his pages, as when he contrasts the "freedom" of the animal creation with the unnatural servitude of man.[67] But his sympathies were called out above all by the weak and the defenceless, and in essay after essay he preached the duty of charity (*ihsan*), especially towards wronged and persecuted women. Yet he attacked Qasim Amin as the corrupter of Egyptian womanhood, and asserted the intellectual inferiority of women to men.[68] The natural tendency in him to melancholy and sentimentality led him to take the most pessimistic view of humanity. Life was indeed to him a vale of tears, from which he sought an escape in imagination. "I love beauty in imagination more than in reality," he writes. "The description of a garden gives me more pleasure than to view it. I like to read about fine cities ... and care not at all to see them, as though I wished to preserve unspoilt this imaginative delight, and were afraid that the reality would rob me of it."[69] But too often his sense of social injustice issued in an unqualified cynicism, which was the gravest fault in his character as a writer. Nothing escaped his lash; even the reformers fared no better than the wealthy and powerful, and in his impatience he denied human loyalty altogether.[70] But it was against politicians that his bitterest scorn was directed. "Can a man be a politician without being a liar and a knave?" he exclaims, in seeking to justify his abstention from political debate.[71]

It was less the content of his essays, however, than the style in which they were written that won for Manfaluti his singular pre-eminence. Of this it is perhaps difficult for a European to judge quite fairly. Manfaluti had a clear perception of the need for a change in Arabic literary methods and repeatedly expressed his conviction that the secret of style lay in the truthful representation to the reader of the ideas which occupied the writer's mind. With this he held strongly to the necessity of studying the great models of Arabic eloquence, asserting that the poverty of so much contemporary writing was due to ignorance and lack of confidence. For himself he disclaimed any sort of imitation; he expressed his ideas with complete freedom in the language which pleased his own ear.

This resulted, as might be expected, in a characteristic mixture of medieval and modern. Modern is the general smoothness of his writing, especially in narrative passages, and the framework of the essays. He delights to begin with a homely illustraton or a simple parable, which serves as the text of his discourse, and is often expanded into a complete story. A humorous scene with mosquitoes serves as prelude to a denunciation of inhumanity. At another time he bids farewell to humor with playful gravity before launching on a diatribe against Westernism. Modern, too, are his imaginative metaphors and similes, though European readers may often fail to realize how novel they are in Arabic. The influence of the Syro-Americans is obvious in the passages of "prose poetry" to be found in his earlier work, but in spite of the popularity of these passages, the prose poem seems to have followed regular poetry into the limbo of neglect.

With all this, he could not completely throw off inherited mannerisms. Though he criticized rhymed prose, he fell into it automatically whenever the emotional tone of his writing rose. The effect is often not unpleasing, and to those who (like the present writer) regard rhymed prose as a natural and legitimate ornament of Arabic style, it gives, when properly used, a cadence and a finish that is sadly lacking in most of his contemporaries. But the use of rhymed prose is open to criticism when it is employed simply for its own sake, and becomes mere highfalutin— a fault from which Manfuluti was by no means free. Unfortunately, too, he showed a tendency in his later essays to restrict rhymed prose to just such passages of padding. A still more insidious fault, which he shared with almost all Arabic writers, was the habit of balancing words and phrases by rhyming or unrhymed synonyms, which add nothing to the sense, and hinder the development of the narrative or thought. Occasionally, but not often, his excess of detail resulted in clumsy sentences.[72] How far Manfaluti is to be charged with the pedantry which he condemned in others is a question which, in the present state of Arabic letters, can be answered only by those who knew him personally.

The later essays differ to some extent from the earlier, both in style and matter, but in an unfavourable sense. The writing is more mechanical and less humorous, the decoration more artificial; there is more effort at symmetry and balance. His imagination has no longer the same wide play, and the didactic purpose is more stressed. Along with this went a certain stereotyping of his ideas. His Islamic patriotism and antipathy to the spread of Western influences were more pronounced,[73] and led him at times to idealize the old manners and even the old political organization.[74] Yet he himself remained completely under the influence of Western thought in his interpretation of religious and social ethics, and seemed quite unconscious of the contradiction.

Nevertheless, taken as a whole, Manfaluti's work marks an immense advance on that of all his predecessors. It was the first really successful attempt to adapt the classical tradition to the new demands of popular literature, however much room it left for improvement. There is certainly little in modern Arabic writing that affords so much pleasure as the *Nazarat,* and its brilliant qualities frequently disguise the inadequacy and lack of originality of the ideas which it clothes. Only when it is read in bulk does the repetition of ideas, of phrases, even of metaphors, and still more the querulous and critical tone which pervades it from cover to cover, pall at length on the reader, and leave him with the feeling that with the *Nazarat* Manfaluti had worked himself out.

As the peculiar virtues of Manfaluti's style must largely be lost in translation, the contrast which he offers to his Syrian predecessors may perhaps be best illustrated by comparing two essays which show a general similarity of plan in developing the text that "Riches do not confer happiness."

Gurgi Zaydan begins his essay[75] with a simple warning that happiness must not be sought in riches, though there is nothing reprehensible in the acquisition of wealth by rightful means. To marry for money, on the other hand, brings evil moral and material consequences in its train. "Do not be dazzled by the outward pomp of wealth," he says in effect, "but come with me and visit one of these imposing palaces," and having drawn a picture of a dispirited husband, whose wife cares only for dress and spends the night out dancing with more attractive partners, he returns to draw the lessons of the danger of riches. The tone never rises above a pleasant conversational level, with an occasional touch of lightness.

Manfaluti, on the other hand, opens[76] with two pages of brilliant description of a luxurious palace, "whose towering battle-

ments soar to the heavenly spheres," written in elaborately inter-
laced rhyming prose. He then passes to a picture in simple but
dignified language of a dying man awaiting through the night the
return of his frivolous wife and depraved son. From a faithful
black servant he learns that their callousness is the direct outcome
of his earlier life of dissipation. As he leans out to drink in the
fresh dawn breeze he overhears the gardener and his wife contrasting their simple happiness with his wealth and misery, and
in his death agony sees the wreckage of his life fall about him. The
contrast between the two writers is intensified by Manfaluti's
melodramatic exaggeration and absence of shading in his characters, who are little more than personifications of virtues or
vices.[77]

The other prose writings of Manfaluti consist of a volume of
short stories entitled *al-Abarat* ("Tears")[78] and several versions of
French romances, presumably made from Arabic drafts.[79] Several
of the stories in the *Abarat* are also based on translated material,
as are several essays in the *Nazarat*. But it seems that the translations in the *Nazarat* are intended partly as object lessons or experiments in the capacity of Arabic to render exalted passages of
Western literary style (e.g., Hugo's discourse on Voltaire, and the
speeches of Brutus and Antony from "Julius Caesar"). In the
Abarat, on the other hand, Manfaluti abandoned himself to the
sentimental pessimism of the extreme romantic school, with the
same absence of light and shade in his character drawing which
he had already displayed in the *Nazarat*.[80] In spite of the popularity which the work has enjoyed, largely on account of its stylistic
qualities, it ranks very far below the *Nazarat* as a contribution to
modern Arabic literature.

III   Egyptian Modernists

The period 1914-1919, though one of relative quiescence,
marks a turning point in the development of modern Arabic literature, but, in spite of the coincidence of dates, the European war
was not responsible, either directly or indirectly, for initiating
the change. The new element by which the change was brought

about was the rise of a distinctive Egyptian school of writers, which, from small beginnings in the years immediately preceding the war, gathered strength in the interval, and emerged into sudden prominence on the resumption of literary activities. To understand the significance of this movement we must look back for a moment at the situation as it was about 1912. At that time, as has been seen, there was a sharp opposition between two contrasting schools of thought in Arabic letters. On the one hand were the modernists, almost all Syrians, and Christian Syrians at that, headed by the new Syro-American school; on the other were the classicists, who still clung to the medieval Islamic tradition, and who were dominant in Egypt and in Muslim Syria. Between the two extremes were varying intermediate grades, including several writers who individually exercised considerable influence, but did not form a body sufficiently united in method or aim to counterbalance either of the opposing schools. The most prominent of these intermediate figures were Gurgi Zaydan and Manfaluti, but, as the preceding section has shown, neither Zaydan nor Manfaluti, in spite of their great gifts and popularity, could establish a definite literary movement. Zaydan's writing was too colorless and didactic, and Manfaluti was too superficial in thought and too strongly inclined to the classical tradition in style, to attract readers who sought in Arabic literature something comparable to the books with which they were familiar in the languages of the West.

The outcome of this state of affairs was that the sympathies of the educated reading classes were attracted to those Syro-American writers who by their boldness and originality had established themselves as the leaders of the modernist movement, and who thus gained a predominant position in neo-Arabic literature, in spite of the violent attacks of the classicists,[81] It is unnecessary at this point to enter into a full discussion of their views and literary methods, since they have been made the subject of an admirable article by Professor Kratchkowsky in *Le Monde Oriental*.[82] Within the last ten years, however, their leadership has been challenged, and on the whole successfully, by the new Egyptian school.[83]

The beginnings of the new school date from the foundation of the newspaper *al-Garidah* in 1907, as the organ of the now defunct "Popular Party" (*hizb al-ummah*). The tone of the new journal was set by its political director, Ahmad Lutfi Bey as-Sayyid, under whose influence *al-Garidah*, unlike its Egyptian-edited contemporaries, Mustafa Kamil's *Liwa*, with its purely political aims, and the conservative *Muayyad*, opened its columns to the social and literary reform movements of the day. Around Lutfi Bey as-Sayyid gathered the young Muslims of the new generation in Egypt, who were not only inspired by the growing nationalist ideals, but who had been more thoroughly educated on western lines than their predecessors, and had in many cases absorbed much of the spirit of western culture through prolonged contacts with it during student years, for the most part in France. The aspiration of these young writers was to see their country not only politically free, but able to take a worthy place in world civilization. At the same time, they were Muslims, but Muslims in whom the legacy of Muhammad Abduh was working towards a new adaptation of the fundamental positions of Islam to the demands of modern life and thought. Deeply conscious of the present contradiction, they were yet convinced that it could and must be resolved, not by a return to the past, nor, like the Syro-Americans, by cutting adrift from the past, but by the slow process of education and reform, and it was to this task that they felt themselves called. *Al-Garidah* thus served as the training ground of some of the most prominent members of the new school, including Muhammad Husayn Haykal, at that time a law student in Paris, and afterwards the principal mouthpiece of its ideals.

Down to 1914, however, the new movement was still in its infancy, and overshadowed in its own country by the Syrian writers and the nationalist-conservative movement. The war put a temporary stop to most of its outward activities. *Al-Garidah* suspended publication, though its place was to some extent taken by the weekly *as-Sufur*, edited by Abdal-Hamid Hamdi, a former member of the staff of *al-Garidah* and subsequently one of Haykal Bey's collaborators in *as-Siyasah*. The movement nevertheless continued to grow in strength, and at length came to fruition during the early post-war years. Two important steps in its advance were marked by the reorganization of the Egyptian University, with Lutfi Bey as-Sayyid as its director,[84] and the formation of the

Liberal Constitutional party, with its organ *as-Siyasah* founded in 1922 under the editorship of Husayn Bey Haykal. Through these two organizations, which were moreover in fairly close touch with one another, the scattered forces of education and reform were enabled to concentrate and co-operate, and thus to gain an increasing influence over Egyptian public opinion. At the same time the increased vigor of the nationalist movements in the Arabic East as a result of the war, and the enthusiasm which they generated, not only gave fresh driving force to the activities of the new school, but gained for their writings universal sympathy in the Arabic lands, as the literary exponents of the aims and ideals with which all, in greater or less degree, were imbued. Though in the political sphere they were temporarily overborne by the more extreme elements in Egypt, and were often constrained to yield to force of circumstances, educated circles in all the civilized Arab lands were impressed by their activities and earnestness, as by the closer contact with the realities of the situation and truer reflection of their own aspirations which the Egyptian writers showed, in contrast to the detachment of the Syro-American writers,[85] and were sympathetically attracted by their stand upon the common ground of the Muslim and Arabic heritage.

It is true that, taken singly, none of the elements which have gone to make up the Egyptian school, and few of its ideals, were new or original in modern Arabic literature—a fact which goes some way to explain the obscurity of its beginnings. It is equally true that to speak of these writers as a school is to use a misleading, though convenient, term, since not only do they fall into various sub-groups, but the individual writers show such wide divergencies of methods, background, and temperament, that their association appears to be largely haphazard. Yet in practice they do form a group as well defined, for instance, as the Syro-Americans, among whom similar individual differences are found, in that certain distinctive aims and characteristics are shared by them all, to greater or less degree. All of them are striving to give greater depth and range to modern Arabic writing, and to rescue it from the fluent superficiality to which a literature based on journalism is peculiarly liable. Most of them aim at applying modern aesthetic and literary criteria to the rich stores of old Arabic literature, as well as to modern productions, and so at bringing out all that they can contribute to the building-up of a new civilization. They are distinguished also by a new comprehensiveness, in which the sharpness of the old antagonism between modernist and classicist has been blunted, and made to serve the purpose of creating a new literary technique, which shall be in harmony with modern aims and standards, and yet preserve the familiar rhythms of Arabic. They have already achieved so much that the old wrangles of classicists and modernists on points of linguistic usage have lost their meaning, and have give place to a fresh alignment between conservatives and liberals on the fundamental principles of culture. From the literary point of view, what now determines the extent to which any writer is a modernist is not the superficial features of his writing but the answer which he gives to the question, how far Arabic literature is to draw its sole or main inspiration from traditional Islamic sources. But there can scarcely be found one Muslim Egyptian writer of note who rejects the Islamic past entirely, in the manner of the Syro-Americans; it is in fact one of the distinctive features of the Egyptian school as against the latter, that even the most modernist amongst them aim at what Jibran Khalil Jibran has scornfully called "patching the outworn garment."

None of these characteristics, however, is necessarily or in fact limited to Egyptian writers. The appropriateness of the description "Egyptian school" lies not so much in the fact that the leaders of the new school are all Egyptians, as in the gradual emergence of a further feature which they have in common, a feature which is difficult as yet to define and liable to assume exaggerated prominence. At present it may perhaps be termed "Egyptian particularism," which shows itself in a tendency to think in terms of Egypt rather than of the Arab world. Egypt, they feel, is still a part of the Arabic-speaking world, but has nevertheless to create its distinctive culture, and to make its distinctive contribution to literature and thought. In certain spheres of popular literature, and more especially in the drama, this attitude is still more explicit, and goes the length of using as a medium the colloquial Egyptian dialect. It is not surprising that the other Arabic-speaking countries try to shut their eyes to this—from their point of view—unwelcome tendency among modernist Egyptian writers.[86] Yet the tendency is there, and is increasingly marked, partly by reflection from the political situation, and partly as a result of the new interest and pride in the ancient Egyptian civilization, which has been deliberately cultivated by the leaders of the Egyptian nationalist movement. At the present moment, the strength of this feeling varies greatly from writer to writer, but it may eventually prove a decisive factor in the development of neo-Arabic thought.[87]

The majority of modernist Egyptian writers fall naturally into two groups, one composed of writers whose western background is mainly French, the other of writers who have been more strongly, though not exclusively, influenced by English literature. Of the former group the principal mouthpiece is Muhammad Husayn Bey Haykal, now editor of *as-Siyasah*, which, together with its weekly edition started in 1926, has become the leading organ of liberal thought amongst Egyptian Muslims, rivaling in this respect the old established Syrian-owned *Ahram* and *Muqattam*. It was only comparatively recently that Dr. Haykal began to devote himself to journalism.[88] His first large scale publication was a notable incursion into the field of imaginative literature, a novel of Egyptian peasant life, entitled *Zaynab*, published anonymously in 1914.[89] For some years after this he was absorbed in legal practice, but in 1921 he published the first two parts of a study on the life and works of Rousseau.[90] Since 1922 the editorship of the *Siyasah* has left him little time to give to more elaborate literary tasks, and his only later publications in book form so far are a collection of essays and studies reprinted from various journals, under the title of *In Leisure Hours*,[91] and a narrative of his visit to the Sudan at the opening of the Makwar dam, entitled *Ten Days in the Sudan*.[92]

It is less through his books, however, than through his journals[93] and his own descriptive articles and studies, that Dr. Haykal exerts the great influence which he enjoys throughout the Arabic world. His first and immediate object is to discipline the Arabic language into a flexible idiom which will express the thoughts and ideals of modern civilization. Long ago it was borne in on him that the vocabulary of Arabic put it at a disadvantage compared with the language of Western Europe. "I used," he has written, "to rebel inwardly when I found myself unable to express in my own language what I felt in my heart and pictured in my mind's eye, and the shape of its French or English expressions formed themselves in my imagination."[94] This is a service which the journalist is peculiarly fitted to render, and it is partly with this object that Dr. Haykal exercises his pen week by week in long descriptive and critical essays, in which the capacity of Arabic for expressing delicate shades of meaning are tested and supplemented.[95] Language is but an instrument, which must be kept "polished" or it becomes rusty; considerations of "classical" usage must not be allowed to stand in the way of adaptation to modern ideas. "The true *adib*," so runs his creed, "is not the person who is familiar with obscure and antiquated words, but the person who can clothe beautiful ideas or fine shades of thought or imagery . . . in a garment, through which their beauty and originality can be perceived. The simpler the words, the sweeter they are to the ear, the nearer to the heart, and the more attractive to the mind."[96]

The working out of a new technique, however, is in his view no more than a preliminary step to a wider aim, which is shared by all the leaders of the Egyptian school. In the existing cleavage between writer and public they see the gravest danger to the future of Egyptian literature. One cannot help sympathizing with al-Aqqad when, in a moment of despondency, he cries, "Readers in Egypt are all in one of three groups: readers of novels and brain-ticklers (*nawadir*), readers of [classical] Arabic literature, and readers of Western literature."[97] Each writer in his own way is trying to bridge the gap, and to raise the standard of literary taste in Egypt. They feel that the wider public would willingly come to their side and second their efforts, if only some inner contact could be made.[98] To Dr. Haykal the only sure method of achieving unity is to work for the development of a truly national culture. At present there is no indigenous culture in the Arab lands— nothing but sham antique and imitations of the West.[99] This national culture is not to be achieved by pseudo-antiquarianism: "The Arab peoples and the Arabic language have plunged irrevocably into the race, and are preparing their shoulders to bear the whole civilization of humanity, in all its manifestations of science, art, and literature."[100] Nor can it be achieved by disregarding the past.[101] In realizing this aim both modernist and classicist must co-operate; otherwise victory will rest with the Syro-Americans, and Islamic culture will vanish.[102] The task will be long and arduous. It calls for the labor and self-sacrifice of generations; premature haste, the besetting sin of the Orient of today, can lead only to disaster.[103] Meanwhile, something may be done by familiarizing the reading public with the principles of objective criticism and teaching it, if not to think for itself, at least to turn its attention, not in the first place to the language of a writer, but to his ideas and thoughts, and only secondarily to his methods of expression.

Though Dr. Haykal often speaks in this connection of Arabic culture as a whole, and frequently insists on the need of strengthening the cultural ties among the Arabic-speaking peoples,[104] he believes that each Arabic-speaking country will in due course develop a literary life of its own.[105] His own hopes and energies, consequently, are centered mainly on the creation of a modern Egyptian culture.[106] In all his writings, from the first fervent dedication of his early novel *Zaynab* "To Egypt," there glows an intense love of his country. Scarcely any other modern writer shows such interest in the ancient history of Egypt, and the pride which he so often expresses in the ancient East is really a pride in the achievements of ancient Egypt. So strong is this feeling in him that it results in a certain jealousy of the Arabs, and a peculiar insensibility to ancient Arabic literature; indeed, he has confessed that since 1910 he has ceased to pay much attention to it.[107] He complains that Egyptian literature and thought are neglected in the Egyptian University, and of the absence of Egyptian feeling in the writings of both classicists and modernists.[108] Yet with him this Egyptian feeling is totally distinct from the effervescent froth so prominent since 1919 among a section of Egyptians. Though he shares, as deeply as any man, their political aspirations, and though he has exploited, as he was perhaps entitled to do, the inflamed national sentiment for his own purposes, he realizes that no enduring political progress is possible without a social and intellectual regeneration which is as yet only in its beginnings. The men and women of this generation are precursors, and upon their success in effecting a change of mind in the rising generation depends the future of Egypt.

In this aim Dr. Haykal finds his closest collaborators among his former colleagues in the new Egyptian University and a number of the teachers in the higher training colleges. Though their work is by its nature more concentrated, and does not lend itself as a rule to literary productions other than technical manuals, it is none the less important in its bearing on the future of Egyptian literature. To them also this is an age of preparation rather than achievement, "an age of translation, not of composition," in the words of Lutfi Bey as-Sayyid, Director of the University and the present Minister of Public Instruction. But one teacher at least, Dr. Taha Husain, has created for himself in modern Arabic letters a position as prominent as that occupied by Dr. Haykal, in a manner which often contrasts oddly with the moderation and supple methods of his colleague.

Taha Husain was born into a home which preserved all the traditional features of up-river village life. At an early age his sight was completely lost, and he was destined for a theological career. After the usual elementary instruction in the village *kuttab* he was entered as a student at al-Azhar and spent some years there, in the course of which he acquired a thorough grasp of Arabic from the linguistic side. Under the guidance of Shaikh Sayyid b. Ali al-Marsafi he began to show a special partiality for Arabic literature, and subsequently continued his studies under European professors in the newly-founded Egyptian University. Here he was initiated into modern western methods of literary criticism and historical study, and he rapidly threw off the prejudices and cramped outlook of the Azharite. The first fruits of these studies was a thesis on Abul-Ala al-Maarri,[109] in the introduction to which he already displayed his characteristic audacity by attacking the methods of teaching Arabic literature in Egypt. During the war years he studied at the Sorbonne, specializing in French literature and literary criticism, and in classics. His university career, after a narrow escape from disaster on account of an impetuous criticism which gave some offence in Egypt,[110] closed in 1919, with the production of a doctoral thesis on Ibn Khaldun.[111] On his return to Egypt he was appointed to the new chair of Classical (Greek and Roman) History at the Egyptian University, and on the reconstitution of the university was transferred to the Professorship of Ancient Arabic literature.

At the very outset of his teaching career the new professor had need of all his natural courage. His appointment gave the signal for the opening of a campaign directed against him and his work on the part of all the conservative educational elements in Egypt. Although he was already, as has been seen, *persona ingratissima* to the shaikhs, the main attack was directed against the new chair, probably the first of the kind in any Muslim institution. For although every student of the Middle Ages is aware of the debt which Islamic civilization owed to Hellenism, it was a debt which the Islamic world never recognized, and in any case that aesthetic legacy of Greece which so profoundly influenced the evolution of modern Europe had found no acceptance in the Orient. Even when the modern westernizing movement gained momentum in Egypt and Syria and passed from the stage of translation to that of imitation and closer study, it was only the outward modern manifestations of western thought and literature that were studied. Gradually the history of European thought began to be better appreciated, but the foundations still remained unknown. The first attempt to familiarize the Arabic world with something of the classical literary background was made by Sulayman al-Bustani in his translation of the *Iliad*.[112] The attempt was perhaps premature, and the subject ill-chosen. Epic poetry has never attracted the Arab, whose language lacks even a suitable metrical scheme for poems of such length and quality, and the technical difficulties were enhanced by the necessity of transliterating and fitting into Arabic meter all the Greek names. The result was that Bustani's translation was appreciated more as a *tour de force* than for the intrinsic qualities of either the original or the Arabic version.[113] Egypt, striving after western democracy and western science, remained ignorant of and indifferent to, even a little contemptuous towards, their source.

This paradox was brought vividly home to Dr. Taha Husain. His students at first showed some hostility to the new imposition, as they regarded it, but gradually his eloquence and enthusiasm began to effect a change. Now he came boldly forward with the claim that if Egypt was to gain self-respect and was to progress in the ways of modern life, she must go to school and begin again with the foundations. In a series of works intended for the general public[114] he stressed again and again the necessity of classical studies as the basis of a living culture. "We cannot live in this age demanding all the political and intellectual independence enjoyed by the peoples of Europe, while we remain dependent on them for all that nourishes the intellect and the feelings in science, philosophy, literature, and the arts."[115] It might perhaps have gone hard with him had the attention of Egypt not been distracted by the political crisis through which it was passing; as it was, however, he found strong support in a section of educated opinion and especially among his own colleagues. Indeed, at this very time, the Director of the University, Ahmad Lutfi Bey as-Sayyid, was engaged in a translation, from the French, of the *Nicomachean Ethics,* which appeared in 1924.[116] But if the political situation eased his path, it also affected the success of his propaganda, and with his transference to the chair of Arabic literature, the projected continuations of his classical studies came to an untimely and regrettable end. It is too soon yet to say that the effort to bring classical studies to bear on Arabic literature has failed; it is to be hoped at least that the professor's example of enthusiasm for learning and intellectual courage has not been lost on the rising generation.

Even after his transference to Arabic studies, however, Dr. Taha Husain was not to find himself in smoother waters. Following up his principle of introducing modern French methods of critical study into Egypt, he began to apply a sort of Cartesian analysis to Arabic literature, with results which became more and more radical. So far from emulating Dr. Haykal's cautious adaptation of European methods to the existing level of general education in Egypt, he jumped down the throats of the conservatives, and at length carried the method of philosophic doubt to a point for which Egyptian opinion was totally unprepared. His gradual progress towards radicalism can be traced in the first two series of studies which he published on Arabic poets;[117] on the publication of the third, however, entitled *On Pre-Islamic Poetry,*[118] such an outcry was raised that the book had to be withdrawn, and a process for heresy was begun against the author.[119] Again his good fortune saved him from the worst effects of his audacity, and the result of the attempted persecution of the conservatives was only to enhance his popularity and prestige with the liberals and make him the idol of the students. Nothing daunted, therefore, he republished the work, slightly revised as a concession to public opinion, and considerably enlarged, under a different title (*On Pre-Islamic Literature*) in the following year.[120]

Scholastic though all these works are, they form an important contribution to contemporary Egyptian literature, not only by their qualities of style and method, but by the skilful way in which the needs of a wider public are kept in view. The style is peculiar in the sense that, being dictated, not written, it presents characteristics, such as frequent repetition of phrases, which belong to oratory rather than to prose. Yet the happy choice of words, the smoothness and facility of the argument, and the humorous and masterly handling of the subject, give it an attractive quality which is rarely equaled in Egyptian writing. Nevertheless, it is in their educational aspect that the main value of these studies lies, and whether or not all the conclusions to which Dr. Taha Husain has come are accepted, the wide influence which he enjoys must in due course lead to the strengthening in Egyptian thought and literature of the principles for which he stands.[121]

It is not only in virtue of these works, however, that Dr. Taha Husain occupies an outstanding position in contemporary letters. Outside the sphere of his professional studies, he has found the time to make fairly extensive contributions to periodical literature, among which may be mentioned the lengthy critical analyses of modern French plays, published in *al-Hilal*, a number of which have been reprinted in book form.[122] In 1922 he issued a translation of Gustave le Bon's *Psychologie de l'Education*.[123] Much more important from every point of view is the literary autobiography, entitled *Al-Ayyam* ("Days"), a work which is justly praised for its depth of feeling and for the truth of its descriptions, and has a good claim to be regarded as the finest work of art yet produced in modern Egyptian literature.[124]

Together with the writers already mentioned there are a number of others who belong to the same group, but are less prominent in the world of letters. Among the other professors at the Egyptian University, several, including Mansur Bey Fahmi, Dr. Ahmad Amin, Dr. Ahmad Dayf,[125] and Shaikh Mustafa Abd ar-Raziq, are known to a fairly wide public. The last named,[126] whose masterly introduction to the French translation of Muhammad Abduh's *Risalat al-Tawhid* is familiar to European scholars, probably stands in the truest line of development from Muhammad Abduh, as a modernist who yet holds firmly to the bases of Islamic tradition. At the opposite extreme to him is Mahmud Azmi, sub-editor of *as-Siyasah,* and the most advanced of all Muslim Egyptian modernists.

The same school of thought is represented also among the teachers at other higher colleges, and though in most cases their individual influence is bounded by their immediate students and their particular subject, yet cumulatively their effect on the evolution of Egyptian taste is considerable. It extends still further into the ranks of more popular writers, who, whether or not they make any claim to familiarity with French literature, show in their output the influence of their contacts with French thought. As Lord Cromer observed several years ago,[127] French culture has exercised a peculiarly powerful attraction on educated Egyptians, and while there is nothing regrettable in this fact itself, the study of Egyptian literature shows that it is open to question whether its effects have been altogether good.

The reasons for this criticism lie in the attraction of Egyptian writers and readers towards particular currents in French literature, rather than towards French literature as a whole. It could hardly be expected that Egyptians should feel any natural sympathy with the productions of the classical school, while, on the contrary, there is a real kinship between the spirit of Arabic literature and the works of the Romanticists. The previous section has shown how strongly Manfaluti fell under the influence of such writers as Chateaubriand, and in this Manfaluti was by no means exceptional. The range of better educated Egyptians has widened, but the student cannot help noticing how often the names of Rousseau, Alfred de Vigny, de Musset, and Hugo recur, and still more how widespread is the admiration for Anatole France, even among the best of the Egyptian writers mentioned above.[128] When one considers what might be the fruit of this inoculation with the more negative and skeptical sides of modern French culture, one can sympathize with the fear of the conservatives that the influence of European studies is wholly destructive. Fortunately, however, among the leaders of the liberal school, these tendencies are balanced by a wider grasp of the vital and constructive process within which the European reader is able to give the Romanticists their fitting place. There are even one or two writers who stress the doctrine of progress through suffering,[129] though they fail to convey a vivid impression of actuality.

An important share in the propagation of healthier and more constructive elements of western thought is taken by the second group of Egyptian modernists, those writers whose European background is mainly English. The reason for this is not to be sought in any comparisons between French and English culture as a whole, but rather in the fact that the English writers with whom Egyptians are most familiar—Shakespeare, Carlyle, Dickens, Tennyson, Bernard Shaw—are essentially writers of a healthy and constructive outlook. The leading literary figures in this group are Abbas Mahmud al-Aqqad and Ibrahim Abd al-Qadir al-Mazini. The gap which separates al-Aqqad from the majority of those already named is fairly wide, and has unfortunately been widened by political differences, though the latter of course cut across all literary divisions. Al-Mazini occupies a more intermediate position, but in the controversies to which they, in common with many others, have devoted a disproportionate share of their energies, he is distinguished by a vigor which amounts at times to violence.

In their literary careers al-Aqqad and al-Mazini have developed along closely similar lines. Both of them began as poets of a modernist type,[130] whose lyrics are inspired by definite subjective emotions, and not in any way influenced by the traditional methods and subjects of Arabic poetry. At the same time, that is from 1912 onwards, they engaged in a certain amount of poetic criticism, which led up to their joint publication in 1920-1921 of vigorous critical essays on such leading literary figures of the conservative school as Manfaluti and the poet Ahmad Shawqi, under the misleading title of *ad-Diwan*.[131] Their subsequent publications consist of collections of articles of different dates, reprinted from various journals, and ranging over a wide field.[132] In general they share the aims and characteristics already noted as common to all the Egyptian modernists, and do not hide their conviction that a literary revival, reflecting a revolution in the ideas and outlook of the people, is a necessay preliminary to a full revival of national life, and that it is the present task of the writer and thinker to guide the people towards the formulation and achievement of their national contribution to civilization. But both of them stand appreciably nearer to the conservative position than either Dr. Haykal or Dr. Taha Husain; they are less insistent on the evolution of a purely Egyptian culture, and lay more weight on the grafting of congruent European elements on the Arabic stock in order to produce a modernized Arabic-Islamic culture.[133] One of the main features of their work, consequently, is a careful study of such poets as Ibn ar-Rumi and Mutanabbi, and the valuation of their productions somewhat on the lines of Hazlitt.

Yet in spite of a certain general similarity of aim and methods and even of subject, there is a marked difference in tone, no less than in style, between the work of al-Aqqad and that of al-Mazini. Hitherto al-Aqqad appears by far the more original writer and his work leaves the more satisfying impression.[134] The keynotes of his writings are freedom and truth. These are the things of which Egypt stands in greatest need.[135] Freedom lies in the power of the mind to overcome obstacles; to begin by seeking political "freedom" is to begin at the wrong end. Truth is the reality behind the outward shows of life, and truth and freedom issue in beauty. "Without love of beauty there is no freedom;" the mind of Egypt hitherto is symbolized by the cultivation of the soil of Egypt—entirely given up to necessary and materially useful things; but now there is a growing appreciation of beauty and art.[136] The larger number of al-Aqqad's essays, outside those devoted to purely literary criticism, are given up to the elaboration of these ideas.[137] It is in this reaction to the views of the realistic school that the chief importance of his work as a prose writer lies. The same conceptions underlie his literary methods. "Literature and the arts are the highest expression of freedom."[138] The object of literature is not to amuse or entertain, but to widen the reader's hold on life.[139] The writer of natural genius (matbu) is one who follows his natural bent without seeking to copy others.[140] But it is not enough to present a faithful picture, a mere photograph;

the writer must be an artist who strives after an ideal of beauty. Simplicity alone is not the supreme art in style; it is not to be demanded of a writer that his language should be easy to everyone.[141] In accordance with this principle al-Aqqad has forged for himself a style which is peculiar in contemporary Arabic literature, a style which is elaborate and rather of a western type in texture, yet slightly archaic in language, and which demands the utmost concentration on the part of the reader. Some such new form of expression he feels to be necessary for his purpose, since old Arabic had no real literary style, what did duty as such (excluding works dealing with plain recitals of fact) being in reality rhetorical in its origin and manner, and open to serious criticisms.[142] True renovation must, however, be based on a thorough grasp of classical Arabic;[143] the writer who has acquired this mastery may then at his own will enrich it by the adaptation of congruent elements from other languages.[144] Unadorned statement is not literature; only that is worthy of the name which expresses thought in a garb of beauty and dignity.

Al-Mazini shares al-Aqqad's views on "freedom," but not his artist's idealism. He is at heart a realist, whose vision is, however, tempered by a touch of fantasy. His earlier literary essays are for the most part straightforward in subject and manner, and scarcely call for special remark. It is more interesting to follow up the evolution of his style. In his earliest work[145] he is still strongly influenced by the classical Arabic style, though his treatment of the subject is determined by his English reading. The post-war essays in the same collection show a marked improvement in the direction of simplicity and concentration; the style resembles on the whole that of Dr. Haykal and other modernist authors, the choice of words is careful, but there is no attempt to imitate al-Aqqad's elaborate syntax and rather studious diction. In his next book,[146] however, the tone of his writing has begun to change. It is altogether lighter, gayer, and more sparkling, and in a few passages the essay form is exchanged for short sketches and dramatic dialogues. It seems as if al-Mazini had realized that the literary essay was not his real bent, and was beginning to find his feet in a new form of composition. Since 1928 he has regularly contributed to the weekly *Siyasah* and other journals sketches and dialogues written in this crisp and witty style, and there can be no question that as a definite contribution to imaginative literature, in which modern Arabic is still exceedingly weak, these rank much higher than his critical essays. Whether he will eventually take the next step and emerge as an Arabic novelist, remains to be seen,[147] but there is none among the modern Arabic writers mentioned so far who possesses, at least from the point of view of style, better qualifications.

The place occupied by German literature in this revival is still restricted, though in view of the numbers of Egyptian students in Germany it may be expected to expand. References to Goethe, Schiller, Nietzsche, and so on are frequently found in the pages of the essayists, but there is little evidence of any real influence exerted by German thought on Egyptian writers. It is interesting, however, to see how the distinction between the two groups observed above maintains itself in relation to German literature. Al-Aqqad is attracted to Kant,[148] and frequently discusses Schopenhauer and Nietzsche, while the French school is attracted rather to the romantic writers. From the latter group emanates the only notable translation yet made of a German work, Goethe's *Werther*, and that itself on the basis of French translations.[149]

Within the ranks of the Egyptian modernists whose activity has been discussed up to this point there are, of course, varying degrees of western adaptation. Shaikh Mustafa Abd ar-Raziq and Professor Mansur Fahmy are still to a large extent in touch with conservative feeling; al-Aqqad and Dr. Haykal are less so, while Dr. Taha Husain inclines still more to the left. The extreme left wing of Egyptian modernism, however, is formed by another group, composed hitherto largely of Egyptian Christians, in which the principal figure is Salamah Musa, the present editor of the monthly journal *al-Hilal*. Salamah Musa first came into prominence by his writings in defence of the theory of evolution and of socialism, which he had studied during some years of residence in England.[150] His post-war publications consist so far of collections of essays, reprinted from *al-Hilal* and other journals, and dealing not only with literary matters, but with such assorted subjects as Malthus, the Ice Age, psychoanalysis and the subconscious mind, and especially with evolution.[151] His favorite authors are Bernard

Shaw and H. G. Wells; like them, he speaks his mind out fearlessly, and even provocatively, on subjects which even the most advanced of the Muslim modernists treat with caution. Perhaps the best example is furnished by his essay on Monotheism,[152] in which he argues for the naturalistic origin of *tawhid* and boldly applies the doctrine of evolution to religion. His attitude to Arabic literature and literary style is characterized by the same boldness and vigor of thought. In both classical and contemporary Arabic literature he finds a lack of sound knowledge and of contact with the facts of life, and while at first he was content to allow the classical tradition some share, though a subordinate one, in the formation of a modern Arab culture,[153] in his latest writings he pronounces for complete severance from the past.[154] English and French style he declares roundly to be better than Arabic style, and he has made it his aim to produce what he calls the "telegraphic" form of writing, "in which the words do not outnumber the ideas."[155] But while he is distinguished from his Egyptian colleagues by his more extreme views (though to the European they are often the ordinary views of an educated man), he is, unlike the Syro-American school, careful to observe in his writings the familiar rhythms of Arabic. The "vulgarity" of language, for which he is violently criticized in certain quarters, amounts to no more than the taking up into the written language of a few popular words, which serve his purpose better than unfamiliar classicisms.[156] Yet he is not entirely a partisan of the "Egyptian culture" school; on the contrary his aim is to bring Arabic thought generally into line with western thought. Like his predecessor Gurgi Zaydan, his work is rather didactic than literary, but it may be said with truth that he is the worthy successor of Zaydan in the altered circumstances of present day Egypt. His popularity with, and the influence which his work exerts on, a section of the rising generation of Egyptians, both Muslim and Christian, show that he is a factor to be reckoned with in the evolution of modern Egyptian thought and literature.[157]

If it is asked to what, after all, this literary activity in Egypt amounts, the answer will not be found merely by reckoning up the number of productions which will bear comparison, from the point of view of interest or profit, with those of any other country. It must be judged, not from the standpoint of a highly developed

Western literature, but in relation to its background, audience, and environment. It has brought into Arabic literature new values and ideals, towards which it strives to direct the political and cultural aspirations of the Egyptians, and which at the same time link it up with the thought of the civilized world outside. These writers have shown that it is not possible, but, humanly speaking, certain, that in due course a body of Arabic literature will be created which will express the distinctive contribution of Arabs and Egyptians to modern civilization, not as imitators of an alien culture, but as members of an original and vigorous organism, in the same way that Russian literature has expressed the distinctive contribution of the Russian genius. All of them are conscious that they stand at the beginnings of this development, that they are precursors of that newer Arabic literature yet to be, but each seeks to bring to it his own offering of experiment and thought. They know that what they are expressing is not the feeling of the people as a whole, but the views of a small minority who are striving, with increasing success and a strong assurance of ultimate victory, to convert and educate the people. In this alone they see the hope of the future, and their part is to unify, broaden, and extend the influence of these forces. For their final aim, as al-Aqqad has well said,[158] is not to create an intellectual culture, a culture of decadence and mere words, but a natural culture, a culture of progress.

IV   The Egyptian Novel

The beginnings of the novel as a literary art in Egypt are so recent that the student of contemporary Arabic literature might well be excused for seeking to trace some genetic connection between its development and the earlier productions of the Syrian school of writers. But except for the possibility that the success of the Syrian novelists (whose works have been admirably described by Professor Kratchkowsky in the work frequently quoted in the previous sections of these studies, and now available in a German translation[159]) may have encouraged the Egyptian writers to produce a class of works which would appeal to the same public, the literary movement which forms the subject of the present article

has remained in general entirely independent of the Syrian historical novel. Western influences, which are very marked in the later
stages, have been exercised directly, but Egyptian recreational
literature continued for a long time to lean rather on classical and
conventional models. It is only very slowly and hesitatingly that it
has emancipated itself, and its progress in this direction has been
sporadic and individual rather than the result of a steady evolution. We can, in fact, speak of a "development" of the novel in
Egypt only by stretching the term "novel" to include a rather
wide range of works with a fictional framework, many of which
are not, strictly speaking, novels at all.

The tardiness of Egypt in this field of literature, as compared
with Turkey and India, the other two main centers of Islamic
culture, may be traced to several causes. The general educational
and literary-aesthetic factors which hindered the rise of a new
type of recreational literature have been examined earlier; the
greater variety and satisfaction to be enjoyed in classical Arabic
literature than in either Turkish or Urdu may also have played
a part. Added to this were several special or local causes, which
will be discussed more fully below. But at least part of the explanation lies in the fact that the rather narrow sections of the
Egyptian public which had received a modern education were
able to find for themselves all that they wanted in French (and to
a lesser extent English) literature. The incentive was thus lacking
in literary circles to the composition of works of a similar kind in
Arabic. As the demand grew, the most natural course was to meet
it by translating French and English novels, instead of setting to
the ungrateful task of building up an indigenous novelistic literature, which involved the creation of an entirely new literary technique.[160] Bald and jejune as these translations may have been,
and ill-adapted to Egyptian social and cultural conditions and
literary taste, their reception showed that there was a public which
appreciated them. With what skill, on the other hand, a translator
of genius could adapt a European novel to a Muslim Egyptian
public may be seen in Osman Galal's version of *Paul et Virginie*.[161]
The translation, though slightly abridged and shorn of its more
exotic features, remains on the whole faithful to the word and
spirit of the original, while the use of simple but elegant rhymed

prose throughout and the replacement of the numerous philosophical reflections by short poetic pieces give it a natural Arabic flavour, which is sadly lacking in most of the contemporary and later translations.[162] Amidst the many hundreds of these there are, of course, not a few in which the translators have adapted the original to a greater or less extent, notably the well-known translations of al-Manfaluti; but in spite of the brilliance of the latter's style, his versions lack the quality of Osman Galal's work.[163] A full investigation into the character and circulation of the translated fictional literature would no doubt yield important results for the social study of modern Egypt, but for its relation to the literary problem of the Egyptian novel it is not necessary to do more at this point than to note its very large output and apparent popularity.

The characteristic tendency of Egyptian writers to remain faithful to the traditional forms and graft new elements upon them is clearly to be seen, though in a very unusual combination, in the first Egyptian romance with literary pretensions which I have traced, an early production of the famous poet Ahmad Shawqi (1868-1932), entitled *The Maid of India*.[164] The traditional background of this work, however, is neither the classical belles-lettres nor the romance of the *Arabian Nights* or *Sira* types, but the fantastic popular stories known as *hawadith*,[165] supplemented and expanded along the lines of the historical novel. The story is frankly preposterous, not so much in plot as in the portentous supernatural machinery of magicians and sorcerers invoked on nearly every page. But it inherits from its popular ancestry a keen instinct for movement and adventure which offers some compensation, and where the supernatural is not too forcibly obtruded there is real pleasure to be got out of the vivid narrative. To its other parent, the historical novel, it owes its quasi-historical setting, which, as the expression of a new sense of pride in the greatness and glory of ancient Egypt, is worthy of notice. The feature, however, which gives this romance its special literary interest is that it is written with all that mastery of language and verbal artifice which has gained for Shawqi his outstanding place in modern Arabic poetry. The rhymed prose in which much of it is composed is of the most elaborate kind, the rhymes often recurring four or five times (more solemn passages, such as prayers and invocations, are generally rhymed throughout), and interspersed with long or short pieces of original verse, and one can only regret that so much virtuosity could not find better materials on which to expend itself.

While Ahmad Shawqi's romance has remained a solitary *tour de force,* a much more successful attempt was made a few years later to adapt to the new requirements the literary genre known as *Maqamat,* familiar to students of medieval Arabic literature as its nearest approach (at least in the domain of belles-lettres) to the novel.[166] The *maqama* in its traditional form continued to be cultivated right down to the end of the nineteenth century, notably by Nasif al-Yaziji and Abdallah Pasha Fikri,[167] but with these and other writers of the same school it still moved within the old circle of established themes, and had but little connection with the life and problems of the age. Totally distinct from this was the new function of social criticism, to which the *maqama* form, more or less modified and simplified, was now applied by several Egyptian writers in a series of works which constitute one of the characteristic types of Egyptian literary production in the decade prior to 1914.

The earliest and best work of this group, and the one which approaches most closely in conception and treatment to the novel in the strict sense, is the well known and still popular *Hadith Isabni Hisham* of Muhammad Ibrahim al-Muwaylhi (1858-1930),[168] already referred to. In this work too (as in all the others of its kind to be mentioned shortly) the supernatural is invoked, as the thread of the narrative hangs upon the experiences of a Pasha of Muhammad Ali's time who rises from the grave and finds himself, to his confusion and astonishment, in an unfamiliar and Europeanized Cairo. By means of this device the author is enabled to deal in turn with different aspects of the social life of his time, depicting it in lively dialogue, comparing it with the past, and criticizing its falsity and aping of the worst European standards. Such a work lacks, of course, as Mahmud Taymur has remarked,[169] the essential characteristics of the novel, namely development and plot, but succeeds to a remarkable degree in the delineation of character. In its original form the work was unfinished, ending abruptly in the middle of an episode. The fourth and last edition rounded off this episode rapidly, and added a short second part (*ar-rihla ath-thaniya*), in which the scene is changed to Paris at the time of the Great Exhibition in 1900, and the evils of westernization are attacked at their source. Even at the end of this, however, the Pasha is not safely relaid in his grave, and there are suggestions in the course of the book that the author had forgotten the scene with which his narrative opens.

It is less the story itself and its moral than its brilliant style and power of description that have won for it a deserved reputation. It forges together all the best characteristics of the *maqama* prose with a modern smoothness and humor. The rhyming prose of the narrative sections (which, by being put in the mouth of that incomparable master of Haririan *saj*, Isa b. Hisham, openly challenges his creator) is skillfully broken up by dialogue in simple modern language, which does not disdain at times the colloquial idiom, even though the dialogue itself occasionally develops into lengthy explanatory monologue. The *saj* likewise is a skillful blend of ancient and modern,[170] by which the impression of archaizing is avoided and the reader is left free to enjoy what is in effect a very original and lively work, which can afford to bear comparison in style with al-Manfaluti and far outdistances him in depth and range of feeling.

Of the other works which follow al-Muwaylhi in applying the *maqama*-form to the function of social criticism, though without his humanity and lightness of touch, two may be mentioned here. The first is by Shawqi's rival in the firmament of Egyptian poetry, Muhammad Hafiz Ibrahim (1871-1932), issued under the title of *Layali Satih*.[171] The framework and plan are simple; a number of persons on successive evenings bring some grievance against the prevailing state of things in Egypt, and to each in turn a mysterious voice addresses a discourse in rhymed prose with occasional verse, analyzing the causes of his grievance and pointing out the remedy. Gradually, however, the plan of the book changes, until the greater part of it is taken up with a series of conversations in plain unrhymed prose, in which the original scheme is completely lost from sight. The work was warmly received in Egyptian literary circles,[172] but it is interesting to ob-

serve that already voices were raised in criticism of the use of *saj*
in such productions.[173]

The *maqama* plan is more strictly adhered to in the second
work, *Layali r-Ruh al-Hair,* by the publicist and playwright Muhammad Lutfi Guma.[174] But it is a *maqama* without rhymed
prose, and the influence of the Syro-American school of writers is
strongly marked, especially in the form of composition known as
Shir manthur, or free verse. The interlocutor in this work is a
disembodied spirit, as the title suggests, and the greater part of
his discourses is devoted to criticism of Egyptian social conditions.
Zaydan justifiably draws attention to its beauty and elegance of
phrase, which, it must be admitted, somewhat outweigh the depth
of the ideas it expresses.[175]

In all these works we can trace a cumulative effort to evolve
a new type of literary production which would satisfy the requirements of a new reading public, which should bear some relation to
its problems and outlook, be readily intelligible, and above all
rouse its interest and appeal to its imagination. But they did not,
in fact, meet the problem successfully. Their appeal was too literary and appreciated only by a small class of educated readers;
instead of opening new horizons and serving as an antidote to the
cares of life, they concentrated attention precisely on those cares,
and, worst of all, their object and tone was too frankly didactic.
The medieval view of literature as an intellectual luxury or
vehicle of edification was shared by them all—the adapters of the
classical tradition as well as such translators as Osman Galal and
al-Manfaluti. The Syrian novelists themselves were not entirely
exempt from it. Even the writers of the numerous novellettes,
whose works have long since been consigned to a merited oblivion,
were obsessed by, or proclaimed their adhesion to, this moral and
educational aim.[176] The contemptuous attitude of the medieval
scholars to the popular romances and tales seemed still to govern
the outlook of literary circles in Egypt, and did more than anything else to delay the development of the novel as an Arabic
literary art.

Thus the first real Egyptian novel crept into life anonymously and little noticed by the learned.[177] Its author, Dr. Husain
Haykal, then a young and ambitious advocate, was unwilling to

acknowledge its paternity, lest it should stand in the way of his career. *Zaynab* broke away decisively in language, style, subject, and treatment from anything that had gone before in Arabic literature. It bore no relation to the historical novels of Zaydan or the philosophical novels of Farah Antun, but, as its title implies, set out to portray the social life of the Delta in a series of episodes centered on the fortunes of a peasant girl. The story itself can be briefly told. Zaynab, a beautiful and sensitive girl, after an innocent flirtation with an educated youth (Hamid), son of the village landlord, falls in love with a youth in the village (Ibrahim), but is married by her parents to his friend (Hasan). She remains loyal to her husband, but the conflict between love and duty preys upon her health, and when Ibrahim is drafted into the army the bitterness of her loss brings on consumption, of which she dies. A subsidiary theme is introduced by the relations between Hamid and his cousin, a town-bred girl, and his disappearance when his hopes of marriage with her are frustrated. The plot is, on the whole, too thin to sustain four hundred pages of type, and the book has other defects as a novel, which will be discussed immediately. *Zaynab*, however, is not only the first effort of a young man, but the first effort of a young literature, and must be judged accordingly. Such details as may be open to criticism are of little importance compared with the fact that the effort was made, and that a new and, in its setting, original kind of literary production was added to Arabic literature.

The construction of the novel is interesting from two aspects, the psychological and the descriptive. The plot is evidently designed with a view to the study of the reactions of certain typical Egyptian characters in face of adverse circumstances. It does not entirely succeed, since the characters themselves are not sufficiently complex (except that of Hamid, who undoubtedly reflects to some extent the author himself) and the dramatization both of persons and incidents is rather weak on the whole.[178] The result is that the psychological comment has generally to be supplied by the author himself, and is set out rather in textbook fashion in the first person plural.

The intervention of the author is still more marked in the descriptive element. In his introduction to the second edition Haykal Bey recalls the circumstances under which he composed the book. As a student in Paris, overcome by strong homesickness, he deliberately set himself to recall every aspect of country life and of nature in Egypt. This effort of affectionate recollection betrays itself on nearly every page by lengthy descriptions of natural scenery—sun, moon, stars, crops, streams, and ponds—sometimes rising to lyrical eloquence and dignity, but cumulatively distracting and oppressive. Every action, every scene, is accompanied by similar descriptive asides, which inevitably cause the narrative to drag painfully at times. Trifling episodes, without significance for the story, are often introduced simply, it would seem, as a peg on which to hang another descriptive interlude, and here and there sentences, overloaded with trivial photographic detail, lose shape and substance. But it must not be forgotten that to Egyptian readers such passages of description convey much more than they do to any outsider, and that in their direct aesthetic appeal lies one of the main reasons of their appreciation of the work.

More integral to the plot of the novel are the sociological excursions which it contains. It is inevitable that the causes of the maladjustments and final tragedy should be traced back to their origin in the social habits of the people. The novel is dominated throughout by an insistence on the evils created by "outworn customs," but the social criticism is seldom allowed to obtrude in the same manner as the psychological and descriptive passages. This more natural effect is obtained by the device of representing it through the eyes and reflections of the character of Hamid, an educated young man of liberal and reformist tendencies, strongly under the spell of Qasim Amin and the social reformers, though the author occasionally reverts here too to the textbook idiom. The organization of the family and seclusion of women form naturally the main theme of his social criticism, but not the exclusive theme. Amongst other aspects of Egyptian life which he criticizes are the faulty type of education, divorced from the realities of life,[179] the type of country doctor—this half-humorously[180]—and more bitterly the impostors who trade on the credulity of the peasantry as Shaikhs of the *turuq*.[181] His nationalist feeling is implicit, rather than explicit, but occasionally finds outward expression, especially in regard to the humiliation of military service under the control of the foreigner.[182]

No less remarkable than the general character of the novel

is the style of its composition. Its basis is the ordinary modern literary style, but substantially modified both in vocabulary and syntax. The influence of the colloquial idiom of the Delta, on the one hand, is seen in the abruptness of the sentences and transitions and in many details of usage;[183] that of French, on the other hand, in the long and complex sentences, with the principal clause interrupted by numerous subordinate clauses and apocopes.[184] The impression which it leaves on the whole is rather tortured, and corresponds to the admission made by Haykal Bey himself of the obstacles which he experienced to the expression of his thought in Arabic.[185] In regard to the vexed question of the idiom to be employed in the dialogue, he struck out boldly for the use of the colloquial dialect when the conversation is between the peasantry, while the educated characters, on the other hand, speak in modern literary idiom.

It will be clear from what has been said that the imaginative element in *Zaynab* is more limited than in the average modern European novel, and that the various sentimental and intellectual components, which together constitute the personal element, tend to predominate over the narrative. It is admitted also by the author in his preface to the second edition that behind many of its peculiar features lie the influence and example of the modern French psychological novel.[186] But unless it can be shown that this influence has been so strong in detail, as well as in method and style, as to make the work in effect an adaptation from the French, it is impossible to deny to *Zaynab* the credit of being the first Egyptian novel, written by an Egyptian for Egyptian readers, and whose characters, settings, and plot are derived from contemporary Egyptian life.

Although on its first appearance in 1914 the book attracted little notice, it apparently met with appreciation from an increasing circle of readers.[187] Its republication in 1929 was the result of a public demand, stimulated by several factors, amongst which may be included the strengthening of that national self-consciousness which it already foreshadowed, the literary eminence attained by the now confessed author, and the adaptation of the book as the subject of the first cinematograph film produced in Egypt.[188] On this occasion it naturally became the subject of numerous articles and critiques, mostly laudatory;[189] but of much greater importance for the problem of the development of the novel in Egypt is a series of articles by Haykal Bey and Muhammad Abdallah Inan, which appeared in the weekly edition of *as-Siassa* early in 1930.[190]

How is it, asks Haykal Bey, that modern Arabic literature shows such a strange poverty and weakness in the field of the novel and the story, although Egyptians possess a natural talent for story-telling? Several reasons have been put forward; lack of imaginative staying power, the difference between the idioms of literature and of conversation, the slackness of Egyptian writers. But none of these is the true cause, though the second reason given may possibly play a small part. He then suggests four contributory causes: (1) the relatively high proportion of illiteracy in Egypt, which prevents any real appreciation on the one hand, and offers inadequate material recompense to the writer on the other; (2) the lack of support from the upper classes and the wealthy, perhaps because they are not encouraged to give support by the women (in this connection he recalls the part played by women in seventeenth and eighteenth century France, and the value of the encouragement and patronage of women in old Arabic literature); (3) the persistent and public depreciation of leading men in Egypt by their rivals and inferiors; (4) the preoccupation of the people with political and economic questions, and consequent tendency of writers to serve political rather than literary aims. The net result of all these causes is to hinder writers from the necessary specialization and long-maturing preparation, the necessity of which in novel writing is not yet realized in Egypt.

Inan in turn agrees with the general tenor of this analysis, but insists that the second of Haykal Bey's four causes is the most important. The real key to the development of the novel lies in the social position of women. The part played by women in stimulating the old Arabic poetry has no relation to their encouragement of the novel, whose material basis is found only in a society in which women play an important part and which is permeated by their influence, especially in dictating standards of morals and manners. For lack of this influence the old Arabic literature, like medieval European literature, moves in a narrow field and is lacking in fineness of feeling and emotion. In modern Arabic literature this narrowness still persists, since the social standards remain unchanged. *Zaynab* is an exception which proves the rule, since its success is due to the relative freedom enjoyed by women in the conditions of life in the Delta. He refuses therefore to share Haykal Bey's optimism; under present conditions the Arabic novel can only be maimed, limited, and individual, and is unable to offer any true representation or interpretation of the emotions and the character of social life. There can be no future for it in the modern literary revival so long as Muslim life remains in its traditional mold.[191]

This article produced a reply from Haykal Bey in which he abandoned the arguments based upon external causes, which he had previously adduced, and went straight to the psychological root of the matter in an article which deserves to be read with the most sympathetic attention. The real weakness of the short story and the novel in Egypt, he asserts, corresponds to the failure to get the most out of life, and goes back to the lack of any sound training of the emotions. The finer emotions cannot come to flower in a social life in which feeling is blunted to a point at which the physical desires take the place of any higher sentiment in the human soul. No art which does not spring in the mind of the artist from love for some aspect of life can possibly be a flourishing art. The development of the instinct of love to a human emotion in the higher sense demands a long and arduous training, for which one or even many generations may not suffice. Even charity and sympathy in their more developed social aspects are still rare in Egypt; love still remains close to the primitive instinct, and the existence of a finer ideal is hardly thought of or even imagined. Finally he seeks the reason for this defective training of the emotions in the absence of educative influences in the home, and in the character of the old type of education, which was purely vocational, not humane.

Such arguments could not pass, of course, without meeting a considerable current of opposition from different quarters. One of the more obvious and pertinent criticisms will be illustrated a little later in dealing with al-Mazini's novel *Ibrahim al-Katib*. But it is scarcely surprising that the most fundamental criticism came from the ranks of the classically educated. Why all this talk about novels? Arabic literature got on very well in the past without them, and the craving for the novel is simply another instance of that insane imitation of the West which has wrought such havoc in the foundations of eastern life. The western novel, with its false and meretricious glamour, and its incompatibility with the traditional standards of the East, has exercised a debasing and destructive influence on Egyptian social life—why should she nurse the serpent in her bosom? This opposition, in more temperate and reasoned form, may be illustrated from a recent article by Dr. Zaki Mubarak.[192] Accepting the argument that the novel will not come into existence in Arabic literature until women have a recognized social position, he condemns the writers of Arabic stories as belonging "to the lowest class of literary writers," lacking all literary training and independence of thought, and mere spongers on foreign literatures. Worse still, they mislead the youth into despising other forms of literature. But, in fact, true literature, by which is meant a truthful and artistic appreciation of life, may find expression in other forms as well, such as a *risala or qasida*. Arabic literature is not to be judged by French or English literature, but by the temperament of its own people, and by its success in expressing their minds, visions, and desires. The journalistic literature of Egypt even now illustrates many sides of their intellectual, spiritual, and emotional crises, and is only hindered from fuller discussion by the censorship of the government and the reactionaries. But there is another side to the question: as heirs of the past "it is our duty to look at the past when we think of the present," and while moving on from the ancient styles and methods, to give due attention to their legacy of literature, whch is often deeper and more valuable than "the empty froth thrown in the face of modern literature."

But however instructive such discussions may be for the purpose of elucidating the various opinions actually held and laying bare the social and intellectual background of contemporary Egyptian literature, that literature itself—and herein it proves its vitality—has not waited upon their issue, but has taken its own independent way. The existence of the "middle-class reader" is a fact which, ignored as it may be in discussion, demonstrates its reality by creating a demand which has somehow to be satisfied. To invite his attention to the *Iqd al-Farid* and the works of the Golden Age is to offer him a stone instead of the bread he wants and will have; if the writers in his own tongue will not supply him with it, he will continue to import it from abroad, however indigestible it may be in the view of his doctors. The article, essay, or *risala*, and even, it is to be feared, the average *qasida*, is either too solid or deficient as a stimulus to the imagination; it lacks above all the essential quality of living interest, and of all these only the poem offers anything that can enter into the imaginative heritage of the people.

The problem, in essence, has very little to do with deliberate imitation of the West. It is a problem conditioned by the natural consequences of an increasingly wide extension of primary education. For the similar problem in Europe the solution has, to a great extent, been found in the novel, and if Arabic writers find themselves unable to put forward any other satisfactory solution (and neither the magazine article nor the literary essay is a satisfactory solution), then no course is open to them but to fall back, provisionally at least, upon the Western solution. The idea that there should be anything derogatory to the dignity or self-respect of a people in the transference of a particular kind of literary production from without into their own literature would be indeed a strange extension of chauvinistic extravagance, and it has still to be shown that either Turkish or Indian literature has lost in depth and fidelity by the introduction of the novel. Hence it is that the novel and the story have been steadily driving their roots into the field of Egyptian letters, however ungrateful the soil or ungracious the welcome. But for the full development of the novel one essential condition is adaptation to its environment, and here lies, so far as the recent history of the Arabic novel is concerned, the main difficulty.

Leaving aside the social factors discussed above, the Arabic novelists and story-writers were confronted with a further problem, already referred to, that, namely, of creating a modern novelistic technique. Of the earlier writers al-Manfaluti and Gurgi Zaydan illustrate different approaches towards a solution, the one by the color, the other by the simplicity, of his style. But neither touched the central difficulty, that of presenting a realistic representation of contemporary social life, in vocabulary, forms of expression, and especially in dialogue. This task was now taken up and experimented with by a group of writers of short stories, beginning with Muhammad Taymur (1892-1921).[193] The general study of the works of these writers, apart from the fact that they constitute one of the most interesting orientations of modern Egyptian literature, is thus essential for following up the development of a new technique, but such a study would overstep the limits of the present study.[194] For our purposes it must suffice at present to examine briefly their handling of one of the most crucial problems, that of the idiom of dialogue.

Here again the problem is not one which is peculiar to Arabic literature, but has its analogies both in an earlier stage of most Western European literatures and in those of all countries in which the ordinary speech of daily social intercourse has not yet become standardized under the influence of the literary usage. The question at issue is whether the dialogue is to run the risk of appearing artificial and stilted by being expressed in the literary idiom, or whether it is to aim at realism at the expense of the aesthetic dislocation involved in using one idiom for narrative and descriptions and another for dialogue. The first alternative is that adopted in all the early novels, not only the translated novels (where indeed it was quite natural), but also in those of the Syrian writers, with the result that they give even the Western reader the same impression of formality and affectedness which he finds in the early novels in his own language. *Zaynab* was the first work of fiction, to my knowledge, in which the dialogue was phrased in the colloquial idiom. The same striving after realism influenced also the writers of short stories, at least to begin with, and in the first edition of Mahmud Taymur's collection entitled *Ash-shaykh Guma*, for example, the dialogue is also in colloquial Egyptian. But there has gradually grown up a tendency to adopt a compromise, by graduating the speech of the characters from pure literary to pure colloquial idiom according to the education and station of the speakers, and, further, even in the case of the former, to avoid in general words and phraseology of too literary a stamp, in favour of simpler and more colloquial turns of phrase.[195] By this means the impression of naturalism is maintained, at a very slight sacrifice of realism, and it is in fact no great task for the reader, if he so desires, to transpose the written symbols in many cases into the spoken forms. We may, however, expect at no very distant date to see this problem solve itself, both by the general extension of primary education and still more through the influence of the Egyptian broadcasting stations.

It remains only to inquire how far the problems, needs, and aspirations to which we have referred have been met in the most recent examples of the Egyptian novel. As may be gathered from the discussion summarized above, these are very few indeed if we are to take into account only genuinely original productions of a certain literary value.

The most prolific and also, according to Mahmud Taymur, the most popular Arabic novelist of the present day is Niqula'l-Haddad,[196] editor of the journal *As-Sayyidat war-Rigal,* in which most of his works were originally published serially. Although he is himself Syrian, the tone and feeling of his writing is markedly Egyptian, much more so than that of most other Syrian publicists. To judge by his historical novel *Firawnat al-Arab indat-Turk.*[197] he possesses the *feuilleton* writer's gift of keeping the reader's interest on the stretch by rapidity of movement and frequent dramatic climaxes, but his plot is loosely constructed and the figures lack characterization, and it is questionable whether he has any contribution to make, either in style or treatment, to the literary development of the Egyptian novel.

Much greater literary interest attaches to another historical novel, the first strictly Egyptian work of its kind, entitled *Ibnat al-Mamluk* ("The Mamluk's Daughter"), by Muhammad Farid Abu Hadid.[198] This work does not seem to be in any sense dependent upon the type of historical novel written by Zaydan, and represents in some respects an advance upon him. The heroic element gives way to a more subdued realism, and the story is not wrapped round historical events, but placed in a historical setting, the period selected being that of the struggle of Muhammad Ali and the Mamluks between 1805 and 1808. The course of historical events is fitted naturally into the background, and not forced upon the reader's notice; even the most important military action during this period, the English expedition to Alexandria and its defeat at Rosetta in 1807, is only referred to briefly in two or three lines, although the hero, a young Arab refugee from the Wahhabis in Arabia, is represented as having taken part in the struggle. Although the book does not succeed altogether in avoiding the stiffness of the older historical novels, there is more life and movement in the characters, and it holds the reader's attention right down to its tragic conclusion.

The most recently published, and in every respect the most important, Arabic novel since *Zaynab* is the long-awaited work of al-Mazini, issued in 1931 under the title of *Ibrahim al-Katib*.[199] According to the author's statement in the preface, the novel was written partly in 1925 and finished later on in 1926,[200] then thrown aside, and a portion of the second half was hurriedly rewritten during printing owing to the loss of the original manuscript, which may explain a certain unevenness referred to below. The preface deals also in an interesting manner with the questions discussed above. In regard to the language of dialogue, al-Mazini rejects the colloquial idiom as lacking flexibility of expression and not being sufficiently stabilized, whereas the literary idiom is daily acquiring greater flexibility and polish. He also criticizes the views of Haykal Bey as to the obstacle offered by Egyptian social life to the creation of the Egyptian novel. Such a view assumes, wrongly, that the Western novel is the only possible model for the novel; but why should there not be an Egyptian novel, possessing its own distinctive character? The social life of Egypt offers no obstacle to any writer with the requisite capacity for imagination. Moreover, granted that the emotion of love is felt and conceived of in Egypt in a manner different from that in the West, why must this be a fatal difficulty, or why even must the emotion of love be the mainstay of the novel? Such a limitation is "sheer hysteria, neither more nor less."

The novel itself does not wholly fulfil the expectations aroused by these arguments. Not that it is defective from the point of view of plot, development of situation and characters, and other technical aspects; in these respects it is certainly the best original novel in Arabic to my knowledge. There is the same lightness of touch, the same humor, sometimes subtle, sometimes more on the

surface, the same rather defiant cynicism,[201] which, as already remarked in the preceding study, distinguishes al-Mazini's work
from that of all other contemporary writers in Arabic. The narrative moves rapidly and easily, the dialogue is crisp and natural,
and the social criticism and philosophical implications of the story
are implicit rather than explicitly expressed.[202] But it is not, except for its characters and setting, an Egyptian novel in the sense
which al-Mazini himself appears to postulate. The hero, who gives
his name to the work, is entirely a Westernized creation, in whom
few Egyptians would be likely to recognize themselves—perhaps
the publisher has some justification for claiming, in spite of the
author's disclaimer, that the identity of names between hero and
writer is not entirely fortuitous. The novel itself is Western in
feeling and ideas as well as in literary background, and the subject
round which it revolves is a psychological study of the emotion of
love in its Western rather than its Egyptian conception. Even the
external features of form and style confirm this impression, such
as the frequent use of Western images and phrases,[203] and com.
parative absence of the corresponding Arabic phrases, and, most
curious of all, the practice of heading each chapter with a verse
from the Bible. The phrasing itself diverges in many details from
the normal usages of literary Arabic, though without doing actual
violence to the genius of the language. There is, however, a certain
difference in tone and subject between the first and second halves
of the book. The former moves entirely within the framework of
Egyptian social life, and in its harmonious blending of humor and
sympathy could come only from the pen of an Egyptian writer.
The latter depicts another atmosphere in much harder tones, and
the color gradually fades out, as if the author's style were affected
by the closing in of the shadows upon his hero.

Without denying, therefore, the imaginative originality of
the author, the literary parentage of *Ibrahim,* like that of *Zaynab,*
is obviously to be sought in the Western novel. But the rather
sentimental prototypes of *Zaynab* are not the sort of production
which would appeal to al-Mazini, whose inclinations are altogether
towards a robuster view and more realistic presentation. In this
case, his habit of literary reminiscence[204] gives a clue to the origin
of at least part of the conception, and points directly to M. P.

Artzybashev's *Sanine*. The plot and development of *Ibrahim al-Katib* are (it should be noted) entirely different from those of Artzybashev's story, but the character of Ibrahim has certainly borrowed something from that of *Sanine* (though what in *Sanine* is romantically portrayed as the result of natural training is in *Ibrahim* the outcome of a matured philosophy), and one scene in particular is practically a literal translation of the climax of the Russian novel.[205]

Thus the Egyptian novel, in the work of its two chief representatives, still falls short of the ideal which they, along with others, have visualized. The link between technical competence and Egyptian inspiration has yet to be satisfactorily forged. So long as this is absent the mass of readers in Egypt will continue to gather up the crumbs which fall from the tables of others—unless, indeed, the writers of Egypt succeed in creating some entirely new literary form, a much harder task, of which there is no indication at present. So far from the novel serving as the stalking-horse of Western "materialism," I can conceive of no effective barrier to the flood of Western literary influences in Egypt but the development of the truly Egyptian novel, and perhaps we may yet see a Department of Journalism and Novel writing at the University of al-Azhar.

NOTES

[1] George Young, *Egypt* (London, 1927), p. x.

[2] *Ibid.*, p. 284.

[3] Except for a few scattered articles, the only European sources of reference are a number of studies in various Russian journals by Professor I. Kratchkowsky (whose personal encouragement I would here gratefully acknowledge), and the review pages of recent numbers of the *Mittheilungen* of the Berlin Oriental Seminary (*MSOS.*), due to Professor G. Kampffmeyer. See also *MSOS.*, xxviii (1925), 249-52.

[4] For this see Zaydan iv, 152-57; Muhammad Bey Taymur حاتنا التمثيلية (Cairo, 1922), esp. 22-6, 47-112; al-Aqqad مطالعات 259-62; *BSOS.*, ii, 255-56.

[5] The most complete account of Arabic literature in the nineteenth century is Père Louis Cheikho's *al-Adab al-arabiya fil-qarn at-tasi-ashar* (2 vols., second ed., Beirut, 1924-1926; a supplementary volume including writers who died between 1901 and 1926 is in course of republication from *al-Machriq*, 1925-1927). This work is quoted below as Cheikho. The fourth volume of Gurgi Zaydan's *Tarikh adab allughah al-arabiya* (Cairo, 1914) devotes the greater part of its space to the literary organizations of the nineteenth century, schools, libraries, societies, etc. Neither of these works offers a general study

and analysis of the various movements. More detailed accounts of the principal
writers are given in Gurgi Zaydan's collection of biographies (mainly reprinted
from the journal *al-Hilal*) entitled *Mashahir ash-Sharq* (second ed., Cairo,
1911) , quoted below as *M.Sh.* Similar biographies are scattered through various
Arabic periodical publications, complete sets of any of which are scarcely to be
found in London.

There are no European studies of comparable scope. The sections devoted to nineteenth century literature in C. Huart's *Littérature arabe* (pp.
404-435) and C. Brockelmann's *Geschichte der Arabischen Litteratur* (vol. ii,
469-496; pp. 241-250 of his handbook) are little more than random catalogues
of names and books, meaningless when divorced from the movements that
alone give them significance. English works on Arabic literature treat exclusively of classical literature. A series of articles from the pen of my honoured
teacher, Shaykh M. H. Abd ar-Raziq, in *BSOS* (Vol. II, pp. 249-265, 755-762) has
unfortunately remained uncompleted. An excellent general analysis by Professor Kratchkowsky appeared in *Vostok,* vol. i (Peterburg, 1922), pp. 67-73.

Since this was written the Leningrad Oriental Institute has issued (1928)
an anthology of modern Arabic literature, *Obraztsy Novo-arabskoi Literatury,
1880-1925, I. Tekst,* edited by Mdme. Ode-Vasil'eva (Kulthum Nasr Awdah, on
whom see *Majallah al-Majma al-Ilmi,* viii (1928) , 756-757) , with an introduction of twenty-five pages by Professor Kratchkowsky, describing the literary
developments of the period, with brief characterizations of the authors from
whom extracts have been taken. The latter part of this introduction is available
also in a five-page English summary.

Professor Kratchkowsky also draws attention to the value of the well-
known work of Comte Philippe Tarrazi, *Tarikh as-sahafah al-arabiyah* (Beirut,
1913) , as a source for the history of modern Arabic literature in the nineteenth
century.

[6] *M.Sh.*, ii, 19-24; Cheikho ii[2], 8. An excellent study of him from the pen
of Muh. as-Sadiq Husayn Bey appeared in *as-Siassa*, weekly edition, 28 May,
1927.

[7] Cheikho, ii[2] 100-2; Zaydan, iv, 245; *BSOS.*, ii, 256-257; Brockelmann, ii,
476-477; esp. Vollers, *ZDMG.*, xlv (1891) , 36 ff.

[8] As a figure typical of many we may take Fransis Marrash of Aleppo
(1836-1873) (Cheikho, ii[2], 45-8; *M.Sh.*, ii, 285-8) . His works, which are chiefly
on social and philosophical subjects, but include one novel, were inspired
by his studies, not in Arabic, but in French literature. Cf. Qustaki al-Himsi,
Udaba Halab (Aleppo, 1925) , pp. 20-30.

[9] *M.Sh.* ii, 81-92; Cheikho, ii[2], 86-88; Huart, *Littérature arabe*, 408-409.
Mr. Amin ar-Rayhani suggests that Ahmad Faris ash-Shidyaq "deserves more
than a passing notice. He is, with all his faults, one of the outstanding figures
in the Arabic literature of the nineteenth century. He has in him a Yaziji, a
Hariri, and a modern thinker of uncommon ability."

[10] *M.Sh.*, ii, 9-18; Cheikho, ii[2], 27-35. See also Chenery, *The Assemblies
of al-Hariri* (London, 1867) , 98-101; Kratchkowsky, *Vostok*, ii, 91.

[11] *M.Sh.*, ii, 119-136; Cheikho, ii[2], 38-43. To the works there enumerated
there is now to be added the selection from his letters, etc., published in Cairo
in 1920 under the title of رسائل اليازجى .

[12] Of the many institutions which contributed to the spread of western
studies in Beirut, the Syrian Protestant College (now the American University) ,
founded in 1866, stood in the closest relation with the leaders of the literary

movement and exercised the most far-reaching influence. In its early years it was directed by a group of notable scholars, the most remarkable of whom was Dr. Cornelius van Dyck (1818-1895; see *M.Sh.*, ii, 40-54; Cheikho, ii², 4), a close friend of Butrus al-Bustani, and author of a number of educational works in Arabic, chiefly in the physical sciences. For the American Press (1834), the Catholic Press (1848), and other printing presses in Syria prior to 1870 see Cheikho, i², 48, 76-78.

[13] *M.Sh.*, ii, 25-32; Cheikho, ii², 126-127.

[14] See on this Dozy, *Supplément aux Dictionnaires arabes,* p. xi.

[15] Cheikho, ii², 127-128; Zaydan, iv, 274.

[16] Kratchkowsky in the Bagaly-Festschrift of the Ukrainian Academy of Sciences (Kiev, 1927); *al-Machriq*, xxiii. (1925), 778 ff.

[17] The social and intellectual effervescence of the Lebanon between the sixties and nineties, which is one of the most remarkable phenomena in modern Arabic history, still awaits a historian.

[18] On this see Kratchkowsky in article cited above (note 3), and review by Prof. Margoliouth in *JRAS.*, 1905, 417-423.

[19] Zaydan, iv, 64-65. For a list of works dealing with Arabic journalism see *BSOS.*, ii, 257-258.

[20] كانت الصحافة المصرية قبل المؤيّد وقفاً على السوريين المسيحيين *Manar* xvi [1331], 875). See also the chapter *La Presse* by Achille Sĕkalÿ Bey in the volume entitled *L'Egypte* (Cairo, 1926), especially pp. 431-432: "Il est générale- ment admis que l'élément syrien a joué un rôle prépondérant dans la création et le développement de la presse périodique aussi bien que dans la renaissance des Lettres arabes en Egypte. Jusqu'à ces dernières années, ses journeaux ont montré le plus de vitalité, d'initiative, d'esprit, d'organisation et de progrès. Mais, après la guerre surtout, ces qualités ont commencé à se manifester parmi l'élément purement égyptien."

[21] The fact may be accepted without prejudice to the ultimate results of ethnographical research into the population of the Lebanon.

[22] See *al-Wasit* by Shaykh Ahmad al-Iskandari, pp. 339-342.

[23] On his *qasida* see Goldziher's remarks in *Abh. Arab. Phil.*, i, 173.

[24] *M.Sh.*, ii, 305-310; Cheikho, ii², 95-96; *al-Wasit*, 333-335.

[25] لوتقدم به الزمان لكان فه بديعان، ولم ينفرد بهذا اللقب علامة همذان

[26] *M.Sh.*, ii, 33-39; *al-Wasit*, 335-337; Cheikho, ii², 97; *BSOS.*, ii, 755-756; *ZDMG.*, xlvii (1893), 720-722; and review by Goldziher in *WZKM.*, iv, 347-352.

[27] See on this subject the pungent criticisms of Dr. Taha Husayn, في الادب الجاهلى (Cairo, 1927) pp. 2-13.

[28] The Arabic writers themselves have not been slow to recognize the debt which the classical movement in the east owes to European orientalists during the nineteenth century, by their editions of classical Arabic texts and their researches into the history and literature of the Middle Ages. It is not too much to say that, but for the facilities they placed within the reach of all (aided by the piratical activities of Egyptian publishers) a great part of classical Arabic literature would still be a closed book to the majority of modern Arabic intellectuals. See also Cheikho, ii², 72; and especially M. Kurd Ali in *Majallah al-majma al-ilmi al-arabi* (Damascus, 1927), vol. viii, 433-456.

[29] *Rissalat al Tawhid* (see note 30), pp. xviii-xix.

[30] A considerable literature has already arisen round Muhammad Abduh, both in Arabic and in European languages. The principal biography in Arabic is in vol. viii (1333) of *al-Manar*. An excellent biographical sketch from the

pen of Shaikh Mustafa Abd ar-Raziq will be found in the preface to the French translation of his *Risalat al-Tawhid* (Paris, 1925) , together with analyses of his works and other biographical references.

[31] *M.Sh.*, ii, 55-66; M. Abduh in *al-Jamiah*, vol. v, 122-129; I. Goldziher, art. "Djamal ad-Din" in *Encyc. of Islam*, with citations of authorities. See also an article by Shaykh Mustafa Abd ar-Raziq in *as-Siassa*, weekly edition, 4 June, 1927.

[32] Zaydan, iv, 78-104.

[33] *M.Sh.*, ii, 75-80; Cheikho, ii², 133-135.

[34] *M.Sh.*, ii, 105-112; Cheikho, ii², 99-100.

[35] Even before Nadim the colloquial had been used for nationalist propaganda by the Jewish journalist James Sanua (جمس سانوا), author of the notorious *Travels of Abu Naddara* (رّحْلَةُ أبي نظّارَةِ زَرْقَا-sic) , a weekly broadsheet lithographed in Paris between August, 1878, and March, 1879, and of its continuation, the monthly broadsheet *Abu Naddara*.

[36] Cromer, *Modern Egypt*, ii, 180 note (one-vol. ed., p. 600, n. 1) .

[37] *Hilal*, xxii (1914), 148-151; *Manar*, xvi (1331) , 873-878, 947-956; *Machriq*, 1926, 225-226; al-Aqqad, *al-Fusul*, 207-213.

[38] There is an interesting passage in the long decree of judgment given by Shaikh Ahmad Abul-Khatwah (a leading modernist, d. 1906; see *Manar*, ix, 880) against Shaikh Ali Yusuf, in a suit brought against him by Shaikh Abd al-Khaliq Sadat (on whom see Cromer, *ibid.* 178, one-vol. ed., 598) . The passage deserves to be cited in its entirety, not for its severe castigation of Shaikh Ali, but as an *ex cathedra* statement of the attitude of the *Shar'* to the Press. (Quoted from *al-Liwa*, 1904, No. 3, pp. 43-44.)

حيث ان حرفة الصحافة التى نسبها المدعى عليه لنفسه قسمان قسم يبحث
فيه عن فنون وعلوم مخصوصة للارشاد عما تبحث فيه كالمجلات الغير اليومية
وهذه شرفها بمقدار شرف ما تبحث فيه وهى صحافة جليلة وهذا القسم لا يدعيه
المدعى عليه لنفسه، وقسم لا يختص بموضوع مخصوص وهو عبارة عن ارشاد

من تكون منهم الامة اى المملكة بارشاد الافراد والعائلات والهيئة الاجتماعية
والحكومة فهى معدة لارشاد الامة فى اخلاقها ونظام عائلاتها وهيئتها
الاجتماعية وآدابها وسياسة مملكتها وبالجملة فهى عبارة عن الارشاد بما يلزم
من سياسة النفوس والعائلات والملك والمراقبة على ذلك اذ وظيفة هذه الصحافة
هى الارشاد العام والمراقبة عليه وهى صحافة جليلة جداً ولا يمكن القيام بها الا
بعد استحصال على كل معداتها من العلوم الاقتصادية وغيرها وعلوم تهذيب
الاخلاق وسياسة المنزل والمملكة ودراسة اخلاق الناس وعوائدهم وسياسة
الحكومات والتمييز فيما هى عليه والصحيح منه ومعرفة كيف يعالج الفساد

وكيف يزيله ويرقي الأمة ويهذب الاخلاق ويلزم لذلك ان يكون القائم بها
من اشد الناس محافظة على الكمالات والآداب حتى يمكنه ان ينفع بنصحه
وارشاده وان يرقي الأمة المنحطة ويستمر في ترقيتها ان لم تكن منحطة وهذا
لا يتأتى الا اذا كان القائم بها من الطبقة الاولى ذكاء وعلما بالسياسة الداخلية
والخارجية وعلما بالاخلاق و تهذيبها وان يعلم كيف ينصح وكيف يستفاد من
نصحه ولذلك اشتغل بها في غير هذه الديار اكابر الناس عقلا وفضلا واشتغل
بها في هذه الديار بعض الفضلاء برهة من الزمان ولا يمكن المدعي عليه ان
يدعي لنفسه هذه الصحافة لان تقلبه في المبادئ لغير سبب وتعرضه للشخصيات
في ثوب المصالح العامة وسكوته عن بعض ما يلزم الكلام فيه لاغراض بعض
من يهمه رضاه وكثرة اضراره عندما يريد ان ينفع وغير ذلك مما هو
معروف يمنعه من دعوى القيام بهذه الصحافة لنفسه الخ

[39] Few would subscribe to Cromer's dictum: "I suspect that my friend Abdu ... was in reality an Agnostic" (*op. cit.*, ii, 180; one-vol. ed., 599). He was rather a Mutazilite; cf. *Rissalat al-Tawhid*, xlviii, lxii, lxiv, lxviii, lxxxiv; and Goldziher, *Die Richtungen der islamischen Koranauslegung* (Leiden, 1920), 322 ff. Professor D. B. Macdonald writes: "Muhammad Abduh was plainly a Maturidite. He never mentions Maturidi in his *Risala*, but while he refers with devotion to al-Ashari, his theological positions are straight Maturidite."

[40] Dr. Husayn Bey Haykal, *Fi awqat al-faragh*, p. 116.

[41] *M.Sh.*, i, 335-347; Haykal, *op. cit.*, 96-148; *Machriq*, 1926, 224-225; Kratchkowsky, *Kasim Amin. Novaya zhenschina*, suppl. to *Mir Islama*, i (St. Petersburg, 1912). A German translation of Qasim Amin's epoch-making work has now been issued by O. Rescher, *Tahrir el-mara* (Ueber die Frauemenancipation), Stuttgart, 1928. Cf. also Rescher's translation of *an-Nisaiyat* of Malak Hifni Nasif (*Ueber die aegyptische Frauenfrage*, Constantinople, 1926).

[42] *M.Sh.*, i, 310-325; Haykal in *as-Siassa*, weekly, 18 June, 1927.

[43] The phrase is C. H. Becker's (*Der Islam*, ii, 408).

[44] *Hilal*, xxii (1914), 628-632. *MSOS.*, xxix (1926), 249-251. A collection of his articles, mostly of the class called 'Reflections," on aspects of social life, was issued under the title of الآثار الفتحيّة.

[45] It was founded at Beirut in 1876 and transferred to Cairo in 1885, on account of the Turkish censorship. On Sarruf see now Prof. Margoliouth in *JRAS*, 1927, 937-938.

[46] Zaydan, iv, 323-326 (appended by his son); *R.M.M.*, iv, 837-845.

[47] Two have been translated into French, one into German, and several into other oriental languages (see رواية عزوس فرغانة, pp. 1-2). A detailed account of these and other contemporary Egyptian novels is given by Kratchkowsky, *Istoricheskii roman, etc.*, in *Journal of [Russian] Ministry of Education* (June, 1911), 260-288.

[48] For translations of this into Persian, Turkish, Urdu, French and English, see *al-Hilal*, xx (1912), 567-568.

[49] Criticisms by Haykal, *Fi awqat al-faragh*, 221-247; *al-Machriq*, 1911, 582-595; 1912, 597 ff.; 1913, 792-794.

[50] First published in 1892. A selection from his articles in this journal was published under the title of مختارات جرجي زيدان in 3 vols. (Cairo, 1919-1921) ; review by Cheikho, *al-Machriq*, 1921, 157, 715-716.

[51] Cf. Cheikho, ii², 68, 4-6.

[52] There were also scattered colonies in other parts, e.g. in Santiago, Chile. For Syrian emigration see also Cheikho in *al-Machriq*, 1910, 926 ff. The Syrians now (1930) resident in the United States alone number, at the lowest estimate, 200,000.

[53] See on this subject an excellent analysis of Egyptian educational methods by Professor Ahmad Amin in *Majallah al-Majma al-Ilmi* (Damascus, 1927), vii, 481 ff.

[54] *Ibid.*

[55] *an-Nazarat,* iii, 145.

[56] This statement refers of course to the general body of literates, not to scholars such as Ahmad Pasha Zaki and Ahmad Pasha Taymur.

[57] Cf. the English translation of selected *Quatrains of Abul-Ala* by Ameen F. Rihani (New York, 1903) .

[58] See below, section IV.

[59] On Farah Antun see Kratchkowsky, *Istorichesii roman etc.*, in *Zhurnal Min. Narod. Prosvyescheniya*, June, 1911, pp. 282-284, and in the Introduction to *Obraztsy Novo-arabskoi Literatury* (1928) , pp. xiii-xiv; Cheikho in *al-Machriq*, 1927, 115; al-Aqqad, مطالعات (Cairo, 1924) , 61-66.

[60] See in *Le Monde Orientale*, xxi (1927) , 193-213, Professor Kratch-kowsky's article "Die Literatur der arabischen Emigranten in Amerika (1895-1915) ," and the slightly extended Russian version of the same in *Izvyestiya Leningradskovo Gosudarstvennovo Universiteta*, vol. i (1928) .

[61] Fourth edition, 3 vols. (Cairo, 1923) . The most judicial of contemporary reviews is that of Salah ad-Din al-Qasimi in *al-Muqtabas*, v. (1910) , 325-334, 371-382. An interesting study from a more recent point of view has been written by al-Aqqad, مراجعات (Cairo, 1926) , 170-184 (see *MSOS*. [Berlin, 1926], xxix², 241) . See also Kratchkowsky in Introduction to *Obraztsy*, etc., p. xv.

[62] i, 213. In iii, 68, however, which was written in 1913, he speaks of Muhammad Abduh in terms of profound respect.

[63] i, 324-329.

[64] i, 204-215. Cf. also his eulogy of Omar Khayyam, ii, 235-241.

[65] i, 286-288; iii, 131-145.

[66] i, 101-113.

[67] i, 184-185.

[68] i, 212; ii, 62-69. Cf. also *Abarat* [see below], pp. 61 ff. (الحجاب).

[69] ii, 355.

[70] ii, 17-18.

[71] ii, 102.

[72] e.g., i, 194.

[73] iii, 216-217, 237, and *passim*.

[74] e.g., iii, 126, 243 ff. It is instructive to compare this with Muwaylhi, *Isa b. Hisham*, third edition (Cairo, 1923) , 103 ff.

[75] *Mukhtarat Gurgi Zaydan* (Cairo, 1920) , i, 136 = *Hilal*, viii (1900) , 325.

[76] i, 150-161 (عبرة الدهر).

[77] The same tendency in him to absolute judgments in moral questions may be exemplified by comparing his essay on Truth (i, 166-179) with the balanced judgment of Zaydan (*Mukhtarat*, i, 26-29 = *Hilal*, xi (1902-1903), 149).

[78] Fifth edition (Cairo, 1926).

[79] For four of these (Rostand's *Cyrano de Bergerac*, A. Karr's *Sous les Tilleuls*, Coppee's *Pour la Couronne*, and Saint-Pierre's *Paul et Virginie*) see *MSOS.*, xxix², 246-248. The last-named had already been translated by Farah Antun (Alexandria, 1902).

[80] A brief critical examination of Manfaluti's qualities as a writer of short stories is contained in the Introduction to الشيخ سيد البيطا by Mahmud Taymur (Cairo, 1926), 44-45, reproduced in translation in *MSOS.*, *ibid.*, 254.

[81] Not only among Muslim traditionists; the organ of the Jesuit Fathers, *al-Machriq*, repeatedly indulged in violent diatribes against them from the pen of the late Père Cheikho, e.g., against Jibran 1912, 315-316; 1923, 487-493; 1924, 555; against Rayhani 1909, 716-718; 1910, 389-392, 703-710; 1922, 746; 1924, 478-479, 623-629, 755-757.

[82] *Die Literatur der Arabischen Emigränten in Amerika*, xxi (1927), 193-213; see also on Rayhani, Jibran, Abd al-Masih Haddad (the editor of the New York Arabic journal *Al-Sayeh*) and Mikhail Naima, his introduction to the Chrestomathy of modern Arabic Literature (*Obraztsy Novo-arabskoi Literatury*, Leningrad, 1928), pp. xv-xviii. Professor Kampffmeyer has rendered a valuable service by publishing a German translation of this preface in *MSOS.*, xxxi (1928), pp. 180-199; the passage referred to is on pp. 191-194. Here also attention may be called to the German translation of an introductory study by Professor Kratchkowsky referred to in a former article in this series (*ESOS.*, iv, 747 note), published by Professor Kampffmeyer under the title of "Entstehung und Entwicklung der neu-arabischen Literatur" in *Die Welt des Islams*, xi (1928), 189-199. A summary of other studies by Professor Kratchkowsky on the work of Amin ar-Rayhani is contained in the same issue, pp. 179-180.

[83] The last of the late Père Cheikho's articles on modern Arabic literature (*al-Machriq*, xxv [1927], pp. 941-949) contains a list of contemporary Muslim poets and prose writers, but shows an unusual number of inaccuracies in detail.

[84] On the Egyptian University, see *al-Machriq*, xxvi (1928), pp. 284-288.

[85] Ar-Rayhani, who was resident in Arabia and Syria during this period, forms, of course, an exception.

[86] Syrian writers sometimes refer to it, with a touch of half-humorous deprecation, as a kind of modern مصرولوجية ("Egyptology"!).

[87] An interesting counter-movement to this tendency is furnished by the formation (in 1922) of the "Oriental League" (الرابطة الشرقية), which aims at strengthening the links between all the peoples of Asia and Africa in the face of European aggression, and at present yokes many of the modernist writers discussed below in a somewhat uneasy fellowship with "moderates" and "conservatives." Since 1928 the League has issued a journal under the same title, edited by Ahmad Shafiq Pasha, the general tone of which is hitherto pronouncedly "modernist." The editor of the *Journal of the Oriental League* is the well-known publicist, Ali Abd ar-Raziq (on whom see Khemiri and Kampffmeyer, *Leaders in Contemporary Arabic Literature*, pp. 9-10).

[88] In sketching the careers of the writers mentioned in this article, I have had to rely almost entirely on the indications contained in their own publications.

[89] زينب. مناظر واخلاق ريفية بقلم مصرى فلاح. (Garidah press, n.d.) . A second edition was published in 1929; of this I have not yet seen a copy.

[90] جان جاك روسو حياته وكتبه. I have not seen a copy of this book.

[91] فى اوقات الفراغ. (Asriyah press, n.d. [1925]) . See an analysis of the contents of this book in *MSOS.*, xxix^2 (1926) , 242-244.

[92] عشرة ايام فى السودان. (Asriyah press, 1927) .

[93] The daily *Siassa* (as the name is spelt on the cover) is an ordinary newspaper of six or eight pages. The weekly *Siassa*, on the other hand, is a literary review, generally of 28 pages, about 2,000 words to the page, containing articles of literary, social, legal, historical, or other interest, translations of foreign articles, reviews of literature, art, and. drama, essays, and short stories. Since the political *coup d'état* in 1928, the articles on internal politics have been discontinued.

[94] *As-Siassa*, weekly edition, 13 August, 1927, p. 11, cols. 1-2. The period referred to is about 1912. In the issue of 23 July, 1927, p. 10, col. 2, the same idea is more fully expressed in the present tense:—

فقد اتسعت المدارك ودقت درجات الشعور واصبحت ترى بين الميل لشخص ومحبة وبين العطف على شخص والاشفاق عليه وبين النفور والكراهية وبين الخجل والخوف وبين التردد والجبن درجات متميزة من الاحساس تدركها النفس ادراكا دقيقا وتعبر بعض اللغات عن كل منها تعبيرا يحددها لك تمام التحديد ثم ترى نفسك مطالبا باداء ذلك فى اللغة التى تكتب بها — وهى اللغة العربية — فتشعر بالعجز وترى : « بعد طول الجهد وكثرة الكلام انك قلت شيئا عاديا وان احسن ما فى نفسك بقى فيها مختفيا » .

(The last words are a quotation from Qasim Amin.) Farther on in the same article (col. 4) he extends this demand for modernization to the syntactical construction of the sentence, which requires to be adjusted to meet modern methods of reasoning and feeling.

[95] See, for example, his description of a sunset: فى اوقات الفراغ, pp. 252-254. In this, he holds, is the true purpose of the study of classical Arabic literature: *as-Siassa* weekly edition, 1 June, 1929, p. 3.

[96] فى اوقات الفراغ, 207.

[97] *al-Fusul* (see below, n. 132) , 121.

[98] See an article by Dr. Haykal in the journal *al-Hadith* of Aleppo, vol. ii (1928) , No, 1, p. 45.

[99] فى اوقات الفراغ, 20.

[100] *Ibid.*, 372.

[101] *Ibid.*, 101.

[102] *Ibid.*, 376.

[103] *Ibid.*, 372-374.

[104] See, for example, his invitation to establish a Pan-Arab congress (العربى مؤتمر الشرق) in *as-Siassa*, weekly edition 8 December, 1928, p. 6.

[105] فى اوقات الفراغ, 363.

[106] He totally scouts, however, the idea expressed by some writers of

advanced modernist views (e.g., by Niqula Yusuf in *as-Siassa*, weekly edition,
2 February, 1929, p. 13, that the germ of the future Egyptian literature is to be
found in the poetry and songs of the people.

[107] *As-Siassa*, weekly edition, 25 June, 1927, p. 10, col. 1; cf. في اوقات الفراغ
p. 372. It is fully in conformity with this feeling that he should regard the
Arabs as foreign invaders of Egypt, much as the average Englishman looks
upon the Romans in England (see the article cited in the following note). The
same idea animates a group of younger writers who are beginning to advocate
the recognition of "Pharaonic literature" as the only true basis of a national
Egyptian literature.

[108] *Ibid.*, 360-361. The argument for a chair of Egyptian studies is developed more fully in *as-Siassa*, weekly edition, 22 December, 1928, pp. 5-6.
Dr. Haykal's Egyptian patriotism is expressed in another fashion in the introduction to his collected biographies, entitled تراجم مصرية وغربية (Matb. as-Siyasa,
1929; cf. Khemiri and Kampffmeyer, p. 22, note *e*) —an eloquent piece of special
pleading, in which he defends Egypt against the charge of having passively
submitted to a succession of foreign conquerors.

[109] ذكرى ابى العلاء (Hilal press, 1915), reprinted 1922.

[110] See في الادب الجاهلي, pp. 3-4.

[111] Subsequently translated into Arabic by another hand: الاجتماعة
فلسفة ابن خلدون tr. Abdallah Inan, together with a translation of an article
on Ibn Khaldun by von Wesendonk. (Itimad press, 1343:1925).

[112] See *BSOS.*, iv, p. 751: *MSOS.*, xxxi², p. 188; *Majallah al-Majma al-Ilmi*,
v (1925), pp. 249-252.

[113] The following comment represents, in spite of its extreme partisan
character, the view of conservative opinion:—

اما شعر الاغريق الذى يفضله المجدد على الشعر العربى وينعى على العرب نبغهم له
وترك الاقتباس من معانيه ... قد كا نحمله قبل ان يترجم لنا سليمان افندى البستانى
الالياذه نظما ... فلما اطلعنا على الالياذه وهى اعلى شعر الاغريق ومفخرتهم التاريخية
حكمنا بان اجدادنا لم ينبنوا شعرهم ورا ظهورهم الا انهم وجدوه دون الشعر العربى فى
حكمه وسائر معانيه وانه على ذلك مشوه بالخرافات الوثنية التى طهرالله عقولهم ومخيلاتهم
منها بالاسلام (*Manar*, xxvii, 1345, p. 397).

[114] (1) صحف مختارة من الشعر التمثيلى عند اليونان (Introductions to
Aeschylus and Sophocles, with extracts in translation). (Tijariyah press, 1920).

(2) نظام الاثنين لارسطاليس (Translation of Aristotle's *Athenian Constitution*, with an introduction) (Hilal press, 1921).

(3) قادة الفكر (Sketches of Greek and Roman thinkers, reprinted from
al-Hilal) (Hilal press, 1925).

[115] *Suhuf Mukhtarah*, p. 9.

[116] علم الاخلاق الى نيقوماخوس Govt. press, 2 vols., 1924 (Y. E. Sarkis,
Bulletin Bibliographique, 1920-1926, No. 562). See also Haykal, *Fi awqat al-
faragh*, pp. 157-163.

[117] حديث الاربعاء (so called, because originally published in *as-Siyasah*

on Wednesdays); 1st series (Tijariyah press, n.d. [1925]) ; 2nd series (Govt. press, 1344:1926) ; critique by M. Kurd Ali in *Majallah al-Majma al-Ilmi* (Damascus, 1925) , v, pp. 147 ff. The reader will note the reminiscence of the *Causeries du Lundi* in the title.

[118] ﻓﻰ‭ ‬اﻟﺸﻌﺮ‭ ‬اﻟﺠﺎﻫﻠﻰ. (Govt. press, 1344:1926) . The book was not sequestrated, but the issue was bought in and withdrawn from circulation. See on this book Lammens, *L'Islam* (Beirut, 1926) , pp. 242-243; English trans. by Sir E. D. Ross (London, 1929) , pp. 223-224.

[119] It should be borne in mind that the Egyptians had taken over the French view of university professors as salaried servants of the State.

[120] ﻟﺠﻨﺔ‭ ‬اﻟﺘﺄﻟﻴﻒ‭ ‬واﻟﺘﺮﺟﻤﺔ‭ ‬واﻟﻨﺸﺮ, Published by the ﻓﻰ‭ ‬اﻷدب‭ ‬اﻟﺠﺎﻫﻠﻰ (Itimad press, 1345:1927) . Reviewed by Professor Margoliouth in *JRAS.* 1927, 902-904. Both these works have provoked a whole series of rejoinders by writers of the conservative school. An interesting discussion of the issues involved will be found in *al-Machriq*, xxvi (1928) , 195 ff., and xxvii (1929) , 434 ff. On the controversy between Dr. Taha Husain and his critics on the subject of pre-Islamic poetry, see the analysis published by Professor Kratchkowsky cited in n. 174.

[121] It is for this reason, of course, that Dr. Taha Husain is the object of the most bitter attacks in conservative and reactionary circles. As a specimen of the outrageous criticism and slander to which he is subjected, the following passages from *al-Manar* (xxvii (1345) , pp. 387-388) , apropos of *Fil-Adab al-Jahili*, may be quoted here, with apologies to him for reproducing such odious —and at the same time ludicrous—personalities:—

جمعية تجديد الالحاد والزندقة والاباحة المطلقة

الفالد كتور طه حسين استاذ تجديد الالحاد والاباحة فى الجامعة المصرية غير الرسمية
فارسية كتبا ... هذا الاعمى البصر والبصيرة ... يريد به تجريد أمتهم من الدين واللغة
والنسب والادب والتاريخ ليجددهم بذلك فيجعلهم امة اوربية !! بل طعمة الدول الاوربية،
كما جدد نفسه ويته بتزوج امرأة غير مسلمة وتسميته اولاده منها باسماء الافرنج رغبة عن
الاسماء العربية القديمة والجديدة واحتقارا لها . وقد حدثنا الثقة عن احد اصدقائه واساتذته
انه قال: لا مانع يحول دون اقناعنا للمصريين بسيادة الانكليز وحكمهم الا الدين ، اى
فلابد من ازالة هذا المانع.

The student will note an interesting example of the survival of traditional methods of Arabic historiography in the last sentence!

[122] ﺑﻴﻦ‭ ‬اﻟﻌﻠﻢ‭ ‬واﻟﺪﻳﻦ، ﻗﺼﺺ‭ ‬ﺗﻤﺜﻴﻠﻴﺔ (Tijariyah press, 1924) . The series published in *al-Hadith*, vol. i (Aleppo, 1927) , is also of interest.

[123] روح‭ ‬اﻟﺘﺮﺑﻴﺔ (Hilal press, 1922) .

[124] Published in *al-Hilal* between December, 1926, and July, 1927. As Dr. Taha Husain's autobiographical work *al-Ayyam* has now been made available in an English translation (*An Egyptian Childhhod*, trans. by E. H. Paxton. London: Routledge, 1932) , supervised by the author himself, there is little to be gained from devoting a special study to it, as I had originally intended. A comparison and study of the relationship between this work and the biographical novels of Dr. Dayf and F. J. Bonjean, note 125, would, however, form an interesting subject.

[125] Dr. Dayf is joint-author of two remarkable novels of Egyptian life published in French, entitled *Mansour* and *El-Azhar*. On his study of Spanish-Arabic literature (بلاغة العرب فى الاندلس) see *MSOS.*, xxix, 240-241.

[126] He is a brother of Ali Abd ar-Raziq, whose book on *Islam and the Principles of Government* (اسلام واصول الدين) (on which see Lammens, *L' Islam*, pp. 121-122, English trans., pp. 109-110) created such a sensation in Egypt in 1925. On Shaikh Mustafa Abdar-Raziq see *al-Hilal*, August, 1929, pp. 1162 ff.

[127] *Modern Egypt*, vol. ii, p. 236. (One volume ed., p. 643.)

[128] Cf. *MSOS.*, xxix, 257.

[129] e.g., Muhammad Sabri, ادب وتاريخ (Govt. press, 1927), pp. 296-300.

[130] For the early productions of al-Aqqad see Sarkis, *Dict. Encyc. de Bibliographie Arabe*, col. 1347; for al-Mazini, *ibid.*, col. 1608 (where the date 1323 given for his *Diwan* is an error for 1333; the edition itself is undated). Al-Aqqad's *Diwan* was republished by the Muqtataf press, 1928; his introduction to al-Mazini's *Diwan* is reprinted in المطالعات, pp. 274-289.

[131] الديوان . كتاب فى النقد والادب. Ten parts were planned, but only two appear to have been issued.

[132] Al-Aqqad: (1) الفصول. (Saadah press, 1341:1922). (Summary of contents in *MSOS.*, xxix², 1926, p. 242.) (2) المطالعات. (Tijariyah press, 1343:1924). (3) المراجعات. (Asriyah press, n.d. [1926]). (Summary of contents in *MSOS.*, ibid., pp. 241-242; review by M. Kurd Ali in *Majallah, etc.*, vi (1926), pp. 334-335.

Al-Mazini: (1) حصاد الهشيم.(Asriyah press, n.d. [1925]). (2) قبض الريح. (Asriyah press, n.d. [1928]).

[133] This to be taken as a general statement, of course; in specific essays here and there al-Aqqad may appear more radical than Dr. Haykal.

[134] On Aqqad see also Professor Kratchkowsky's Introduction, xviii-xix (= *MSOS.*, xxxi², 194).

[135] For this reason he protests against the prominence given to the ideas of Anatole France by writers of the French school (المطالعات, 232 ff.) . The principal weakness which he discerns in the Egyptian character is frivolity and lack of seriousness, and it is perhaps symptomatic of his English background that the remedy which he proposes for this weakness should be *real* play—exercise of the body as well as of the mind (*ibid.*, 272-273) .

[136] المطالعات. pp. 54-57.

[137] e.g. المراجعات, 48-89.

[138] *Ibid.*, 79.

[139] المطالعات, 1-9; cf. المراجعات, 22.

[140] المطالعات, 227. This, of course, is aimed at the conservative school.

[141] المراجعات, 90-99.

[142] المطالعات, 229-230.

[143] Cf. his criticism of Jibran, not only for his language, however, but also for the poverty of his ideas, though he admits the poetic insight of some passages (*al-Fusul*, 46-49) .

[144] المراجعات, 100-108. See also his analysis of modern Arabic literary movements in his letter of acceptance of membership of the Arab Academy; *Majallah, etc.*, vi (1926), pp. 548-550.

[145] A study of Ibn ar-Rumi written in 1913-1914, reprinted in حصاد الهشيم pp. 298-346.

[146] قبض الربع(see above, no. 132) . The greater part is devoted to a criticism of Dr. Taha Husain's في الشعر الجاهلي and حديث الاربعاء*

[147] He has spoken of this possibility in *as-Siassa*, weekly edition, 27 April, 1929, p. 5.

[148] المطالعات, 249-259.

[149] آلام فرتر.Translated by Ahmad Hasan az-Zayyat, with introduction by Dr. Taha Husain. 1342:1924. See on this, and on other translations from the French by az-Zayyat, *MSOS.*, xxix², 248. A translation of Goethe's *Faust*, by Professor Muhammad Awad, of the Egyptian University, has been announced, with a preface by Dr. Taha Husain.

[150] For his earlier works see Sarkis, *Dict. Enc.*, col. 1038. The first exponent of the Darwinian theory in Arabic was the Syrian, Dr. Shibli Shumayl (Shumayyil) , on whom see *al-Machriq*, 1926, p. 526; for his writings, Sarkis, cols. 1144-1145. His work met with very little response in Egypt, and it has fallen to his disciple Salamah Musa to prosecute it with more success. Needless to say, the theory of evolution is still very gingerly handled in ultra-conservative circles. The work and personality of Dr. Shibli Shumayyil have at last been rescued from the semi-oblivion which seemed to surround them, by J. Lecerf: "Sibli Sumayyil, métaphysicien et moraliste contemporain" in *Bull. des Études Orientales*, i, pp. 152-186 and 209-211. On Salamah Musa, as on most of the writers dealt with in the course of this article, the biographical and literary data collected by Khemiri and Kampffmeyer in the very useful publication quoted frequently above.

[151] (1) الفكر وابطالها في مختارات سلامه موسى(Asriyah press, n.d. [1924]) . (2) التاريخ حرة.(Hilal press, 1926) . (3) البوم والغد.(Asriyah press, n.d. [1927]) . I have not seen a copy of this book. There is a violent criticism of it by Cheikho in *al-Machriq*, xxv (1927) , p. 957.

[152] مختارات,pp. 98-103.

[153] "For each look backwards we must look forward twice": *ibid.*, 51.

[154] See his articles قطعية الماضيin *al-Hadith*, vol. ii, 32-34, and في والغرب في الشر in *ar-Rabitah ash-Sharqiyah*, vol. i, No. 2 (Dec. 1928) , 46-50.

[155] مختارات, p. 8.

[156] See his article on the literary use of Egyptian colloquial terms in *al-Hilal*, July, 1926.

[157] According to his own statement (in *al-Hadith*, vol. ii, pp. 285-286) 45,000 copies of his books have been printed.

[158] Introduction to his collected *Diwan*, p. 8.

[159] Ignaz Krackovskij, "Der historische Roman in der neueren arabischen Literatur," translated by G. von Mende, in *Die Welt des Islams*, Band 12, Heft 1-2 (Leipzig, 1930) .

[160] The almost exclusive cultivation of the historical romance by the Syrian writers may possibly be explained by the lighter demands which it made in this direction.

[161] *Al-amani wal-minna fi hadith Qabul wa Ward Janna*, published by Shaikh Mustafa Taj (Cairo, n.d. [but in the reign of Tawfiq, i.e., before 1892]) . On Osman Galal see the article of Sobernheim in *Enc. of Islam*, s.v. Muhammad Bay Othman al-Djalal.

[162] The following extract may serve as an illustration of the style of this rendering and of the translator's success in adapting it, is spite of the slight

deformation of the sentiment at the end. The passage is that in which the
missionary priest persuades Virginia to leave her home: "Mais vous, jeune
demoiselle, vous n'avez point d'excuse. Il faut obéir à la Providence, à nos
vieux parents, même injustes. C'est un sacrifice, mais c'est l'ordre de Dieu. Il
s'est dévoué pour nous: il faut, à son exemple, se dévouer pour le bien de sa
famille. Votre voyage en France aura une fin heureuse. Ne voulez-vous pas bien
y aller, ma chère demoiselle?" The priest is transformed, naturally, into a
"Shaikh faqih" and his argument is rendered thus (p. 44):

وأما أنتِ أيتها الصغيرة فلا عذر لك فى السفر   ولا بد من تسليمك للقضاء. والقدر   وان
تطلبى أمر الأقارب وان ظلموا   وان تسلى لما به حكموا   فان سفرك وان كان لا
أحد يرضاه   فهو على ما حكم الله   فلقد انزل تعالى فى كتابه العظيم   على لسان نبيه
الكريم   قل لا أسئلكم عليه أجرا   الا المودة فى القربى   وان سفرك ان شاء الله
لنعم العقبى   اقتصين الله ما أمر   ام تسلين للقدر .

[163] See the exhaustive and penetrating criticism of M.'s translation of
Paul et Virginie by E. Saussey: "Une adaptation arabe de *Paul et Virginie*," in
Bulletin des Études orientales de l'Institut français de Damas, Tom. I (Paris,
1932), pp. 49-80. It does not appear that M. based his translation in any way
on that of Osman Galal; cf. his version of the passage quoted in the preceding
note, ap. Saussey, p. 71. For a general characterization of the work of recent
translators see Tahir Khemiri and G. Kampffmeyer, *Leaders in contemporary
Arabic literature*, pt. i (Leipzig, Cairo and London, 1930), p. 23.

[164] *Riwayat Adhraal-Hind aw Tamaddun al-Faraina limunshiiha'd-daif
Ahmad Shawqi* (Alexandria: Matb. al-Ahram, 1897), pp. 150.

[165] See on these Mahmud Taymur, Introduction to *Ash-Shaykh Sayyid
al-Abit* (Cairo, 1344:1926), pp. 39-40; revised German translation by G. Widmer, *Die Welt des Islams*, Bd. 13 (Berlin, 1932), 9 ff., and especially pp. 44-46.
This valuable introduction gives a survey of the development of the novel and
short story in Arabic literature, both medieval and modern. Particularly noteworthy are the analyses of the styles and powers of characterization of the
writers mentioned, coming from the pen of one of the most talented and successful of modern Arabic authors.

[166] See Brockelmann's article "Makama" in *Encyc. of Islam*; also L. Mas-
signon, *Essai sur les origines du lexique technique de la mystique musulmane*
(Paris, 1922), p. 298.

[167] See *BSOS.*, IV, 4, pp. 750 and 753. Fikri Pasha's famous *Maqama
Fikriya*, which is a short story, already illustrates the widening scope of the
maqama.

[168] The Muwaylhis came of a mercantile family of Sayyids, and Muh.'s
great-grandfather was *sar-tujjar* of Egypt under Muh. Ali. Muhammad studied
in al-Azhar and Ismail's *madrasat al-anjal*; he joined the party of Arabi Pasha,
and afterwards assisted Jamal ad-Din al-Afghani in Paris in the journal *Mirat
ash-Sharq*. After spending some time in Constantinople, where he published
al-Maarri's *Risalat al-Ghufran* and other early Arabic literary works from
mss. there, he returned to Egypt and engaged in journalism (in *al-Ahram, al-
Muayyad*, etc.), and subsequently held a post in the Ministry of Awqaf until
his retirement in 1915. A number of sidelights on his career will be found in
the *Diaries* of Wilfrid Scawen Blunt (see Index, s.v. Mohammed Moelhi). His

father, Ibrahim Bey, was also a man of literary attainments, and published a volume of essays under the title of *Ma hunaka* (Muqtataf Press, 1896). See also *al-Aqqad, Murajaat,* p. 173. *Hadith Isabni Hisham* was originally published in parts in the journal *Misbah ash-Sharq;* 1st collected ed. Matb. al-Maarif, 1324: 1907; fourth edition Matb. Misr, n.d. (c. 1928-1930).

[169] Introduction to *Ash-Shaykh Sayyid al-Abit,* p. 42; tr. Widmer, *W.I.,* xiii, pp. 47-48.

[170] E.g., the dirty fingernails of a painter are كالكاحل علقت بها المراود او كطوط الحداد على صفحات الجرائد (fourth edition, p. 411).

[171] *Layali Satib li-munshiihi Muhammad Hafiz Ibrahim* (Matb. Muh. Mitr., Cairo, n.d. [1907]), pp. 128. Cf. M. Taymur, *loc. cit.,* p. 42; Widmer, p. 48. For the legendary and half-mythological character of Satih, see *Encyc. of Islam,* s.v. On Hafiz Ibrahim, see the study by M. Kurd Ali in *as-Siassa,* weekly edition (20 and 27 October, 1928), and *al-Hilal,* xl, 10, and xli, 1 (October-November, 1932), where the reader will find some account of the personal experiences which influenced him in his selection of material for this book.

[172] Cf. *al-Manar,* xi, 7 (August, 1908), p. 530; Zaydan, in *al-Hilal,* xvi, 10 (July, 1908), p. 583, refers to its اسلوب جديد فى اللغة العربية.

[173] *Al-Muqtabas,* vol. iii, 9 (October, 1908), p. 598.

[174] (Cairo, Matb. at-Talif, 1912), pp. 192. The work is enthusiastically reviewed by Zaydan in *al-Hilal,* xx (1912), pp. 551-555. For other early works of the author see Sarkis, *Dict. Biog.,* coll. 1692-1693 (very incomplete). His plays are criticized by Muhammad Taymur in the collected volume حياتنا التمثيلية, pp. 94-103, and a later book of his entitled تاريخ فلسفة الاسلام in *as-Siassa,* weekly edition, 29 October, 1927, by Mahmud Muhammad al-Khudayri, who declares it to be plagiarized from S. Munk's *Mélanges de Philosophie Juive et Arabe* (Paris, 1859). On his most recent work entitled الشهاب الراصد (Cairo, Matb. al-Maqtataf, 1926, pp. 324), in reply to Taha Husain's work on pre-Islamic poetry (see *BSOS.,* V, 3, p. 457), see Professor Ignaz Kratchkowsky's article "Taha Husein o doïslamskoï poëzii arabov i ego kritiki" in *Bull. Ac. Sciences URSS.,* 1931, pp. 604-607, and M. Kurd Ali in *RAAD.,* vii (1927), pp. 89-90.

[175] To the same class as these works, though distinct in inspiration and to some extent in style, belongs the celebrated treatise ابن الانسان: (Cairo, Matb. al-Maarif, n.d. [1911], pp. 272), composed by Shaikh Tantawi Gawhari and offered to the International Congress of Peoples, which met in London in 1911. The interlocutor in this book is a celestial spirit, and the subject is the wider one of human progress and fraternity. The author avoids the use of rhymed prose but has retained the traditional balanced and antithetical style. Although this is one of the works which do most honor and credit to modern Arabic literature and deserves to be made the subject of an independent study, it is unnecessary to do more than refer to it here, since it falls outside the scope of the present article. It has, moreover, already been analyzed and made known to wider circles by D. Santillana (*RSO.,* iv, pp. 762-773) and Baron Carra de Vaux (*Les Penseurs de l'Islam,* v. (Paris, 1926), pp. 281-284), preceded by a description of the first part of the author's remarkable commentary on the Koran, now complete as far as Sura 49 in twenty-two volumes (Cairo, Matb., Mustafa al-Babi al-Halaki, A.H. 1341-   ). See further the author's own comments on the above-mentioned work in vol. xxii, pp. 239-247.

[176] Cf., e.g., the introduction to *Riwayat Nihayat al-Gharam aw Fatat al-Minya,* a dull and rather primitive type of novelette by Muh. Sadiq al-Antabli, apparently a Syrian Christian, (Cairo, Matb. Khadiwiya, 1905) :—

ليس الغرض من تاليف الروايات سرد الحكاية لتسلى بها الأفكار ويخرج القارئ منطبعا
فى ذاكرته هذا الموقف الغرامى انئ يجب ان تكون النصيحة وجهة الكاتب يتها فى خلال
كتاباته لتميل الأذواق السليمة للمستحسن وتبتعد عن القبيح.

[177] *Zaynab. Manazir wa-akhlaq rifiya. Biqalam misri fallah.* (Cairo, Matb. al-Jarida. n.d. [1914]). My copy has 416 pages, but has possibly lost the last sheets, as the second edition (Matb. al-Jadid, n.d. [1929], pp. 296) has the equivalent of four pages more. On Haykal Bey see *BSOS.*, V, 450-456; Khemiri and Kampffmeyer, *Leaders*, i, 20-21; Widmer, 48-49.

[178] Cf. for the characters of the two women the article by K. V. Ode-Vasil'eva, "Otrazhenie byta sovremennoi arabskoi zhenstchiny v'novelle," in *Zap. Koll. Vostokovedor*, v (Leningrad, 1930), pp. 300-301.

[179] 1st ed., p. 19; 2nd. ed., pp. 22-23.

[180] 1st ed., pp. 401-403; 2nd ed., pp. 283-284.

[181] 1st ed., p. 322; 2nd ed., pp. 229-230.

[182] 1st ed., pp. 293, 296; 2nd ed., pp. 209, 211.

[183] E.g. *abu* retained in oblique cases; fondness for participles governing the accusative; tendency to omission of relative conjunction (*alladhi*, etc.); the ungrammatical use of the oblique case of the dual (e.g., وعلى مقربة منه ثوريه p. 408; قد بقى على الفجر ساعتين, p. 275; both corrected in 2nd ed., pp. 287, 197). There can be little doubt that these offences against literary usage, together with the type of sentence illustrated in the following note, were partly responsible for the negative attitude adopted towards it by the literary public on its first appearance. Moreover, the novelty in literary style of many details of usage and vocabulary has been blurred at this distance of time by the fact that they have come to be more and more extensively used in contemporary writing.

[184] E.g., the sentence beginning معد الغلام رواة 1st ed., p. 37; 2nd ed., p. 34; or that beginning ولم تكن الالحظات 1st ed., pp. 89-90; 2nd ed., p. 70.

[185] See the passages quoted in section III above.

[186] It would scarcely serve any useful purpose to attempt to trace out its origins in detail. Dr. Rudi Paret, in a private letter, suggests that an interesting comparison might be made between *Zaynab* and Th. Fontane's *Effi Briest*, but the comparison could hardly go beyond general situation and atmosphere, and it is not likely that Fontane entered into Dr. Haykal's course of reading in Paris.

[187] Already in 1927 I found great difficulty in procuring a copy.

[188] It was adapted and produced by the Ramsis Film Co. of Egypt in 1929, having been selected as the only novel amongst the works of "two hundred or more writers" which was worthy of consideration (see the article by the technical producer, Muhammad Karim, in *as-Siassa*, weekly edition, 17 August, 1929, p. 7).

[189] The most interesting of these, in view of what follows, are the two long articles by al-Mazini in *as-Siassa*, weekly edition, 27 April and 4 May, 1929.

[190] 22 February (pp. 3-4); 1 March (p. 10); 8 March (pp. 3-4). On Muh. Abd. Inan see Khemiri and Kampffmeyer, *Leaders*, pp. 22-23. The question of modern literary tendencies in Arabic and of the novel in particular is discussed *ad nauseam* in every production of the Arabic periodical press, but it would neither be possible nor profitable to analyze all these views here. The three articles dealt with here stand out from the rest, as having been written by authors with practical experience, and as facing the problem frankly and fully.

191

استطعنا ان نقطع بان المجتمع الاسلامى لا يمكن٠ متى بقى تطوره وتقدمه محصورًا فى
المبادى٠ الاسلامية الخالدة أو فى التقاليد التى كانت أثرًا لهذه المبادى٠ ان يعد كتاب
القصص العربى يوما بمادة واسعة او غزيرة كالتى قدّمها المجتمع الغربى الى كتاب الغرب٠
أو ان يغدو الأثر الذى يخصه للمرأة ذات يوم وحيًا للفن٠ أو للخيال.

[192] حياتنا الأدبية : al-Marifa, i, 11 (March, 1932), pp. 1326-1328. The article
is written in reply to a pessimistic article by Dr. Taha Husain under the same
title in the special number of the journal الدنيا المصوّرة, 10 January, 1932, in the
course of which he quotes a casual remark made by the present writer on the
subject of the Egyptian novel.

[193] See the biography by his brother Mahmud in the Introduction to vol.,
i of his collected works, وميض الروح   (Cairo, Matb. al-Itimad, 1922), pp. 11-88;
Cheikho in al-Machriq (1926), pp. 862-863; further the Introduction to
الشيخ سيد البيط, p. 45; Widmer, p. 52. The following section of the latter Introduction contains a list of the principal recent writers of short stories in Arabic, to
whom must be added—and that in the first place—Mahmud Taymur himself;
for him see Widmer, pp. 3-9, and the literature cited there on p. 8. Two of
Muh. Taymur's stories (Nos. 2 and 7 of the collection entitled ما تراه العيون),
translated into English by the poet Ahmad Rami, are contained in the last
chapter of Egypt in Silhouette, by Trowbridge Hall (New York: Macmillan,
1928), together with two sketches by Manfaluti, an essay by Aqqad, and poems
by Aqqad, Shawqi, Hafiz Ibrahim, and Rami himself.

[194] Cf. the article of Mme. Ode-Vasil'eva cited above, p. 9, n. 1.

[195] In the second edition of Ash-shaykh Guma (Cairo, Matb. as-Salafiya,
1345:1927) the dialogue has been revised in accordance with this method. See
on this subject the Introduction to this edition and·Widmer, p. 7.

[196] Introduction to الشيخ سيد البيط, pp. 46-47; Widmer, p. 53, where the
titles of his principal works are cited. He is known also as a translator of
sociological works.

[197] Published originally in 1922-1923; issued in one volume, Matb. Yusuf
Kawwa, n.d. The scene is laid in Constantinople during the war of 1914-1918.
This was intended as the first volume of a series, the second of which appeared
later under the title of Gamiyat ikhwan al-ahd.

[198] Cairo, Matb. al-Itimad, 1926, p. 435.

[199] Riwayat Ibrahim al-Katib biqalam Ibrahim Abd al-Qadir al-Mazini
(Cairo, Matb. at-Taraqqi, 1350:1931), pp. 384.

[200] The greater part thus belongs to the period during which his new
style was still in process of formation, and is earlier than the sketches collected
under the title of صندوق الدنا (Cairo, Matb. at-Taraqqi, 1929), pp. 320. See
further·BSOS., V, 3, 460-464; Khemiri and Kampffmeyer, Leaders, 27-29.

[201] The reader can already guess something of his spirit from the dedication: "To her for whom I live, on whose behalf I strive, and with whom
alone I am concerned, willy-nilly—my self."

[202] E.g., in reference to magical spells and the like, "... in spite of his
Azharite education ... he had no belief in all that" (p. 241).

[203] E.g. "a 'Homeric' sight" (p. 147); "his words were like ... pearls cast
before swine" (p. 375).

[204] This free adaptation of episodes or methods from well-known books is characteristic of al-Mazini's work (see for example the reminiscences of Mark Twain's *The Innocents Abroad* in his travel sketches entitled رحلة الحجاز— originally published by him as Special Correspondent for *as-Siassa*—signalized by Umar Abun-Nasr in *al-Hadith*, vi, 5 [Aleppo, May, 1932], pp. 359-366) but appears to me in no way to detract from his literary craftsmanship.

[205] *Sanine* was translated into Arabic (? by al-Mazini himself) from the discreetly abridged English version (by P. Pinkerton, 1915) and published *en feuilleton* under the title of ابن الطبيعة. I have not seen this Arabic translation, but a detailed comparison between phraseology and episodes from it and from al-Mazini's novel will be found in an article in *al-Hadith*, vi, 3 (Aleppo, March, 1932), pp. 194-201, by the Iraqi novelist Mahmud Ahmad (for whose writings see M. Taymur, tr. Widmer, p. 53).

14. The Reaction in the Middle East Against Western Culture

In approaching a study of the reaction against Western culture which is beginning to appear in the Middle East, even if as yet only a glimmer on the horizon, we must be careful to avoid two opposing errors. One is to imagine that the present conflict is in some way comparable to the struggle which took place in the Middle Ages between Arab culture and the Persian and Greek cultures and that the two oppositions are to be put on the same plane. The other error is to ignore the lessons to be learnt from the past. History always presents two snares, one to the historian, and the other to the man of action. The historian finds it difficult not to read the past into present events; the man of action too readily ignores the past, and is content with a surface appraisal of what confronts him.

To demonstrate that what is termed the impact of Western civilization on the countries of the Middle East is something quite different from the thrust which Muslim thought had to withstand in the Middle Ages from Greek and Persian culture, it is sufficient to draw up a simple list, omitting all details, of the main influences which have impinged on the ancient institutions of Muslim society:

Economic Affairs. (1) In agriculture, specialization in industrial cultures, and the extension of permanent irrigation; (2) in industry, the introduction of modern techniques; state support for new manufacturing industries; (3) in transport and communications; (4) as a consequence of the development of oil resources, the immediate availability of considerable revenues, and, at the same

A lecture delivered in French on April 24, 1951, at the Center for Contemporary Studies of the Institute for Islamic Studies, University of Paris.

time, a future solution to the problem of providing power for heavy industry.

Social Affairs. (1) In the sphere of public order, the reorganization of the armed forces, and of military techniques and discipline; the reform of the police; (2) in the sphere of the administration of justice, the introduction of Western legal codes, and of courts of law and legal procedure copied from Western models; the creation of bars of professional lawyers; the assertion of the right of the state to make laws; (3) in education, the very idea of a system of public education maintained by the state and subject to its control; the creation of elementary and secondary schools, and of Western-style universities; the adoption of compulsory primary education for all children, boys and girls alike, and at the same time the neglect of technical education—a neglect which is, however, being slowly remedied nowadays; (4) in social organization, the replacement by the Western concept of individualism of the ancient corporate groups to which the populations of towns, villages, and regions belonged; the relaxing of social and family traditions; the freedoms which women and young people of both sexes are beginning to acquire in social and economic life, and to demand in political life; (5) as far as the population as a whole is concerned, the rapid, continuous and even excessive increase in the birth rate, favored by the organization of public health services, improved sanitation in the towns, and precautions against fatal epidemics, as a result of which there is even a problem of overpopulation (especially in Egypt, where the number of inhabitants doubles every fifty years); ever-increasing mobility and density in the large towns and the widening of the social gap which has always existed between town and country; also the special case presented by the accumulation of large numbers of workers in towns where there are heavy industries, and the impulse given to the setting-up of syndicates or trades unions; (6) the creation of middle-class professions and the various influences thus created and maintained; above all, journalism, the influence of whose output is sometimes exaggerated by those with no knowledge of the inner powers of resistance of oriental peoples, but which has incontrovertibly widened the general social outlook; (7) recreations, sports, and amusements, football, the scout movement, radio, and above all the cinema, which has proved to be one of the most far-reaching of all Western influences.

Political Affairs. (1) The adoption of forms of constitutional machinery which evolved in Western Europe under the pressure of liberal and French Revolutionary philosophy, and of other concepts originating from the same sources, especially the idea that all citizens have an equal share in both rights and duties, without regard to their religious beliefs and communities, and of their equality before the law; (2) nationalism, i. e., the concept of the sovereign and independent nation state which enjoys absolute supremacy within defined boundaries, and which claims authority over all its inhabitants as of right.

It is true that the Persians and the Greeks did influence the economic, social, and political institutions of the Islamic world; but the list given above shows that what we are now considering is not just a matter of a few influences, limited in greater or lesser degree, but of a complete social revolution.

Can as much be said of cultural influences, using the term in the strict sense, i. e., of the philosophies, literatures and esthetic ideas of the West? Of all that inner structure hidden behind the façade of Western civilization, of that groundwork of ideas which have determined its outward forms, what has passed to the Middle East, and how thorough has been the transfer? Even for ourselves, it is sometmes hard to distinguish between the idea and its manifestation, so closely are they linked together. In the same way, it is quite impossible to dissect Western influences in the Middle East with precision, and to make a distinction between those which are material and those which are cultural. The introduction of new economic, social, and political institutions, and the overthrow or recasting of old institutions carry implications that influence ideas, attitudes, and values; but it is obvious that if we wish to determine the depth of such influences, we must measure not only their mass, but also their density. Where institutions intimately bound up with a body of positive values are concerned—as, for example, civil or constitutional law, or public health services—it would not be possible to believe in their efficacy in any country without a simultaneous and more or less visible transfer of the cultural ideas which justify and confirm them. Thus, among the

educated professional classes, Western values have gained a body
of convinced and firm adherents (at least within their own occupations and environments); and these values have been reinforced
by residence and periods of study in Western countries, and by a
more or less intimate knowledge of Western literature.

The converse of this statement is none the less true. Economic, social, and political borrowings are subject to the influences and to the cultural values of those who adopt them. Here,
as always, the pertinent question is that of ends. For a certain
period of time, external activities and individual actions may
appear to be indifferent and unconnected with any moral system;
but, in the long run, since moral and cultural values determine
motives, and motives determine ends, the results will be in accordance with the values held, and will reveal their true quality.

What I have just written may appear so commonplace and
self-evident that it is not worth stating. My excuse for setting it
down is that many observers of Oriental affairs, and especially
journalists, imagine that a Western institution established in an
Eastern country functions in the same way as at home. We ourselves are inclined to suppose that the introduction of Western
techniques will always have the same results as those which accompanied and followed upon the technological revolution in
Western society, whatever the society into which they are introduced. It is impossible to deny that this may be so; but it must be
pointed out that the assumption is based on what may be a false
premise. It was not the technological revolution in itself which
determined the way in which the Western societies evolved, but
the philosophy, the rationale, of the West which gave direction
to the manner in which the new discoveries and new techniques
were exploited. I do not believe that the acquisition of these techniques is necessarily inseparable from this Western philosophy.
All that one can say with certainty is that they will set in motion
the whole social machinery of the Eastern countries, and that they
will bring about changes in social institutions and a realignment
of social forces.

It is not, then, the institutions and techniques borrowed
from the West, however massive such borrowings may be, nor yet
the external evolution shown in the last century, which will be of

final significance, but the inward reaction towards the cultural values which are seeking to find their place within Muslim society under cover of these borrowings. Everything depends on the capacity of Muslim society to defend and protect its values and cultural traditions against the Western invasions. If it fails in this task, it is lost as a Muslim society; it will inevitably become a more or less faithful copy of Western society with secondary characteristics peculiar to the different countries and languages.

It is sometimes said that this result would be quite a natural one, and that it would be simply a case of the two halves of Western civilization coming togeher again. It is true—and on this point there can be no doubt—that the civilization of the Middle East and that of the so-called "Western" world are closely related; both before and after the rise of Islam there has been interpenetration between them. Greece drew on Oriental sources, and later restored what she had borrowed, incorporating it into the intellectual structure of the Middle East, but in forms so greatly evolved that they were hardly recognizable. Other contributions and influences, on either side, are well known. Medieval Christianity and medieval Islam, thanks to their common heritage and their common problems, were linked by bonds of both spiritual and intellectual affinity.

But, while recognizing that the Arab world was an integral part of the Western world in the broad sense of that term, we must not lose sight of the fact that it has always remained an independent part, that it has taken from the common heritage what it desired or needed, and fused it with the principles of its own culture. In particular, with regard to at least two of the four elements which have been defined as the primary constituents of a society: its philosophy of art, its rationality (or the freedom which it grants to the pursuit of knowledge), its metaphysical beliefs formulated through the intermediary of religion (or the idea which men have of their relationship with the universe), and the common social tradition which links these elements one to the other, the attitude of the Muslims has been in marked opposition to the attitude of the Western peoples.

Surprise has often been expressed that the Arabs should have rejected the art and the artistic literature of the Greeks. I should

hazard the opinion that the most significant reason for this rejection is that Greek art is anthropocentric. Man, the microcosm
in the strictest sense, is the center of its universe. On its higher
levels, Greek art is richly humanist, but (and this is astonishing)
it was never, in spite of the Platonists, deeply moved by the philosophical vision of the Great Mover of the universe, by the wonder
and mystery of the world, and rarely by the sense of a human
destiny beyond the visible and tangible. Such things were fundamental in Arab Muslim thought. In their daily lives, certainly, the
Arabs were not less "materialistic" than the Greeks, but they were
aware, as few Greeks were aware, that man is not the measure of
all things. This attitude, which is called "religious," is not in itself
derived from religion; it would be more correct to say that religion has given form and stability to what is an integral element
of any Middle Eastern culture and to its conception of life.

The distinction which I have just indicated is still the cardinal one between the Muslim community and the Western
Christian societies. The Christian Church, faithful to its Middle
Eastern origins, has always shared this characteristic attitude of
the Middle East. But even during the Middle Ages, at the height
of its power, it had to wage a relentless and, in the outcome, a
hopeless battle against the humanizing tendencies of its adherents
in the West. The distinction shows itself more particularly in
three cases. In the first place, there was the survival in the West of
Greco-Roman law, with its purely experiential categories, whereas
in the East it was swept away completely except for a few details
which were incorporated in the religious or revealed law. In the
second place, in its role as arbiter of the mysteries, backed by the
imperial heritage of Rome, the Christian hierarchy created authoritarian institutional forms which on the one hand have served
to canalize religious thought, and, on the other, have integrated
the hierarchy itself into its secular environment. By contrast, Islam
has never tolerated formal regulatory institutions, and has trusted,
in the majority of cases, in the influence of a body of "doctors" in
order to constrain the individualism of the religious conscience
within the rational bounds of Koranic monotheism.

The third difference is perhaps the most characteristic and
the most instructive. This is the difference between the motives

and productions of the artistic spirit or the imaginative life in the two groups. In the medieval Christian world, the aesthetic impulse was able to find most vigorous expression in the external form of religious architecture and, above all, in painting. Even the imaginative literature of the Christian Middle Ages is almost dominated by architectonic qualities. I think one can see in this appeal to the sense of architectural proportion and of visual representation the first signs of the renascence of those tendencies which we have already observed in Greek art. They are still subordinated to the church and to church doctrine, they are anthropomorphic rather than anthropocentric, but, as their development in the Renaissance century was to show, they were already preparing to lay claim to the rank which they had formerly enjoyed, as independent and autonomous expressions of the human mind.

In the Arab Muslim world, the aesthetic senses found an outlet in subtler forms and emotions: first of all in the art of words and the pursuit of verbal harmonies affecting the imagination through the ear, later in the pursuit of the mystic unity of the universe, of the identification of the Allah of the Koran with the principle hidden not only behind all things, but in all things. Mysticism in Islam corresponds to painting in the West; both are attempts to make the mystery of the divinity, which reason can grasp only in a weak and confused manner, accessible, if not explicit, to the senses. But each approaches its task in quite different ways: painting, by means of visual metaphors, which limit and humanize their object, whereas in Islam, in so far as this object emerges from a state of pure sensation, it is represented by verbal metaphors which preserve its mystery and emphasise its superhuman character. That there have been mystics in the West and architects in the East does not detract from the validity or the scope of this general judgment. All that we have attempted to do here is to set out as clearly as possible those elements in the makeup of the medieval Islamic synthesis which distinguish it from the Western European synthesis; but while we define their distinctive characteristics in this way, we should never forget that they emerge from a common cultural base.

Towards the end of the medieval period, each of the two societies underwent a shift in the balance of its constituent ele-

ments; each set off down the paths which presented the strongest
appeal to it, and followed them even to the point of exaggeration.
In the West, the Renaissance, by its rationalism, provided the
means by which the humanist impulse broke free from the bonds
imposed on it by the church, and, like reason itself in the West,
soon ceased to concern itself with realities outside and greater
than man. In the Middle East, Islamic culture, when it combined
the rational and aesthetic elements of human life, had integrated
them into an extremely fragile organization of thought that
lacked a solid external prop which, although it might have made
it more gross, would yet have saved it from the process of volatili-
zation which it did in fact undergo. Its heritage of rationality, now
stereotyped, and therefore sterile and inert, was no longer capable
of serving as a check upon the upsurge of the imagination nor of
maintaining its intellectual balance. Its thought, excessively subjective, voluntarily or involuntarily lost itself in a variety of by-
ways; it became unhinged, and in its misdirection rendered its
votaries powerless in the modern world, incapable of distinguishing the real (where material facts are concerned) or the just (where
values are concerned) from fantasy, hypothesis, or even deception.
The Arab world had lost the faculty of reasoning in scientific and
concrete terms based upon verified postulates, and at the same
time the sensitivity of its intuitive perception became blunted,
and its imaginative and spiritual life revolved at random.

Suddenly, in the middle of the eighteenth century, the Wahhabi movement threw down its challenge to this degradation of
the Arab Muslim world, to this national apostasy. It would be
difficult to exaggerate the importance of its role in clearing away
the accumulated abuses of centuries and restoring the bases for
the reconstruction of Muslim thought. But before the Wahhabi
movement was able to finish its task, the Middle East had to withstand the massive assault of the military, economic, and scientific
techniques of the West, as set out above.

Oriental writers nowadays usually claim or imagine that
Western influences, with all the resultant changes, were forcibly
imposed upon the Middle East. This idea is true only within certain narrow limits. The changes were most frequently introduced
and carried out, and the resultant new institutions are maintained

today, by groups and classes belonging to the countries concerned. They acted in this way because they felt a need, or an attraction towards them; this amounts to saying that they set a higher value on the new ideas than on traditional ones.

The success of the invasion of Western institutions and values, and the inability of the old society to put up an effective opposition, must be imputed to some hidden weakness within Muslim society itself. Islamic civilization in the Middle East managed to create, down the centuries, a social equilibrium which was remarkable from every point of view, but it was never able to achieve a true cultural unity. The organs of power and the governing classes practiced for centuries a morality based on values drawn from the ancient imperial traditions of Western Asia and far removed from the Islamic values. Against this "inverted culture" the representatives of Islamic culture struggled unceasingly but unavailingly. To put it briefly, the defects which Eastern critics never tire of pointing out in the Western world under the heading of "materialism" were already deeply rooted in the ruling classes of the Muslim world, and had found not a few adherents among the so-called middle classes, among businessmen, and even among the Muslim jurists.

It was thus into a society already characterized by this half-hidden internal conflict that the West forced its way. The ruling classes, far from attempting to resist the intrusion, encouraged it. It was not Napoleon who introduced military and industrial techniques into Egypt, it was Muhammad Ali who asked for them. It was not Westerners who advocated the adoption of legal codes, parliamentary institutions, compulsory education, and freedom of the press; all these institutions were demanded by the peoples of the East themselves. Does anyone seriously believe that cinemas have sprung up in every town in the Middle East exclusively because of the Westerners' love of gain, or that it was only to please them that bathing beaches have been laid out? The facts are much more complex than the oversimplifications of publicists, and in each country or region one must allow for local nuances, or even greater divergences.

In a general way, one can distinguish two phases in this evolution. The first is that in which new military and administrative methods were accepted by the ruling classes, whose powers were greatly increased as a result. The "materialist" values of Western civilization, transplanted into Middle Eastern society, reinforced the "materialist" values already there, and opened up vast new fields for exploitation, whether by the Westerners or by the Orientals themselves. This reinforcement not only sharpened the internal conflict and unbalanced the social structure, but also disconcerted the opposition, so that the split within Muslim society became henceforward obvious to all. Seen from the outside the task of those who were defending traditional Muslim culture must have appeared hopeless; it was for this reason that Western writers at the end of the nineteenth century so frequently foretold the decadence and collapse of Islam.

The second phase clearly displays a Western inspiration, but here too the agents are Orientals. They are the new literate and professional classes, who, educated in Western schools, became imbued with a passionate faith in the humanitarian and perfectionist ideals of the liberals, or, at a lower level, thought they had found in Western-style legal and governmental institutions a means of defense against absolutism at home and the Western invasion from abroad.

We do not propose to spend much time in an analysis of this phase, which is principally the phase between the two wars, and of which the details are well known. The most remarkable aspect of this evolution is the prodigious effort towards Westernization which has been displayed in every country in the Middle East, not on the initiative of the European powers, but almost entirely pressed on by the professional middle classes, with lawyers and journalists at their head. This activity is the result of two generations of Western education. All key positions are now in the hands of men who are Westernized, and who have introduced Western methods into all departments of national life, not because they have carefully calculated the advantages of doing so, but because it seemed natural to them to do so, something which was unquestionably right. No one laid down regulations for the entry of girls to the new Egyptian university, but they got in all the same.

The means whereby the Westernized classes have secured

their surprisingly firm grip upon power has been (paradoxical though it may seem) nationalism. For nationalism also is a Western concept, and to achieve its ends nationalists have had to create organizations to obtain mass support. This they have gained, and thereupon have considered themselves authorized to model the institutions of their countries on those of the nation-states of the West. But, so true it is that in success itself lie hidden the seeds of decadence, the stronger the hold which nationalism has gained upon the masses, the more it has lost its Western character and become orientalized. The masses have not, of course, become Westernized; while supporting the programs of the nationalist leaders, they have interpreted these programs in the light of their own traditional concepts of the state and of society. As soon as the nationalists come to power, there opens a hidden inner conflict between the handful of leaders and the relentless omnipresent pressure of those surrounding them, a pressure which has become all the more insistent since the moral bankruptcy of the West and of the Westernized classes has become apparent.

I do not think I am going too far when I use the term "moral bankruptcy." The movement of revulsion had already started after World War I, which exposed the discrepancy between the humanitarian ideals paraded by the West and its indifference to human values in wartime. But this discrepancy was only revealed in part by World War I. It was at that time possible to believe that this had been a special case, and that the democracies, at least, would regain their moral strength, so that the Westernized classes still believed that they had joined the right side. As we have seen, it was at that exact moment that the new or second generation of nationalist leaders was in power. But the gap became more and more apparent to Eastern eyes when they saw Western society rotting from inner forces of corruption; they beheld with astonishment all the economic perversions, the exploitation of scientific and technical discoveries to create instruments of destruction, bitter party strife, the hypocrisy that combined outward declarations of good will and co-operation with increasingly intense competition, the efforts to further the interests of some at the expense of others (and it was precisely in the Middle East, unfortunately, that this was most obvious); in short, they could see all the insecurities within our society. This spectacle has fostered an attitude of cynical incredulity towards the whole system of Western morality, both public and private. All this was reinforced by the defects which appeared when Western institutions were applied in the Arab countries: the selfishness of political parties, their bankruptcy in face of social problems, administrative corruption, the inadequacy of the new forms of justice (which were, in any case, scarcely comprehensible to the average Muslim),[1] the dislocation of formerly united communities, the setting-up of barriers between the new nation-states, the lack of social sensitivity in the individualist system, and the disregard of established social conventions. Because of all these grievances, a wave of antipathy, if not contempt, for everything to do with Western civilization has of late become manifest in the Arab world. We must not, of course, lose sight of the element of hostility towards Western encroachments in the political sphere; but this hostility must not be confused with the subject we are considering here, although it does have its relevance as a heightening, and sometimes complicating, factor in the internal conflict. We have seen the rise of movements such as the "Muslim Brotherhood" (the *Ikhwan al-Muslimin*), which are clearly of popular inspiration, and whose program aims to sweep away all Western influences. All these movements pass over the main question in silence. It is no longer possible to make a clean sweep of all Western contributions; the whole of public life and a good part of economic life are geared to the Western system. The plain truth of the matter is that "modernization" means "Westernization." But, on the other hand, it would be impossible for the Arabs to follow the path taken by the Turkish Republic without losing their identity completely. This, then, is the question: how, in a world in which technology is making progress at an unprecedented pace, where industry is organized on an ever vaster scale, can the social values and cultural ideals of Islam be reaffirmed in such a way as to rebuild a stable society endowed with a vigorous and homogeneous social order capable of playing an active and constructive role?

At the root of the confusion to be seen in the Arab countries today there lies a confusion of thought. There is scarcely to be found any meticulous analysis of the facts; instead, writers and orators are content to repeat such platitudes as the hackneyed saying that the West is materialist and the East spiritual—a platitude which Dr. Taha Husain (Pasha) has termed "utter folly."[2] He is the only one, as far as I am aware, who has made any attempt to expose the realities of the situation, and to say outspokenly that if Egypt wishes to create an independent way of life in the modern world, the only way is "to share Western civilization in its good aspects and its bad aspects, in what we like and what we do not like."[3]

Nevertheless, this analysis itself has not been carried far enough. We must first admit that those elements of Western civilization which have been introduced into the Middle East so far are material elements, which was, of course, inevitable. But, since every action is linked in some way with social and moral values, the habitual use of Western techniques implies a conscious or unconscious adjustment of personal attitudes. That the underlying Western values are not understood is explained by two facts. First, those who have creatively assimilated the Western techniques are a tiny minority; for the others, these are simply acquired skills which remain external. Then again, those who exercise these skills have been for the most part, up to the present time, members of the old ruling classes or of the land-owning class (except, perhaps, in the Lebanon); that is to say, that they belong to the "materialist" wing of Muslim society which we have defined above. They have, therefore, transferred to their new professions their old "materialist" values and attitudes, combining them in varying proportions with the external "materialist" aspects of the Western techniques which they have acquired. Because of their own "reversed" or negative culture, they have been incapable of appreciating, or even of recognizing, the cultural attitudes and moral values associated with these techniques, as in medicine, for example. It is precisely here that I think we can find the inner reason which explains the faulty working of Western institutions in Middle Eastern countries, and their cultural sterility.

The most serious aspect of this situation concerns not the attitudes of Muslims towards the West, but the social and cultural results in their own society. On the one hand, the Western influ-

ences, which daily strike deeper roots in Arab society, have been
severed from Western social thought and morality; on the other
hand, they have not entered into any relationship with Muslim
thought. For values can only establish relationship with other
values. Those who claim that only "materialism" lies behind the
things of the West thwart their own plan to infuse "the spiritual
values of the East" into Western borrowings.

How, then, is the average Muslim, or even the educated
Muslim, to form some conception of Western cultural values, and
of those which underlie even material techniques? How are they
to set about adapting them to Muslim values? Here it is that the
past can give us some guidance by reminding us that the life of
societies is measured not in years but in generations. From the
beginning of the invasion of the East by Western ideas and techniques there have been three generations: the first, which felt a
shock of surprise, a second, dazzled by what it saw, a third, which
adopted the innovations *de facto*. The way in which this adoption
was carried out has shown itself to be far from satisfactory to the
mind of the Muslim masses, and even to the mind of educated
Muslims. The struggle has already begun; as usual, its first manifestations have been in impulsive forms, like that of the *Ikhwan*,
befitting the unconscious and blind needs of the masses. In themselves, these movements can end only in absolute moral bankruptcy; but the significant fact is that they do exist. To save Muslim society, then, and to obviate the disadvantages of these movements, it is necessary that an opposition more conscious of what
it is doing should enter the field, an opposition which knows how
to make use of the weapons of both adversaries, which will claim
for the masses (even against their will) the essential part of their
demands, and which will retain for the educated elements the
cultural and material values of the adversary, while yet recasting
them in the molds of the Muslim mind.

If we wish to make comparisons with the struggle carried on
in the Middle Ages to free the Muslim mind from the intellectual
and cultural control of the Persians and the Greeks, we must
remember the relevant facts: that many generations had to come
and go before a solution was reached, that this solution was never
100 per cent perfect, and that even while saving the principles of

Islam and preserving the artistic and social values of the Middle East, it had yet to allow that "reversed" culture to continue in the ranks of the ruling classes. This period of history passes quickly enough in our textbooks, but it took several centuries, after, as well as before, al-Ashari's conscious attempt to re-evaluate the Greek contributions to Muslim culture.

The task today will be no less difficult, and it would be absurd to expect it to be completed in any shorter space of time. The nature of the factors in the situation is much more complex than those in the medieval conflict; one cannot foresee any of its vicissitudes, and only an astrologer would be so bold as to foretell the outcome. But I think we can already distinguish two signs of a conscious cultural revival in the Arab world. First, in spite of the fact that technological progress in the East must depend for many years to come on the West, a new class of technical experts is in the process of formation. In intercourse with such men, I feel quite certain that in time energies and capacities which still remain latent will one day blossom forth, with consequent reactions not only on institutions and attitudes, but also on thought. At the same time I think we can see the emergence of a new generation of leaders of the community and of social thought, a generation which comes, not from the old ruling classes, but from strata of society which have remained Muslim, in the strict sense, up to the present day. These new elements, because they do still maintain their links with the old Islamic culture, will be able to perceive and understand the values latent in Western civilization, and to come at last to grips, in concrete terms, with the overriding problem of the Arab peoples.

All this is hidden in the future. The new generation is still young, groping its way uncertainly forward, and one cannot foretell what course it will take. It is already rejecting the deep and unthinking Westernization of the previous generation, and even, I think, the more subtle Westernism of the man who can, in many respects, be considered as their precursor, Dr. Taha Husain (Pasha). It is a noteworthy phenomenon that the highly Western-ized trend of Egyptian literature in the period between the two wars has not continued, or, at most, continued only in a very attenuated form. Taking into account the external causes of this apparent retreat, it seems to me that writers are seeking, very hesitatingly, for new and more "Oriental" formulas. They are not content, either, with the rather strident, somewhat secondhand orthodoxy which was so widespread in the nineteen-forties. It is the rights, not of an outward and fossilized orthodoxy, but of the inward reason of Islam, which must be restored. It is in this fashion, and this fashion alone, that Muslim thought will be able to re-establish its position in this age of technological revolution, and impose its own values on the new institutions of social life. This will be a long-term undertaking, and it has scarcely yet more than begun. But it has begun, and until it is successfully completed there will be no solution for the social and cultural problems of the Arab world.

NOTES

[1] See Tawfik el-Hakim's remarkable book, *The Maze of Justice*.
[2] *Mustaqbal al-thaqafa fi Misr*, I, 65.
[3] *Ibid.*, I, 45.

15. Problems of Middle Eastern History

The first, and certainly most important, problem in modern Middle Eastern history is to find, and then to find a living for, a few historians fully qualified to investigate its problems. It must be realized that the great majority of those who write on Middle Eastern history, medieval or modern, are strictly not historians, but orientalist amateurs of history. The principal tasks of the orientalist lie in the fields of language, literature and general culture, and history is a by-product of our work in these fields. In England and Europe there are at most only some three or four orientalist scholars who are professional historians; the difference this makes can be easily seen when their production is compared with the usual orientalist works on Middle Eastern history. In the United States it would be hard to find as many. The study of any period of Middle Eastern history, medieval or modern, calls for a continuous and concentrated search for and study of considerable bodies of historical documents. The amateur is physically unable to do this because his attention is continually being drawn off to other tasks. Because orientalists have some of the competences necessary for historical study, and because the field was otherwise empty, they have been drawn into it; but the patchwork that we produce, and the gaps in our technical equipment are painfully obvious even (and especially) to ourselves.

From the statesman's and economist's point of view, no less than from the historian's, the outstanding fact in the modern Middle East is that during the last fifty to one hundred fifty years all the social institutions—in the widest sense—have been deeply affected by the impact of a number of internal and external factors. As a result of these impacts many of the traditional older institutions (such as trade guilds) have been broken up, many others (such as legal institutions and land tenures) have been invaded by disturbing innovations, and many new professions have come into existence whose place in and relation to the national societies as a whole is still experimental. These changes have been accompanied by new political and social philosophies which are not yet integrated with the deep-rooted social ideologies in the Islamic world or with its economic life and potentialities. Both on the physical and on the psychological planes, every social and functional group has been profoundly affected. This has produced a complex of physical and emotional reactions which generate and perpetuate a broad area of instability, particularly marked in political life.

What is the historian to make of a situation like this? If the term "historian" means a student who attempts to trace the story of contemporary or near-contemporary political events, who differs from a journalist in that his technique involves a search in diplomatic and other so-called primary sources and an effort to link up these events with earlier events culled from secondary sources, his product will be, it is true, a more or less realistic description of the external manifestations of this instability. But it is questionable whether this product is any better, if as good, as the work of the competent professional journalist who has closely observed these same events on the spot and who has the advantage of a much better acquaintance with the local factors.

In either case, what the reader gets from this kind of production is a more or less meaningless sequence of facts—meaningless because inorganic. That it is of necessity inorganic will be seen presently. Whatever it is, it is not and cannot be history. For history is a search for the patterns on the web of human life. Every historian is an artist, but not every artist is a historian. The artist weaves his patterns out of his own imagination, and the same too often seems to be true of the journalist and contemporary "historian" of the Middle East. The real historian is one who tries first to discover and then to investigate the patterns that are already there, woven into the web of human life in time past by the actions of innumerable individuals. It is true that the innumerable individual facts can never be known. But out of the recurring patterns the historian selects as his master patterns those which appear to him to be the most significant, in that they, more than the rest of their contemporary patterns, determine the pattern of the next length of the web. It is here, of course, that historians of equal merit will often disagree, but out of their disagreement there should emerge in time a clearer perception of the real master patterns in the historical development of any social group.

Why then should a historian of real competence and insight be unable, on the basis of a thorough knowledge of the patterns woven into the history of the Middle East in the last century, to select from among the thousands of contemporary facts those which constitute significant developments of those patterns? The attempt to answer this question will reveal an astonishing situation. There exists hardly a single work of genuine historical research into any aspect of the inner historical development of the Middle East in the nineteenth century.[1]

The history of Muhammad Ali in Egypt has been written by many hands in many volumes; there is not one which traces the development of the internal social and economic institutions on the basis of the available documents. The late Georges Douin produced a history of Ismail Pasha in six bulky volumes, partly utilizing the archive materials; but only two volumes deal with Egypt proper, and one will search through them in vain for any analysis of social developments within Egypt. The remaining four are concerned exclusively with the Sudan. The full and true history of the British Occupation has still to be written. As for Syria, the case is even worse. The Egyptian archives relating to the period of the Egyptian Occupation, 1832-1840, have been published but remain unstudied. The Lebanese troubles of 1860 produced a mass of polemical and partisan publications, but have not yet been investigated by a historian worthy of the name. As for Iraq, the answer is silence. The Wahhabi movement in Arabia has found a monographer in Philby, but unless recent works by the research department of ARAMCO have filled the gaps, there remain large blank spaces in our knowledge of the peninsula.

The conclusion to be derived from this brief survey need not be labored. The historian of the Arab world in the twentieth century (and much the same is true for Persia and Turkey also) has at his disposal few—and in all cases incomplete—materials of a genuinely historical nature upon which to base his study of twentieth century trends. His facts hang in mid-air. But in all truth the situation is worse still. Even in relation to the twentieth century, political and diplomatic history has all but monopolized the interest of students or observers of the Middle East, to the exclusion of fact-finding studies on the actual phenomena and mechanisms of human life. This glaring deficiency is, to be sure, beginning to be remedied. A few monographs have been published on peasant life in Egypt and Syria, and on Bedouins, semi-nomad, and sedentarized groups, though there is still surprisingly little on the development of the cities and their populations, and nothing at all on the evolution of the modern professional classes: doctors, lawyers, journalists, school teachers, industrialists, and civil servants. Further testimony may be found, if required, in a work recently published under the auspices of the Social Science Research Council, under the title of *Social Forces in the Middle East*.[2] Although it enlisted the co-operation of a highly qualified team of observers and students of different social and functional groups, the editor bluntly admits that, "Each chapter both explicitly and implicitly demonstrates with renewed clarity the inadequacy of the present state of our knowledge concerning the peoples of the Near East."

Even so, the study of functional groups has gone further than that of the social institutions in general. The central importance of legal institutions in any society, for example, needs no emphasis. Yet no study has appeared of the actual working of any modern legal institution in the Middle East in the light of its social implications and effects. We have studies of the legal codes themselves and of the changes introduced into the religious jurisdictions, but if we wish to understand how they work in terms of human lives, the only materials at our disposal are literary productions—novels and stories by Middle Eastern writers—or an industrious combing through files of periodicals. Whatever value we may attach to the works of novelists for illustrative purposes, it needs no argument that they throw only partial and broken lights on such a complex subject. Too often, also, the studies made by Arab writers other than novelists of the economic, educational, religious and other institutions are tracts, more or less purposefully and skillfully designed to support a policy or a point of view.

One can understand, and sympathize with, the ambition of many history students and social scientists to be "up to the minute." But imagine what a history of the United States since 1920 would be like if the writer possessed no more than a bare outline of its earlier history, derived exclusively from De Tocqueville and other foreign sources, with perhaps the works of Jefferson thrown in. An "up to the minute" history of the Middle East is only too likely to be of the same order of value. To say this is by no means to cast aspersions on the teachers in American universities who valiantly strive with the poor materials at their disposal to give their students some understanding of the more recent evolution of the Middle East. But it remains inexorably the case that "the hungry sheep look up and are not fed." Even when it comes to current history, no real student needs to be told how hopelessly muddied many of his sources are. He is necessarily forced to rely for everything outside the small range of his personal experience either on books written by others in the same situation as himself, or on an intelligent use of the press. And just how little reliance may be placed on the press for Middle Eastern news has been authoritatively and impartially shown by the International Press Institute's survey of *The News from the Middle East,* published at Zürich in October 1954.

It may be thought that the picture drawn in the preceding paragraphs is an exaggerated one. The writer does not believe it to be so; but even if it were only half true, it still poses a problem. Is the attempt to work towards a genuinely historical and clearly focused approach to the modern history of the Middle East to be given up as a bad job? Or will historians not rather see in this situation a challenge to cultivate a field which they have hitherto been content to leave to others?

If this challenge is to be met, the task falls into two divisions. The first is the historical field proper, that is, the careful investigation of the factors which have operated in the life of the societies in the Middle East to produce the social situation as it exists in its entirety. It is vital to stress the word "society"; for, notwithstanding the external impact of the Western powers upon the Middle East, it still remains true that the nature and pressures of the internal social forces engaged have largely determined the working of its political structures. The immense field involved has already been indicated: nothing less than the investigation of the whole of nineteenth century history in the Middle East. What social institutions and mechanisms existed at its beginning, to what extent and how were they deranged in the course of the century? What new social ideas and new social classes arose, in what forms were the new ideas expressed, how deeply were they effective in the society as a whole, what new social tensions did they set up and what new institutions did they create? How was the social balance affected by economic changes, by the settlement of nomads, the rise of urban proletariats, the activities of foreign groups, new legal codes and jurisdictions, new educational programs? On some of these questions no work whatever has yet been done; on several of the larger and more obvious of them there are certainly many currently received generalizations. But the validity of these has never been tested; they are simply assumed to be true and taken as the basis for studies of more recent developments by specialist students, in all good faith and unaware that they are building on foundations which may turn out to be of the flimsiest kind.

The second division is not history in the strict sense, but the gathering of raw materials for future historians. This is the careful description and analysis of all sectors of present-day Middle Eastern societies, penetrating to the mechanisms which operate in each sector and how they are affected by various factors, internal and external, how they measure up to the problems, technical and social, with which they are confronted; what new institutions are developing in each; and how these tie in to the over-all social situations. In view of what has been said above, it should be obvious that any strictly historical evaluation of these social phenomena would still be premature—at least until the study of the present situations can be correlated with an increasingly thorough study of their antecedents.

It follows from this that the true task of the historian in modern Middle Eastern history lies in the investigation of these antecedents. This raises immediately questions of method and of sources. Theoretically, the student should not rest content until he has at his command the entire body of materials for the sector that he wishes to study. But in present circumstances this is an impossible and stultifying condition. The sources may be roughly classified into three groups: (1) Western general materials, in the form of official papers, narratives of eye witnesses, biographies, etc., most of which are more or less accessible; (2) official Arabic, Persian and Turkish archives, which are as yet only partially classified, and can be fully utilized only by the student who can devote years to the task on the spot; (3) documentary materials, both Western and Eastern, such as private papers, trading records, professional reports, press reports. In some respects the third is the most difficult field of all, since in scarcely any sector has the search for such documentary materials as much as begun, and it will be a long and arduous task to bring them together for critical study and evaluation.

These facts in themselves seem to determine the methods of study. It will be a lengthy process, involving the collaboration of both Western and Middle Eastern scholars, in time if not in person, and the confrontation of their conclusions. The Western scholar's first task is to search out, co-ordinate, and critically evaluate the Western sources. The special province of the local scholar is to search out and to organize the local archive and documentary materials. Neither is complete in itself, nor exclusive, but each should ultimately complement the other. If this view is sound, it follows further that the primary aim of history departments in American universities in training Middle Eastern students should be to lay the foundations which will qualify them, on their return to their own countries, to do sound historical research in their own archives.

At the same time, it must be made unequivocally clear that the Western scholar for his part cannot do any work of a genuine scholarly standard in this field unless he possesses an adequate knowledge of Arabic, Persian, or Turkish, as the case may be, and of the general historical and cultural background. This is not to say that at the training stage, at least, he needs to acquire a profound technical knowledge of the literary, religious, and philosophical texts which constitute the special province of the orientalist, but only such a flexible knowledge of the language as will enable him to consult historical texts and to read the studies produced by his Middle Eastern colleagues. Yet this is not quite all that he requires. Because the subject matter of history is the human spirit and its sources are human products, no purely technical investigation, however scrupulously conducted, can ever lead the historian to the whole truth of which he is in search. At every stage he has to relate his materials to the human situations, with all that these imply in personalities, emotions, and other psychological factors, and that too in an age and a society very different from his own. Unless he is equipped, through his knowledge of the native cultural tradition, with a certain intuitive understanding of the people with whom he is dealing, all his technical qualifications will fail to furnish him with a secure guide. The mature student of Middle Eastern history must be, in a certain degree, something of an orientalist.

The conclusion of the argument is thus inescapable. If modern Middle Eastern history is to be taught on a genuinely historical level, the instructor must be a historian with orientalist qualifications, capable, like other university teachers, of conducting original research into his field by an intelligent use of all the materials that lie within his reach. But if it is thought (as sometimes seems to be thought) that an instructor so qualified in Middle Eastern history would be qualified to teach only Middle Eastern history, it is a misconception which cannot be too often or too strongly contradicted. Only if a historian has technical qualifications in a wider field can he be a good historian in the Middle Eastern field. There is no reason therefore why a teacher of Middle Eastern history should not be also as good a general historian as a teacher of German or Russian or any other special branch of history. The preliminary training is more complicated, but once this has been acquired the over-all task of continued study and research is no more difficult.

On the other hand, just because the preliminary training is longer and more difficult, few students are likely to embark on it unless the outlook for future employment is at least somewhat less bleak than it appears to be at present. Those in turn who are charged with general training responsibilities in the Middle Eastern field find themselves confronted with a vicious circle. To encourage promising candidates who have come up through the history schools to adventure into Middle Eastern history is to invite them to risk their economic future. To discourage them is to hinder or to prevent the development of any genuine historical work in this field in American universities. So the argument comes back to its starting point. Until some way of escape can be found from the dilemma, the prospects of making any substantial progress in the field of Middle Eastern history are very far from promising.

NOTES

[1] One exception at least must be made in favor of James Heyworth-Dunne's *Introduction to the History of Education in Modern Egypt*, a work still too seldom consulted by writers on Egyptian history.

[2] Ithaca: Cornell University Press, 1955.

Bibliography

The Publications of Hamilton A. R. Gibb
1923-1961, compiled by Stanford J. Shaw
(* Articles in present volume.)

1923

The Arab Conquests in Central Asia, London, Royal Asiatic Society. (Turkish translation by M. Hakki, *Orta Asyada Arap fütuhati*, Istanbul, Türkiyat Enstitusu, 1930; Persian translation by Hossein Ahmadi Pur, *Futûhât-i A'râb dar Asiyâ Markaci*, Tabriz, 1960.)

"The Arab invasion of Kashgar in A.D. 715," BSOS, II, 467-474.

"Chinese records of the Arabs in Central Asia," BSOS, II, 613-622.

Book Reviews:
G. Ferrand, *Voyage du Marchand Arab Sulayman en Inde et en Chine rédigé en 851* (GJ, LXII, 307).
H. A. Giles, *The Travels of Fa-hsien* (GJ, LXII, 453).

1924

Book Review:
M. Féghali and A. Cuny, *Du Genre Grammatical en Sémitique* (BSOS, III, 571-572).

1925

Book Reviews:
Sir Valentine Chirol, *The Occident and the Orient* (IA, IV, 149-150).
————, *Reawakening of the Orient, and other Addresses* (IA, IV, 252-253).
C. E. Wilson, *The Wall of Alexander against Gog and Magog* (GJ, LXV, 68).

1926

Arabic Literature: an introduction, London, Oxford University Press. (Urdu translation by Sayyid M. Aulad Ali Gilani, *Muqaddama Ta'rikh Edebiyyat Arab*, Lahore, 1959; Russian translation, *Arabskaia literatura: klassicheskiiperiod*, Moscow, Izdatel'stvo vostochnoi literatury, 1960.)

"Qerri," *Encyclopaedia of Islam*.

Book Reviews:
Joseph Hell, *The Arab Civilization*, tr. S. Khuda Bukhsh (IA, V, 261).
B. Shiva Rao and D. G. Pole, *The Problem of India* (IA, V, 262).

1927

Book Reviews:
S. Khuda Bukhsh, *Studies: Indian and Islamic* (IA, VI, 400-401).
S. A. le Prince Omar Toussoun, *La Géographie de l'Égypte à l'Époque Arabe* (GJ, LXX, 493-494).

1928
*"Studies in Contemporary Arabic Literature. I. The Nineteenth Century,"
BSOS, IV, 745-760.
Revision of the English translation of W. Bartold, *Turkistan down to the
Mongol invasion*, E. J. W. Gibb Memorial Series, London.
Obituary: "Canon W. H. T. Gairdner," BSOS, V, 207.
Book Reviews:
W. W. Cash, *The Expansion of Islam* (IA, VII, 290).
G. R. Driver, *A. Grammar of the Colloquial Arabic of Syria and Palestine*
(BSOS, IV, 880-881).
E. E. Elder, *Egyptian Colloquial Arabic Reader* (JRAS, 1928, 220).
W. H. T. Gairdner, *Egyptian Colloquial Arabic* (JRAS, 1928, 220-221).
Marguerite Harrison, *Asia Reborn* (IA, VII, 290).
Sirdar Ikbal Ali Shah, *Afghanistan of the Afghans* (IA, VII, 221).
Shafaat Ahmed Khan, *What are the Rights of the Muslim Minority in India*
(IA, VII, 292).
Hans Kohn, *Geschichte der Nationalen Bewegung im Orient* (IA, VII, 438).
Harold Lamb, *Genghis Khan, Emperor of all Men* (JCAS, XV, 371-372).
Dr. Ditlef Nielsen, *Handbuch der altarabischen Altertumskunde* (BSOS, V,
199-200).
Ibn Fadl Allah al-Omari, *Masalik al-Absar. I. L'Afrique moins l'Egypte*, tr.
Gaudefroy-Demombynes (GJ, LXXII, 294-295).
Revue des Etudes Islamiques, Tome I (BSOS, V, 197-198).
Ameen Rihani, *Ibn Sa'oud of Arabia* (IA, VII, 221-223).
D. C. Phillott, *Manual of Egyptian Arabic* (JRAS, 1928, 220-221).
Dr. Muhammad Sharaf, *An English-Arabic dictionary of Medicine, Biology
and Allied Sciences* (BSOS, IV, 876-880).
A. T. Sheringham, *Modern Arabic Sentences on Practical Subjects* (JCAS, XV,
382).
N. M. Penzer, ed., *Sir John Chardin's Travels in Persia* (GJ, LXXI, 395-396).
E. Trinkler, *Through the Heart of Afghanistan*, tr. B. Featherstone (IA, VII,
221).
Arnold Wilson, *The Persian Gulf* (IA, VII, 439).

1929
Ibn Battuta, *Travels in Asia and Africa, 1325-1354* (tr. and selected by H. A. R.
Gibb), London, Routledge.
"The Foreign Policy of Egypt under the Fatimids," *Oostersch Genoots. in
Nederland, 6de Cong.*, pp. 17-18.
*"Studies in Contemporary Arabic Literature. II. Manfaluti and the 'New
Style,'" BSOS, V, 311-322.
*"Studies in Contemporary Arabic Literature. III. Egyptian Modernists,"
BSOS, V, 445-446.
(with E. D. Ross), "The earliest account of Umar Khayyam," BSOS, V, 467-473.
"Arabic Literature," *Encyclopaedia Britannica* (14th Edition).
Book Reviews:
W. Björkmann, *Beiträge sur Geschichte des Staatskanzlei im Islamischen
Ägypten* (BSOS, V, 627-628).
F. A. Wallis Budge, tr., *The Monks of Kublai Khan* (GJ, LXXIII, 383).
Richard Coke, *The Arab's Place in the Sun* (GJ, LXXIV, 489-490).

H. G. Farmer, *A History of Arabian Music to the XIIIth Century* (BSOS, V, 609-610).
Sir Wolseley Haig, ed., *The Cambridge History of India*, vol. III: *Turks and Afghans* (JCAS, XVI, 255-259).
Hadi Hasan, *A History of Persian Navigation* (GJ, LXXIII, 574).
Sirdar Ikbal Ali Shah, *Westward to Mecca* (IA, VIII, 71-72).
Hans Kohn, *A History of Nationalism in the East* (IA, VIII, 658).
Manuel Komroff, ed., *Contemporaries of Marco Polo* (GJ, LXXIII, 183).
H. Lammens, *Islam: Beliefs and Institutions* (IA, VIII, 658).
Reuben Levy, *A Baghdad Chronicle* (BSOS, V, 629-630).
————, *A Baghdad Chronicle* (GJ, LXXIV, 490).
H. St. J. Philby, *Arabia of the Wahabis* (IA, VIII, 71).
G. R. Potter, tr., *The Autobiography of Ousama* (BSOS, V, 626-627).
Revue des Etudes Islamiques, Tome II (BSOS, V, 628-629).
Eldon Rutter, *The Holy Cities of Arabia* (BSOS, V, 625-626).
C. Stratil-Sauer, *From Leipzig to Cabul* (GJ, LXXIII, 562-563).
Josiah C. Wedgwood, *The Seventh Dominion* (JCAS, XVI, 395-396).

1930
Obituary: "Sir Thomas Arnold" (JCAS, XVII, 398-400).
Book Reviews:
A. Yusuf Ali, *The personality of Muhammed the Prophet* (BSOS, V, 916-917).
Fouad Ammoun, *La Syrie Criminelle* (IA, IX, 274).
H. Armstrong, *Turkey and Syria Reborn* (BSOS, V, 920).
E. Blochet, *Musulman Painting, XIIth-XVIIth Centuries*, tr. C. M. Binyon (JRAS, 1930, 919-921).
H. de Castries, tr., *Et-Tamgrouti* (BSOS, V, 919-920).
Sir Valentine Chirol, *With Pen and Brush in Eastern Lands when I was Young* (IA, IX, 132).
John Garstang, *The Hittite Empire* (BSOS, VI, 229).
J. H. Holmes, *Palestine Today and To-morrow* (IA, IX, 715).
G. Hug, *Pour Apprendre l'Arabe. Manuel du Dialecte Vulgaire d'Egypte* (JRAS, 1930, 921).
J. H. Kann, *Some Observations on the policy of the Mandatory Government of Palestine* (JRAS, 1930, 921).
E. Levi-Provençal, *Documents Inédits d'Histoire Almohade* (JRAS, 1930, 143-147).
H. St. J. B. Philby, *Arabia* (JCAS, XVII, 445-450).
E. Senart, *Caste in India*, tr. Denison Ross (IA, IX, 410-411).
Rev. W. A. Wigram, *The Assyrians and their Neighbors* (IA, IX, 132-133).
Sir Arnold T. Wilson, *A Bibliography of Persia* (BSOS, VI, 237).

1931
"Literature," *Legacy of Islam*, Oxford, pp. 180-209.
"Tulunids," *Encyclopaedia of Islam*.
Book Reviews:
R. Altamira, *A History of Spanish Civilization*, ed. J. B. Trend, (BSOS, VI, 792-793).
Gabriel Audisio, *La Vie de Haroun al-Raschid* (BSOS, VI, 790-791).
F. W. Buckler, *Harunu'l Rashid and Charles the Great* (BSOS, VI, 790-792).
R. Chauvelet, *Où va l'Islam* (IA, X, 567).

Mrs. R. L. Devonshire, *Eighty Mosques and other Islamic Monuments in Cairo* (BSOS, VI, 792).
J. W. Hirschberg, tr. *Der Diwan des as-Samau'al ibn Adija* (BSOS, VI, 795).
Zaki Mubarak, *La Prose Arabe au IVe siècle de l'Hégire* (BSOS, VI, 787-790).
H. St. J. Philby, *Arabia* (BSOS, VI, 794-495).
Aldo Ricci, tr., *The Travels of Marco Polo* (BSOS, VI, 795-796).
W. Rickmer Rickmers, *Alai! Alai! Arbeiten und Erlebnisse der Deutsch-Russischen Alai-Pamir Expedition* (JRAS, 1931, 204-205).
Nathanial Schmidt, *Ibn Khaldun* (GJ, LXXVII, 572).
Bertram Thomas, *Alarms and Excursions in Arabia* (IA, X, 567).

1932

The Damascus Chronicle of the Crusades (Tr. of Ibn al-Qalanisi), London, Luzac
Whither Islam? A Survey of Modern Movements in the Moslem World (ed. H. A. R. Gibb), London, Gollancz. Including articles by Gibb: I. "Introduction," pp. 9-74; VI. "Whither Islam," pp. 313-379.
Note on P. Wittek, "Eine Türkische Fürstin auf dem Wandgemälde von Kusair Amra," *Der Islam*, XX, 196-197.
Final revision and preface to T. W. Arnold, *Old and New Testaments in Muslim religious art*, British Academy Schweich lectures, Oxford.
Book Reviews:
Khan Bahadur Ahsanullah, *History of the Muslim World* (IA, XI, 437).
Norman Bentwich, *England in Palestine* (JRCAS, XIX, 493-495).
General Ed. Brémond, *Le Hedjaz dans la guerre Mondiale* (IA, XI, 436).
F. Duguet, *Le Pèlerinage de la Mecque* (IA, XI, 878).
H. G. Farmer, *Studies in Oriental Musical Instruments* (JRAS, 1932, 225-226).
Dr. Hubert Grimme, *Texte und Untersuchung zur Safatenisch-Arabischen Religion* (JRAS, 1932, 223-225).
P. K. Hitti, tr. *An Arab-Syrian Gentleman and Warrior in the period of the Crusades* (BSOS, VI, 1003-1011).
W. E. Hocking, *The Spirit of World Politics* (IA, XI, 877-878).
H. U. Hoepli, *England in Nahen Osten* (IA, XI, 436-437).
Youssouf Kamal, *Monumenta Cartographica Africae et Aegypti* (GJ, LXXIX, 143-144) (in part).
A. Kammerer, *Pétra et la Nabatène* (BSOS, VI, 1015-1017).
Hans Kohn, *Nationalism and Imperialism in the Hither East* (IA, XI, 878).
A. T. Olmstead, *History of Palestine and Syria to the Macedonian Conquest* (BSOS, VI, 1016).
A. S. Rappoport, *History of Palestine* (BSOS, VI, 1017).
Revue des Études Islamiques, Tome III, IV (BSOS, VI, 1013-1015).
T. H. Robinson, J. W. Hunkin and F. C. Burkitt, *Palestine in General History* (BSOS, VI, 1016).
Otto Spies, *Beiträge zur Arabischen Literaturgeschichte* (BSOS, VI, 1011-1012).
C. A. Storey, *Catalogue of the Arabic Manuscripts in the Library of the India Office*, Vol. II, part I, *Qur'anic Literature* (BSOS, VI, 1012-1013).
Bertram Thomas, *Arabia Felix* (IA, XI, 435-436).

1933

*"The Islamic Background of Ibn Khaldun's Political Theory," BSOS, VII, 23-31.

*"Studies in Contemporary Arabic Literature. IV. The Egyptian Novel," BSOS, VII, 1-22.

(with A. S. Tritton), "The First and Second Crusades from an anonymous Syriac Chronicle" (JRAS, 1933, 69-101, 273-305).

"Muhammad b. Abi'l-Sadj"; "Muhammad b. Sa'ud"; "al-Mu'izz li-Din Allah"; "al-Musta'li-bi'llah"; (with P. Kraus) "al-Mustansir bi'llah," Encyclo-paedia of Islam.

Book Reviews:

Charles C. Adams, Islam and Modernism in Egypt (IA, XII, 565-566).

H. C. Armstrong, Grey Wolf (IA, XII, 133-134).

Sirdar Iqbal Ali Shah, The Tragedy of Amanullah (IA, XII, 567).

H. G. Farmer, Historical Facts for an Arabian Musical Influence (BSOS, VII, 219-220).

Dr. K. Krüger, Kemalist Turkey and the Middle East (IA, XII, 426).

Rudi Paret, Die Legendare Maghazi-Literatur (BSOS, VII, 217-218).

C. Rathjens, Vorislamische Altertumer (BSOS, VII, 218-219).

Michel Sabea, La Réorganisation du Conseil d'État en Syrie (IA, XII, 567).

H. Young, The Independent Arab (IA, XII, 425-426).

1934

"Social Reactions in the Muslim World," JRCAS, XXI, 541-560.

"Na'ib" (with C. C. Davies), Encyclopaedia of Islam.

Book Reviews:

C. C. Adams, Islam and Modernism in Egypt (BSOS, VII, 431-433).

C. H. Becker, Educational Problems in the Far East and the Near East (IA, XIII, 884).

S. Erskine, King Faisal of Iraq (IA, XIII, 133).

K. Grünwald, The Industrialization of the Near East (IA, XII, 884-885).

W. H. Ingrams, Abu Nuwas in Life and in Legend (BSOS, VII, 434).

Khan Sahib Khaja Khan, The Philosophy of Islam (JRAS, 1934, 869).

Ibn Idhari al-Marrakushi, Al-Bayan al-Mughrib, ed. E. Lévi-Provençal (BSOS, VII, 435-436).

L. A. Mayer, Saracenic Heraldry (BSOS, VII, 426-429).

E. Nolde, L'Irak: Origines Historiques et Situation Internationale (IA, XIII, 740).

Dr. W. E. Noordman, Turkije Zooals het was en is (IA, XIII, 132).

Revue des Etudes Islamiques, Tome V (BSOS, VII, 429-431).

C. Sekban, La Question Kurde (IA, XIII, 741).

Shawki, Majnun Layla, tr. A. J. Arberry (BSOS, VII, 433-434).

E. L. Stevenson, tr., Geography of Claudius Ptolemy (BSOS, VII, 424-426).

K. Williams, Ibn Sa'ud, The Puritan King of Arabia (IA, XIII, 132).

Joseph Ben Meir Zabara, The Book of Delight, tr. Moses Hadas (BSOS, VII, 434-435).

1935

"English Crusades in Portugal," Anglo-Portugese Relations, ed., E. Prestage, Watford, England.

"Notes on the Arabic materials for the history of the early crusades," BSOS, VII, 739-754.

"Note by Professor H. A. R. Gibb (on Shiism)," A. J. Toynbee, Study of History, London, I, 400-402.

"Nizar b. al-Mustansir;" "Ruzzik b. Tala'i," *Encyclopaedia of Islam.*
Book Reviews:
A. Mysuf Ali, *The Holy Quran* (BSOS, VIII, 242).
Jalal ud-Din Ahmed and M. Abdul-Aziz, *Afghanistan* (IA, XIV, 442).
N. Bray, *Shifting Sands* (IA, XIV, 440-441).
René Grousset, *Histoire des Croisades et du Royaume Franc de Jerusalem* (BSOS, VIII, 243-249).
Mahmoud Mohtar Katirjoglou, *La Sagesse Coranique* (BSOS, VIII, 242).
R. Levy, *An Introduction to the Sociology of Islam* (JRAS, 1935, 158-161).
P. H. Mamour, *Polemics on the Origin of the Fatimi Caliphs* (BSOS, VII, 984-985).
M. E. Meissa, *Le Message du Pardon d'Abou'l Ala de Maara* (BSOS, VII, 983-984).
Muhammed b. Qassum al-Ghafiqi, *Kitab al-Murshid fil-Kuhl,* tr. Max Meyerhof (BSOS, VII, 985).
H. P. J. Renaud and G. S. Colin, tr.., *Tuhfat al-Ahbab* (BSOS, VII, 985-986).
Revue des Etudes Islamiques, Tome VIII (BSOS, VIII, 241).
Paul Sbath, ed., *al-Dastur al-Bimaristani* (BSOS, VII, 985-986).
R. Tritonj, *L'Unità della Siria e l'Indivisibilità del suo Mandato* (IA, XIV, 586-587).

1936

"The Situation in Egypt," IA, XV, 351-373.
Book Reviews:
N. Bray, *A Paladin of Arabia* (IA, XV, 628).
Ibn ach-Chihna, *Les Perles Choisies,* tr. J. Sauvaget (JRAS, 1936, 161-162).
C. Edmonds, *T. E. Lawrence* (IA, XV, 627-628).
B. S. Erskine, *Palestine of the Arabs* (IA, XV, 475).
R. H. Kiernan, *Lawrence of Arabia* (IA, XV, 628).
H. Kluge, *Das Königreich Irak* (IA, XV, 474).
H. Kohn, *Die Europäisierung des Orients* (IA, XV, 473).
E. Main, *Iraq: From Mandate to Independence* (IA, XV, 473-474).
W. H. Ritsher, *Criteria of Capacity for Independence* (IA, XV, 474).
R. S. Stafford, *The Tragedy of the Assyrians* (IA, XV, 474-475).
C. Sykes, *Wassmuss: The German Lawrence* (IA, XV, 628).

1937

*"Al-Mawardi's Theory of the Khilafah," *Islamic Culture,* XI, 291-302.
"Thomas Walker Arnold," *Dictionary of National Biography, 1922-1930,* pp. 25-26.
Book Reviews:
H. E. Allen, *The Turkish Transformation* (IA, XVI, 164).
F. Awad, *La Souveraineté Égyptienne et la Déclaration du 28 Février 1922* (IA, XVI, 164).
R. Blachère, *Abou T-Tayyib al-Mutanabbi* (BSOS, VIII, 1160).
F. Z. Fahri, *Essai sur la Transformation du Code Familial en Turquie* (IA, XVI, 164).
H. A. Foster, *The Making of Modern Iraq* (IA, XVI, 163).
Francesco Gabrieli, *Il Califfato di Hisham* (BSOS, VIII, 1161-1162).
C. P. Grant, "The Syrian Desert" (*Economic History Review,* VIII, 101).
J. de Monicault, *Le Port de Beyrouth* (IA, XVI, 818).

Revue des Études Islamiques, Tome IX (BSOS, VIII, 1164-1165).
J. Schacht, ed., G. *Bergsträsser's Grundzüge des Islamischen Rechts* (BSOS, VIII, 1163-1164).
Von Norbert von Bischoff, *Ankara* (IA, XVI, 164).
R. F. Woodsmall, *Moslem Women Enter a New World* (IA, XVI, 817).

1938

"Law and Religion in Islam," *Judaism and Christianity*, ed., E. J. Rosenthal, III, London, 145-168.
Editor (with others) of *The Encyclopaedia of Islam: Supplement.* "al-Muhibbi," "al-Muradi," "Ta'rikh," *Encyclopaedia of Islam: Supplement.*
Book Reviews:
George Antonius, *The Arab Awakening* (*The Spectator*, Nov. 25, p. 912).
Alfred Bonné, *Der Neue Orient* (IA, XVII, 585).
S. Chew, *The Crescent and the Rose* (*Modern Language Review*, XXXIII, 580).
Marcel Clerget, *Le Caire* (BSOS, IX, 472-473).
S. D. F. Goitein, *The Ansab al-Ashraf of al-Baladhuri* (BSOS, IX, 468).
Walther Hellige, *Die Regentschaft al-Muwaffaqs* (BSOS, IX, 469).
S. Hillslson, *Sudan Arabic Texts* (BSOS, IX, 471-472).
J. M. Jones, *La Fin du Mandat Français en Syrie et au Liban* (IA, XVII, 872).
D. F. Karaka, *I Go West* (JRCAS, XXV, 307).
M. Muhtar-Katircioglu, *The Wisdom of the Qur'an* (JTS, XXXIX, 209).
Ibrahim Mustafa, *Ihya' an-Nahw* (BSOS, IX, 471).
M. Riad, *La Nationalité Egyptienne* (IA, XVII, 584).
Ronald Storrs, *Orientations* (IA, XVII, 87-88).
Hafiz Wahbah, *Jazirat al-'Arab fi'l-Qarn al-'Ishrin* (JRAS, 1938, 117).
W. W. White, *The Process of Change in the Ottoman Empire* (IA, XVII, 872).

1939

*"Some Considerations on the Sunni Theory of the Caliphate," *Archives d'histoire du droit oriental*, III, 401-410 (reprinted in 1948).
"Nationalism in the Near East," *Nationalism*, London, Royal Institute of International Affairs, 147-151.
"University in the Arab-Moslem World," *University Outside Europe*, ed., E. Bradby, London, 281-297.
Book Reviews:
Zaki 'Ali, *Islam in the World* (IA, XVIII, 135).
A. J. Arberry, ed., *Catalogue of the Arabic Manuscripts in the Library of the India Office*, II. *Sufism and Ethics* (BSOS, IX, 1092).
Centre d'Etudes de Politique Étrangère, *L'Egypte Indépendante* (IA, XVIII, 580-581).
A. E. Crouchley, *The Economic Development of Modern Egypt* (IA, XVIII, 581).
Nabih Amin Faris, tr., *The Antiquities of South Arabia* (GJ, XCIII, 532).
A. M. Husain, *The Rise and Fall of Muhammad bin Tughluq* (JRCAS, XXVI, 533-534).
Rom Landau, *Search for To-morrow* (IA, XVIII, 134-135).
C. N. Johns, *Palestine of the Crusades* (JRAS, 1939, 273).
M. von Oppenheim, *Die Beduinen* (IA, XVIII, 871).
Revue des Études Islamiques, Tome X, XI (BSOS, IX, 1092).

O. Spies, *An Arab Account of India in the Fourteenth Century* (BSOS, IX, 1091-1092).
B. Vernier, *La Politique Islamique de l'Allemagne* (IA, XVIII, 714-715).

1940

The Arabs (Oxford pamphlets on World Affairs, no. 40), Oxford.
Book Reviews:
Dr. A. E. Affifi, *The Mystical Philosophy of Muhyid Din Ibnul 'Arabi* (JTS, XLI, 219-220).
Bernard Lewis, *The Origins of Isma'ilism* (BSOAS, X, 797).
Obituary: "David Samuel Margoliouth, 1858-1940" (JRAS, 1940, p. 392-394).

1941

"Egypt," *Proceedings of the Royal Institute of Great Britain* XXXI, 390-419 (Lecture given on March 4, 1941).
Obituary: "Edward Denison Ross, 1871-1940" JRAS, 1941, p. 49-52.

1942

"Social change in the Near East" and "Future for Arab Unity," P. W. Ireland, ed., *Near East: problems and prospects*, Chicago, pp. 33-64, 67-99.

1943

*"Khawatir fil-Adab al-Arabi, I. Bad' at-Ta'lif al-Nashri," *al-Adab wal-Fann*, I, No. 2, London, 2-18.
Book Review:
F. Rosenthal and R. Walzer, ed., *Alfarabius de Platonis Philosophia* (*The Oxford Magazine*, LXII, 82).

1944

"Islamic archaeology," University of London, Institute of Archaeology, *Occasional Papers*, V, 34-35.
"Middle Eastern Perplexities," IA, XX, 458-469.
Book Review:
V. Minorsky, *Sharaf al-Zaman Tahir Marvazi on China, the Turks and India* (JRAS, 1944, p. 94-95).
Obituary: "Duncan Black Macdonald" (JRAS, 1944, pp. 87-88).

1945

*"Khawatir fil-Adab al-Arabi, II. Nash' et al-Insha' al-Adabi," *al-Adab wal-Fann*, III, No. 1, London, 2-13.
"Toward Arab Unity," *Foreign Affairs*, XXIV, 119-129.

1946

Revision of the English translation of *Claudius Galenus, Galen on Medical Experience* (tr. with notes by R. Walzer), London and New York, 1946.
Obituary: "Reynold Alleyne Nicholson" (JRCAS, XXXIII, 7-8).

1947

Modern Trends in Islam (Haskell Lectures in Comparative Religion), Chicago, University of Chicago Press, 1947. Indonesian tr. by L. E. Hakim,

Aliran-Aliran Modern dalam Islam, Djakarta, 1952; French tr. by B. Vernier, *Les Tendances modernes de l'Islam*, Paris, 1949; Unauthorized Arabic tr. by Kamil Suleyman, *al-Ittijahat al-Haditha fil-Islam*, Beirut, 1954.

Book Reviews:

Prince Aga Khan and Z. Ali, *L'Europe et L'Islam* (IA, XXIII, 271).

G. von Grunebaum, *Medieval Islam* (*English Historical Review*, LXII, 380-381).

Syed Abdul Vahid, *Iqbal, His Art and Thought* (*Oxford Magazine*, LXV, 164).

1948

"Arab poet and Arab philologist," BSOAS, XII, 574-578.

"The argument from design. A mutazilite treatise attributed to al-Jahiz," *Ignace Goldziher Memorial Volume*, I, Budapest, 150-162.

*"The structure of religious thought in Islam," MW, XXVIII, 17-28, 113-123, 185-197, 280-291. Tr. by J. and F. Arin, *La Structure de la Pensée Religieuse de l'Islam*, Paris, Institute des hautes études marocaines, 1950; Tr. by Dr. Adil al-Awwa, *Bunyat al-Fikr al-Dini fil-Islam*, Damascus, 1959.

Book Reviews:

R. Montagne, *La Civilisation du Désert* (IA, XXIV, 454).

E. Taylor, *Richer by Asia* (IA, XXIV, 608).

A. S. Tritton, *Muslim Theology* (JRAS, 1948, pp. 195-196).

1949

Mohammedanism: An historical survey, Oxford University Press, 1949 (second edition, 1953; Mentor book edition, 1955).

In *The Dictionary of National Biography, 1931-1940*, London: "Sir Muhammad Iqbal," pp. 461-462; "Stanley Lane-Poole," pp. 715-716.

Book Review:

E. E. Evans-Pritchard, *The Sanusi of Cyrenaica* (IA, XXV, 539).

1950

"The Arabic sources for the Life of Saladin," *Speculum*, XXV, 58-72.

(with Harold Bowen) *Islamic Society and the West*, I, *Islamic Society in the Eighteenth Century*, part 1 (Oxford University Press).

"The Encyclopaedia of Islam," *Islamic Literature*, II, 334-338.

"Abdul 'Aziz Ibn Sa'ud," "Aden: History," "Alexandria: History" (in part), "Arabia: History," "Arabic Language: History," "Bahrain Islands: History," "Caliphate," "Cyrenaica: History (Mediaeval and Modern)," "Druses," "Egyptian History," "Fatimids or Fatimites," "Fezzan: History," "Hadhramaut: History," "Ibrahim Pasha," "Ismail Pasha," "Kowait: History," "Mamluks," "Mehemet Ali," "Nabateans," "Oman: History," "Omar," "Sabaeans," "Sinai: History" (in part), "Sudan: History," "Transjordan: History," "Tripolitania: History," "Turkestan: History," "Yeman: History," "Zaghlul, Sa'ad," in *Chamber's Encyclopaedia*.

Book Reviews:

Gerald de Gaury, *Arabian Journey* (IA, XXVI, 573).

Philip K. Hitti, *The Arabs: A Short History* (*History*, n.s. XXXV, 111-112).

John La Monte, *The World of the Middle Ages* (MW, XL, 59-60).

Khalil Mardam Bey, ed., *Diwan 'Ali Ibn al-Jahm* (JRAS, 1950, 192-193).
Rhazes, *The Spiritual Physick*, tr. A. J. Arberry (JRAS, 1950, 189).
J. Spencer Trimingham, *Islam in the Sudan* (JRAS, 1950, 85).
W. Montgomery Watt, *Free Will and Predestination in Early Islam* (JRAS, 1950, 86).

1951

"Anglo-Egyptian relations: a revaluation," IA, XXVII, 440-450.
*"The Armies of Saladin," *Cahiers d'histoire egyptienne*, III, 304-320.
*"La reaction contre la culture occidentale dans le Proche Orient," *Cahiers de l'Orient Contemporain*, XXIII, 1-10 (tr. by 'Adil al-Awwa, *Inqadh al-Mujtama'a al-Islami*, Damascus, 1952).
In *Near East and the Great Powers*, ed., R. N. Frye (Harvard University Press, Cambridge, Massachusetts): "Political and economic factors: introductory," pp. 9-10; "Oriental Studies in the United Kingdom," pp. 85-88; "Conclusion," pp. 193-195.
In *Near Eastern Culture and Society*, ed., T. C. Young (Princeton University Press, Princeton, New Jersey), "Near East perspective: the present and the future," pp. 227-239.
Book Reviews:
Joseph Schacht, *The Origins of Muhammedan Jurisprudence* (*Journal of Comparative Legislation*, 3rd series, XXXIII, 113-114).
W. Montgomery Watt, *Free Will and Predestination in Early Islam* (*History*, n.s. XXXVI, 144).

1952

*"The Achievement of Saladin," *Bulletin of the John Rylands Library*, XXXV, 44-60.
"Egypt," *United Empire*, XLIII, 68-76.
"The millenary of Ibn Sina," BSOAS, XIV, 496-500.
"Abbasids," "Abu-Bekr," "Almohades" (in part), "Almoravides" (in part), "Alp Arslan," "Caliphate," "Islam," "Omar," *Encyclopaedia Britannica*.
Book Reviews:
A. J. Arberry, *Sufism: An Account of the Mystics of Islam* (JTS, n.s. III, 148-149).
Marcel Colombe, *L'Évolution de l'Egypte* (IA, XVIII, 252-253).
Harry Hazard, ed., *Atlas of Islamic History* (*English History Review*, CCLXII, 628-629).
Histoire Universelle de Rashid ad-Din Fadl Allah Abul-Khair (ed. and tr. K. Jahn).
Ibn al-Mugawir, *Descriptio Arabiae Meridonalis Pars I* (*Tarikh al-Mustabsir*) (ed. Oscar Löfgren), and
Abd al-Karim ibn Muhammad as-Sam'ani, *Die Methodik des Diktatkollegs* ed., Max Weisweiler (reviewed jointly with A. S. Tritton) (JRAS, 1952, pp. 155-156).

1953

"Al-Barq al-Shami: The History of Saladin by the Katib 'Imad al-Din al-Isfahani," *Wiener Zeitschrift für die Kunde des Morgenlandes*, LII, 93-115.
*"An interpretation of Islamic history," *Journal of World History*, I, 39-62

(reprinted in MW, LXV, 4-15, 121-133; published as a book under the same title, Lahore, Orientalia, 1957).

*"The Social Significance of the Shu'ubiya," *Studia Or.* Pedersen, Copenhagen, pp. 105-114.

"Bi-Mu'alaja Jedida lil-Ta'rikh al-'Arabi," *al-Nada' al-Ijtima'i* (Baghdad), pp. 47-57.

"Seljuks," "Timur," *Encyclopaedia Britannica.*

Editor (with J. H. Kramers) of *The Shorter Encyclopaedia of Islam,* Brill and Co., Leiden.

Book Reviews:

Dwight M. Donaldson, *Studies in Muslim Ethics (Church Quarterly Review,* XLIV, 482-484).

Hisham ibn al Kalbi, *The Book of Idols,* tr. Nabih Amin Faris (JRAS, 1953, pp. 65-66).

E. Jackh, ed., *The Background of the Middle East (Welt des Islams,* n.s. II, 293).

A. A. Vasiliev, *Byzance et les Arabes,* II. *La Dynastie Macédonienne* (JRAS, 1953, pp. 64-65).

1954

"Why we learn the Arabic Language," *al-Islam* (Karachi), II, 39.

Editor (with others), *The Encyclopaedia of Islam: New Edition,* " 'Abd Allah b. al-Zubayr," " 'Abd al-Hamid b. Yahya b. Sa'd," " 'Abd al-Malik b. Marwan," " 'Abd al-Rahman b. Khalid," " 'Abd al-Rahman b. Samura," "Abu'l-Fida," "Abu Firas al-Hamdani," "Abu'l-Sadj," "Abu'l-Saraya al-Shaybani," "Abu 'Ubayda Ma'mar b. al-Muthanna," "Abu 'Ubayda b. al-Djarrah," *The Encyclopaedia of Islam: New Edition.*

"Persia" (in part), *Encyclopaedia Britannica.*

Book Reviews:

A. J. Arberry, *The Holy Koran, An Introduction with Selections* (JTS, n.s. V. 159).

H. G. H. Abu Shaqra, *al-Harakat fi Lubnan ila 'Ahd al-Mutasarrifiya* (JRAS, 1954, pp. 78-79).

Richard Bell, *Introduction to the Qur'an (Hibbert Journal,* LII, 413-415).

A. A. A. Faidi (Fyzee), ed. *Da'a'im al-Islam* (JRAS, 1954, p. 99-100).

Ibn Hazm, *The Ring of the Dove,* tr. A. J. Arberry, and Ibn Sa'id, *An Anthology of Moorish Poetry,* tr. A. J. Arberry (JRAS, 1954, pp. 75-76).

Stephen Longrigg, *Iraq, 1900 to 1950 (Parliamentary Affairs,* VII, 452-453).

James Robson, ed., *An Introduction to the Science of Tradition* (JRAS, 1954, pp. 194-195).

W. Montgomery Watt, *Muhammad at Mecca (Hibbert Journal,* LII, 201-202).

G. M. Wickens, ed., *Avicenna: Scientist and Philosopher* (JRAS, 1954, p. 100).

1955

"Constitutional Organization," in M. Khadduri and J. J. Liebesny, ed., *Law in the Middle East,* I, *Origin and Development of Islamic Law,* Washington, pp. 3-27.

*"The Evolution of Government in Early Islam," *Studia Islamica* IV, 1-17.

"The Fiscal Rescript of 'Umar II," *Arabica,* II, 1-16.

"The Influence of Islamic Culture on medieval Europe," *Bulletin of the John Rylands Library,* XXXVIII, 82-98.

In *A History of the Crusades*, ed. Kenneth M. Setton, Vol. I, *The First Hundred Years* (ed. Marshall W. Baldwin) : "The Caliphate and the Arab States," pp. 81-98; "Zengi and the Fall of Edessa," pp. 449-462; "The Career of Nur ad-Din," pp. 513-527; "The Rise of Saladin, 1169-1189," pp. 563-589. "al-'Adil," "Adjnadayn," "Afamiya," "al-Afdal," "Afghanistan" (in part), "Afrasiyab," "Afshin" (in part), "Agha Khan," *Encyclopaedia of Islam: New Edition.*
"Spain" (in part), "Syria" (in part), *Encyclopaedia Britannica.*
Book Reviews:
Anne S. K. Lambton, *Islamic Society in Persia* (IA, XXXI, 392).
John Marlowe, *Anglo-Egyptian Relations, 1800-1953* (IA, XXXI, 113-114).
V. Minorsky, *Studies in Caucasian History* (BSOAS, XVII, 187-188).
Thomas O'Shaughnessy, *The development of the meaning of spirit in the Koran* (JRAS, 1955, 189).
H. St. John Philby, *Sa'udi Arabia* (JRAS, 1955, p. 190).

1956

*"Problems of Modern Middle Eastern History," *Report on Current Research, Spring, 1956,* The Middle East Institute, Washington, pp. 1-15.
"Social Reform: factor X," *Atlantic Monthly,* 198, pp. 137-141. Reprinted in W.Z. Laqueur, ed. *The Middle East in Transition,* London, 1958, pp. 3-11.
"Ahmed Amin," "Ak Sunkur," "Akhlak" (in part), "Ali b. al-Djahm," *Encyclopaedia of Islam: New Edition.*
"Asma'i," *Encyclopaedia Britannica.*
Book Reviews:
Gustav E. von Grunebaum, ed., *Studies in Islamic Cultural History* (JRAS, 1956, p. 119).
Majid Khadduri, *War and Peace in the Law of Islam* (MEJ, X, 201).
Rudolph Sellheim, *Die Klassisch-Arabischen Sprichwort Ersammlungen* (JR AS, 1956, p. 119).
Eric Schroeder, *Muhammad's People* (MW, XLVI, 69-71).

1957

(with Harold Bowen), *Islamic Society and the West, I, Islamic Society in the Eighteenth Century,* part II (Oxford University Press).
"Government under Law in Muslim Society," American Council of Learned Societies, *Government under Law and the Individual,* Washington, 1957, pp. 16-26.
"Unitive and Divisive Factors in Islam," *Civilisations,* VII, 507-514.
"Antakiya" (in part), " 'Arabiyya. B. Arabic Literature," " 'Arafa" (in part), *Encyclopaedia of Islam: New Edition.*
Foreward to:
Dr. R. Roolvink, *Historical Atlas of the Muslim Peoples* (Djambatan, Amsterdam), v.
Book Review:
K. Cragg, *The Call of the Minaret* (*Religion in Life,* XXVI, 618-620).

1958

"Address (on Teaching in the Humanities)," *Conference on Research and*

Advanced Teaching in the Humanities in Pakistan Universities, Karachi, pp. 7-12.

The Travels of Ibn Battuta, A.D. 1325-1354, I (Hakluyt Society, *Works*, 2nd series, no. 110) , Cambridge, England.

•"Arab-Byzantine Relations under the Umayyad Caliphate," *Dumbarton Oaks Papers*, XII, 219-233.

"Arsuf," "Asad b 'Abd Allah," "Asma," "al-'Attar," "Aydhab," *Encyclopaedia of Islam: New Edition*.

"Esquisse d'un programme d'Etudes sur l'Orient et Occident: Divergence et convergence," *Etudes Méditerranéennes*, IV, 5-9.

Book Reviews:

Nabia Abbott, "Studies in Arabic Literary Papyri," I. Historical Texts (JNES, XVII, 222-224) .

A. J. Arberry, *Reason and Revelation in Islam* (*Welt des Islams*, n.s. V, 272-273.

————, *The Seven Odes: The first chapter in Arabic Literature* (*Welt des Islams*, n.s. V, 271-272) .

H. Birkelund, *Stress Patterns in Arabic* (*Journal of Semitic Studies*, III, 215) .

L. H. Coult, Jr., *An annotated research bibliography of the Fellah of the Egyptian Nile, 1798-1955* (IA, XXXIV, 546-547) .

Wilfred C. Smith, *Islam in modern history* (JAOS, LXXVIII, 126-127) .

Forward To:

Jacob M. Landau, *Studies in the Arab Theater and Cinema* (University of Pennsylvania Press, Philadelphia) , ix-x.

1959

"Islam," *The Concise Encyclopaedia of Living Faiths*, R. C. Zaehner, ed., pp. 178-208.

Book Review:

Hassan Sa'ab, *The Arab federalists of the Ottoman Empire* (MW, XLIX, 323) .

1960

"Politics and Prospects in the Arab Middle East," *University of Toronto Quarterly*, XXIX, 168-180.

"Factors of Cultural Divergence," *Journal of the Pakistan Historical Society*, VIII, 85-89.

Book Reviews:

Ibn Khaldun, *Muqaddamah*, tr. Franz Rosenthal, (*Speculum*, XXXV, 139-142).

Kamel Hussein, *City of Wrong: A Friday in Jerusalem*, tr. Kenneth Cragg (*Religion in Life*, XXIX, 158-159) .

Dominique Sourdel, *Le Vizirat 'Abbaside de 749 à 936*, Vol. 1 (MEJ, XIV, 344-345) .

1961

Foreword to:

Menahem Mansoor, *English-Arabic Dictionary of Political, Diplomatic, and Conference Terms*, New York.

"Islam in the Modern World," Tibor Kerekes, ed., *The Arab Middle East and Muslim Africa*, pp. 9-25.

"Government and Islam under the Early 'Abbasids: the Political Collapse of Islam," *L'Elaboration de l'Islam*, Paris, pp. 115-127.

Index

This Index includes proper nouns, technical terms and book titles mentioned in the text. Words mentioned frequently, such as Arab, Arabic and Muslim, have been omitted